Stress and Coping: An Anthology

Second Edition

STRESS

AND
COPING

an anthology

Edited by Alan Monat
and Richard S. Lazarus

Columbia University Press

New York

Columbia University Press
New York   Guildford, Surrey
Copyright © 1985 Columbia University Press
All rights reserved

Printed in the United States of America

Library of Congress Cataloging in Publication Data
Main entry under title:

Stress and coping.

  Bibliography: p.
  Includes index.
  1. Stress (Psychology)—Addresses, essays, lectures.
2. Adjustment (Psychology)—Addresses, essays, lectures.
I. Monat, Alan, 1945-   .   II. Lazarus, Richard S.
[DNLM: 1. Adaptation, Psychological—collected works.
2. Stress, Psychological—collected works. WM 172 S913]
BF575.S75S77   1985   155.9   85–472
ISBN 0–231–05820–9
ISBN 0–231–05821–7 (pbk.)
p 10 9 8 7 6 5 4 3 2

DEDICATION

AM: To Ian and Murline, Jeff, Ron, and Helene, and My Parents, Harold and Tillie

RSL: To Bunny, David and Mary, Nancy and Rick, Jessica, Adam, and Maiya

Contents

Acknowledgments

The editors would like to thank the following publishers for permission to reprint materials used in this book. It should be noted that, to achieve uniformity, we have in some cases slightly altered the original reference and/or footnote formats to conform with the author-date method of citation used throughout this book. It was also necessary to make some minor editorial changes appropriate to an anthology of this kind.

1. "History and Present Status of the Stress Concept" by Hans Selye: Reprinted with permission of Macmillan Publishing Company from *Handbook of Stress: Theoretical and Clinical Aspects* by Leo Goldberger and Shlomo Breznitz, eds. Copyright © 1982 by The Free Press, a Division of Macmillan Publishing Company.

2. "Stress: A Psychophysiological Conception" by Anis Mikhail: From *Journal of Human Stress* (1981), 7:9–15. Used with permission of Opinion Publications, Inc. and Anis Mikhail.

3. "Stress and Bodily Illness" by Frances Cohen: From *Psychiatric Clinics of North America* (1981), 4:269–86. Used with permission of W. B. Saunders Company.

4. "Anatomy of an Illness (As Perceived by the Patient)" by Norman Cousins: Reprinted by permission of *The New England Journal of Medicine* (1976), 295:1458–63.

5. "The Living World" by Rene Dubos: From *Man Adapting* by Rene Dubos. Copyright © 1965 by Yale University. Used with permission of Yale University Press.

6. "Physiological, Motivational, and Cognitive Effects of Aircraft Noise on Children: Moving From the Laboratory to the Field" by Sheldon Cohen, Gary W. Evans, David S. Krantz, and Daniel Stokols: From *American Psychologist* (1980), 35:231–43. Copyright © 1980 by the American Psychological Association. Adapted by permission of the publisher and author.

7. "Mediating Influences of Social Support on Stress at Three Mile Island" by Raymond Fleming, Andrew Baum, Martha M. Gisriel, and Robert J. Gatchel: From *Journal of Human Stress* (1982), 8:14–22. Used with permission of Opinion Publications, Inc. and the author.

8. "The Psychological Stresses of Intensive Care Unit Nursing" by Donald Hay and Donald Oken: From *Psychosomatic Medicine* (1972), 34:109–18. Used with permission of Harper & Row, Publishers, Inc.

9. "Strategies of Adaptation: An Attempt at Systematic Description" by Robert W. White: From *Coping and Adaptation,* George V. Coelho, David A. Hamburg and John E. Adams, eds. © 1974 by Basic Books, Inc., Publishers. Reprinted by permission of the publisher.

10. "Conceptualizations of Ego: Processes, Functions, Regulations" by Norma Haan: From Chapter 4 of *Coping and Defending: Processes of Self-Environment Organization* by Norma Haan. Copyright © 1977 by Academic Press, Inc. Reprinted by permission of the publisher.

11. "The Costs and Benefits of Denial" by Richard S. Lazarus: From *The Denial of Stress* by S. Breznitz, ed., 1983. Used with permission of International Universities Press, Inc.

12. "Stressful Life Events, Personality, and Health: An Inquiry Into Hardiness" by Suzanne C. Kobasa: From *Journal of Personality and Social Psychology* 37:1–11, 1979. Copyright © 1979 by the American Psychological Association. Reprinted by permission of the publisher and author.

13. "Life Strains and Psychological Distress among Adults" by Leonard I. Pearlin: From *Themes of Work and Love in Adulthood* by N. J. Smelser and E. H. Erikson, eds., by Harvard University Press, 1980.

14. "Some Modes of Adaptation: Defense" by David Mechanic: From *Students Under Stress: A Study in the Social Psychology of Adaptation* by David Mechanic. The University of Wisconsin Press, © 1962, 1978 by David Mechanic. Used with permission of David Mechanic.

15. "The Management of Abhorrent Behavior—Survival Period" by Rex A. Lucas: From Chapter 6, "The Management of Abhorrent Behavior—Survival Period," from *Men in Crisis: A Study of a Mine Disaster,* by Rex A. Lucas, © 1969 by Basic Books, Inc., Publishers, New York. Used with permission of Basic Books, Inc.

16. "A Prediction of Delayed Stress Response Syndromes in Vietnam Veterans" by Mardi J. Horowitz and George F. Solomon: From *Journal of Social Issues* (1975), 31:67–80. Used with permission of The Society for the Psychological Study of Social Issues.

17. "Reactions to the Imminence of Death" by Thomas P. Hackett and Avery D. Weisman: Reprinted from *The Threat of Impending Disasters,* edited by G. H. Grosser, H. Wechsler, and M. Greenblatt, by permission of M.I.T. Press, Cambridge, Mass. Copyright © 1964 by the Massachusetts Institute of Technology.

18. "Behavioral Observations on Parents Anticipating the Death of a Child" by Stanford B. Friedman, Paul Chodoff, John W. Mason, and David A. Hamburg: From *Pediatrics* (1963), 32:610–25. Copyright © 1963 by American Academy of Pediatrics. Used with permission of the American Academy of Pediatrics.

19. "The College Student and Death" by Edwin S. Shneidman: From *New Meanings of Death,* H. Feifel, ed., 1977. Copyright © 1977 by McGraw-Hill, Inc. Used with permission of the publisher.

20. "The Effects of Bereavement on Mortality: A Social Psychological Analysis" by Wolfgang Stroebe, Margaret S. Stroebe, Kenneth J. Gergen, and Mary Gergen: From *Social Psychology and Behavioral Medicine,* J. Richard Eiser, ed. Copyright © 1982 by John Wiley & Sons, Ltd. Reprinted by permission of John Wiley & Sons, Ltd.

21. "The Relaxation Response" by Herbert Benson: From chapter 7 of *The Relaxation Response* by Herbert Benson, M.D., with Miriam Z. Klipper. Copyright © 1975 by William Morrow and Company, Inc. By permission of the publisher.

22. "Strategies for Modifying Type A Behavior" by Margaret A. Chesney and Ray H. Rosenman: From *Consultant* (June 1980), pp. 216–22. Used with permission of the publisher.

23. "Stress Inoculation in Health Care" by Irving L. Janis: From *Stress Reduction and Prevention* by D. Meichenbaum and M. E. Jaremko, eds. Copyright © 1983 by Plenum Press. Used with permission of Plenum Press and Irving L. Janis.
24. "Toward Effective Coping: The Basic Steps" by Robert M. Bramson: Excerpts from *Coping With Difficult People* by Robert M. Bramson. Copyright © 1981 by Robert M. Bramson. Reprinted by permission of Doubleday & Company, Inc.
25. "Stress Management: Averting the Evil Eye" by Ethel Roskies: From *Contemporary Psychology* (1983), 28:542–44. Copyright © 1983 by the American Psychological Association. Reprinted by permission of the publisher and author.
26. "Out of the Habit Trap" by Stanton Peele: Reprinted from *American Health: Fitness of Body and Mind*. Copyright © 1983 by American Health Partners. Used with permission of American Health Partners and Stanton Peele.

Preface to the Second Edition

In the eight years since our anthology first appeared, the stress and coping field has continued to expand at an incredible pace. Courses and seminars on stress and coping are now commonplace; almost routinely, newspaper articles, radio talk shows, and television specials are devoted to topics relevant to stress and coping; and, it is fashionable for corporations, police agencies, and even athletic teams to hire stress management consultants to teach "employees" more effective means for coping with stress.

Because the field has been expanding and evolving so rapidly, a second edition of our anthology is quite appropriate. Like the first edition, the present one is intended by and large for undergraduate students in a variety of disciplines. This second edition is organized much like the first and is similarly characterized by a cognitive perspective. The content of this edition has been significantly revised and updated: e.g., over 75 percent of the articles are new additions. Readers familiar with our earlier anthology will note a greater emphasis in the present edition on illness and stress management.

We are grateful for the wide acceptance of the first edition of *Stress and Coping*. The largely positive and constructive comments of many readers and reviewers have been most helpful as well as reassuring. We hope the present edition proves as useful as the first and gains similar acceptance.

We would like to thank the many authors and publishers who have consented to have their works reprinted here. Our thanks also to Columbia University Press for its support of this project throughout the years and to Columbia's Susan Koscielniak, Theresa Yuhas, and Anne McCoy for their fine efforts.

Preface to the First Edition

For many years the research literature pertaining to stress and coping has been proliferating. General interest in this body of knowledge and ideas has also increased dramatically, partially due, no doubt, to its relevance to our personal lives. Yet, paradoxically, there are few texts or readers offering a systematic presentation of the major issues or findings in this field. While many technical books containing conference papers on the topic have recently appeared, there is currently no general book of readings in the stress and coping area based upon a broad sampling of available writings, theoretical and empirical in nature, and geared primarily to the undergraduate student. Such a book would be highly appropriate not only to courses related directly to stress and coping, but also to those concerned with psychological adjustment and health. This book is designed to help remedy this omission.

Certain considerations were given prime importance in its design. First, readings dealing primarily with humans were given top priority. Although there has been much significant animal research, studies conducted with humans are generally more engaging to the student, and we believe they are ultimately the most relevant for understanding the struggles of humans to cope with the problems of living. Second, the current trend toward naturalistic studies is a healthy and strong one and also deserves emphasis. Third, because of the vast amount of available material, we decided to concentrate primarily upon articles written within the last ten years or so; however, a few earlier articles such as those by Cannon, Lindemann, Menninger, and Selye were included because of their strong and persisting impact. Fourth, while methodological issues, including those pertaining to physiological processes, are represented, they are not emphasized; these topics tend to bore or perplex most students, particularly those who are not yet prepared to grasp their significance. We think the important issues of method need to be dealt with by instructors in other ways, perhaps through lectures or organized commentaries about the readings.

The book begins with an introductory chapter, written by the editors, which systematically presents some of the major issues relevant to the concepts of stress and coping—for example, problems of definition, relationships between stress and illness, etc. This chapter does not summarize the selections in the book but rather provides the reader with a basic and fundamental background for approaching the selections.

At the start of each section of the book we have provided summaries and, often, critical evaluations of the readings. Our comments present what we see as the author's main points and in many cases clarify and elaborate upon theoretical biases, relationships with other research and, to a lesser extent, methodological problems.

The core of the book is divided into five sections, the first two dealing primarily with the concept of stress and the latter three with the nature of coping. The division of stress and coping into separate sections is of course somewhat artificial, as the concepts are intertwined. We found it useful, however, for purposes of organization and clarity of emphasis.

As might be expected, we were faced with a number of critical problems and decisions regarding the organization of this book. First of all, while many would understandably prefer rather narrow working definitions of "stress" and "coping," such a task seems to us to be unnecessarily restrictive here. Though adopting a broad perspective may preserve a certain amount of ambiguity in these terms, we believe a broad approach is more instructive for two reasons: (1) particularly valuable contributions are being made by investigators in fields as diverse as psychology, medicine, anthropology, and sociology, and (2) our understanding of the complex and urgent issues relevant to stress and coping is just only beginning to emerge. Thus, we do not try to give a restrictive definition of the field but treat stress and coping as broad rubrics. In line with this, articles examining stress and coping from many perspectives were selected. Secondly, choice of articles posed a most difficult and distressing problem because of the tremendous variety of interesting and outstanding works. We would have liked to include additional readings but this was prohibited by space limitations.

We express our appreciation to the many authors and publishers who gave us permission to reprint their works and our regrets to the many other investigators whose fine works we were unable to include. John Moore and David Diefendorf of Columbia Press have been most supportive and helpful throughout this project and we thank them sincerely for their efforts and encouragement. Also helpful have been the comments and suggestions of many colleagues and friends including Frances Cohen, Reuven Gal, Murline Monat, and Neil Weinstein. In addition, two anonymous reviewers provided valuable critiques of an earlier draft of the book but, in all fairness, we must assume full responsibility for the final product.

We hope our efforts provide the prospective reader with an accurate, representative, and exciting picture of current theory and research in the stress and coping field.

Introduction

Stress and Coping—
Some Current Issues
and Controversies

War, pollution, unemployment, natural disasters, divorce, "getting ahead," and illness all make us painfully aware of our daily struggles with adversities. Whether we master these stressors and prosper or become their victim, there is little question that they provide the scientist (and layperson) with vital and abundant material for the observation and systematic study of human adaptation.

Interest in the stresses and strains of "modern" life and how we cope with them has increased in recent years. The tremendous popularity of the stress and coping field can be seen by the steady outpouring of rather technical theoretical, empirical, and applied reports (e.g., Goldberger and Breznitz 1982; Kutash, Schlesinger, and associates 1980; Meichenbaum and Jaremko 1983), and of relevant books for the general public (e.g., Brown 1977; Cousins 1979; Friedman and Rosenman 1974; and literally hundreds of self-help books and manuals). Many professional journals are also heavily devoted to research and theory in the stress and coping field.

The present edition of our anthology, as did its predecessor (Monat and Lazarus 1977), pulls together and organizes representative studies to give interested readers a sound and basic introduction to contemporary thought in a field relevant to everyone's concerns about successful living. (A summary and evaluation of each of the readings included in this book can be found in the introduction to the various parts.)

THE CONCEPT OF "STRESS"

Definitions. There has been a tendency to distinguish three basic types of stress: systemic or physiological, psychological, and social. *Systemic stress* is concerned primarily with the disturbances of tissue systems (e.g., Cannon 1929; Selye 1956), *psychological stress* with cognitive factors leading to the evaluation of threat (e.g., Lazarus 1966), and *social stress* with the disruption of a social unit or system (e.g., Smelser 1963). While many believe the three types of stress are related, the nature of this relationship is far from clear (Mason 1975a). Perhaps most surprising (and confusing) is the lack of agreement on a definition of "stress" among those researchers closest to the field. As Mason stated:

Whatever the soundness of logic may be in the various approaches to defining "stress," however, the general picture in the field can still only be described as one of confusion. The disenchantment felt by many scientists with the stress field is certainly understandable when one views two decades in which the term "stress" has been used variously to refer to "stimulus" by some workers, "response" by some workers, "interaction" by others, and more comprehensive combinations of the above factors by still other workers. Some authorities in the field are rather doubtful that this confusion over terminology is correctable in the near future. (1975b:29)

The reasons investigators have been unable to reach any general agreement on a definition of "stress" are undoubtedly complex but revolve largely around the problems inherent in defining any intricate phenomenon. For example, a response-based definition of stress (e.g., one that looks at increased physiological activity as an indicator of stress) suffers from, among other things, the fact that the same response pattern (such as increased blood pressure or heart rate) may arise from entirely different stimulus conditions, for example, from heavy exercise or extreme fright. And, of course, the psychological meanings of these conditions are typically quite different (McGrath 1970b). Likewise, stimulus-based definitions are incomplete because any situation may or may not be stressful, depending on characteristics of the individual and the meaning of the situation for him or her.

Because of these problems some have suggested abandoning the term "stress" (Hinkle 1974; Mason 1975b) while others have argued for using "stress" as a general label for a large, complex, interdisciplinary area of interest and study:

It seems wise to use "stress" as a generic term for the whole area of problems that includes the stimuli producing stress reactions, the reactions themselves, and the various intervening processes. Thus, we can speak of the field of stress, and mean the physiological, sociological, and psychological phenomena and their respective concepts. It could then include research and theory on group or individual disaster, physiological assault on tissues and the effects of this assault, disturbances or facilitation of adaptive functioning produced by conditions of deprivation, thwarting or the prospects of this, and the field of negatively toned emotions such as fear, anger, depression, despair, hopelessness, and guilt. *Stress is not any one of these things; nor is it stimulus, response, or intervening variable, but rather a collective term for an area of study.* (Lazarus 1966:27)

To amplify this, the stress arena refers to any event in which environmental demands, internal demands, or both *tax* or *exceed* the adaptive resources of an individual, social system, or tissue system. However one chooses to define stress, to avoid confusion it seems mandatory that the concepts and procedures employed in a specific study be made explicit—i.e., the antecedent conditions used to induce "stress," the response patterns measured as indices of "stress," and, finally, the intervening processes believed responsible for the nature of the responses must be indicated.

  Other stress-related concepts. When one thinks of stress, other concepts often come to mind and these need to be distinguished from stress and from each other. *Frustration* or psychological harm refers to blockage or delay in progress toward some goal. It implies something that is ongoing or has already happened. *Threat,* like frustration, also involves a harm of some kind, only it is one that has not yet happened. The harm is anticipated, however, on the basis of present cues. The person recognizes, somehow, or believes that future harm portends. The reason this distinction between past or present harm and anticipated harm is so important is that these two types of stress situations require different forms of coping. Harm that has already happened cannot be prevented, so it allows the person only to try to compensate for the damage, make restitution for it, tolerate or accept it, or give up any investment in what he or she has lost (as in the readjustments taking place in grief). On the other hand, future harm might be prevented or prepared for, so threat provides a warning that invites the person to take preventive steps or to do what he or she can to mitigate the impending harm.

  Empirically, the importance of anticipation of harm in the production of stress reactions (physiological and psychological) is well supported. For instance, Shannon and Isbell (1963) have demonstrated that anticipation of a dental anesthetic injection results in the same amount of physiological stress reaction (increases in serum hydrocortisone) as the actual physical injection. Epstein (1967) has indicated that sport parachutists exhibit marked physiological and psychological stress reactions prior to a jump. In the laboratory, Birnbaum (1964) and Nomikos et al. (1968) have shown that unpleasant motion pictures elicit anticipatory physiological stress reactions. Moreover, considerable research has been done on antecedent conditions which may affect the appraisal of threat and the resulting stress reactions such as past experience (Epstein 1967), availability of response options (Averill and Rosenn 1972; Elliott 1965; Pervin 1963), personality dispositions (Hodges and Spielberger 1966; Lazarus and Alfert 1964), and uncertainty (D'Amato and Gumenik 1960; Monat 1976; Monat, Averill, and Lazarus 1972).

It might be noted, as an aside, that accurate assessment of harm and threat is, of course, crucial to the study of psychological stress and typically four classes of response variables are used to infer their presence (Lazarus 1966): negatively toned affect, motor-behavioral reactions, alterations of adaptive functioning, and/or physiological reactions. Unfortunately, each response class is characterized by inherent limitations and problems and, hence, it is desirable to rely upon the simultaneous measurement of several indices of threat (e.g., within and/or between response modalities) whenever feasible. (For a review of many of these measurement problems, the reader should consult Averill and Opton 1968; Brown 1967; Lacey et al. 1963; Sternbach 1966; Venables and Martin 1967; and Weinstein et al. 1968.)

Finally, *conflict* involves the presence simultaneously of two incompatible goals or action tendencies, and so in conflict, frustration or threat of some sort is virtually inevitable. This makes it of great importance in human adaptation. Goals or action tendencies may be incompatible because the behavior and attitudes necessary to reach one such goal are contrary to those necessary to reach the other. If one spends now for enjoyment, saving up for future pleasure is negated. If one goal is attained, the other must be frustrated. Hence, conflict is a major source of psychological stress in human affairs and is a lifelong problem requiring much adaptive effort if one is to achieve a successful and rewarding life.

Summary. The concept of stress has received considerable theoretical and empirical attention in recent years, yet much "confusion and controversy" remain. Attempts have been made to integrate various points of view (e.g., Mikhail 1981) and further efforts along these lines may be forthcoming. Nevertheless, finding consensus among definitions of stress and related concepts (such as frustration, threat, and harm) is still likely to remain a difficult endeavor.

THE CONCEPT OF "COPING"

Definitions and classification systems. While stress and its damaging effects have been studied extensively, less systematic attention has been devoted to the ways in which humans respond to stress positively. More recently, however, there has been a rapid growth of curiosity and concern among researchers about coping and "adaptation" (e.g., Coelho, Hamburg, and Adams 1974; Moos 1976a).

Perhaps because of its common lay usage (there is even a drug named

"Cope"), the term "coping" has accrued a variety of meanings. Nevertheless, there seems to be growing agreement among professionals (e.g., Lazarus, Averill, and Opton 1974; Lazarus and Folkman 1984a, b; Murphy 1962, 1974; White 1974) that coping refers to efforts to master conditions of harm, threat, or challenge when a routine or automatic response is not readily available. Here, environmental demands must be met with new behavioral solutions or old ones must be adapted to meet the current stress. As White notes:

It is clear that we tend to speak of coping when we have in mind a fairly drastic change or problem that defies familiar ways of behaving, requires the production of new behavior, and very likely gives rise to uncomfortable affects like anxiety, despair, guilt, shame, or grief, the relief of which forms part of the needed adaptation. Coping refers to adaptation under relatively difficult conditions. (1974:48–49)

An adequate system for classifying coping processes has yet to be proposed, although initial efforts along these lines have been made (e.g., Haan 1969, 1977; Hamburg, Coelho, and Adams 1974; Lazarus 1966, 1975; Mechanic 1978b; Menninger 1963; Murphy 1974). For example, Folkman and Lazarus (1980) have suggested a taxonomy of coping which emphasizes two major categories, problem-focused and emotion-focused modes. *Problem-focused* coping refers to efforts to improve the troubled person-environment relationship by changing things, for example, by seeking information about what to do, by holding back from impulsive and premature actions, and by confronting the person or persons responsible for one's difficulty. *Emotion-focused* (or palliative) coping refers to thoughts or actions whose goal is to relieve the emotional impact of stress (i.e., bodily or psychological disturbances). These are apt to be mainly palliative in the sense that such strategies of coping do not actually alter the threatening or damaging conditions but make the person feel better. Examples are avoiding thinking about the trouble, denying that anything is wrong, distancing or detaching oneself as in joking about what makes one feel distressed, or taking tranquilizers or attempting to relax. Some modes of emotion-focused coping deploy attention from stressful circumstances (as in thinking about last summer's romance rather than studying for the "big" exam or, as in meditating, relaxing, or jogging), while others alter the meaning or significance of what has happened, or is happening, in order to feel better about it. The latter are similar to strategies traditionally referred to as defense mechanisms.

The above classification in no way implies that we use one kind of coping process or another exclusively. Rather, all of us employ complex combinations of problem-focused and emotion-focused methods to cope with stress. The conditions determining our coping methods in particular situations are undoubtedly complex and largely unknown at this time but likely depend upon the conditions being faced, the options available to us, and our personality.

Coping outcomes. An issue that frequently emerges in discussions of coping is whether some coping processes are more effective than others. Unfortunately, any answer to this problem must be prefaced with a long string of qualifiers due to inherent value questions (Smith 1961), levels of analysis (i.e., physiological, psychological, or sociological), points in time (i.e., short- vs. long-run), and particular situations (Cohen 1975). For instance, behavior which might be effective from, say, the physiological perspective might have devastating consequences for the psychological or sociological domains. Moreover, within any one domain, what is an optimal response in one situation at a particular point in time may be damaging in some other situation or at a different point in time. For example, denial may be effective (in the physiological domain in terms of lowered secretions of stress-related hormones) for parents of terminally ill children prior to the child's death (Wolff et al. 1964) but may prove ineffective after the child dies, i.e., stress-related hormones then increase dramatically (see Hofer et al. 1972). It is clear that what is considered to be an optimal or beneficial response is highly dependent upon one's perspective and judgments.

Traditionally, emotion-focused modes of coping (particularly defense mechanisms such as denial) have been viewed as pathological or maladaptive. This view is often supported in studies where defensive behaviors (such as denial that a suspicious lump in the breast might be cancerous) have actually endangered the lives of individuals (e.g., Katz et al. 1970). On the other hand, denial can initially serve a positive function (cf. Hamburg and Adams 1967) in preventing a person from being overwhelmed by a threatening situation where the possibilities for direct actions are limited and/or of little use (e.g., the person who has suffered severe burns or polio). Cohen states the matter as follows:

Thus we see that denial has been found a useful defense in many situations, lowering physiological response levels and helping the person avoid being overwhelmed by negative life circumstances. However, its usefulness seems most apparent on a short-term basis, in particular situations (such as situations where the person would be otherwise overwhelmed by the unpleasant reality, where the likelihood of threats occurring is small, where there is nothing the individual can do to prepare for the potential threatening event, or where a hopeful attitude prevents feelings of giving up). Further studies must be done to determine the usefulness of denial in other situations and determinations of both long- and short-run consequences of this behavior must be made (1975:14–15)

In general, then, emotion-focused modes of coping may be damaging when they prevent essential direct actions but may also be extremely useful in helping a person maintain a sense of well-being, integration, or hope under conditions otherwise likely to encourage psychological disintegration (see Lazarus 1983, and Taylor 1983, for a fuller discussion of the positive side to defenses and illusions).

Coping dispositions versus strategies. Two different approaches to the study of coping have been pursued by various investigators. On the one hand, some (e.g., Byrne 1964; Goldstein 1973) have emphasized general coping traits, styles, or dispositions, while others (e.g., Cohen and Lazarus 1973; Katz et al. 1970; Wolff et al. 1964) have preferred to study active, ongoing coping strategies in particular stress situations. The former approach, often used by researchers interested in the study of personality, assumes that an individual will utilize the same type of coping (such as repression or sensitization) in most stressful situations. It is for him or her a stable pattern or style. A person's coping style or disposition is typically assessed by personality tests, not by actual observation of what the person says or does in a particular stress situation. Whether the person actually behaves under stress as predicted by the test depends largely on the adequacy of the personality assessment, the generality of the trait being measured, and the myriad internal and external factors affecting the person's actions and reactions in any given situation. It should be noted that many psychological traits, including coping styles, show very limited generality (cf. Cohen and Lazarus 1973; Mischel 1968) and, hence, are poor predictors of behavior in any given situation.

In contrast, those concentrating on active coping strategies prefer to observe an individual's behavior as it occurs in a stressful situation and then proceed to infer the particular coping processes implied by the behaviors. This approach has been largely neglected in the study of coping. Recent research by Folkman and Lazarus (1980, in press) has centered on a process approach to the assessment of coping. Although subjects are not observed in stressful situations, they are asked to reconstruct them and then to provide information about what they actually thought, did, and felt, using the "Ways of Coping" checklist. The coping items to be endorsed (or not) by the person include problem-focused varieties such as "Tried to get the person responsible to change his or her mind" and "Talked to someone to find out more about the situation," and emotion-focused varieties such as "Didn't let it get to me," and "I came out of the experience better than I went in." Increasingly, other researchers (e.g., Collins, Baum, and Singer 1983; Mitchell, Cronkite, and Moos 1983; Parkes, in press; and Stone and Neale 1984) have been using this approach or modified versions of it to describe and measure the actual coping processes people use in the stressful encounters in their lives. We think that assessing coping processes, while time-consuming and often costly, will produce valuable information often unobtainable with the dispositional emphasis.

Summary. While the concept of coping is intimately tied to that of stress, it has been largely neglected by researchers until rather recently. Today much more interest is being expressed in the classification and measurement of coping processes, and the study of their causes and effects. A highly pertinent issue is the "adaptive" value of various coping processes—i.e., are some processes more effective or ineffective than others? There is a growing conviction that all coping processes, including those traditionally considered undesirable (i.e., defense mechanisms), have both positive and negative consequences for an individual, and that any evaluation of coping and adaptation must take into account diverse levels of analysis (physiological, psychological, sociological), the short- versus long-term consequences, and the specific nature of the situation in question. Our understanding of how people cope with specific stress situations will probably be advanced further by assessing coping *in vivo* as well as by generalized trait measurements. With increased interest in the psychology of coping, we shall, no doubt, see rapid advances in our understanding of how people cope with the stresses of living, how their coping patterns are shaped by situational and personality factors, and how these patterns change during the course of development.

STRESS, COPING, AND PHYSICAL ILLNESS

The excitement many find in the study of stress and coping is often attributable to an interest in the biological, psychological, and sociological factors believed to contribute to the development of physical and mental disorders. Although the issues and literature in this area are far too vast to cover here (see Cohen 1975; Coleman, Butcher, and Carson 1980), we would like to point out some basic theoretical positions relating stress and physical illnesses.

Possible links between stress, coping, and illness. There are three main ways in which stress might lead to somatic illness (Holroyd and Lazarus 1982). The first is by the disruption of tissue function through neurohumoral influences under stress. In other words, under stress there are major outpourings of powerful hormones creating dramatic alterations in bodily processes many of which we sense as in the case of a pounding heart, sweating, trembling, fatigue, etc. A second way is by engaging in coping activities that are damaging to health, for example, by trying to advance occupationally or socially by means of a pressured style of life (e.g., Type A behavior), by taking minimal rest, by poor diet, heavy use of tobacco or alcohol, etc. Intrinsically noxious styles of living can increase the likelihood of disease by damaging the tissues of the body. A third way stress and coping might lead to disease is by psychological and/or sociological factors which consistently lead the person to minimize the significance of various symptoms. That is, a person may frequently interpret pain or illness symptoms in such a way as to neglect to seek medical aid when it is crucial. Avoidance of doctors or of medical regimens can come about as a defense mechanism, for example, denial, or merely because the individual is a member of a culture or subculture that values stoicism (Mechanic 1978a; Zborowski 1969). Such avoidance can be fatal in certain instances, as in the case of heart attack victims who delay seeking medical attention, thereby decreasing their chances of survival (Hackett and Cassem 1975).

The issue of generality versus specificity. The way in which stress produces somatic illness via hormonal secretions that alter tissue function has been of tremendous recent interest. This interest has no doubt received its greatest impetus from the work of Hans Selye (e.g., 1956). In his studies, Selye has attempted to demonstrate how physical and psychological "stressors" may lead to "diseases of adaptation" via a series of "nonspecific" biological responses, called the "General Adaptation Syndrome" (GAS). The GAS is the defensive physiological reaction of the organism which is set in motion by any noxious stimulus. Its characteristic pattern includes three stages: an alarm reaction, a stage of resistance, and a stage of exhaustion. This sequence is invariant, although it need not be carried to completion if the stressor is terminated early enough, and involves increased secretions of the pituitary gland. These secretions in turn stimulate the production of hormones by the cortex or outer shell of the adrenal glands. If the stressor (e.g., heat, cold, exercise, psychological threat) persists or is severe, diseases of adaptation, such as stomach or intestinal ulcers, increased susceptibility to infection, etc., will occur and eventually, if the stressor is unabated, the organism dies.

Until the last decade or so, Selye's work was widely accepted and largely unchallenged. Recently, however, several researchers (e.g., Lazarus 1974; Mason 1971, 1975a, 1975b) have criticized aspects of Selye's position, particularly his total commitment to the concept of the physiological nonspecificity of the stress response. Selye distinguishes

between the *specific* effects induced by a stressor agent and the effects induced by such stimulation which are *not* specific to it. Thus he observes that whereas one stimulus (e.g., cold) may produce a vasoconstriction and a second stimulus (e.g., heat) a vasodilation, both (or either), if applied intensely or long enough, produce(s) *effects in common* and therefore not specific to either stimulus. These common changes, taken together, constitute the stereotypical response pattern of systemic stress. Selye "operationally" defines stress as "*a state manifested by a syndrome which consists of all nonspecifically induced changes in a biologic system.*" (Cofer and Appley 1964:442)

Mason and Lazarus have offered theoretical viewpoints and presented empirical evidence which strongly suggest Selye has overstated the role of nonspecificity in the production of illness. Mason (1975b) suggests that the pituitary-adrenal cortical system is remarkably sensitive and responds easily to emotional stimuli. This is important, for many laboratory situations designed to study physical stressors very often elicit discomfort or pain. Therefore, what would happen to the GAS if psychological factors were minimized?

When special precautions are taken, however, to minimize psychological reactions in the study of physical stimuli, such as heat, fasting, and moderate exercise, it now appears that the pituitary-adrenal cortical system is *not* stimulated in nonspecific fashion by these stimuli which are generally regarded as "noxious," "demanding," or as appreciably disturbing to homeostatic equilibrium. . . . [In] heat studies with both human and monkey subjects, it appears heat *per se* either does not change or actually *suppresses* adrenal cortical hormone levels when measures are taken to avoid such factors as novelty or extremely sudden or severe temperature changes. (Mason 1975b:24)

These findings are important, for they imply that somatic illness may depend on quite specific reactions to specific stressors. As Lazarus points out, the role of specificity in illness creates more varied options, since

the nature and severity of the stress disorder could depend on at least three factors: (1) the formal characteristics of the environmental demands, (2) the quality of the emotional response generated by the demands, or in particular individuals facing these demands, and (3) the process of coping mobilized by the stressful commerce. (1974:327)

It may be too early to evaluate adequately the role(s) of nonspecific and specific factors in the etiology of illness, but clearly there is a growing belief in the importance of the latter.

Summary. Stress, coping, and physical illness have been linked by a variety of theories. Most basically, these viewpoints tend to emphasize one or another of the following: (1) the short- and long-term disruption of stress hormones on bodily processes; (2) unhealthy coping activities, such as substance abuse to reduce anxiety and tension; and, (3) the potentially damaging consequences of psychological or social values minimizing the significance of bodily symptoms—e.g., minimizing threatening bodily signs because one has been taught it is "unmanly" to worry or show fear. There is still much to be learned about each of these possibilities and controversy abounds. (See Stone, Cohen, and Adler 1979, for discussions of the stress, coping, and illness literature.)

STRESS MANAGEMENT

It is now commonly believed that all illness is, in part, stress related (Davison and Neale 1982). Given this wide-spread belief, it is not surprising that a new, multi-billion dollar stress management industry (mainly in the form of consulting firms and self-help manuals) has emerged to help contain the menacing "stress bug." As noted by Roskies, "It would be un-American to accept a new cause for disease without seeking to cure or control it" (1983:542).

Stress management attempts to reduce or prevent stress and its harmful effects (like excessive, chronic levels of catecholamines and steroids) by advocating either the use of a particular technique or a potpouri of techniques. There are three general (and somewhat overlapping and arbitrarily defined) categories of such stress management techniques: (1) alterations of environment and/or lifestyle; (2) alterations of personality and/or perception; and, (3) alterations of biological responses to stress. Table 1 lists examples of each category—cf. Girdano and Everly 1979, and Greenberg 1983.

Two points should be made about the stress management field. First, its growth has been largely the result of perceived need and demand rather than the availability of empirically supported "cures." There unfortunately have been rather weak efforts to determine clearly the effectiveness of the various techniques for different stress-related disorders or for different kinds of people. While practicing thought stopping, breathing exercises, etc. may usually not be harmful, one could (and should?) legitimately ask whether such techniques actually do any good, and about the conditions under which they might help or harm people. With some exception (e.g., stress inoculation or biofeedback), there have been woefully few research efforts along these lines.

A second point is whether or not by offering "ready-made" and overly simplistic cures, we "trivialize" distress. Are professionals not mocking the vic-

Table 1. Some Stress-Management Techniques

Environment/ Lifestyle	Personality/ Perceptions	Biological Responses
Time management	Assertiveness training	Progressive relaxation
Proper nutrition	Thought stopping	Relaxation response
Exercise	Refuting irrational ideas	Meditation
Finding alternatives to frustrated goals	Stress inoculation	Breathing exercises
Stopping smoking, drinking, etc.	Modifying Type A behavior	Biofeedback
		Autogenics

Discussion of these and other stress-management techniques may be found in Davis, Eshelman, and McKay (1982), Girdano and Everly (1979), Greenberg (1983), and Steinmetz et al. (1980).

Note that one could easily place some of the techniques in more than one of the above categories. For example, exercise may be seen as a technique altering one's biological responses to stress, as well as a change in one's lifestyle (if exercise has indeed been absent).

tims of distress or illness when they rather patly provide (or prescribe) techniques of unproven validity or which fail to acknowledge individual differences and life agendas? As noted by Lazarus:

it would be well for professionals, of all people, not to fall into the trap of popularization which now plagues media treatments of stress, coping and adaptation, and programs of stress management. When professionals take their simplistic formulas for intervention too seriously and oversell their product, thereby encouraging the public to think in terms of mechanical solutions that fail to address the most important sources of distress, they help create a culture in which distress is trivialized, or at the least encourage public acceptance of an already existing pattern of trivialization. The goal of realizing effective intervention requires more sophisticated thought than presently exists and a deep respect for the person who receives our help. (in press)

Overview: A Look at This Book

In the following sections of our book, we have assembled articles capturing the flavor of the issues and controversies currently dominating the stress and coping field—many of which were highlighted in the present chapter. The articles are organized into six parts: Stress and Some of Its Effects, Stress and the Environment, The Concept of Coping, Coping with the Stresses of Living, Coping with Death and Dying, and Stress Management. It is our intention that the present collection of readings not only stimulate your interest, but also foster a critical outlook on the stress and coping field.

Part I

Stress and Some of Its Effects

The readings in Part I present divergent and controversial viewpoints about the stress concept, including its possible relationship with disease processes. The first article, written by Hans Selye (1982), is a succinct introduction to the history of the stress concept and its current status. Selye describes briefly his own theory, which we discussed critically in our Introduction, and also presents his philosophical views about living a healthy life. Note that Selye discusses several psychological and behavioral stress-management techniques that the general public might use (without professional assistance) to combat the negative effects of stress. Selye's attention to psychology and philosophy (an apparent shift in his professional interests as he grew older) should not lead one to overlook the fact that his theory of stress is essentially a biologically-based one.

Mikhail's (1981) article is an excellent attempt at integrating Selye's approach to stress with those emphasizing psychological and sociological factors. Mikhail elaborates on the controversy, discussed in our Introduction, surrounding Selye's concept of nonspecificity. Mikhail believes there is no logically inherent reason why the biologically and psychologically based viewpoints cannot be integrated into a "holistic" one. Mikhail's proposed definition suggests that the stress concept must be understood to include *both* the conditions (environmental and psychological) that bring about stress *and* the actual stress reactions (or syndrome).

Cohen's (1981) article addresses theories of stress and bodily illness. She begins with some general comments regarding the stress concept and then proceeds to highlight several interesting and important methodological issues characterizing this field. Cohen's discussions of theories linking stress and disease are directed to "generality approaches," namely to those which link stress with diseases of all types. There are many other theories of stress and illness that emphasize specific disorders (such as heart disease or cancer)—see Cohen (1979) for a description of some of these viewpoints.

Of the theories discussed by Cohen, the most influential has probably been that proposed by Holmes and Rahe (1967b). They and their colleagues have reported evidence that illnesses of all kinds increase following periods of "stressful" life changes because of the major coping activities such changes require. Both positive and negative changes, such as marriage and divorce, are considered to be stressful by Holmes and Rahe because they all presumably demand adjustments by the individual to a new life style or pattern. To measure these life changes, Holmes and Rahe developed a self-administered questionnaire, the Social Readjustment Rating Scale (SRRS), which the person uses to report whether any of the indicated life changes have occurred during the past few months or years (usually the preceding one or two-year period)—see table 2. Each change is assigned a Life Change Unit (LCU) score and a total LCU score for each person is then obtained. Numerous studies (e.g., Rahe 1972; Rahe, McKean, and Arthur 1967; see reviews by Holmes and Masuda 1974, and Rahe 1974) have demonstrated that the likelihood of future illness (and even accidents and athletic injuries) increases when a person experiences a considerably high number of life change units.

Table 2. The Social Readjustment Rating Scale

Life Event	Mean Value
1. Death of spouse	100
2. Divorce	73
3. Marital separation from mate	65
4. Detention in jail or other institution	63
5. Death of a close family member	63
6. Major personal injury or illness	53
7. Marriage	50
8. Being fired at work	47
9. Marital reconciliation with mate	45
10. Retirement from work	45
11. Major change in the health or behavior of a family member	44
12. Pregnancy	40
13. Sexual difficulties	39
14. Gaining a new family member (e.g., through birth, adoption, oldster moving in, etc.)	39
15. Major business readjustment (e.g., merger, reorganization, bankruptcy, etc.)	39
16. Major change in financial state (e.g., a lot worse off or a lot better off than usual)	38
17. Death of a close friend	37
18. Changing to a different line of work	36
19. Major change in the number of arguments with spouse (e.g., either a lot more or a lot less than usual regarding child-rearing, personal habits, etc.)	35
20. Taking out a mortgage or loan for a major purchase (e.g., for a home, business, etc.)	31

Life Event	Mean Value
21. Foreclosure on a mortgage or loan	30
22. Major change in responsibilities at work (e.g., promotion, demotion, lateral transfer)	29
23. Son or daughter leaving home (e.g., marriage, attending college, etc.)	29
24. Trouble with in-laws	29
25. Outstanding personal achievement	28
26. Wife beginning or ceasing work outside the home	26
27. Beginning or ceasing formal schooling	26
28. Major change in living conditions (e.g., building a new home, remodeling, deterioration of home or neighborhood)	25
29. Revision of personal habits (dress, manners, associations, etc.)	24
30. Trouble with the boss	23
31. Major change in working hours or conditions	20
32. Change in residence	20
33. Changing to a new school	20
34. Major change in usual type and/or amount of recreation	19
35. Major change in church activities (e.g., a lot more or a lot less than usual)	19
36. Major change in social activities (e.g., clubs, dancing, movies, visiting, etc.)	18
37. Taking out a mortgage or loan for a lesser purchase (e.g., for a car, TV, freezer, etc.)	17
38. Major change in sleeping habits (a lot more or a lot less sleep, or change in part of day when asleep)	16
39. Major change in number of family get-togethers (e.g., a lot more or a lot less than usual)	15
40. Major change in eating habits (a lot more or a lot less food intake, or very different meal hours or surroundings)	15
41. Vacation	13
42. Christmas	12
43. Minor violations of the law (e.g., traffic tickets, jaywalking, disturbing the peace, etc.)	11

SOURCE: T. H. Holmes and R. H. Rahe, "The Social Readjustment Rating Scale," *Journal of Psychosomatic Research* (1967), 11:213–218. Used with permission of Pergamon Press.

As Cohen notes, there has been much concern over theoretical and methodological weaknesses associated with the "Accumulation of Life Changes" approach—see, for example, Dohrenwend and Dohrenwend 1974, 1978; Rabkin and Struening 1976; and Sarason, de Monchaux, and Hunt 1975. To illustrate, many people undergo considerable change in their lives without becoming ill. Moreover, research suggests that the negative events predict future illness better than the positive ones do. Clearly, this popular view of stress and illness needs further clarification and research.

The final selection in this section describes the heroic efforts taken by Norman Cousins in his bout with a life-threatening disease. In this influential paper, Cousins (1976) details his efforts at directing his own treatment procedure and course of recovery. Believing that his illness was stress related, Cousins attempted to halt the spread of his collagen disease by inducing positive emotions. He watched, for example, old comedy classics to help him laugh vigorously. This "treatment," along with massive doses of vitamin C, and a strong will to live, was largely responsible for Cousins' remarkable recovery—at least that is Cousins' belief.

As fascinating and encouraging as Cousins' account is, we will never know the exact cause (or causes) for his cure—see Holden (1981) for an overview of some criticisms of Cousins' conclusions. Nevertheless, Cousins has greatly spurred the holistic health movement and today's trend of patients playing a greater role in their own recovery procedures. Cousins' views provide an important source of optimism in the treatment (and perhaps in the prevention) of stress-related diseases. A fuller accounting of Cousins' experiences may be found in his 1979 book, *Anatomy of An Illness as Perceived by the Patient*.

1

History and Present Status of the Stress Concept

HANS SELYE

N owadays, everyone seems to be talking about stress. You hear about this topic not only in daily conversation but also on television, via radio, in the newspapers, and in the ever increasing number of conferences, centers, and university courses devoted to stress. Yet remarkably few people define the concept in the same way or even bother to attempt a clearcut definition. The businessperson thinks of stress as frustration or emotional tension; the air traffic controller, as a problem in concentration; the biochemist and endocrinologist, as a purely chemical event; and the athlete, as muscular tension. This list could be extended to almost every human experience or activity, and, somewhat surprisingly, most people— be they chartered accountants, short-order cooks, or surgeons—consider their own occupation the most stressful. Similarly, most commentators believe that ours is the "age of stress," forgetting that the caveman's fear of attack by wild animals or of death from hunger, cold, or exhaustion must have been just as stressful as our fear of a world war, the crash of the stock exchange, or overpopulation.

Ironically, there is a grain of truth in every formulation of stress because all demands upon our adaptability do evoke the stress phenomenon. But we tend to forget that there would be no reason to use the single word "stress" to describe such diverse circumstances as those mentioned above were there not something common to all of them, just as we could have no reason to use a single word in connection with the production of light, heat, cold, or sound if we had been unable to formulate the concept of energy, which is required to bring about any of these effects. My definition of *stress* is the *nonspecific* (that is, common) *result of any demand upon the body*, be the effect mental or somatic. The formulation of this definition, based on objective indicators such as bodily and chemical changes that appear after any demand, has brought the subject (so popular now that it is often referred to as "stressology") up from the level of cocktail party chitchat into the domain of science.

One of the first things to bear in mind about stress is that a variety of dissimilar situations—emotional arousal, effort, fatigue, pain, fear, concentration, humiliation, loss of blood, and even great and unexpected success—are capable of producing stress; hence, no single factor can, in itself, be pinpointed as the cause of the reaction as such. To understand this point, it is necessary to consider certain facts about human biology. Medical research has shown that while people may face quite different problems, in some respects their bodies respond in a stereotyped pattern; identical biochemical changes enable us to cope with any type of increased demand on vital activity. This is also true of other animals and apparently even of plants. In all forms of life, it would seem that there are common pathways that must mediate any attempt to adapt to environmental conditions and sustain life.

HISTORICAL DEVELOPMENT

Even prehistoric man must have recognized a common element in the sense of exhaustion that overcame him in conjunction with hard labor, agonizing fear, lengthy exposure to cold or heat, starvation, loss of blood, or any kind of disease. Probably he soon discovered also that his response to prolonged and strenuous exertion passed through three stages: first the task was experienced as a hardship; then he grew used to it; and finally he could stand it no longer. The vague outlines of this intuitive scheme eventually were brought into sharper focus and translated into precise scientific terms that could be appraised by intellect and tested by reason. Before turning to contemporary science, it will be helpful to review some of the intervening developments that laid the foundation for the modern theory of stress.

In ancient Greece, Hippocrates, often considered the "father of medicine," clearly recognized the existence of a *vis medicatrix naturae,* or healing power of nature, made up of inherent bodily mechanisms for restoring health after exposure to pathogens. But early investigations were handicapped by the failure to distinguish between distress, always unpleasant, and the general concept of stress, which also encompasses experiences of intense joy and the pleasure of self-expression.

The nineteenth-century French physiologist Bernard enormously advanced the subject by pointing out that the internal environment of a living organism must remain fairly constant despite changes in the external environment: "It is the fixity of the *milieu intérieur* which is the condition of free and independent life" (1879:564). This comment had enormous impact; indeed, the Scottish physiologist Haldane was of the opinion that "no more pregnant sentence was ever framed by a physiologist" (1922:427). But this influence was due largely to various meanings that subsequently were read into Bernard's formulation. Actually, inanimate objects are more independent of their surroundings than are living beings. What distinguishes life is adaptability to change, not fixity. Bernard's more enduring legacy was the stimulation of later investigators to carry forward his pioneering studies on the particular adaptive changes by which the steady state is maintained.

The German physiologist Pflüger crystallized the relationship be-. tween active adaptation and the steady state when he noted that "the cause of every need of a living being is also the cause of the satisfaction of that need" (1877:57). The Belgian physiologist Fredericq expressed a similar view: "The living being is an agency of such sort that each disturbing influence induces by itself the calling forth of compensatory activity to neutralize or repair the disturbance" (1885:34).

In this century, the great American physiologist Cannon suggested the name "homeostasis," from the Greek *homoios,* meaning similar, and *stasis,* meaning position, for "the coordinated physiologic processes which maintain most of the steady states in the organism" (1939:333). Homeostasis might roughly be translated "staying power." Cannon's classic studies established the existence of many highly specific mechanisms for protection against hunger, thirst, hemorrhage, or agents tending to disturb normal body temperature, blood pH, or plasma levels of sugar, protein, fat, and calcium. He particularly emphasized the stimulation of the sympathetic nervous system, with the resulting hormonal discharge from the adrenal glands, which occurs during emergencies such as pain or rage. In turn, this autonomic process induces the cardiovascular changes that prepare the body for flight or fight.

It was against this cumulative background that, as a medical student, I eventually was drawn to the problem of a stereotyped response to any exacting task. The initial focus of my interest was what I thought of as the "syndrome of just being sick." In my second year of training I was struck by how patients suffering from the most diverse diseases exhibited strikingly similar signs and symptoms, such as loss of weight and appetite, diminished muscular strength, and absence of ambition. In 1936, the problem presented itself under conditions suited to analysis. While seeking a new ovarian hormone, co-workers and I at McGill University injected extracts of cattle ovaries into rats to see whether their organs would display unpredictable changes that could not be attributed to any known hormone. Three types of changes were produced: (1) the cortex, or outer layer, of the adrenal glands became enlarged and hyperactive; (2) the thymus, spleen, lymph nodes, and all other lymphatic structures shrank; and (3) deep, bleeding ulcers appeared in the stomach and upper intestines. Being closely interdependent, these changes formed a definite syndrome.

It was soon discovered that all toxic substances, irrespective of their source, produced the same pattern of responses. Moreover, identical organ changes were evoked by cold, heat, infection, trauma, hemorrhage, nervous irritation, and many other stimuli. Gradually, I realized that this was an experimental replica of the "syndrome of just being sick," which I had noted a decade earlier. Adrenal enlargement, gastrointestinal ulcers, and thymicolymphatic shrinkage were constant and invariable signs of damage to a body faced with the demand of meeting the attack of any disease. These changes became recognized as objective indices of stress and furnished a basis for developing the entire stress concept.

The reaction was first described in *Nature* as "a syndrome produced by diverse nocuous agents." Subsequently it became known as the *general adaptation syndrome* (GAS) or *biologic stress syndrome* (Selye 1936). In the same report, I also suggested the name "alarm reaction" for the initial response, arguing that it probably represented the somatic expression of a generalized call to arms of the body's defensive forces.

THE GENERAL ADAPTATION SYNDROME

The alarm reaction, however, was evidently not the entire response. After continued exposure of the organism to any noxious agent capable of eliciting this reaction, a stage of adaptation or resistance ensues. In other words, a state of alarm cannot be maintained continuously. If the agent is so drastic that continued exposure becomes incompatible with life, the animal dies during the alarm reaction (that is, within the first hours or days). If the organism can survive, this initial reaction is necessarily followed by the *stage of resistance.* The manifestations of this second phase are quite different from, and in many instances the exact opposite of, those that characterize the alarm reaction. For example, during the alarm reaction, the cells of the adrenal cortex discharge their secretory granules into the bloodstream and thus become depleted of corticoid-containing lipid storage material; in the stage of resistance, on the other hand, the cortex becomes particularly rich in secretory granules. In the alarm reaction, there is hemoconcentration, hypochloremia, and general tissue catabolism, whereas during the stage of resistance there is hemodilution, hyperchloremia, and anabolism, with a return toward normal body weight.

Curiously, after still more exposure to the noxious agent, the acquired adaptation is lost. The animal enters into a third phase, the *stage of exhaustion,* which inexorably follows as long as the demand is severe enough and applied for a sufficient length of time. It should be pointed out that the triphasic nature of the general adaptation syndrome gave us the first indication that the body's adaptability, or *adaptation energy,* is finite, since, under constant stress, exhaustion eventually ensues. We still do not know precisely what is lost, except that it is not merely caloric energy: food intake is normal during the stage of resistance. Hence, one would think that once adaptation had occurred and ample energy was available, resistance would go on indefinitely. But just as any inanimate machine gradually wears out, so does the human machine sooner or later become the victim of constant wear and tear. These three stages are reminiscent of childhood, with its characteristic low resistance and excessive response to any kind of stimulus, adulthood, during which the body has adapted to most commonly encountered agents and resistance is increased, and senility, characterized by loss of adaptability and eventual exhaustion, ending with death.

Our reserves of adaptation energy might be compared to an inherited bank account from which we can make withdrawals but to which we apparently cannot make deposits. After exhaustion from excessively stressful activity, sleep and rest can restore resistance and adaptability very close to previous levels, but complete restoration is probably impossible. Every biologic activity causes wear and tear; it leaves some irreversible chemical scars, which accumulate to constitute the signs of aging. Thus, adaptability should be used wisely and sparingly rather than squandered.

Mechanisms of Stress

Discoveries since 1936 have linked nonspecific stress with numerous biochemical and structural changes of previously unknown origin. There has also been considerable progress in analyzing the mediation of stress reactions by hormones. However, the carrier of the alarm signals that first relay the call for adaptation have yet to be identified. Perhaps they are metabolic by-products released during activity or damage, or perhaps what is involved is the lack of some vital substance consumed whenever any demand is made upon an organ. Since the only two coordinating systems that connect all parts of the body with one another are the nervous and the vascular systems, we can assume that the alarm signals use one or both of these pathways. Yet, while nervous stimulation may cause a general stress response, deafferented rats still show the classic syndrome when exposed to demands; so the nervous system cannot be the only route. It is probable that often, if not always, the signals travel in the blood.

The facts that led us to postulate the existence of the alarm signals would be in agreement with the view that the various cells send out different messengers. In that case the messages must somehow be tallied by the organs of adaptation. Whatever the nature of the *first mediator,* however, its existence is assured by its effects, which have been observed and measured. The discharge of hormones, the involution of the lymphatic organs, the enlargement of the adrenals, the feeling of fatigue, and many other signs of stress can all be produced by injury or activity in any part of the body.

Through the first mediator, the agent or situation disruptive of homeostasis eventually excites the hypothalamus, a complex bundle of nerve cells and fibers that acts as a bridge between the brain and the endocrine system (see figure 1.1). The resulting nervous signals reach certain neuroendocrine cells in the median eminence (ME) of the hypothalamus, where they are transformed

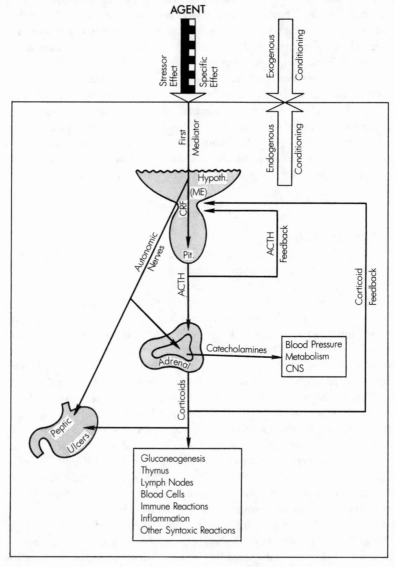

Figure 1.1. Principal pathways of the stress response.

into CRF (corticotrophic hormone releasing factor), a chemical messenger that has not yet been isolated in pure form but is probably a polypeptide. In this way, a message is relayed to the pituitary, causing a discharge into the general circulation of ACTH (adrenocorticotrophic hormone).

ACTH, reaching the adrenal cortex, triggers the secretion of corticoids, mainly glucocorticoids such as cortisol or corticosterone. Through gluconeogenesis these compounds supply a readily available source of energy for the adaptive reactions necessary to meet the demands made by the agent. The corticoids also facilitate various other enzyme responses and suppress immune reactions and inflammation, thereby helping the body to coexist with potential pathogens.

Usually secreted in lesser amounts are the pro-inflammatory corticoids, which stimulate the proliferative ability and reactivity of the connective tissue, enhancing the *inflammatory potential.* Thus, they help to build a strong barricade of connective tissue through which the body is protected against further invasion. Because of their prominent effect upon salt and water metabolism, these hormones have also been referred to as *mineralocorticoids* (e.g., desoxicorticosterone and aldosterone). The somatotrophic hormone (STH), or growth hormone, of the pituitary likewise stimulates defense reactions.

This chain of events is cybernetically controlled by several feedback mechanisms. For instance, if there is a surplus of ACTH, a short-loop feedback returns some of it to the hypothalamus-pituitary axis and this shuts off further ACTH production. In addition, through a long-loop feedback, a high blood level of corticoids similarly inhibits too much ACTH secretion.

Simultaneously with all these processes, another important pathway is utilized to mediate the stress response. Hormones such as catecholamines are liberated to activate mechanisms of general usefulness for adaptation. Adrenaline, in particular, is secreted to make energy available, to accelerate the pulse rate, to elevate the blood pressure and the rate of blood circulation in the muscles, and to stimulate the central nervous system (CNS). The blood coagulation mechanism is also enhanced by adrenaline, as a protection against excessive bleeding if injuries are sustained in the state of affairs eliciting stress.

Countless other hormonal and chemical changes during stress check and balance the body's functioning and stability, constituting a virtual arsenal of weapons with which the organism defends itself. The facts known today may lead us to believe that the anterior pituitary and the adrenal cortex play the cardinal roles in stress, but this view probably reflects the active part endocrinologists have taken in elucidating the syndrome. Also, the techniques required to investigate the role of the nervous system are much more complex than those heretofore used. It is considerably easier, for example, to remove an endocrine gland and substitute injected extracts for its hormones than it is to destroy minute nervous centers selectively and then restore their function to determine the role they may play.

Syntoxic and Catatoxic Responses

In the course of human evolution, the body has developed two basic mechanisms for defense against potentially injurious aggressors, whether of external or internal origin. These two types of reactions, on which homeostasis mainly depends, are known as *syntoxic*, from *syn*, meaning together, and *catatoxic*, from *cata*, meaning against. The former help us put up with the aggressor while the latter destroy it. Syntoxic stimuli, acting as tissue tranquilizers, create a state of passive tolerance, which permits peaceful coexistence with aggressors. In the case of catatoxic agents, chemical changes, mainly the induction of destructive enzymes, generate an active attack on the pathogen, usually by accelerating its metabolic degradation.

Corticoids, substances produced by the adrenal cortex, are among the most effective syntoxic hormones. Of these, the best known are the anti-inflammatory group, including cortisone, and related substances that inhibit inflammation and many other defensive immune reactions such as the active rejection of grafted foreign tissues, that is, hearts or kidneys.

The main purpose of inflammation is to prevent the spread of irritants into the bloodstream by localizing them within a barricade. However, when the foreign agent is itself innocuous and causes disease only by inciting an exaggerated defense reaction, the suppression of inflammation is advantageous. Thus, anti-inflammatory corticoids have proved effective in treating diseases whose major complaint is inflammation of the joints, eyes, or respiratory passages.

On the other hand, when the aggressor is dangerous, the defensive reaction should be increased above the normal level. This is accomplished by catatoxic substances carrying a chemical message to the tissues to fight the invader even more actively than usual.

Stressors

The agents or demands that evoke the patterned response are referred to, quite naturally, as *stressors*. Something is thus a stressor to the same degree that it calls forth the syndrome. Stressors, it should be noted, are not exclusively physical in nature. Emotions—love, hate, joy, anger, challenge, and fear—as well as thoughts, also call forth the changes characteristic of the stress syndrome. In fact, psychological arousal is one of the most frequent activators. Yet it cannot be regarded as the only factor, since typical stress reactions can occur in patients exposed to trauma, hemorrhage, etc., while under deep anesthesia. Anesthetics themselves are commonly used in experimental medicine to produce stress, and stress of anasthesia is a serious problem in clinical surgery.

STRESS AND DISEASE

In general, the nervous and hormonal responses outlined above aid adaptation to environmental change or stimuli. Sometimes, however, they are the cause of disease, especially if the state of stress is prolonged or intense. In the latter case, the body passes through successive stages of the GAS, described earlier.

As we have seen, a fully developed GAS consists of the alarm reaction, the stage of resistance, and the stage of exhaustion. Yet it is not necessary for all three stages to develop before we can speak of a GAS; only the most severe stress leads rapidly to the stage of exhaustion and death. Most of the physical or mental exertions, infections, and other stressors that act upon us during a limited period produce changes corresponding only to the first and second stages. At first the stressors may upset and alarm us, but then we adapt to them.

Normally, in the course of our lives we go through these first two stages many, many times. Otherwise we could never become adapted to all the activities and demands that are man's lot. Even the stage of exhaustion does not always need to be irreversible and complete, as long as it affects only parts of the body. For instance, running produces a stress situation, mainly in our muscles and cardiovascular system. To cope with this, we first have to limber up and get these systems ready for the task at hand; then for a while we will be at the height of efficiency in running; eventually, however, exhaustion will set in. This sequence could be compared with an alarm reaction, a stage of resistance, and a stage of exhaustion, all limited primarily to the muscular and cardiovascular systems; yet such an exhaustion is reversible—after a good rest we will be back to normal.

It nevertheless remains true that the adaptive response can break down or go wrong because of innate defects, understress, overstress, or psychological mismanagement. The most common stress diseases—the so-called diseases of adaptation—are peptic ulcers in the stomach and upper intestine, high blood pressure, heart accidents, and nervous disturbances. This is a relative concept, however. No malady is just a disease of adaptation. Nor are there any disease producers that can be so perfectly handled by the organism that maladaptation plays no part in their effects upon the body. Such agents would not produce disease. This haziness in its delimitation does not interfere with the practical utility of our concept. We must put up with the same lack of precision whenever we have to classify a disease. There is no pure heart disease, in which all other organs remain perfectly undisturbed, nor can we ever speak of a pure kidney disease or a pure nervous disease in this sense.

The indirect production of disease by inappropriate or excessive adaptive reactions is well illustrated by the following example drawn from everyday life. If you meet a loudly insulting but obviously harmless drunk, nothing will happen if you take the syntoxic attitude of going past and ignoring him. But if you respond catatoxically, by fighting or even only preparing to fight, the outcome may be tragic. You will discharge adrenalinelike hormones that increase blood pressure and pulse rate, while your whole nervous system becomes alarmed and tense. If you happen to be a coronary candidate, you might end up with a fatal brain hemorrhage or cardiac arrest. In that case, your death will have been caused by your own biologically suicidal choice of the wrong reaction.

THE PRESENT STATUS OF RESEARCH

In this short chapter, it is impossible to give a meaningful sketch of all that has been learned about the structure of stress hormones, the nervous pathways involved, the medicines that have been developed to combat stress, and the diagnostic aids that this approach has offered. Nevertheless, the medical, chemical, and microscopic approaches to the problem have all been extremely fruitful. Since the very first description of the GAS, the most important single discovery was made only recently: the brain produces certain simple chemical substances closely related to ACTH. These substances have morphinelike, painkilling properties, and since they come from the inside (*endo*), they have been called *endorphins*. (I am especially proud that one of my former students, Dr. Roger Guillemin, was one of the three American scientists who shared the 1977 Nobel Prize for this remarkable discovery, although it was made at the Salk Institute quite independently of me.) The endorphins have opened up an entirely new field in medicine, particularly in stress research. Not only do they have antistress effects as painkillers, but also they probably play an important role in the transmission of the alarm signal from the brain to the pituitary, and their concentration is especially high in the pituitary itself. Thus, they may shed some light on the nature of the first mediator.

Significant breakthroughs have also been made with the discovery of tranquilizers and psychotherapeutic chemicals to combat mental disease. These have reduced the number of institutionalized mental patients to an unprecedented low. Also worth mentioning are the enormously potent anti-ulcer drugs that block the pathways through which stress ulcers are produced.

However, all these purely medical discoveries are applicable only by physicians, and the general public cannot use them in daily life without constant medical supervision. Furthermore, most of these agents are not actually directed against stress but rather against some of its morbid manifestations (ulcers, high blood pressure, or heart accidents). Therefore, increasing attention has been given to the development of psychological techniques and behavioral codes that anybody can use, after suitable instruction, to adjust to the particular demands made by his life.

Among these not strictly medical approaches are the relaxation techniques. We should spend a little time each day at complete rest, with our eyes closed and our muscles relaxed, breathing regularly and repeating words that are either meaningless or heard so often that they merely help us not think of anything in particular. This is the basis of Transcendental Meditation, Benson's relaxation technique, and an infinite variety of other procedures. These practices should not be underestimated merely because science cannot explain them; they have worked for so long and in so many forms that we must respect them.

More recently, biofeedback has added a great deal to the psychological approach. A number of highly sophisticated instruments have been developed that inform the user constantly about body changes characteristic of stress, for example, in blood pressure, pulse rate, body temperature, and even brain activity. We do not yet have a scientific explanation for biofeedback, but if people learn to identify, instinctively or through instrumentation, when they are under stress, they can automatically avoid, or at least reduce, their responses.

A SCIENTIFIC ETHICS

The drunk illustration I used earlier shows how certain well-known facts about the demands of everyday life can make clearer some of the principles involved in the unconscious, wired-in stress responses mediated by the neurohumoral system. Yet it is also true that the latter can refine our knowledge of the former. Laboratory observations on the body's methods for fighting distress have already helped us to lay the foundations for a biologically justifiable code of behavior, one designed to achieve the pleasant stress of fulfillment (known technically as *eustress*—from the Greek *eu* meaning good, as in euphemia and euphoria) without the harmful consequences of damaging stress, that is, *distress* (Selye 1974).

At first it seems odd that the laws governing life's responses at such different levels as the cell, the whole person, and even the nation should be so essentially similar. Yet this type of uniformity is true of all great laws of nature. For example, in the inanimate world, arrangement of matter and energy in orbits circulating around a center is characteristic of the largest celestial bodies, as well as of individual atoms. Why is it that on these opposite levels, the smallest and the largest, the satellites circling a huge planet and the minute electrons around an atomic nucleus, should go around in orbits? We find comparable similarities in the laws governing living matter. Countless phenomena run in cycles, such as the periodically recurring needs for food, water, sleep, and sexual activity. Damage is unavoidable unless each cycle runs its full course.

In formulating a natural code of behavior, these thoughts have fundamental importance. We must not only understand the profound biological need for the completion and fulfillment of our aspirations but also know how to handle these in harmony with our particular inherited capacities. Not everybody is born with the same amount of adaptation energy.

Work: A Biological Necessity

Most people consider their work their primary function in life. For the man or woman of action, one of the most difficult things to bear is enforced inactivity during prolonged hospitalization or after retirement. Just as our muscles degenerate if not used, so our brain slips into chaos and confusion unless we constantly use it for work that seems worthwhile to us. The average person thinks he works for economic security or social status, but at the end of a most successful business career—when he finally has achieved this goal—there remains nothing to fight for. There is no hope for progress and only the boredom of assured monotony. The question is not whether we should or should not work, but what kind of work suits us best.

In my opinion, today's insatiable demand for less work and more pay does not depend so much on the number of working hours or dollars as on the degree of dissatisfaction with life. We could do much, and at little cost, by fighting this dissatisfaction. Many people suffer because they have no particular taste for anything, no hunger for achievement. These, and not those who earn little, are the true paupers of mankind. What they need more than money is guidance.

Without the incentive to work out his role as *homo faber*, a person is likely to seek destructive, revolutionary outlets to satisfy the basic human need for self-assertive activity. Man may be able to solve the age-old problem of having to live by the sweat of his brow, but the fatal enemy of all utopias is boredom. What we shall have to do after technology makes most "useful work" redundant is to invent new occupations. Even this will require a full-scale effort to teach "play professions," such as the arts, philosophy, crafts, and science, to the public at large; there is no limit to how much each man can work on perfecting himself and on giving pleasure to others.

"Earn Thy Neighbor's Love"

Each person must find a way to relieve his pent-up energy without creating conflicts with his fellow men. Such an approach not only insures peace of mind but also earns the goodwill, respect, and even love of our neighbors, the highest degree of security and the most noble status symbol to which the human being can aspire.

This philosophy of hoarding a wealth of respect and friendship is merely one reflection of the deep-rooted instinct of people and animals to collect— a tendency as characteristic of ants, bees, squirrels, and beavers as of the capitalist who collects money to put away in the bank. The same impulse drives entire human societies to build systems of roads, telephone networks, cities, and fortifications, which they view as necessary ingredients of their future security and comfort.

In man, this urge first manifests itself when children start to amass matchboxes, shells, or stickers; it continues when adults collect stamps or coins. This natural proclivity is not artificial. By collecting certain things, one acquires status and security in the community. The guideline of earning love merely attempts to direct the hoarding instinct toward what I consider the most permanent and valuable commodity that man can possess: a huge capital of goodwill that protects him against personal attacks by others.

To live literally by the biblical command to "love thy neighbor as thyself" leads only to guilt feelings because this teaching cannot be reconciled with the laws of objective science. Whether we like it or not, egoism is an inescapable characteristic of all living beings. But we can continue to benefit by the wisdom of this time-honored maxim if, in the light of modern biological research, we merely reword it. Let our guide for conduct be the motto "Earn thy neighbor's love."

2

Stress:
A Psychophysiological
Conception

ANIS MIKHAIL

In the article "A Historical View of the Stress Field," Mason wrote: "It is tempting to suggest that we might be better off without the term 'stress' at all, given our present crude level of insight, but perhaps the notion of a generic term which somehow ties together the threatening or taxing demands of the environment on living organisms strikes some deep, responsive chord within us which keeps alive the use of stress terminology in spite of all the confusion it creates" (1975b:35).

The question of whether the stress concept should have a place in science requires the evaluation of two opposing views. The first maintains that the term should be abandoned altogether, as suggested by Mason and several psychologists. Dr. Robert Ader, for example, argued at a recent symposium on ulceration (1979) that the effects attributed to stress do not seem to follow any predictable direction. From his perspective, stress is a useless concept which may confuse rather than clarify scientific inquiry. The second view finds stress a useful concept which should be retained despite its present ambiguity. The expectation of this position is that future theoretical growth in the stress field will sharpen the meaning of the concept.

What do philosophers of science say about these conflicting opinions which appear, also, in other areas of science? Kaplan clearly supports the second position. He argues that "we may prudently let vagueness persist" until pressure arises for a new verbal construction that resolves the vagueness in the relevant portion of the concept. While Kaplan concedes "that the progress of science is marked by successive closures" of meaning and precise definitions, he points out that "it is just the function of inquiry to instruct us how and when closure can best be achieved," and that "the scientist is in no hurry for closure. Tolerance of ambiguity is as important for creativity in science as it is anywhere else" (1964:71).

Added to this philosophical view are the contributions of Hans Selye (1950) whose stress concept has achieved a recognized place inside and outside the technical scientific literature and has encouraged research by scientists in many disciplines into the effects of stress on health and behavior. Indeed, the publication of two journals, the *Journal of Human Stress* and recently Selye's *Stress,* reflects the increasing interest in stress as a concept.

HOW STRESS EVOLVED
IN SELYE'S CONCEPTION

To a great extent the concept of stress as presently understood in medical sciences has been the outcome of Selye's theoretical and empirical work (1936) on the effects of nocuous agents. In its formative stage, the concept was ever so vague. However, as Selye explained, "You must first have a concept derived from observation and symbolized by a name—before you can even try to delimit it more precisely by a definition" (1976:61).

In Selye's attempt to define stress, the concept went through several modifications. At the beginning, there was an inclination to define stress as "the rate of wear and tear in the body caused by life at any one time" (p. 65). Selye noticed that this formulation could not provide the concept of stress with an objective operational base. In another attempt, he defined stress more simply "as the sum of all nonspecific changes caused by function or damage." The nonspecificity of the changes is Selye's theoretically significant characterization of stress that appears in this formulation and in an improved version: "Stress is the state manifested by a specific syndrome which consists of all the nonspecifically induced changes within a biologic system" (p. 64).

Unlike the earlier formulation, no reference was made in the foregoing definition to the causation of the "nonspecific changes." The expression "caused by function or damage" was omitted altogether. Obviously, the focus of Selye's theory is on the stress response (reactions) rather than on its stimulus (antecedent causative agents). The lack of interest in the stimulus side is evident, but to a lesser degree, in the latest definition: "Biologic stress is the nonspecific response of the body to any demand made upon it." It should be observed that the expression "any demand" does not specify with sufficient clarity the conditions that are necessary to activate the stress mechanism and the nonspecific response. This vagueness in the conception of stress can be reduced markedly when current psychological literature is taken into account as will be mentioned later. At any rate, Selye's latest definition has attractive simplicity and is generally acceptable in the medical sciences. So far, no alternative theoretical definition of stress has been proposed.

Is Stress Response Nonspecifically Induced?

As noted earlier, Selye attached great theoretical significance to the nonspecificity of stress reactions and disease. This view contrasts sharply with the older specificity position of Pasteur's theory which maintained that each disease could be induced only by its specific causative agent or microbial infection.

The nonspecificity of the stress response, however, has been the subject of some controversy. Mason (1971), for instance, found that the nonspecificity of the pituitary-adrenocortical activity, the stress response, was not as broad as Selye had suggested. The effects of several kinds of nocuous agents—fasting, muscular exercise, heat, hemorrhage and cold exposure—on the secretion level of urinary 17-hydroxycorticosteroid (17-OHCS) of monkeys were tested. According to Selye's theory, it would be predicted that elevation in 17-OHCS should result from all the noxious agents despite their qualitative differences. Contrary to expectation, neither fasting nor heat raised 17-OHCS level. The failure of 17-OHCS to rise, however, was noted only when psychological influences were minimized— that is, when fasting monkeys were isolated from nonfasting ones and when nonnutritive cellulose diet pellet was given to them to provide some bulk within the gastrointestinal tract. But when psychological factors were included as in the condition wherein monkeys were suddenly deprived of their daily food while their neighbors were eating next to them as usual, a marked rise in 17-OHCS was observed.

The inability of the physically harmful stressors, fasting and heat, to raise 17-OHCS could be interpreted by the opponents of the theory as evidence against it. On the other hand, advocates of the theory could argue that what appeared in this experiment to be a test of different kinds of stressors in eliciting the nonspecific response was really no more than a test of different levels of stressor intensity. The lower levels failed to activate the stress response simply because they were weak. When fasting was strengthened by psychological factors, the nonspecific response occurred.

Mason's experiment did not reach an unequivocal conclusion about the nonspecificity of the stress response because it tested a theory which is not formulated in a testable form. Before we can reasonably be asked to test the nonspecificity notion we should at least be able to induce stress with some certainty. To do so, the conditions which constitute a stressor must be stated independently of the stressor's effect. Not any demand is stressful. Demands that evoke stress are only those which tax the organism's capability and which appear to be of value to the individual. The extent of stress depends largely on the individual's evaluation of the consequences of unfulfilled demands.

It is necessary to point out that the study of stress requires that the researcher or clinician be aware of its psychological determinants. The ambiguity of this aspect of stress in Selye's formulation impairs the design of sensitive experiments and the attainment of reliable findings.

A second line of research (Lacey 1967) challenged what Selye described as the "specific syndrome" of stress. On the basis of several studies (Lacey et al. 1963), Lacey could not support the idea that an overall activation syndrome of autonomic and hormonal stress reactions exists, as suggested by Cannon (1953) and recently by Selye. He found that, during stress, changes in physiological measures such as heart rate and skin conductance were not uniformly in the same direction. The opposing directions of these autonomic measures were described as "directional fractionation." To illustrate (Lacey 1959), skin conductance level of subjects who were tested in four stimulus conditions—visual attention, empathic listening, thinking and pain—increased. Heart rate, on the other hand, in visual and auditory attending situations, decreased. It is worth noting that the direction of heart rate was not consistent across all test situations. That is, in the visual and auditory tasks deceleration was observed, but in the thinking and pain situations cardiac acceleration was noted.

The foregoing findings argue against an identifiable pattern of stress reactions that displays monolithic change. As indicated by Lacey, the stress syndrome is not stereotyped; it varies depending on the nature of the situation and on characteristics of the individual. This means that stress is not manifested by a single specific syndrome (The General Adaptation Syndrome) but by a multiplicity of patterns whose compositions and form are determined by situational and organismic variables. Each stress pattern is a product of a *specific* causative interaction between situational and organismic determinants.

Despite the validity of the above argument, Selye's position can be easily defended. "Specificity is always a matter of degree" (1976) both within stress reactions and among the causes which induce them. The high level of specificity of form and nonspecificity of cause appear to occur under conditions of intense stress, such as those employed in Selye's early research. Mild stress, on the other hand, may not be strong enough to activate all the reactions that characterize Selye's stress syndrome. As noted in Lacey's work, less demanding tasks (e.g., visual attending) led to a decrease rather than an increase in heart rate. Unlike intense stress, mild stress is distinguishable by nonspecificity of form (i.e., absence of stereotyped patterning) and by specificity of cause (i.e., particularization).

The difference between the characteristics of mild and intense stress may account for part of the inconsistency in stress literature. A more serious charge is that specificity and nonspecificity are fluid concepts which cannot be of value to objective scientific inquiry. What is specific could be judged nonspecific and vice versa so long as no criterion has been set to determine the degree of specificity. This argument carries some weight, but as Selye remarked (1976), many useful concepts such as "green" reflect no more than a judgment. In a perfect color spectrum, no one could state exactly where green starts and where it ends. The judgment that stress reactions are nonspecifically induced is useful in drawing the attention of researchers and medical practitioners to the fact that some diseases, diseases of adaptation, have less specific causation than Pasteur's infectious diseases. Unlike microbial infections, stress diseases are functional disorders that are brought about by a wider range of causative agents.

General Adaptation Syndrome

As mentioned earlier, the focus of Selye's theory is on the adaptive reactions of the body to stressful conditions. It maintains that the body reacts with a specific syndrome: the General Adaptation Syndrome (GAS). The value of the theory is in the description it offers to the biochemical mechanisms of adaptation to stress. It describes also the temporal course of the GAS in terms of three stages: alarm, adaptation, and exhaustion.

The theory does not attempt, however, to answer fundamental questions such as under what conditions stress occurs, or what constitutes a demanding stressor that is capable of eliciting the GAS. This theory is not designed to account for the role of situational and organismic variables involved in the activation of a stress state. It does not state the necessary and sufficient conditions for the induction of stress. Hence, it should be described more accurately as a theory of *adaptation* to stress rather than a stress theory.

PSYCHOLOGICAL STRESS THEORY

A major source of stress is the psychological environment. A biochemical stress theory, such as Selye's, cannot provide answers to research or practical problems which evoke stress psychologically. To illustrate, a frequently quoted statement which Selye used as a practical advice to business executives is that "it is not what happens to you that matters but how you take it." Certainly, this advice is not derived from biochemical theory. The psychological component, however, is clearly detectable in it.

Progress in psychological theorizing has been slow. Early work on psychological stress was represented by two significant publications: *Men under Stress* by Grinker and Spiegel (1945) and *Psychological Stress* by Janis (1958). The presence of psychological stress literature, however, was overshadowed by Selye's theory and writings which dominated the entire stress scene around the mid-fifties. Stress at that time had mainly physiological connotations of hormonal and autonomic nature. It was perhaps the appearance of Lazarus' *Psychological Stress and the Coping Process* in 1966 that marked a change in stress conception. This work which integrated a wide range of literature was in fact a culmination of views which had been expressed earlier by several writers. Haggard's view in 1949 was a good portrayal of what the stress concept would become three decades later:

> An individual experiences emotional stress when his overall adjustement is threatened, when his adaptive mechanisms are severely taxed and tend to collapse. Some of the factors which influence an individual's ability to tolerate and master stress include: the nature of his early identifications and his present character structure, and their relation to the demands and gratifications of the present stress-producing situation; the nature of his reactions to the situation; his ability to master strong and disturbing emotional tensions; the extent to which he knows about all aspects of the situation, so that he is not helplessly unaware of the nature and source of threat; his available skills and other means of dealing effectively with it; and the strength and pattern of his motivation to do so (p. 458).

In the fifties, it could be seen that three important aspects of stress were identified.

1. *Individuals differ in their reactivity to stress.* The recognition of the role of individual differences was noticeable in Lazarus' statement in 1952 that "while great individual differences in response to stress have been recognized, few fruitful attempts have been made to discover their nature" (Lazarus, Deese, and Osler 1952:307).

2. *Stress is determined by the perception of the stressful situation rather than by the situation itself.* This determinant can be traced back to Pascal's conception of stress "in terms of a perceived environmental situation which threatens the gratification of needs . . ." (1951:177). Similarly, Basowitz et al. noted in a study of stress in paratroopers that "in future research . . . we should not consider stress as *imposed* upon the organism, but as its response to internal or external processes which reach those threshold levels that strain its physiological and psychological integrative capacities close to or beyond their limits" (1955:288–289).

3. *The extent of stress depends partly on the capability of the individual to cope.* This determinant appeared in Basowitz' previous quotation and in another of Cofer and Appley who defined stress as "the state of an organism where he perceives that his well-being (or integrity) is endangered and that he must divert all his energies to its protection" (1964:453).

These aspects of stress have been expressed more articulately in recent literature. Lazarus (1976), for example, indicated that "stress occurs when there are demands on the person which tax or exceed his adjustive resources." Likewise, McGrath defined stress "as the *anticipation* of inability to respond adequately (or at a reasonable cost) to perceived demand, accompanied by anticipation of negative consequences for inadequate response" (1970a:23). The same kind of thinking appeared in Sells' monograph in which he stated that a state of stress arises when the "individual has no adequate response available" to meet a demand and "when the consequences of failure to respond effectively are important to the individual." According to Sells, "stress intensity depends on the importance of individual involvement and the individual's assessment of the consequences of his inability to respond effectively to the situation" (1970:138).

The view that emerges from the above is that the necessary and sufficient condition for psychological stress is a cognitive appraisal of a demand-capability imbalance. This conception of psychological stress which represents the position of several writers (Cox 1978; Lazarus 1976; McGrath 1970a; Sells 1970) prevailed in a symposium (McGrath 1970c) on *Social and Psychological Factors in Stress* (1967). In contrast to Selye's biologic stress, the emphasis of psychological stress is on the input side, in particular, on the kind of situation and individual interaction that evokes a stress state.

There are many indications that the interest in psychological stress is developing rapidly. In recent introductory psychology texts, for instance, reference to stress and adjustment literature is common, while in the majority of older texts (i.e., published about 15 years ago) the term *stress* was not even mentioned. The present interest in stress, however, seems to be limited to psychological and social sciences. In this regard, Mason mentioned "that the popularity of stress concepts has gradually dwindled in the physiological field during the past 15 years, while the use of stress terminology and concepts has continued to flourish in the psychological and social sciences" (1975a:11). He pointed out further that "a key insight in understanding the present state of stress research is the recognition that the overwhelming bulk of interest and effort in the field is concerned with *psychological stress,* i.e., with the impact of psychosocial influences upon the organism" (p. 11).

AN INTEGRATED APPROACH

A look at contemporary stress literature in psychology and in physiology shows that hardly any logical link exists between them. The theoretical interests are unrelated. Adaptive reactions of the stress state are the domain of physiological stress, while conditions essential for stress activation are the domain of psychological stress. Undoubtedly, psychological stress theory can maintain its present direction independent of Selye's physiological conception. This opinion was expressed earlier by Mason who mentioned that "the evolution of psychological stress terminology and theory could proceed more purely on the basis of assessment of psychological data without the present pressures of trying to link psychological stress concepts to Selye's essentially physiological stress concepts, unless there is really a compelling rationale for doing so" (1975b:31).

Is there a compelling reason for integrating psychological and physiological stress theory? Should psychological theorizing assimilate or repel what has emerged in physiological stress research? Should the old order as represented by Selye's concepts be retained or discarded? A sound answer to these questions is provided by Kaplan when he states that "even scientific revolutions preserve some continuity with the old order of things" (1964:304). The tendency to reject older concepts and theories is an uncommendable peculiarity of behavioral sciences. As Kaplan noted, "Much of the theorizing in behavioral science is not building on what has already been established so much as laying out new foundations, or even worse, producing only another set of blueprints" (1964:304).

There is no logical incompatibility that stands in the way of integrating psychological stress theory with Selye's theory. Both approaches are, in fact, complementary. Psychological stress theory outlines the conditions which determine the evocation of stress while Selye's theory describes its form. To portray what is significant in these approaches, the following definition of stress is suggested.

Holistic Definition of Stress

Stress is a state which arises from an actual or perceived demand-capability imbalance in the organism's vital adjustment actions and which is partially manifested by a nonspecific response.

An objective of this new definition is to emphasize the continuity between psychological and physiological theorizing. The older conception is remade but not refuted. As Kaplan wrote, "In an important sense, new scientific theories do not refute the old ones but somehow remake them" (1964:304).

Merits of Integration

Mason aptly remarked, "that the question of the extent to which there may be logical continuity or compatibility of concepts developing in the psychological stress field with Selye's concept of stress as a nonspecific physiological response pattern is an issue which very much needs to be confronted directly and resolved" (1975a:12). Does the continuity position as implied in the proposed stress definition improve the present state of thought? To answer this question, the merits of continuity should be looked at against a background of present thinking.

Undoubtedly, Selye recognizes the influence of the interpretive psychological processes on determining the stress level. This is evident in his previously quoted advice to business executives. In his formal definition of stress, however, the significant role of perceptual processes was not expressed. Selye's medical training in sciences that excluded psychology was obviously responsible for the restrictive biological influence on his stress conception. An integrated approach provides Selye's formulation with the breadth needed to encompass the stress of living.

Psychological processes appear to serve also as the main first mediator of stress. This issue was noted by Lazarus in 1966 and was discussed more fully in 1980 (see Lazarus et al. 1980). Quoting Lazarus, "It is altogether possible that the extensive findings of stress biochemists that physiologically noxious agents produce changes in the hormonal secretions of the adrenal cortex are the result of their psychological impact" (1966:398). To support his opinion, Lazarus cited the observation (Symington et al. 1955) that adrenocortical stress reactions do not occur under the conditions of unconsciousness and anesthesia. Mason's position is similar to that of Lazarus. He wrote, "The unrecognized first mediator in many of Selye's experiments simply may have been the psychological apparatus involved in emotional arousal . . ." (1975b:25). A transition from the physiological to psychological level, Mason remarked, would mean a shift from a "relatively simple 'physiological' arc, involving afferent inputs directly into the final common neuroendocrine pathways in the diencephalon, to that involving the higher, more complex, 'psychological' processes . . ." (p. 26).

The nonspecificity aspect of stress is not overstated in the integrated definition of stress, because not all stress reactions are nonspecifically activated. This fact is well recognized by Selye as expressed in this statement: "Every conceivable agent which can act upon the human body, from without or from within, does certain things more than others. Those which it does more are relatively specific or characteristic for it, as compared to those which it does less" (1976:103). For theoretical considerations, Selye chose to devote his attention to the nonspecific stress response. Likewise, Cannon was particularly interested in the sympathico-adrenal system which is similar to the pituitary-adrenocortical response in its nonspecific induction.

There is no logical reason, however, to limit our conception of stress to its nonspecific response. For a broader understanding of stress, specific responses are not less significant than the nonspecific ones. Indeed, the nonspecificity which attracted Selye's attention so much seems to reflect no more than a natural characteristic of the hormonal system. The relative nonspecificity of many hormones is an emerging principle in endocrinology as noted by Mason: "The response of many hormones, including cortisol, epinephrine, norepinephrine, thyroxine, growth hormone, insulin, testosterone, and others, may be described as 'nonspecific,' in the sense that more than one stimulus is capable of stimulating the secretion of each of them" (1975b:27).

Whatever the level of nonspecificity of hormonal reaction is, it should be emphasized that the entire hormonal system is not the only one which reacts to stress. Others such as the cardiovascular, the digestive, and the motor systems react to stress also but with greater specificity. The picture that emerges from the above is that specificity and nonspecificity of stress responses represent two ends of a continuum rather than two dichotomous classes of distinctly different forms of reactions. The specificity level of these reactions increases as we follow the evolution of adjustment systems of the old and new brain (MacLean 1958) from the stone age response to civilized behavior.

3

Stress and Bodily Illness
FRANCES COHEN

I n recent years there has been increasing interest in the role that stress plays in the precipitation and prevention of physical illness. Some writers claim that stress is the major killer of our time; however, it appears that the relationship between stress and the development of illness is not that simple or straightforward. To understand the role of stress in a multifactorial disease model, and to pinpoint areas in which psychological interventions might be useful, we must evaluate the empirical work supporting a link between stress and disease and specify the mechanisms that might be involved. To set the stage for this discussion, what is meant by the word "stress" needs to be clarified and some methodologic problems in the data base must be considered.

THE RUBRIC OF STRESS

The word "stress" has been used to refer to (1) an aversive stimulus event, (2) a specific physiological or psychological response, or (3) a special type of transaction between the person and the environment. Confusion is avoided if each of these is specified separately. Thus we distinguish stressors (or stress events) from the psychological state of stress (i.e., feelings of threat, harm or loss, or challenge, as described by Lazarus and Launier 1978), and from stress responses (on physiological, psychological, or social levels).

Types of Stressors
Stressors include specific events that involve change, ongoing negative environmental conditions, and certain types of situations where no change

EDITORS' NOTE—We have omitted numerous references from this paper. Please consult the original source for a complete accounting of citations.

occurs. The latter category includes situations of monotony (Frankenhaeuser 1976) where no change has occurred when change might have been expected, as when a life-course event does not occur "on time" (Gersten et al. 1974) and when differences exist between expectations and actualities (Coover, Goldman, and Levine 1971).

It is important to keep in mind that stressors are not homogeneous in nature. Four types of stress events can be distinguished, based primarily on their duration (F. Cohen et al. 1980): (1) acute time-limited events (e.g., awaiting surgery, parachute jumping); (2) stress event sequences—one particular event initiates a series of different events which occur over an extended period of time (e.g., bereavement, being fired from a job); (3) chronic intermittent stressors (e.g., things that may occur once a day, once a week, once a year, such as sexual difficulties or conflicts with neighbors or in-laws); and (4) chronic stress conditions (e.g., being disabled, chronic job stress) which may or may not be initiated by a discrete event. In both stress event sequences and conditions of chronic stress, psychological and physiological reactions to stressors may occur over an extended period of time. In the former condition the person may be responding to different stressors over time, while in the latter case the same stressors persist. Important research questions concern the psychological and physiological effects of each of these types of stressors. For example, we do not know if different coping strategies are effective for dealing with acute as compared to chronic stressors. Nor do we know if the mobilization that occurs in response to time-limited stressors has negative long-term consequences on health or whether chronicity of physiological response is necessary for pathophysiological outcomes to occur. In the case of chronic stressors, the individual may reach an equilibrium in which constant coping efforts are not required. Some hormones (e.g., cortisol) rarely show chronic elevations, suggesting that an adaptive process occurs. Other hormones (e.g., catecholamines, testosterone) do show sustained alterations in response to chronic stress conditions. We need to learn more about the adaptive processes and physiological responses to chronic stressors in human beings.

Types of Stress Responses

Stress responses can occur on physiological, psychological, or social levels. Physiologically, there can be changes in autonomic nervous system, hormonal, immunologic, and neuroregulatory (both neurotransmitter and neuromodulator) reactions. *Autonomic nervous system* reactions include increased heart rate, blood pressure, blood volume, and respiration rate, and changes in electrical skin resistance. The most studied *hormonal* responses to stressors are the increased secretion of adrenocortical hormones (e.g., cortisol), stimulated by adrenocorticotropic hormone (ACTH) from the pituitary, and of adrenal-medullary hormones (i.e., the catecholamines, especially epinephrine and norepinephrine), stimulated by sympathetic nerve activity. There may also be increases in growth hormone and prolactin, and a biphasic response of luteinizing hormone and testosterone. In recent years there has been increased interest in how the *immunologic* system responds to stressors. Both cell-mediated responses (involving T lymphocytes) and humoral immune responses (involving B lymphocytes) have been studied. The central nervous system, endocrine, neurotransmitter, and other physiological processes may be involved as intermediate steps in the pathway from stressors to immune response. Stressors may also influence *neurotransmitters* (chemical compounds that transfer information between nerve cells) such as dopamine, norepinephrine, and epinephrine, and *neuromodulators* (chemicals that alter interneuronal communication but do not act within the synapse itself). Neuromodulators influence the activity of a neurotransmitter by affecting its synthesis, release, reuptake, or interaction with a receptor. Other neuroregulater compounds that may function as neurotransmitters or neuromodulators include serotonin and endorphins and other peptides.

On the psychological level, stress responses can be reflected in negatively toned affect (e.g., anxiety, fear), motor-behavioral reactions (both expressive and instrumental actions), and alterations in adaptive performance (Lazarus 1966). On a social level, evaluation can be made of antisocial behavior, difficulties in meeting social role requirements, and so forth.

Stress as Growth-Enhancing

Although most researchers emphasize the deleterious effects of stress, there is increasing interest in the role that stress may play in enhancing personal development. Certain stresses are inevitable throughout the life cycle, yet most people do not appear to suffer adverse effects. People may have to feel distress at certain time periods in order to develop competencies, increase self-esteem, enhance later performance, learn empathy, and so on. In some cases stress can enhance personal development and lack of it can result in diminished capabilities in later life (Block 1971; Murphy 1962).

Whether a stressful event leads to growth, temporary difficulty or trauma is a function of a number of factors, including the following: (1) the pervasiveness and persistence of the event, (2) the timing of the event, (3) one's personal resources, (4) the nature of the surrounding environment including one's relationships with significant others, (5) the opportunities available for acting on the environment, and (6) the meaning that can be given to the experience (Benner, Roskies, and Lazarus 1980).

Further, some people seek out highly stressful environments (Klausner 1968). Stress-seeking may be a way to test one's competence, build feelings of mastery, or relieve boredom. Systematic studies are needed in this area. Important questions include: Under what conditions are stressful experiences growth-enhancing? For whom? Do those with few personal or social resources have the most difficulty? Do early stressful experiences inoculate a person so he or she is better equipped to cope with later stressors? As we understand more about the positive effects of stressful life experiences we will be in a better position to evaluate if particular interventions are likely to be beneficial or if they may interfere with needed growth and development of coping skills.

METHODOLOGICAL PROBLEMS
IN THE RESEARCH BASE

There are three major methodological problems in most of the research relating stress and disease: (1) the inadequacy of current measures of stressors, (2) the problem of distinguishing between illness and "illness behavior" (Mechanic 1962), and (3) the inadequacy of studying etiologic factors in disease through retrospective studies.

Problems in Measurement of Stressors

The most commonly used measure of stress events in humans is the Holmes and Rahe (1967a) Schedule of Recent Experience (SRE). The SRE lists 43 life changes (e.g., promotion, divorce, being fired) and the subject indicates how many times in the preceding time period each has occurred. Each event is given a Life Change Unit (LCU) score and the sum of LCU's is obtained. The LCU weightings for each life event were obtained by having different groups of subjects rate for each item the amount of readjustment they thought would be required (Holmes and Rahe 1967b). The empirical research using this scale will be discussed later in this article. However, the adequacy of the SRE as a measure of stress has come under considerable attack. The reliability of reporting of life events is low and may be adequate only for events in the 6-month time period prior to administration of the test (Jenkins, Hurst, and Rose 1979). Further, the scale confounds life events with what could be considered presymptomatic manifestations of incipient illness (e.g., changes in sleeping habits, physical illness). This confounding does not provide a clear measure of stressors and would artificially inflate the association between "life changes" and illness (Hudgens 1974).

More importantly, the SRE represents only one way of conceptualizing stress—that is, as life change. Excluded from this instrument are chronic ongoing stress situations as well as acute stressors and minor daily problems. Researchers have found that chronic conditions such as sex role conflicts (Pearlin 1975a), status incongruity between spouses (Pearlin 1975b), and work overload and underload (Frankenhaeuser and Gardell 1976) have important relationships to health and morale. Yet since these situations do not involve change, they are not measured by the SRE. It has further been argued that the seemingly minor hassles of everyday life may be quite powerful predictors of health outcomes (Kanner et al. 1981; Pearlin and Schooler 1978) and might have more deleterious health consequences than the relatively rare life events measured by the SRE.

Problems in Criterion Measures of Illness

In studies of the role of stress in the development of disease, the following types of illness indicators have been used (Cohen 1979): (a) number of visits to a physician (without confirmation of the existence of organic disease), (b) physical illness confirmed in patients who have self-selected for treatment, (c) subjects' reports of physical symptoms or illness (without confirmation of the existence of organic disease), and (d) illness confirmed by medical examination in a population sample which includes those with no complaints of physical symptomatology. Some researchers argue that the first three indicators tap "illness behavior" rather than illness (Mechanic 1962, 1978a). Illness behavior refers to those processes whereby individuals perceive, interpret, and respond to physical symptoms. There are considerable individual differences in people's sensitivity to symptoms, likelihood of defining them as serious, and likelihood of seeking treatment (Zola 1972). Many people may have physical symptoms without seeking treatment. Thus the treatment-seekers may represent a special, small percentage of those who actually are ill. Even severe symptoms such as those involved in angina pectoris or myocardial infarction may go unreported in a substantial number of cases (Margolis et al. 1973).

When physician visits are used as the indicator of illness, there is both self-selection for treatment and the inclusion of a group without organic disease—those Garfield (1970) refers to as the "worried well." Patients whose illness is diagnosed because they have elected to seek treatment may represent only a small percentage of all persons with that illness. The third indicator—questionnaire reports of illness—has similar problems and undoubtedly underreports some disorders and may overreport others (Chambers et al. 1976). To be sure that one is studying the development of illness itself rather than illness behavior or self-report, it may be necessary to perform medical examinations on a representative sample of the population. The need for population samples, not just those who self-select for treatment, is increasingly being emphasized by researchers in the field (Rahe and Arthur 1978; Weiner 1977).

Retrospective Reports of Life Events

The third methodological problem concerns the inadequacy of looking at stressors as etiologic factors by utilizing retrospective reports of life events.

The knowledge that one is ill or the disease process itself may affect the independent variables hypothesized to be causal factors . . . Once disease has been diagnosed, patients may reinterpret their past experiences. For example, Down's syndrome was once thought to be the result of emotional stress in early pregnancy because mothers of children with Down's syndrome reported a high number of stressful events when interviewed about their pregnancy after the child was born. It was not until the discovery that a chromosomal defect produced this disease that the stress-related etiologic hypothesis was finally discarded (Brown 1974). Further, many of the studies focusing on diagnosed cases have not utilized control groups or tried to minimize observer bias, raising further questions about the adequacy of this type of design.

THEORIES LINKING STRESS AND DISEASE

The literature linking psychological factors and disease falls into two broad categories: studies that focus on general susceptibility to illness (generality approaches) and those that focus on the development of specific illnesses (specificity approaches). The basis of the distinction is whether generalized or specific somatic effects are predicted to result from the particular psychological factors under study: generality approaches posit factors which affect a general susceptibility to illness—which would increase the probability of developing diseases of many types—whereas specificity approaches examine physiological mechanisms directly implicated in the development of a particular disease. Our review will focus on theories with a generality focus. Discussion of the role of stress as a factor in specific diseases, such as cancer, coronary heart disease, or psychosomatic disorders can be found in other sources (Cohen 1979; Fox 1978; Jenkins 1976; Weiner 1977).

There are several different hypotheses about which stress-related factors are most likely to lead to disease . . . The research focuses on three types of events (Cohen 1979): (1) *loss events*—which involve loss of important gratifications (e.g., bereavement); (2) *accumulation of life changes*—the occurrence within a limited time period of different life events that require readjustment; and (3) *stress-appraised* events. The third approach emphasizes that life events themselves are not necessarily stress-producing; only if they are perceived as stressful is disease likely to be an outcome.

Loss Events

The notion of giving-up has often been implicated in studies showing sudden death after severe losses (Engel 1973; Seligman 1975) or the breaking of a taboo (Cannon 1942), although there are no systematic studies in this area. Some studies have focused on morbidity or mortality after the death of a spouse. In a number of studies, increased mortality among widows or widowers was found for the first 6 months or 1 year after the death (see Jacobs and Ostfeld 1977; Rowland 1977, for reviews). However, Clayton (1974) did not find increased mortality for a widowed group. Rees and Lutkins (1967) compared the mortality rate of 903 bereaved relatives with a control group of 878. They found the death rate during the first year after bereavement was seven times higher for the bereaved relatives than for the control group. In two studies, decreased immune function in one parameter of immune response was found in bereaved spouses a few weeks after the loss occurred (Bartrop et al 1977; Schleiffer et al. 1980). Although a number of studies have found an increased death rate, it is not clear whether the findings are due to the effects of jointly sharing a deleterious environment or to the losses involved in widowhood.

The results as to whether morbidity also increases after the loss of one's spouse are mixed. During the year following bereavement, widows reported more physical symptoms such as headaches, indigestion, shortness of breath, and palpitations (Clayton 1974; Maddison and Viola 1968), but there was little change in the frequency or severity of major diseases, the number of physician visits, or the frequency of hospitalization (cf. Parkes and Brown 1972).

In another study, student nurses who initially had the worst response to separation from home later showed increased utilization of health care services (Parens, McConville, and Kaplan 1966). In a retrospective study Schmale (1972) found that 80 percent of patients who were physically ill gave evidence in an interview of a recent actual, threatened, or symbolic loss with feelings of either hopelessness or helplessness. Serious questions can be raised about the retrospective studies, as we indicated earlier. Other studies have not found significant relationship between separation experiences and utilization (Imboden, Canter, and Cluff 1963). Although some have suggested that the losses involved in institutional relocation hasten death among the elderly, the results of research studies are not clear-cut. It appears that relocation is related to increased mortality only for those initially in poor health (Rowland 1977).

Separation experiences are frequent in the lives of normal subjects, especially in changes from one life stage to another. Thus control groups are essential to determine if separation or loss increases the probability of disease. It may be that how one copes with loss may be more important than the occurrence of loss itself (see later discussion of Schmale and Engel's helplessness-hopelessness dimension).

Accumulation of Life Changes

Holmes and Rahe and their associates (Holmes and Masuda 1974; Rahe 1974; Rahe, McKean, and Arthur 1967) have investigated the relationship between stressful life events and the onset of illness. Using the SRE (described earlier) they look at life stress in terms of life changes that require a significant readjustment in the individual's life pattern. The SRE includes life changes that are both positive (e.g., promotion) and negative in nature (e.g., divorce). In a number of retrospective and prospective studies, it has been found that life events cluster significantly in a period preceding the onset of illness, and that illness onset can be predicted from the total number of life events . . . Significant relationships have also been found between reports of life changes and reports of psychophysiological symptoms (Markush and Favero 1974; Vinokur and Selzer 1975).

Although there has been considerable research using the SRE the life change approach has come under considerable attack for methodological and theoretical reasons (Brown 1974; Rabkin and Struening 1976). Earlier we discussed some of the weaknesses with the scale as a measure of stressors. Additional criticisms concern the nature of the empirical relationships. First, although significant results are often found, the magnitude of relationships is small, generally below .30. For example, a correlation of .12 (as reported by Rahe 1974, in various Navy samples) was found to be significant in samples of 800 but explains less than 2 percent of the variance. In some studies the correlations are even lower and other variables (e.g., characteristics of the occupational environment and demographic variables) were found to be significantly better predictors of illness reporting (Rahe et al. 1972). Second, as discussed earlier, if many of the life events on the SRE could represent presymptomatic manifestations of illness, this would artificially inflate the association between life changes and illness outcomes. Third, the indicators of illness used in these studies are subjective measures. Thus it is possible that these studies are tapping the relationship between reported life stress and illness behavior, not illness (Cohen 1979).

The SRE has also been criticized from a theoretical perspective (Cleary 1974). Although Holmes and Rahe and their colleagues (Holmes and Masuda 1974) posited that both positive and negative life events had deleterious effects, there is evidence that the two types of events may have different physiological consequences. For example, while cortisol, catecholamines, and growth hormone rise after negative life events, only the catecholamines show a rise after events of a pleasureable nature (Rose 1980). Further, the undesirable life events are stronger predictors of disease outcomes (Vinokur and Selzer 1975).

In addition, the life change approach overemphasizes the impact of the occurrence of events and underemphasizes other factors that determine the consequences of life changes. A substantial number of people undergo many severely stressful events without becoming ill (Hinkle 1974). As we will discuss in the next section, reaction to life changes depends also on the capacity of the person to deal with the life changes and on the nature of the surrounding environment.

It is theoretically and practically important to determine whether life changes, both positive and negative, increase a person's risk of becoming ill. The evidence is not yet in that the accumulation of life changes significantly increases pathophysiology. Counseling patients to maintain the status quo and to limit life changes in an attempt to prevent illness seems quite inappropriate considering the weakness of the evidence. This approach also ignores the negative consequences of no change. Before such interventions are made, further research is needed.

Stress-Appraised Life Events

Whereas the life change approach suggests that any life change will increase the likelihood that illness will develop, other researchers suggest that illness is more likely among people who have difficulty successfully adapting to negative life experiences. For example, Hinkle and his colleagues found that episodes of illness are not randomly distributed among the population. In several groups in which they studied the illness distribution episodes, it was found that about 25 percent of the members experienced about 50 percent of the episodes over a 20 year period of time (see Hinkle 1974, for a review). It also appeared that illnesses were not distributed at random over the life of a person but often appeared in clusters. These clusters of illness were most frequent when a person perceived he or she was having difficulty adapting to the environment.

The stress-appraisal viewpoint suggests that there is not a simple relationship between life change and illness, and that other mediating variables must be taken into account. These include biological predispositions to illness or a history of preexisting illness, the person's appraisal of the situation, resources for dealing with the event, the social supports received from others, the coping strategies used in dealing with the stress, and whether the life change results in significant modification of the person's activities, diet, and so on (Cohen 1979). We shall briefly discuss the literature showing the impact of some of these mediating variables on illness outcomes.

Cognitive Appraisal. Lazarus (1966; Lazarus, Averill, and Opton 1970) has emphasized the central role of cognitive appraisal, as have other researchers in recent years. Events that may be stressful for one person may not be stressful for another. If a person has adequate resources to meet the challenge, or does not believe that danger exists, no stress reaction may be found. The meaning of an event is critically important. For example, Hinkle and his colleagues (Hinkle et al. 1959) found that refugees from the Hungarian Revolution of 1956 reported less illness following their social upheaval and flight to the United States than prior to these changes. For soldiers seriously wounded in battle, surgery can mean release from the battlefield and a return home; the positive meaning associated with the surgery may be one reason why wounded soldiers require less narcotics for postsurgical pain than civilians with incisions of comparable size (Beecher

1956). Even in animals, one's expectancies and prior experiences influence the physiological reponse to stressors (Levine and Coover 1976). A consensus is growing that stress responses are dependent on a person's appraisal that a stressor exists, and that except in extreme situations, researchers cannot a priori determine that a stimulus or event will be perceived as stressful by all who encounter it.

Coping. Numerous studies have shown that the way an individual copes may reduce physiological arousal in response to stressful events (Rose 1980). For example, successful defenses lower levels of 17-hydroxycorticosteroids (17-OHCS) in persons in combat situations (Bourne, Rose, and Mason 1967), in parents whose child is dying of leukemia (Friedman, Mason, and Hamburg 1963), and in patients awaiting surgery (Katz et al. 1970). Being engaged in motor activity in situations of threat is related to increaseed physiologic arousal especially of the adrenocortical hormones (Gal and Lazarus 1975). There is also substantial evidence that cardiovascular and psychoendocrine systems show increased physiologic reactivity in situations where people are "engaged" (Singer 1974). Some of the animal studies suggest that the inability to cope with an environmental stressor may influence immunologic processes (Sklar and Anisman 1979). There is also evidence that the way people cope with illness or surgery can affect the process of their recovery (Cohen and Lazarus 1979).

Engel (1968) and Engel and Schmale (1967) suggest that a giving-up—given-up complex in response to situations of loss may precede the development of illness of all types in those with somatic predispositions. In their theory a psychological state of helplessness or hopelessness mediates the development of illness although this state is not a necessary or sufficient condition. Although Engel and Schmale focus much of their work on the occurrence of loss, the aspect they emphasize is the inability to cope in the face of negative environmental events. There has been much interest in their work; however, serious methodological problems exist with the research, including the lack of truly predictive studies, absence of control groups, possibility of observer bias, and other alternative explanations (Cohen 1979).

In both the human and the animal literature the evidence seems strong that the way one copes with stress is an important modifier of the stress-disease relationship. Further work is needed to determine which coping processes are effective in altering the links between stress and disease and to unravel the mechanisms involved.

Personality. A few studies have investigated those personality factors that may protect people from a wide variety of physical diseases. Kobasa (1979) found that those who did not get ill after undergoing many stressful experiences (high LCU) had a stronger sense of meaningfulness and commitment to self, a more vigorous attitude toward life, and an internal locus of control—a constellation she termed "hardiness." On the other hand, Hinkle (1974) suggested that those who remained healthy, as compared with those more likely to become ill, were emotionally insulated and showed lack of concern for others. Further research is needed to investigate the role of other personality factors in buffering the effects of stressors.

Personal Resources. It has been suggested that those with many personal resources, assets, and competencies are better able to meet life challenges and deal effectively with loss (Beiser, Feldman, and Engelhoff 1972; Cassel 1976). The factors that provide protection against life stressors are still poorly understood. Important positive influences probably include genetic factors, high intelligence, special talents, calm temperament, high self-esteem, and a large repertoire of coping skills. In studying these factors it will be important to distinguish a person's internal resources from his or her access to external resources. With knowledge of which factors build social competence and protect against illness, we might be better able to intervene with those who are deprived to help build important sources of strength.

Social Supports. Recent research evidence suggests that those who have social supports are protected in crisis from a variety of pathologic states. It is thought that supports buffer the individual from the potentially negative effects of crisis and can facilitate coping and adaptation. There is evidence that those who have social supports or social assets may live longer (Berkman and Syme 1979), have a lower incidence of somatic illness (see reviews by Cassel 1976; Dimsdale et al. 1979; Kaplan, Cassel, and Gore 1977), as well as more positive mental health (Cobb 1976). For example, studies have suggested that social support can prevent posthospital psychological reactions in children undergoing tonsillectomy, reduce psychological distress and physiological symptoms following loss of a job or bereavement, and aid recovery from congestive heart failure, myocardial infarction, surgery, tuberculosis, asthma, and other diseases.

Supports are thought to modify the potentially negative effects of stress either by reducing the stress itself or by facilitating the individual's efforts to cope. Several studies have reported interactions between life stress and social assets. Nuckolls, Cassel, and Kaplan (1972) found that while neither extensive life changes (as measured by the SRE) nor low psychosocial assets were individually predictive of higher rates of complications during birth of a baby, those women with many life changes and few psychosocial assets were at much greater risk. Among men who lost their jobs, those with high levels of emotional support from their wives had fewer symptoms of illness and lower levels of serum cholesterol and serum uric acid (Gore 1973).

Although the studies in this area are generally consistent, the research base is weak. Confounding factors are rarely controlled and there are many studies in which the expected relationships are not found. Further, some of the most positive findings are open to alternative explanations since other factors (such as the person's physical state) may result in lack of support rather than vice-versa.

On the other hand, close relationships with others can involve a high potential for conflict, and some relationships may inhibit personal growth, thereby leaving the individual less able to cope with life stressors. In evaluating social support, one may need to consider the fit between need and availability. For people who are hard to get along with, or who do not like being with others, providing supportive relationships may intensify stress rather than reduce it.

Broader Environmental Factors. Moos (1976b) reviews the work relating physical and architectural features, organization factors, human aggregate factors, and social climate variables to health outcomes. The findings suggest that climate, organizational factors in industrial settings, community structure, and social characteristics of the environment are significantly associated with health and disease. Further, the impact of the environment may differ for people of different types. For example, the environmental docility hypothesis suggests that people who are disabled, impaired, or under stress are more likely to be influenced by environmental conditions (Lawton and Nahemow 1973). The notion that certain groups of individuals are more responsive to their environment suggests that such groups might be most likely to benefit from interventions.

COMPLEXITY OF THE PHYSIOLOGICAL RESPONSE

There is a large body of literature that shows that stressors can influence autonomic nervous system, hormonal, central nervous system, and immunologic processes. A forthcoming report will review this research in detail (National Academy of Sciences 1982). It is impossible to summarize this large data base in a few pages. Here we will address some important issues in the research findings.

Lines of evidence from studies of each of these physiologic systems indicate that the effects of stressors on the organism are extremely complex. Within each physiological system, not all indicators respond in a similar fashion. For example, Mason (1974) has found that different profiles characterize the neuroendocrine responses of rhesus monkeys to different noxious stressors. Epinephrine, norepinephrine, testosterone, thyroxine, insulin, growth hormone, 17-hydroxycorticosteroids and other hormones responded in differential patterns to different stressor agents. Mason (1968) suggests that in evaluating the neuroendocrine response to stressors, researchers should focus not on the secretion of any one hormone, but rather on the relative overall balance among several hormones. Similar arguments have been made against studying the response of just one neurotransmitter substance or one facet of immunologic response.

Laboratory work with animals suggests that certain types of stressors can lead to decreased resistance to some microorganisms and increased resistance to others:

"Handling, for example, increases resistance to experimentally induced gastric erosions and retards the growth rate of a transplanted tumor, but handling decreases subsequent resistance to a transplanted leukemia and to electroconvulsive shock while having no effect on susceptibility to alloxan diabetes, encephalomyocarditis virus, or the spontaneous development of leukemia in AKR rats (Ader and Grota 1973:401)." The effects of stressful experiences on later illness susceptibility further depend on the type of early stimulation given, the lapse of time between the stressor and the inoculation, the acuteness or chronicity of the stressor, the timing of the stressor, the outcome measure examined, and the species of animal used.

Further, although many researchers focus on only one physiologic system, it is increasingly evident that an extensive network of central nervous system, autonomic nervous system, endocrine, neuroregulator, opioid peptide, and immunologic responses may be involved. Not only may reactions on one level modify responses on another, but the relationships between systems may be complex. For example, in most cases high levels of corticosteroids are immunosuppressive. However, in some circumstances both high and low levels of corticosteroids suppress the immunological response while intermediate levels enhance it (Solomon 1969).

Another issue concerns the relationship between response to acute stressors and long-term disease outcomes. Just because behavioral stimuli can produce acute physiological changes, this does not establish a cause-and-effect relationship between the stressor and subsequent disease. We need to understand better how acute physiological responses can lead to permanent changes in a person's health. There is a normal variation in most physiological systems; they fluctuate in relation to time of day and sleep patterns, as well as diet, stage of the life cycle, and so forth. We need to determine at what point variations may be pathological. In discussing the immunologic system, for example, lack of information about the immunologic variability in normal baseline patterns makes it difficult to assess the impact of psychological stressors. It could be that changes in immunological rhythms are more significant than the changes found to occur in response to specific stressors studied (Rogers, Dubey, and Reich 1979).

Further, increased physiologic activation may also have positive consequences. For example, Frankenhaeuser (1975b) reviews studies that show that those who habitually secrete high levels of epinephrine have higher IQ and better school performance, are rated as happier and livelier, receive higher scores on ego strength, and perform better on laboratory tasks, as compared with those with low epinephrine levels. Gal and Lazarus (1975) and Frankenhaeuser (1976) also suggest that the magnitude of the physiologic response may not be a good measure of adaptive outcome compared to the time it takes for the return to baseline hormonal levels. Successful adaptation may involve both efficient mobilization and demobilization of physiologic systems.

CLINICAL IMPLICATIONS

The literature reviewed suggests that stressors may produce many short-term physiologic changes, but that the relationship between these acute reactions and long-term health consequences is not yet clearly established. Significant findings have been reported in the animal literature, but the generalizability of much of this research is unclear. The types of stressors used in animal studies are usually extreme ones; whether the less overwhelming types of stressors characteristic of our daily lives can have similar deleterious effects is by no means understood. Further, the physiologic response to stressors is quite complex, sometimes increasing disease susceptibility, sometimes decreasing it, and sometimes showing no overall effect. Important factors that modify the relationship between stressors and disease were reviewed: How the stressor is appraised, the way individuals cope, the resources they have available to deal with the environment, the nature of their surrounding environment including the amount of social support available all appear to play a significant mediating role. The clinical implications of these findings are important. They suggest that in prevention approaches we should not focus exclusively on stressors, with the hope of eliminating all negative events. Stress events are ubiquitous in life and are almost always involved in important life transitions. Although some stressors can be avoided, removed, or destroyed, others may need to be adapted to on an ongoing basis (White 1974). Learning to cope with stressors and challenges seems essential for human growth and development. Trying to intervene by altering mediating factors instead of by altering the occurrence of stressors is an important strategy to consider.

It may also be useful to think of etiology of disease in terms of a sequence of causal events, with multiple factors involved. Intervention may be possible at several points along the chain. For example, stressful life events could increase anxiety and thus the number of cigarettes smoked (Horowitz et al. 1979). Smoking may increase susceptibility to illness. The areas of intervention could be many: One could prevent the stressful events, reduce the person's anxiety, help him or her find a way of coping other than smoking, or help the person stop smoking altogether. Prevention programs that are set up to affect several factors simultaneously may be most effective. Helping the individual learn more effective coping skills while simultaneously altering high risk environments would improve the chances for success.

This article has focused exclusively on the relationship between stress and physical disease. However, it is important to keep in mind that stressors can produce effects in several domains of functioning—psychological and social as well—and that these responses may reflect different aspects of adaptation. Disease, disrupted social relationships, mental distress, and criminal acts are all possible responses to stressors, and the way one copes with stress may have differential effects on outcome. For example, while Type A behavior pattern may increase the risk of coronary heart disease (Jenkins 1976) it may also produce feelings of satisfaction and earn the person community respect. Trying to reduce the risk of physical disease by altering the person's behavior may have negative social and personal consequences. The positive and negative effects of various changes in life style must be carefully considered.

As health care professionals working with patients, we might try to increase our efforts to help patients learn and use effective coping skills, develop resources they can draw on, and improve the social support available. Social supports can be increased through our relationship with the patients and with their family, our referral to supportive community resources (such as Reach to Recovery and other self-help groups) and the ways we structure hospital environments. All members of the health care team can contribute to these efforts.

Being ill is stressful for many people. Being ill can involve threats not only to life and to one's physical well-being, but also to one's self-image, beliefs, social functioning, values, and emotional equilibrium (Cohen and Lazarus 1979). Efforts to cope may be directed toward these threats as well as toward doing something about the physical illness itself . . . We can try to reduce the stress of hospital environments by reducing sensory deprivation effects in special care units, helping patients gain some degree of autonomy and control in the hospital environment, clarifying confusing medical details by presenting information in simple, non-technical language, and helping patients think through important medical decisions that they must make based on informed consent procedures. As we work to reduce those stressors that we can influence, increase the support we provide to others, and help patients improve their resources and ways of coping, the influences of stressors on the development of physical illness may be significantly reduced.

4

Anatomy of an Illness (As Perceived by the Patient)

NORMAN COUSINS

Ever since the publication of Adam Smith's much-talked-about *Powers of the Mind* some months ago, people have written to ask whether his account of my recovery from a supposedly incurable illness was accurately reported (Smith 1975:11–14). In particular, readers have been eager to verify Mr. Smith's statement that I "laughed" my way out of a crippling disease that doctors believed to be irreversible.

I have not written until now about my illness, which occurred in 1964, largely because I was fearful of creating false hopes in other persons similarly afflicted. Moreover, I knew that a single case has small standing in the annals of medical research. I had thought that my own episode might have anecdotal value—nothing more. However, since my case has surfaced in the public press, I feel justified in providing a fuller picture than was contained in Mr. Smith's account.

In August 1964, I flew home from a trip abroad with a slight fever. The malaise, which took the form of a general feeling of achiness, rapidly deepened. Within a week it became difficult to move my neck, arms, hands, fingers, and legs. I was hospitalized when my sedimentation rate hit 80 mm per hour. The sedimentation rate continued to rise until it reached 115.

There were other tests, some of which seemed to me to be more an assertion of the clinical capability of the hospital than of concern for the well-being of the patient. I was astounded when four technicians from four different departments took four separate and substantial blood samples on the same day. That the hospital didn't take the trouble to coordinate the tests, using one blood specimen, seemed to me inexplicable and irresponsible. When the technicians came the second day to fill their containers with blood for processing in separate laboratories, I turned them away and had a sign posted on my door saying that I would give just one specimen every three days and that I expected the different departments to draw from it for their individual needs.

I had a fast-growing conviction that a hospital was no place for a person who was seriously ill. The surprising lack of respect for basic sanitation, the rapidity with which staphylococci and other pathogenic organisms can run through an entire hospital, the extensive and sometimes promiscuous use of x-ray equipment, the seemingly indiscriminate administration of tranquilizers and powerful painkillers, more for the convenience of hospital staff in managing patients than for therapeutic needs, and the regularity with which hospital routine takes precedence over the rest requirements of the patient (slumber, when it comes for an ill person, is an uncommon blessing and is not to be wantonly interrupted)—all these and other practices seemed to me to be critical shortcomings of the modern hospital.

Perhaps the hospital's most serious failure was in the area of nutrition. It was not just that the meals were poorly balanced; what seemed inexcusable to me was the profusion of processed foods, some of which contained preservatives or harmful dyes. White bread, with its chemical softeners and bleached flour, was offered with every meal. Vegetables were often overcooked and thus deprived of much of their nutritional value. No wonder the 1969 White House Conference on Food, Nutrition, and Health made the melancholy observation that the great failure of medical schools is that they pay so little attention to the science of nutrition.

My doctor did not quarrel with my reservations about hospital procedures. I was fortunate to have as a physician a man who was able to put himself in the position of the patient. Dr. William Hitzig supported me in the measures I took to fend off the random sanguinary assaults of the hospital laboratory attendants.

We had been close friends for more than twenty years, and he knew of my own deep interest in medical matters. We had often discussed articles in the medical press, including the *New England Journal of Medicine* and *Lancet*. He felt comfortable about being candid with me about my case. He reviewed the reports of the various specialists he had called in as consultants. He said there was no agreement on a precise diagnosis. There was, however, a general consensus that I was suffering from a serious collagen illness. I had considerable difficulty in moving my limbs and even in turning over in bed. Nodules appeared on my body, gravel-like substances under the skin, indicating the systemic nature of the disease. At the low point of my illness, my jaws were almost locked.

Dr. Hitzig called in experts from Dr. Howard Rusk's rehabilitation clinic in New York. They confirmed the general opinion, adding the more particularized diagnosis of ankylosing spondylitis.

I asked Dr. Hitzig about my chances for full recovery. He leveled with me, admitting that one of the specialists had told him I had one chance in 500. The specialist had also stated that he had not personally witnessed a recovery from this comprehensive condition.

All this gave me a great deal to think about. Up to that time, I had been more or less disposed to let the doctors worry about my condition. But now I felt a compulsion to get into the act. It seemed clear to me that if I was to be that "one case in 500" I had better be something more than a passive observer.

I asked Dr. Hitzig about the possible cause of my condition. He said that it could have come from any one of a number of causes. It could have come, for example, from heavy-metal poisoning, or it could have been manifested by the aftereffects of a streptococcal infection.

I thought as hard as I could about the sequence of events immediately preceding the illness. I had gone to the Soviet Union in July 1964 as chairman of an American delegation to consider the problems of cultural exchange. The conference had been held in Leningrad, after which we went to Moscow for supplementary meetings. Our hotel was in a residental area. My room was on the second floor. Each night a procession of diesel trucks plied back and forth to a nearby housing project in the process of round-the-clock construction. It was summer, and our windows were wide open. I slept uneasily each night and felt somewhat nauseated on arising. On our last day in Moscow, at the airport, I caught the exhaust spew of a large jet at point-blank range as it swung around on the tarmac.

As I thought back on that Moscow experience, I wondered whether the exposure to the hydrocarbons from the diesel exhaust at the hotel and at the airport had anything to do with the underlying cause of the illness. If so, that might account for the speculations of the doctors concerning heavy-metal poisoning. The trouble with this theory, however, was that my wife, who had been with me on the trip, had no ill effects from the same exposure. How likely was it that only one of us would have reacted adversely?

There were two possible reasons, it seemed to me, for the different responses. One had to do with individual allergy. The second was that I was probably in a condition of adrenal exhaustion and I was less apt to tolerate a toxic experience than someone whose immunologic system was fully functional.

Was adrenal exhaustion a factor in my own illness?

Again, I thought carefully. The meetings in Leningrad and Moscow had not been casual. Paper work had kept me up late nights. I had ceremonial responsibilities. Our last evening in Moscow had been, at least for me, an exercise in almost total frustration. A reception had been arranged by the chairman of the Soviet delegation at his dacha, located 50 to 65 km outside the city. I had been asked if I could arrive an hour early so that I might tell the Soviet delegates something about the individual Americans who were coming to dinner. The

Russians were eager to make the Americans feel at home, and they had thought such information would help them with the social amenities.

I was told that a car and driver from the government automobile pool in Moscow would pick me up at the hotel at 3:30 P.M. This would allow ample time for me to drive to the dacha by 5:00P.M., when all our Russian conference colleagues would be gathered for the social briefing. The rest of the American delegation would arrive at the dacha at 6:00.

At 6:00, however, I found myself in open country on the wrong side of Moscow. There had been a misunderstanding in the transmission of directions to the driver, the result being that we were some 130 km off course.

We didn't arrive at the dacha until 9:00 P.M. My host's wife looked desolate. The soup had been heated and reheated. The veal was dried out. I felt pretty wrung out myself. It was a long flight back to the States the next day. The plane was overcrowded. By the time we arrived in New York, cleared through the packed customs counters, and got rolling back to Connecticut, I could feel an uneasiness deep in my bones. A week later I was hospitalized.

As I thought back on my experience abroad, I knew that I was probably on the right track in my search for a cause of the illness. I found myself increasingly convinced, as I said a moment ago, that the reason I was hit hard by the diesel and jet pollutants, whereas my wife was not, was that I had had a case of adrenal exhaustion, lowering my resistance.

Assuming this hypothesis was true, I had to get my adrenal glands functioning properly again and to restore what Walter Cannon, in his famous book *The Wisdom of the Body* (1963), called homeostasis.

I knew that the full functioning of my endocrine system—in particular, the adrenal glands—was essential for combating severe arthritis or, for that matter, any other illness. A study I had read in the medical press reported that pregnant women frequently have remissions of arthritic or other rheumatic symptoms. The reason is that the endocrine system is fully activated during pregnancy.

How was I to get my adrenal glands and my endocrine system, in general, working well again—both physically and emotionally?

I remembered having read, ten years or so earlier, Hans Selye's classic book, *The Stress of Life* (1956). With great clarity, Selye showed that adrenal exhaustion could be caused by emotional tension, such as frustration or suppressed rage. He detailed the negative effects of the negative emotions on body chemistry. He wrote, for example, about the increase of hydrochloric acid in the stomach. He also traced changes in corticoids and anticorticoids under conditions of emotional stress.

The inevitable question arose in my mind: What about the positive emotions? If negative emotions produce negative chemical changes in the body, wouldn't the positive emotions produce positive chemical changes? Is it possible that love, hope, faith, laughter, confidence and the will to live have therapeutic value? Do chemical changes occur only on the downside?

Obviously, putting the positive emotions to work is nothing so simple as turning on a garden hose. But even a reasonable degree of control over my emotions might have a salutary physiologic effect. Just replacing anxiety with a fair degree of confidence would be helpful.

A plan began to form in my mind for systematic pursuit of the salutary emotions, and I knew that I would want to discuss it with my doctor. Two preconditions, however, seemed obvious for the experiment. The first concerned my medication. If that medication were toxic to any degree, it was doubtful whether the plan would work. The second precondition concerned the hospital. I knew I would have to find a place somewhat more conducive to a positive outlook on life.

Let's consider these preconditions separately.

First, the medication. The emphasis had been on painkilling drugs—aspirin, phenylbutazone (Butazolidin), codeine, colchicine, sleeping pills. The aspirin and phenylbutazone were anti-inflammatory and thus were therapeutically justifiable. But I wasn't sure they weren't also toxic. With Dr. Hitzig's support, we took allergy tests and discovered that I was hypersensitive to virtually all the medication I was receiving. The hospital had been giving me maximum dosages: 26 aspirin tablets a day; and 3 phenylbutazone tablets four times a day. No wonder I had hives all over my body and felt as though my skin was being chewed up by millions of red ants.

It was unreasonable to expect positive chemical changes to take place so long as my body was being saturated with, and toxified by, painkilling medications. I had one of my research assistants at the *Saturday Review* look up the pertinent references in the medical journals and found that drugs like phenylbutazone and even aspirin levy a heavy tax on the adrenal glands. I also learned that phenylbutazone is one of the most powerful drugs being manufactured. It can produce bloody stools, the result of its antagonism to fibrinogen. It can cause intolerable itching and sleeplessness. It can depress bone marrow.

The hazards of phenylbutazone are explicit. Aspirin enjoys a far more auspicious reputation, at least with the general public. The prevailing impression of aspirin is that it is not only the most harmless drug available but also one of the most effective. When I looked into research in the medical journals, however, I found that aspirin is quite powerful in its own right and that it warrants considerable care in its use. The fact that it can be bought in unlimited quantities without prescription or doctor's guidance seemed indefensible. Even in small amounts, it can cause internal bleeding. Articles in the medical press reported that the chemical composition of aspirin, like that of phenylbutazone, impairs platelet function. Did the relation between platelets and collagen mean that both drugs do more harm than good for some sufferers from arthritis?[1]

It was a mind-boggling train of thought. Could it be, I asked myself, that aspirin, so universely accepted for so many years, was actually harmful in the treatment of collagen illnesses? (Sahud and Cohen 1971)[2]

The history of medicine is replete with instances involving drugs and modes of treatment that were in use for many years before it was recognized that they did more harm than good. For centuries, for example, people believed that drawing blood from patients was essential for rapid recovery from virtually every illness. Then, midway through the nineteenth century, it was discovered that bleeding serves only to weaken the patient. King Charles II's death is believed to have been caused in large part from administered bleedings. George Washington's death was also hastened by the severe loss of blood resulting from this treatment.

Living in the second half of the twentieth century, I realized, confers no automatic protection against unwise or even dangerous drugs and methods. Each age has had to undergo its own special nostrums. Fortunately, the human body is a remarkably durable instrument and has been able to withstand all sorts of prescribed assaults over the centuries, from freezing to animal dung.

Suppose I stopped taking aspirin and phenylbutazone? What about the pain? The bones in my spine and practically every joint in my body felt as though I had been run over by a truck.

I knew that pain could be affected by attitudes. Most people become panicky about almost any pain. On all sides they have been so bombarded by advertisements about pain that they take this or that analgesic at the slightest sign of an ache. They are largely illiterate about pain and so are seldom able to deal with it rationally. Pain is part of the body's magic. It is the way the body transmits a sign to the brain that something is wrong. Leprous patients pray for the sensation of pain. What makes leprosy such a terrible disease is that the victim usually feels no pain when his extremities are being injured. He loses his fingers or toes because he receives no warning signal that he is being injured.

I could stand pain so long as I knew that progress was being made in meeting the basic need. That need, I felt, was to restore the body's capacity to halt the continuing breakdown of connective tissue.

There was also the problem of the severe inflammation. If we dispensed with the aspirin, how would we combat the inflammation? I recalled having read in the medical journals about the usefulness of ascorbic acid in combating a wide number of illnesses—all the way from bronchitis to some types of heart disease. Couldn't it also combat inflammation? Did vitamin C act directly, or did it serve as a starter for the body's endocrine system—in particular, the adrenal glands? Was it possible, I asked myself, that ascorbic acid had a vital role to play in "feeding" the adrenal glands?

I had read in the medical press that vitamin C helps to oxygenate the blood (Hamburger 1962; Kinderlehrer 1974; Klenner 1971). If inadequate

or impaired oxygenation was a factor in collagen breakdown, couldn't this cir-
cumstance be another argument for ascorbic acid? Also, according to some medical
reports, people suffering from collagen diseases are deficient in vitamin C (Sahud
and Cohen 1971). Did this lack mean that the body uses up large amounts of
vitamin C in the process of combating collagen breakdown?

I wanted to discuss some of these ruminations with Dr. Hitzig. He
listened carefully as I told him of my speculations concerning the cause of the
illness, as well as my layman's ideas for a course of action that might give me a
chance to reduce the odds against my recovery.

Dr. Hitzig said it was clear to him that there was nothing undersized
about my will to live. He said that what was most important was that I continue
to believe in everything I had said. He shared my sense of excitement about the
possibilities of my recovery and liked the idea of a partnership.

Even before we had completed arrangements for moving out of the
hospital, we began the part of the program calling for the full exercise of the
affirmative emotions as a factor in enhancing body chemistry. It was easy enough
to hope and love and have faith, but what about laughter? Nothing is less funny
than being flat on your back with all the bones in your spine and joints hurting.
A systematic program was indicated. A good place to begin, I thought, was with
amusing movies. Allen Funt, producer of the spoofing television program "Candid
Camera," sent films of some of his "CC" classics, along with a motion-picture
projector. The nurse was instructed in its use.

It worked. I made the joyous discovery that ten minutes of genuine
belly laughter had an anesthetic effect and would give me at least two hours of
pain-free sleep. When the painkilling effect of the laughter wore off, we would
switch on the motion-picture projector again, and, not infrequently, it would lead
to another pain-free sleep interval. Sometimes, the nurse read to me out of a trove
of humor books. Especially useful were E. B. and Katherine White's *Subtreasury
of American Humor* (1962) and Max Eastman's *The Enjoyment of Laughter* (1971).

How scientific was it to believe that laughter—as well as the positive
emotions in general—was affecting my body chemistry for the better? If laughter
did in fact have a salutary effect on the body's chemistry, it seemed at least
theoretically likely that it would enhance the system's ability to fight the inflammation. So we took sedimentation-rate readings just before as well as several hours
after the laughter episodes. Each time, there was a drop of at least five points.
The drop by itself was not substantial, but it held and was cumulative.

I was greatly elated by the discovery that there is a physiologic basis
for the ancient theory that laughter is good medicine.

There was, however, one negative side effect of the laughter from the
standpoint of the hospital. I was disturbing other patients. But that objection
didn't last very long, for the arrangements were now complete for me to move my
act to a hotel room.

One of the incidental advantages of the hotel room, I was delighted to find, was that it cost only about one-third as much as the hospital. The other benefits were incalculable. I would not be awakened for a bed bath or for meals or for medication or for a change in the bed sheets or for tests or for examinations by hospital interns. The sense of serenity was delicious and would, I felt certain, contribute to a general improvement.

What about ascorbic acid and its place in the general program for recovery? In discussing my speculations about vitamin C with Dr. Hitzig, I found him completely open-minded on the subject, although he told me of serious questions that had been raised by scientific studies. He also cautioned me that heavy doses of ascorbic acid carried some risk of renal damage. The main problem right then, however, was not my kidneys: it seemed to me that, on balance, the risk was worth taking. I asked Dr. Hitzig about previous recorded experience with massive doses of vitamin C. He ascertained that at the hospital there had been cases in which patients had received up to 3 g by intramuscular injection.

As I thought about the injection procedure, some questions came to mind. Introducing the ascorbic acid directly into the bloodstream might make more efficient use of the vitamin, but I wondered about the body's ability to utilize a sudden massive infusion. I knew that one of the great advantages of vitamin C is that the body takes only the amount necessary for its purposes and excretes the rest. Again, there came to mind Cannon's phrase—the wisdom of the body (1963).

Was there a coefficient of time in the utilization of ascorbic acid? The more I thought about it, the more likely it seemed to me that the body would excrete a large quantity of the vitamin because it couldn't metabolize it that fast. I wondered whether a better procedure than injection would be to administer the ascorbic acid through slow intravenous drip over a period of three or four hours. In this way we could go far beyond the 3 g. My hope was to start at 10 g and then increase the dose daily until we reached 25 g.

Dr. Hitzig's eyes widened when I mentioned 25 g. This amount was far beyond any recorded dose. He said he had to caution me about the possible effect not just on the kidneys but on the veins in the arms. Moreover, he said he knew of no data to support the assumption that the body could handle 25 g over a four-hour period, other than by excreting it rapidly through the urine.

As before, however, it seemed to me we were playing for bigger stakes: losing some veins was not of major importance alongside the need to combat whatever was eating at my connective tissue.

To know whether we were on the right track, we took a sedimentation test before the first intravenous administration of 10 g of ascorbic acid. Four hours later, we took another sedimentation test. There was a drop of nine full points.

Seldom had I known such elation. The ascorbic acid was working. So was laughter. The combination was cutting heavily into whatever poison was attacking the connective tissue. The fever was receding, and the pulse was no longer racing.

We stepped up the dosage. On the second day we went up to 12.5 g of ascorbic acid, on the third day, 15 g., and so on until the end of the week, when we reached 25 g. Meanwhile, the laughter routine was in full force. I was completely off drugs and sleeping pills. Sleep—blessed, natural sleep without pain—was becoming increasingly prolonged.

At the end of the eighth day I was able to move my thumbs without pain. By this time, the sedimentation rate was somewhere in the 80s and dropping fast. I couldn't be sure, but it seemed to me that the gravel-like nodules on my neck and the backs of my hands were beginning to shrink. There was no doubt in my mind that I was going to make it back all the way.

Two weeks later, my wife took me to Puerto Rico for some sustained sunshine. On the first day, friends helped support me in the breaking surf. Within a few days I was standing up by myself. At first the soles of my feet were so sensitive that I felt as though I were standing on my eyeballs. But walking in the sand was the best possible therapy, and within a week I was able to jog—at least for a minute or two.

The connective tissue in my spine and joints was regenerating. I could function, and the feeling was indescribably beautiful.

I must not make it appear that all my infirmities disappeared overnight. For many months I couldn't get my arms up far enough to reach for a book on a high shelf. My fingers weren't agile enough to do what I wanted them to do on the organ keyboard. My neck had a limited turning radius. My knees were somewhat wobbly, and, off and on, I had to wear a metal brace.

But I was back at my job at *Saturday Review* full time again, and this was miracle enough for me.

Is the recovery a total one? Year by year the mobility has improved. During the past year I have become fully pain free, except for my knees, for the first time since I left the hospital. I no longer feel a sharp twinge in my wrists or shoulders when I hit a tennis ball or golf ball, as I did for such a long time. I can ride a horse flat out and hold a camera with a steady hand. And I have recaptured my ambition to play the Tocata and Fugue in D Minor, though I find the going slower and tougher than I had hoped. My neck has a full turning radius again, despite the statement of specialists as recently as 1971 that the condition was degenerative and that I would have to adjust to a quarter turn.

It was seven years after the onset of the illness before I had scientific confirmation about the dangers of using aspirin in the treatment of collagen diseases, which embrace the various forms of arthritis. In its May 8, 1971 issue, *Lancet* published a study by Drs. M. A. Sahud and R. J. Cohen (1971) showing that aspirin could be antagonistic to the retention of vitamin C in the body. The authors said that patients with rheumatoid arthritis should take vitamin C supplements since it has often been noted that they have low levels of the vitamin in their blood. It was no surprise, then, that I had been able to absorb such massive amounts of ascorbic acid without kidney or other complications.

What conclusions do I draw from the entire experience?

The first is that the will to live is not a theoretical abstraction, but a physiologic reality with therapeutic characteristics. The second is that I was incredibly fortunate to have as my doctor a man who knew that his biggest job was to encourage to the fullest the patient's will to live and to mobilize all the natural resources of body and mind to combat disease. Dr. Hitzig was willing to set aside the large and often hazardous armamentarium of powerful drugs available to the modern physician when he became convinced that his patient might have something better to offer. He was also wise enough to know that the art of healing is still a frontier profession. And, though I can't be sure of this point, I have a hunch he believed that my own total involvement was a major factor in any recovery.

People have asked what I thought when I was told by the specialists that my disease was progressive and incurable.

The answer is simple. Since I didn't accept the verdict, I wasn't trapped in the cycle of fear, depression and panic that frequently accompanies a supposedly incurable illness. I must not make it seem, however, that I was unmindful of the seriousness of the problem or that I was in a festive mood throughout. Being unable to move my body was all the evidence I needed that the specialists were dealing with real concerns. But deep down I knew I had a good chance and relished the idea of bucking the odds.

Adam Smith, in *Powers of the Mind* (1975), says he discussed my recovery with some of his doctor friends, asking them to explain why the combination of laughter and ascorbic acid worked so well. The answer he got was that neither laughter nor ascorbic acid had anything to do with it and that I probably would have recovered if nothing had been done.

Maybe so, but that was not the opinion of the specialists at the time.

Two or three doctors, reflecting on the Adam Smith account, have commented that I was probably the beneficiary of a mammoth venture in self-administered placebos.

Such a hypothesis bothers me not at all. Respectable names in the history of medicine like Paracelsus, Holmes and Osler have suggested that the history of medication is far more the history of the placebo effect than of intrinsically valuable and relevant drugs. Physicians in the past who favored such modalities as bleeding (in a single year, 1827, France imported 33 million leeches after its domestic supplies had been depleted); purging through emetics; physical contact with unicorn horns, bezoar stones, mandrakes or powdered mummies—the physicians prescribing such treatments no doubt regarded them at the time as specifics with empirical sanction. But today's medical science recognizes that whatever efficacy these treatments may have had—and the records indicate that the results were often surprisingly in line with expectations—was probably related to the power of the placebo.

I have wondered, in fact, about the relative absence of attention given the placebo in contemporary medicine. The literature on the subject is remarkably sparse considering the primacy of the placebo in the history of medicine. The late Henry K. Beecher (1955) and Arthur K. Shapiro (1964) are among the small number of contemporary medical researchers and observers who have done any noteworthy thinking and writing about this phenomenon. In connection with my own experience, I was fascinated by a report citing Dr. Thomas C. Chalmers (Blake 1976), of the Mount Sinai Medical Center in New York, which compared two groups that were being used to test the theory that ascorbic acid is a cold preventive. "The group on placebo," says Dr. Chalmers, "who thought they were on ascorbic acid had fewer colds than the group on ascorbic acid who thought they were on placebo."

I was absolutely convinced, at the time I was deep in my illness, that intravenous doses of ascorbic acid could be beneficial—and they were. It is quite possible that this treatment—like everything else I did—was a demonstration of the placebo effect. If so, it would be just as important to probe into the nature of this psychosomatic phenomenon as to find out if ascorbic acid is useful in combating a high sedimentation rate.

At this point, of course, we are opening a very wide door, perhaps even a Pandora's box. The vaunted "miracle cures" that abound in the literature of all the great religions, or the speculations of Charcot and Freud about conversion hysteria, or the Lourdes phenomena—all say something about the ability of the patient, properly motivated or stimulated, to participate actively in extraordinary reversals of disease and disability. It is all too easy, of course, to raise these possibilities and speculations to a monopoly status—in which case the entire edifice of modern medicine would be reduced to little more than the hut of an African witch doctor. But we can at least reflect on William Halse Rivers' statement, as quoted by Shapiro, that "the salient feature of the medicine of today is that these psychical factors are no longer allowed to play their part unwittingly, but are themselves becoming the subject of study, so that the present age is serving the growth of a rational system of psychotherapeutics" (1964).

What we are talking about essentially, I suppose, is the chemistry of the will to live. In Bucharest in 1972, I visited the clinic of Ana Aslan, described to me as one of Rumania's leading endocrinologists. She spoke of her belief that there is a direct connection between a robust will to live and the chemical balances in the brain. She is convinced that creativity—one aspect of the will to live—produces the vital brain impulses that stimulate the pituitary glands, triggering effects on the pineal glands and the whole of the endocrine system. Is it possible that placebos have a key role in this process? Shouldn't this entire area be worth serious and sustained attention?

If I had to guess, I would say that the principal contribution made by my doctor to the taming, and possibly the conquest, of my illness was that he encouraged me to believe I was a respected partner with him in the total undertaking. He fully engaged my subjective energies. He may not have been able to define or diagnose the process through which self-confidence (wild hunches securely believed) was somehow picked up by the body's immunologic mechanisms and translated into anti-morbid effects. But he was acting, I believe, in the best tradition of medicine in recognizing that he had to reach out in my case beyond the usual verifiable modalities. In so doing, he was faithful to the first dictum in his medical education: *primum non nocere.* He knew that what I wanted to do might not help, but it probably would do little harm. Certainly, the threatened harm being risked was less, if anything, than the heroic medication so routinely administered in extreme cases of this kind.

Something else I have learned. I have learned never to underestimate the capacity of the human mind and body to regenerate—even when the prospects seem most wretched. The life-force may be the least understood force on earth. William James (1948) said that human beings tend to live too far within self-imposed limits. It is possible that those limits will recede when we respect more fully the natural drive of the human mind and body toward perfectibility and regeneration. Protecting and cherishing that natural drive may well represent the finest exercise of human freedom.

NOTES

1. I realize, of course, that the implications here are not entirely negative in view of the fact that the same properties of aspirin that prolong bleeding also prevent clotting. Aspirin is therefore useful to some patients with cardiac disease and those for whom clotting is a danger.

2. The scientific verification that aspirin can be harmful in the treatment of collagen diseases came in 1971 and is discussed later in this article (Sahud and Cohen 1971).

Part II

Stress and the Environment

There is currently a great deal of interest in the ways environmental factors determine and influence our behavior. Appropriately, the selections in Part II deal with the ways in which two broad classes of environmental stimuli, physical and social, operate in the production of stress reactions.

In the selection by biologist Dubos (1965), the stresses of overpopulation are discussed. As may be seen from Dubos' analysis, much of our knowledge about the harmful effects of crowding is based on animal studies (e.g., Calhoun 1962) and may or may not be relevant to humans. Dubos makes an important distinction (see also Stokols 1978), one often overlooked by others, between population density and crowding. *Density* is defined in terms of objective physical or spatial conditions (e.g., number of people per acre), while *crowding* is a psychological or experiential state in which the individual is troubled by the spatial conditions. While density and crowding may go together sometimes, it is surely not always the case. A packed gymnasium is a highly dense setting, but one in which most do not feel crowded. Understanding the effects of "crowding" on human behavior is extremely difficult, especially in comparison with animals, because the effects are so strongly determined by cultural, social, contextual, and psychological factors. (For additional studies and information on crowding and stress, see Baum and Valins 1977, Freedman 1975, and Holahan 1982).

Cohen, Evans, Krantz, and Stokols (1980) address several significant issues in their article on the effects of noise on elementary school children. They begin with a discussion of the importance of an interplay between laboratory research and naturalistic studies. Much of the research on noise (and, stress in general) has been laboratory based. One might legitimately ask whether or not the findings from such efforts are relevant or generalizable to the "real" world. Cohen et al. believe it is necessary to move from the laboratory setting to the naturalistic one, and their study is an attempt to do so. The findings of the Cohen et al. study suggest that children exposed to frequent and uncontrollable (aircraft) noise suffer negative consequences (such as higher blood pressure and poorer performance than control subjects). These findings, obtained in a field study, are in accord with those obtained in laboratory settings (e.g., see Cohen and Weinstein 1981; Glass and Singer 1972).

Natural disasters ranging from tornadoes to volcanic eruptions have created havoc for scores of victims throughout the years, and stress researchers have certainly taken an interest in the victims' stress reactions and their ways of coping. Haunting many today, however, is a fear not only of natural disasters, but also of "human-made" ones, like the fear of a nuclear accident involving a power plant, waste dump, or a nation's defense system. This form of environmental disaster, likely a by-product of error or neglect, may prove to be far more devastating to the human race than any disaster yet created by nature.

In March 1979, there was an accident at a nuclear reactor on Three Mile Island near Middletown, Pennsylvania. Radioactive gases escaped through a venting system, threatening the lives of many local residents. As noted in the paper by Fleming, Baum, Gisriel, and Gatchel (1982), stress reactions were found in area residents immediately following the accident and even years later. Yet, not all residents were prone to these reactions. Fleming et al. suggest that one reason for this difference in individual susceptibility may be social support. *Social support* involves a sense of being loved, accepted, and cared for by significant others and appears to be associated with many positive outcomes (outlined by Fleming et al.). In terms of stress reactions to the Three Mile Island accident, it seems that having high or moderate levels of social support protected individuals from some of the psychological and behavioral symptoms of stress (like poor task performance and complaints about anxiety). Interestingly, Fleming et al. did not find a protective function of social support for biochemical functioning (e.g., catecholamine levels). Their explanation for the discrepancy between the psychological and behavioral symptoms and the biochemical ones—which emphasizes the consequences of having to cope over a long period of time with an unchangeable stressor—is intriguing and deserves further exploration.

While many jobs may be characterized as "high pressured," health-related jobs seem to be particularly stress-inducing (Colligan, Smith, and Hurrell 1977). And, perhaps no job is more demanding than that of intensive care unit (ICU) nursing. In their interesting paper, Hay and Oken (1972) have portrayed graphically the special problems faced by the ICU nurse (e.g., formidable work load, heavy responsibility for life and death, patient pain and distress, and repeated observation of death) and how she copes with them. (Hay and Oken dealt only with female nurses.) To protect herself from many stress-related emotions (e.g., grief, anxiety) the ICU nurse often uses defense mechanisms, particularly gross denial and detachment. The nature of the ICU work situation also promotes breakdowns in communication between the nurses and other hospital personnel and with relatives of the patients, adding further to the overall stress. (For a more recent look at sources of stress among nurses from various hospital units, see Numerof and Abrams 1984).

5

The Living World

RENE DUBOS

The word "crowd" has unpleasant connotations. It evokes disease, pestilence, and group-generated attitudes often irrational and either too submissive or too aggressive. Congested cities call to mind unhealthy complexions and harassed behavior; city crowds are accused of accepting despotic power and of blindly engaging in acts of violence. In contrast, rural areas and small towns are thought to foster health and freedom. The legendary Arcadia and the Utopias of all times are imagined as comfortably populated by human beings enjoying vast horizons. The nature and history of man are far too complex, of course, to justify such generalizations, but there is some truth nevertheless in the belief that crowding generates problems of disease and behavior. However, these problems are poorly understood and their formulation is rendered even more difficult by a number of oversimplified and erroneous concepts inherited from the late nineteenth century.

During the Industrial Revolution, the crowding in tenements, factories, and offices was associated with tremendous increases in morbidity and mortality rates. Along with malnutrition, the various "fevers" were the most obvious causes of ill health. Epidemic outbreaks and chronic forms of microbial disease constituted the largest medical problems of the late nineteenth century because they were extremely prevalent, not only among the economically destitute but also among the more favored classes. The new science of microbiology that developed during that period provided a theory that appeared sufficient at first sight to explain the explosive spread of infection. The germ theory made it obvious that crowding facilitates the transfer of microbes from one person to another, and this led to the reasonable conclusion that the newly industrialized communities had been caught in a web of infection, resulting from the increase in human contacts.

The expression "crowd diseases" thus became, and has remained ever since, identified with a state of affairs conducive to the rapid spread of infective agents, particularly under unsanitary conditions. Epidemiologists have built their science on the hypothesis that the pattern of microbial diseases in a given community of animals or men is determined by the channels available for the spread of microbes. In reality, however, the rise and fall of animal populations, both in confined environments and in the field, present aspects that cannot be entirely accounted for by these classical concepts of epidemiology. The reason, as we shall now see, is that crowding has several independent effects. On the one hand, it facilitates the spread of infective agents; on the other hand, it also modifies the manner in which men and animals respond to the presence of these agents and thereby increases indirectly the prevalence and severity of microbial disease. In fact, crowding affects the response of the individual and social body, not only to infection, but also to most of life's stresses.

In many species, the numbers of animals increase continuously from year to year until a maximum population density is reached; then suddenly an enormous mortality descends. This phenomenon, known as "population crash," has long been assumed to be caused by epidemics corresponding to those which have been so destructive in the course of human history, for example plague or yellow fever. Indeed, several different kinds of pathogens have been found to attack animal populations at the time of the crash. Pasteurellae and salmonellae are among the bacterial organisms that used to be most commonly incriminated; two decades ago a particular strain of *Mycobacterium muris* (the vole bacillus), isolated from field mice in England, was thought for a while to be responsible for population crashes in these rodents. Now that viruses have taken the limelight from bacteria, they in turn have been made responsible for occurrences of widespread mortality in several animal species.

It has become apparent, however, that the relation between population crashes and microbial diseases is far less clear than was once thought. On the one hand, several different types of pathogens can be associated with crashes in a given animal species. On the other hand, there are certain crashes for which no pathogen has been found to account for the pathological picture. These puzzling observations have led to the theory that the microbial diseases associated with population crashes are but secondary phenomena, and that the primary cause is a metabolic disturbance. . . .

Food shortages, or at least nutritional deficiencies, were long considered as a probable cause of drastic population decline. It is well known, in fact, that when wild animals multiply without check under natural conditions they exhaust their food supply, lose weight, and bear fewer young; this occurs for example when their predators are eliminated. However, a poor nutritional state can hardly account alone for population crashes. Its effect is rather to limit reproduction, either by failure of conception or by abortion; the overall result is an automatic adjustment of population size to the food supply instead of a massive crash. In fact, drastic population declines commonly occur even when the food supply is abundant.

The trend during recent years has been to explain population crashes by a "shock disease" related in some obscure way to overactivity of the adreno-pituitary system. A notorious example of this type of crowd disease is the mass migration of the Norwegian lemmings from the mountaintops of Scandinavia. According to an ancient Norwegian belief, the lemmings periodically experience an irresistible "collective urge" either to commit suicide or to search for their ancestral home on the lost Atlantic Continent, and consequently they march unswervingly into the sea. In reality, such migrations take place whenever the lemmings become overcrowded, a situation that occurs every third or fourth year, as each mating pair produces 13 to 16 young annually. The migration of Norwegian lemmings was so massive in 1960–61 that a steamer entering the Trondheim Fjord took one hour to pass through a two-mile-long pack of swimming and sinking rodents!

Although the nature of the initial stimulus that prompts the lemmings to migrate is not understood, crowding is almost certainly one of its aspects. As the rodents become more and more crowded they fall victim to a kind of mass psychosis. This results in a wild scrambling about that, contrary to legend, is not necessarily a march toward the sea but merely random movement. The animals die, not by drowning, but from metabolic derangements associated with stress; lesions are commonly found in the brain and the adrenals.

Profound changes have also been observed to occur at more or less regular intervals in the population of snowshoe hares. According to a classical description, these animals observed in Minnesota during periods of crash

characteristically died in convulsive seizures with sudden onset, running movements, hind leg extension, retraction of the head and neck, and sudden leaps with clonic seizures upon alighting. Other animals were typically lethargic or comatose. . . . This syndrome was characterized primarily by decrease in liver glycogen and a hypoglycemia preceding death. Petechial or ecchymotic brain hemorrhages, and congestion and hemorrhage of the adrenals, thyroid, and kidneys were frequent findings. (Deevey 1960)

Interestingly enough, many of the signs and symptoms observed in wild animals dying during population crashes have been reproduced in the laboratory by subjecting experimental animals to crowding and other forms of stress. Voles placed for a few hours a day during a month in cages containing another pair of aggressive voles eventually died, but not of wounds. The main finding at necropsy was a marked increase in the weight of their adrenals and spleen and a decrease in the weight of the thymus. Similar findings have been made on captive and wild rats.

Crowding can act as a form of stress in most species of experimental animals. In chickens, mice, rats, and voles, it causes an enlargement of the adrenals chiefly through cellular hyperplasia in the cortical areas; in addition it interferes with both growth and reproductive function.

Crowding affects many other biological characteristics of animal population; for example, the reproducibility of the response to various abnormal states, such as barbiturate anaesthesia, is affected by population density. The toxicity of central nervous system stimulants such as amphetamine is remarkably enhanced when the animals are placed in a crowded environment; central depressants protect to some degree against this aggregation effect. The experimental hypertension produced in rats bearing regenerating adrenals is increased by crowding, and coronary arteriosclerosis develops more rapidly and more intensely in chickens that are grouped than in animals kept isolated.

Field studies of voles in England have revealed the puzzling fact that their population continues to fall the year after the crash. It would appear, therefore, that the reduced viability reponsible for the crash is transmitted from one generation to another. This finding is compatible with other observations which indicate that crowding of the mother affects the physical development and behavior of the offspring.

The response to almost any kind of stimulus can be modified by crowding, as is illustrated by the production of experimental granuloma. Cotton pellets impregnated with turpentine were introduced subcutaneously into groups of mice that were then either caged individually or in groups. The granulomas that developed in the grouped mice weighed 19 percent less than in the other animals, a result probably due to the fact that the greater adrenocortical activity in the grouped mice had exerted a suppressive effect on the inflammatory reaction.

It is probable that the effect of crowding on tissue response accounts for the decrease in resistance to infection. In order to put this hypothesis to the test, mice were infected with a standardized dose of *Trichinella* and then were either isolated in individual jars or caged in groups immediately after infection. When these mice were sacrificed fifteen days later, it was found that all the grouped animals had large numbers of worms (15 to 51) in their intestines, whereas only 3 out of 12 of the isolated animals showed any sign of infection. Although exposure to infection had been identical, crowding had therefore increased the ability of trichinella to invade the intestinal wall, probably by decreasing the inflammatory response to the parasite. Analogous observations have been made with regard to infantile diarrhea of mice. The incidence of clinical signs of this disease remains small or is nil when the population density in the animal room is low, but it increases as the colony approaches peak production. The infection is endemic in most colonies, but the disease does not become overt until the animals are crowded.

The grouping of several organisms of one given species has certainly many physiological consequences more subtle than those mentioned above. One such curious effect has been observed in male ducks kept constantly either in the dark or exposed to artificial light for periods of over two years. In both cases, these abnormal conditions of light exposure resulted in marked disturbances of the sexual cycles, which were no longer in phase with the seasonal rhythms. However, the animals within each group exhibited a remarkable synchronism of testicular evolution, thus revealing a "group effect" on sexual activity that was independent of light, of season, and of the presence of animals of the opposite sex.

Territoriality, Dominance, and Adaptation to Crowding

As we have just seen, the epidemiology of "crowd" diseases involves factors other than those affecting the spread of infectious agents. Association with other living things modifies the total response of the organism to the various environmental forces and thereby affects susceptibility to a multiplicity of noxious influences, including infection.

A quantitative statement of population density is not sufficient, however, to forecast the effects of crowding on human beings or animals. Even more important than numbers of specimens of a given species per unit area is the manner in which each particular person or animal responds to the other members of the group under a given set of conditions. The response to population density is determined in large part by the history of the group and of its individual members; furthermore, it may be favorable or unfavorable, depending upon the circumstances.

Many types of rodents, such as laboratory rats and mice, prefer to be somewhat crowded. In fact, individually housed rats and mice usually behave in a more "emotional" or "frightened" manner than their group-housed counterparts; they are also less able to adapt to a variety of experimental procedures such as food restriction, food selection, or cold stress. Isolated mice are less able than grouped mice to overcome the disturbances in intestinal ecology caused by antimicrobial drugs and other physiological disturbances (unpublished observations). . . . The practice of mutual cleaning accelerates wound healing in many animal species, and isolation has unfavorable effects on the behavior and personality structure of animals and man.

In most animal species, probably in all, each group develops a complex social organization based on territoriality and on a social hierarchy comprising subordinate and dominant members, the so-called pecking order. The place of each animal in the hierarchy is probably determined in part by anatomical and physiological endowments and in part by the history of the group. In any case, the behaviorial differences that result from the pecking order eventually bring about anatomical and physiological differences far more profound than those initially present. For example, the dominant animals usually have larger adrenals than the subordinates and they grow more rapidly because they have more ready access to food. It appears also that in rhesus monkeys the young males issued from females with a high social rank have a better chance than other males to become dominant in the colony.

Under a given set of conditions, the relative rank of each individual animal is fairly predictable. Social competition is often restricted to the male sex, the reproductive fortunes of the female being determined by the status of the male which selects her. Females associated with subordinate males in experimental populations may entirely fail to reproduce. However, the pecking order is valid only for well-defined environmental conditions. For example, each canary bird is dominant in the region near its nest; and similarly chickens in their home yard win more combats than strangers to that yard. The successes of animals on their own territorial grounds bring to mind the better performance of baseball teams on their home fields.

Successful competition within the group naturally confers advantages. The despot has first choice with regard to food and mates, and its position may even increase its resistance to certain forms of stress such as infection. In a particular experiment involving tenches, one fish in the group was found to dominate the whole territory and to be the first one to feed. This dominance had such profound physiological consequences that when all the tenches were infected with trypanosomes, the infection disappeared first from the dominant fish. When this fish was removed from the tank, fighting started among those remaining; the fish that became dominant in the new grouping in its turn had first access to the food, and soon got rid of its trypanosome infection.

The phenomenon of dominance has a social meaning which transcends the advantages that it gives to the dominant individuals. Acceptance of the hierarchical order reduces fighting and other forms of social tensions and thus provides a stability that is beneficial to the group as a whole. In an undisturbed organized flock of chickens, for example, the individual animals peck each other less frequently and less violently, eat more, maintain weight better, and lay more eggs than do chickens in flocks undergoing social reorganization through removal of some animals or addition of new ones. Furthermore, the subordinate animals do not suffer as much as could be expected from their low rank in the pecking order. There is no direct competition for food or for mates in the well-organized group; the subordinates readily yield their place to the dominants at the feeding box; they exhibit no sexual interest, often behaving as if they were "socially castrated." Thus, the establishment of an accepted hierarchy in a stable group of animals almost eliminates the stresses of social tension and results in a kind of social homeostasis.

Needless to say, there are limits to the protective efficacy social organization can provide against the dangers created by high population density. Excessive crowding has deleterious effects even in the most gregarious rodents. When laboratory rats are allowed to multiply without restriction in a confined space, an excess of food being available at all times, they develop abnormal behavior with regard to mating, nest building, and care of the young as soon as the population becomes too dense. However, such conditions of life are extremely artificial. Under the usual conditions of rodent life in the wild, animals migrate or are killed when the population becomes too large for the amount of food available.

Although man is a gregarious animal, sudden increases in population density can be as dangerous for him as they are for animals. The biological disturbances created during the Industrial Revolution by lack of sanitation and by crowding in tenements and factories were aggravated by the fact that most members of the new labor class had immigrated from rural areas and were totally unadapted to urban life. In contrast, the world is now becoming more and more urbanized. Constant and intimate contact with hordes of human beings has come to constitute the "normal" way of life, and men have eagerly adjusted to it. This change has certainly brought about all kinds of phenotypic adaptations that are making it easier for urban man to respond successfully to situations that in the past constituted biological and emotional threats.

There may be here an analogy with the fact that domesticated animals do not respond to various types of threatening situations in the laboratory as do wild animals of the same or related species. In any case, the effects of crowding on modern urban man are certainly very different from those experienced by the farmer and his family when they were first and suddenly exposed a century ago to the city environment of industrialized societies.

The readiness with which man adapts to potentially dangerous situations makes it unwise to apply directly to human life the results of experiments designed to test the acute effects of crowding on animals. Under normal circumstances, the dangerous consequences of crowding are mollified by a multiplicity of biological and social adaptations. In fact, crowding per se, i.e. population density, is probably far less important in the long run even in animals than is the intensity of the social conflicts, or the relative peace achieved after social adjustments have been made. As already mentioned, animal populations in which status differences are clearly established are likely to reach a greater size than those in which differences in rank are less well defined.

Little is known concerning the density of population or the intensity of stimulation that is optimum in the long run for the body and the mind of man. Crowding is a relative term. The biological significance of population density must be evaluated in the light of the past experience of the group concerned, because this experience conditions the manner in which each of its members responds to the others as well as to environmental stimuli and trauma.

Laying claim to a territory and maintaining a certain distance from one's fellow are probably as real biological needs in man as they are in animals, but their expressions are culturally conditioned. The proper distance between persons in a group varies from culture to culture. People reared in cultures where the proper distance is short appear "pushy" to those coming from social groups where propriety demands greater physical separation. In contrast, the latter will appear to the former as behaving in a cold, aloof, withdrawn, and standoffish manner. Although social anthropologists have not yet adequately explained the origin of these differences, they have provided evidence that ignorance of them in human relations or in the design of dwellings and hospitals can have serious social and pathological consequences.

The problems posed by crowding in human populations are thus more complex than those which exist in animal populations because they are so profoundly conditioned by social and cultural determinants. Indeed, there is probably no aspect of human life for which it is easier to agree with Ortega y Gasset that "man has no nature. What he has is a history." Most experimental biologists are inclined to scorn discussions of mob psychology and related problems because they feel that the time is not yet ripe for scientific studies on the mechanisms of collective behavior. Yet the phrase "mob psychology" serves at least to emphasize that the response of human beings to any situation is profoundly influenced by the structure of the social environment.

The numerous outbreaks of dancing manias that occurred in Europe from the fourteenth to sixteenth century constitute a picturesque illustration of abnormal collective behavior; such an event was witnessed by P. Breughel the Elder and became the subject of one of his most famous paintings, "The Saint Vitus Dancers," now in Vienna. Even today, revivalists, tremblers, and shakers often outdo the feats of the medieval performers during the dancing manias. And millions of people can still be collectively bewitched by the antics of a Hitler or other self-proclaimed prophet, to whom they yield body and soul. What happens in the mind of man is always reflected in the diseases of his body. The epidemiology of crowd diseases cannot be completely understood without knowledge of mob psychology.

REFERENCES

Allee (1951); Barnett (1960, 1963, 1964); Barrow (1955); Benoit, Assenmacher, and Brard (1955, 1956); Bernardis and Skelton (1963); Bronson and Eleftheriou (1965a, 1965b); Calhoun (1949, 1962); Carpenter (1958); Chitty (1958); Christian and Davis (1956); Christian, Flyger and Davis (1960); Christian and Williamson (1958); Curry-Lindahl (1963); Davis and Read (1958); Deevey (1960); Ellis and Free (1964); Elton (1958); Etkin (1964); Flickinger and Ratcliffe (1961); Greenwood (1935); Hall (1959,

1964); Hediger (1950); Hinde (1960); Keeley (1962); Koford (1963); Lasagna (1962); Mackintosh (1962); Mason (1959); McDonald, Stern, and Hahn (1963); McKissick, Flickinger, and Ratcliffe (1961); Siegal (1959); Thiessen (1963); Tinbergen (1953); Washburn and Devore (1961); Welty (1957); Zeuner (1963).

6

Physiological, Motivational, and Cognitive Effects of Aircraft Noise on Children: Moving from the Laboratory to the Field

SHELDON COHEN, GARY W. EVANS,
DAVID S. KRANTZ, and DANIEL STOKOLS

S cience's contribution to social policy decisions regarding noise pollution has been primarily limited to the documentation of the impact of high-intensity sound on hearing. Acceptable noise standards used in both national and local statutes are based on research that assesses magnitude of hearing loss at varying intensities and durations of sound. Yet during the last ten years it has become clear that noise can alter nonauditory systems as well as auditory ones. Thus laboratory research has established effects of noise on cognitive, motivational, and general physiological processes. For example, noise is associated with alterations in task performance (cf. Broadbent 1978; Loeb 1979), decreased sensitivity to others (e.g., S. Cohen and Lezak 1977; Mathews and Canon 1975), and elevation

The research reported in this article was supported by grants from the National Science Foundation (BNS 77–08576 and SOC 75–09224), the National Institute of Environmental Health Sciences (1 RO1 ES0176401 DBR), the Society for the Psychological Study of Social Issues, and the University of Oregon Biomedical Fund.

The authors are indebted to Sheryl Kelly, Laurie Poore, Jerry Lukas, Rich Haller, and Nick Garshnek; to the administrative staffs of the Los Angeles, Lennox, and Inglewood (California) School Districts; to the staff, teachers, children, and parents of the participating schools; to the California Assessment Program; and to the California Department of Health. We also wish to thank Michael Posner and Myron Rothbart for their comments on an earlier draft.

of a number of nonspecific physiological responses (cf. Glass and Singer 1972; Kryter 1970). Exposure to noise that is unpredictable and uncontrollable (cannot be escaped or avoided) can also reduce one's perception of control over the environment (e.g., Glass and Singer 1972; Krantz, Glass, and Snyder 1974). This loss of control is often accompanied by a depression of mood and a decrease in one's motivation to initiate new responses (Seligman 1975).

One argument against serious consideration of this evidence when making policy decisions is that it is largely derived from laboratory studies. Since laboratory subjects typically experience a single short period of exposure to high-intensity sound and are aware that their exposure is only temporary, the applicability of these findings to experiences of chronic noise exposure is questionable. Because of a lack of well-controlled studies of persons routinely living and working under noise, we are unable to say with any certainty if similar effects occur in individuals exposed to noise for prolonged periods.

Our own lack of confidence in the generality of the effects of noise that occurs in laboratory settings translates into a lack of influence in the policy-making process. Legislation restricting noise levels in industrial and community settings usually imposes a heavy economic burden on those responsible for the noise. To convince policymakers that such burdens are justified, there must be substantive evidence that community and/or industrial noise deleteriously affects health and behavior.

Naturalistic studies of the effects of noise that occurs in home, school, or office seem like the obvious alternative to investigations carried out in laboratory settings. However, such studies are correlational. Subjects are not randomly assigned to noisy or quiet settings, and the settings often vary on dimensions other than noise exposure. These problems can be substantially reduced by carefully matching the noise and quiet samples on important dimensions and by statistically controlling for other possible confounds. It is always possible, however, that some unknown factor covaries with exposure to the noise setting and actually causes the effects that the investigator associates with noise. Thus, in isolation, naturalistic studies also provide insufficient evidence for a link between community noise and measures of health and behavior.

It is clear that neither laboratory nor naturalistic studies can in themselves provide what either scientists or politicians would consider convincing evidence for noise-induced effects. What is necessary is an interplay between laboratory and field methodologies. This interplay can take at least two forms. On the one hand, an effect can first be established as reliable within laboratory settings where causal links can be inferred. Then, the robustness of this relationship can be established in a number of naturalistic settings. On the other hand, by first conducting field research, it is possible to isolate important dimensions of a particular problem. At that point, laboratory studies may be useful to rule out plausible alternate explanations often inherent in naturalistic research. Laboratory and field approaches are often pursued to the exclusion of one another, but only by combining these two strategies can we begin to understand the impact of environmental variables in naturalistic settings. Moreover, only when evidence from the laboratory and field converges can a credible scientific case be presented in order to influence public policy.

This emphasis on the interplay between the laboratory and the field is consistent with Campbell and Stanley's (1966) discussion of the inevitable trade-off between well-controlled experimental settings (internal validity) and our ability to generalize across persons and settings (external validity). The laboratory provides the opportunity for an internally valid investigation, but the generality of laboratory findings is severely restricted. Naturalistic studies provide the opportunity to generalize findings to a greater range of persons and settings but often lack the strict control of the laboratory.

The study presented in this article examines the effects of aircraft noise on children. It is particularly concerned with exploring the generality of laboratory work on noise-induced shifts in attentional strategies, feelings of personal control, and nonauditory physiological responses related to health. Our purpose in reporting this study is twofold. First, it is presented as evidence for relationships (or lack of relationships) between aircraft noise exposure and a number of cognitive, motivational, and physiological measures. The article includes short discussions of laboratory and field research in each of the areas of concern. Second, it is presented as an example of an attempt to examine the generality of laboratory effects in a naturalistic setting. In this regard, the study employs an individual testing procedure in a field setting. It uses a matched-group design and attempts to control statistically for a number of possible alternative explanations for correlations between community noise and the various criterion variables.

OVERVIEW OF THE STUDY

The subjects were children attending the four noisiest elementary schools in the air corridor of Los Angeles International Airport. Peak sound level readings in these schools are as high as 95 dB (A), and the schools are located in an air corridor that has over 300 overflights a day—approximately one flight every 2.5 minutes during school hours (Lane and Meecham 1974). Three control schools (quiet schools) were matched with the experimental schools for grade level, for ethnic and racial distribution of children, for percentage of children whose families were receiving assistance under the Aid to Families with Dependent Children program, and for the occupations and education levels of parents. Thus we were able to compare samples of children attending noise schools and quiet schools who were relatively similar in terms of age, social class, and race. . . .

The study focused on effects occurring outside of noise exposure (i.e., aftereffects). Thus all tasks and questionnaires (except the achievement test records gathered from school files) were administered in a quiet setting—a noise-insulated trailer parked directly outside the school. These data were collected during two 45-minute sessions on consecutive days. Three cognitive tasks were administered during the test periods. One was designed to assess feelings of personal control and the others to determine whether the children employed some common attentional coping strategies. A questionnaire concerned with responses to noise and two blood pressure measures were also given during the testing sessions. A parent questionnaire dealing with parent response to noise, mother's and father's level of education, and the number of children in the family was sent home with each child. Scores on standardized reading and math tests and data on absenteeism were collected from school files.

The study included children from all noise-impacted third- and fourth-grade classrooms in each noise school as well as children from an equal number of classrooms in quiet schools. To ensure that performance differences between children from noise schools and those from quiet schools could not be attributed to noise-induced losses in hearing sensitivity, an audiometric pure-tone threshold screening was administered to each child. Children were screened at 25 dB for select speech frequencies (500, 1000, 2000, and 4000 Hz). Children failing to detect 25 dB tones at any one of these frequencies in either ear were not included in the study. Six percent of the noise-school children and 7 percent of the quiet-school children failed the screening. A total of 262 subjects (142 from noise schools and 120 from quiet schools) remained in the study. Individual analyses, however, sometimes contain fewer subjects because of missing data.

Data compiled from the parent questionnaire allowed us to determine the degree of similarity of the prematched noise and quiet samples. Analyses of variance indicated that there were no differences between the samples on the various social class factors. The mean number of children per family was 3.54 in the noise sample and 3.88 in the quiet sample. Levels of parent education were also equivalent, falling between some high school (scaled as 3) and high school graduate (scaled as 4). The mean level of education for fathers was 3.75 for noise-school children and 3.41 for quiet-school children, and for mothers, 3.64 and 3.35, respectively. The racial distributions, however, differed significantly, . . . with the noise group containing more blacks (32 percent vs. 18 percent) and the quiet group more Chicanos (50 percent vs. 33 percent). Noise and quiet samples had nearly equal percentages of whites (32 percent and 29 percent, respectively) and of unidentifiable or mixed-race children (3 percent in each sample).

The two samples also differed on mobility, with children in the quiet sample having lived in their homes longer (a mean of 49.6 months vs. 41.4

months) and attended their schools for longer periods (a mean of 43.2 months vs. 36.0) than noise children, . . . Length of school enrollment was not related to father's education, mother's education, or the number of children in the family. Moreover, the noise and quiet samples were relatively equal on these various social class factors across all durations of exposure. This finding suggests that the decision to continue living in the noise-impacted area was not determined by the parents' socioeconomic status. There were, however, more blacks and whites in the noise group with less than 2 years' exposure than there were in the equivalent quiet group, . . . There were no differences in racial distribution for other exposure durations.

. . . .

NOISE MEASURES

Interior sound levels (without children) were measured inside each classroom with Tracoustics (SLMS2A) sound level meters. Sound levels were monitored for a 1-hour period in the morning and a 1-hour period in the afternoon. Peak sound levels in terms of dB (A) were recorded for both morning and afternoon sessions. The overall mean peak for classrooms in noise schools was 74 dB and in quiet schools 56 dB. The highest reading in a noise-school classroom was 95 dB, while the highest reading in a quiet school was 68 dB.

The questionnaire administered to each child assessed his or her perception of classroom and home noise levels. The parent questionnaire also included questions on perception of home noise level as well as queries on how long the child had been enrolled in the present school and how long he or she had lived at their present address. Data on school enrollment were also available from school files. Noise contours (compiled by the Los Angeles International Airport) provided approximations of the sound levels outside the homes of noise-school children.

. . . Children in noise schools reported that their classrooms were noisier, . . . and that airplanes bothered them more in the classroom . . . than children in quiet schools did. They did not, however, report having more trouble hearing their teacher.

In regard to home noise, children from air-corridor schools were more bothered by airplane noise than their quiet-school counterparts were . . . However, noise- and quiet-school children did not differ in ratings of home noise.

. . . Parents of children from the air-corridor schools indicated both that there were higher levels of noise in the home . . . and that they were bothered more by noise . . . than the parents of children attending quiet schools indicated. The home noise level reported by the parents of noise-school children increased with the number of years they had lived in their present residence . . .

EFFECTS OF NOISE

Physiological Response and Health

Aside from temporary and permanent effects on hearing, previous research provides little convincing evidence for noise-induced physical disease (cf. S. Cohen, Glass, and Phillips 1979; Kryter 1970). It is well established, however, that short-term exposure to relatively high sound levels in laboratory settings can alter physiological processes. Physiological changes produced by noise consist of nonspecific responses typically associated with stress reactions, including increases in electrodermal activity, catecholamine secretions, vasoconstriction of peripheral blood vessels, and diastolic and systolic blood pressure. Because such changes, if extreme, are often considered potentially hazardous to health, many feel that pathogenic effects of prolonged noise exposure are likely. Laboratory evidence that some components of the physiological response to noise do not habituate (Jansen 1969) lends fuel to this argument, but is difficult to interpret in light of evidence from other laboratories indicating complete habituation (Glass and Singer 1972).

A number of studies of workers in noisy industries have indicated health problems for those exposed to intense noise levels. Included are respiratory problems, such as sore throat, and allergenic, musculoskeletal, circulatory, neurological, cardiovascular, and digestive disorders (e.g., Anticaglia and Cohen 1974; A. Cohen 1973). However, all of the industrial noise studies are subject to serious criticism because of their failure to control for other adverse workplace or job factors, for example, task demands and risks, that often covary with the noisiness of the job (cf. S. Cohen, Glass, and Phillips 1979; Kryter 1970). It is also important to note that several industrial surveys have failed to find a relation between noise and ill health (e.g., Finkle and Poppen 1948; Glorig 1971).

There are no existing controlled studies on the impact of noise on nonauditory health in children (Mills 1975). Recent theoretical work, however, argues that children (along with the old, individuals in institutions, and persons suffering from other sources of stress) may be particularly susceptible to noise-induced illness because they lack the ability to temporarily escape their noisy environments (S. Cohen, Glass, and Phillips 1979). It is suggested that this inability to escape at will can cause both an increase in overall duration of noise exposure and an increase in feelings of helplessness. This effect is important, since feelings of helplessness have been implicated as possible causal factors in illness (Seligman 1975).

Each child's resting blood pressure (systolic and diastolic) was taken on an SR-2 Physiometrics automated blood pressure recorder.[1] To accustom the children to the blood pressure measurement technique, an initial measurement was made at the beginning of the first day of testing. A short explanation of the technique and the concept of blood pressure was given at this time, and questions were solicited and answered. This initial measurement was not recorded. Each child's blood pressure was measured again on the first day and once more on the second day. The blood pressure data are based on the mean systolic and diastolic pressures for these two measurements. The graphic output of the machine was coded after the study was completed, with coders blind to experimental condition. Each child's height and weight were also measured. Absenteeism was used as an indirect measure of health, since absence from school is often attributable to illness. These data were available from school files.

Health measures were separated into two multivariate clusters: general health measures and blood pressure. This procedure was necessary because two of the general health measures—height and ponderosity (weight/height)— were required as controls for the blood pressure analyses (cf. Voors et al. 1976). Although noise-school children were shorter and weighed less than quiet-school children, neither of these differences reached significance . . . Surprisingly, noise-school children attended school a higher percentage of the time (97.5 percent vs. 94.2 percent) than their quiet-school counterparts did . . .

As is apparent from figure 6.1, children from noise schools had higher blood pressure than their quiet-school counterparts did . . . Unadjusted means for systolic pressure were 89.68 mm for the noise group and 86.77 mm for the quiet group. Diastolic means were 47.84 mm for the noise group and 45.16 mm for the quiet group. A marginal interaction . . . between noise and months in school suggests that systolic pressure differences between noise and quiet groups are greatest during the first few years of school enrollment; differences after this point remain constant. Figure 6.1 reflects a similar pattern for diastolic pressure. This interaction does not, however, reach even marginal statistical significance.[2]

Helplessness

Both laboratory and community noise research suggests the possibility that high-intensity noise exposure induces feelings of helplessness. According to Seligman (1975), a psychological state of helplessness frequently results when we continually encounter events (especially aversive ones) that we can do nothing about. The state of helplessness includes a perception of lessened control over one's outcomes, a depression of mood, and a decrease in one's motivation to

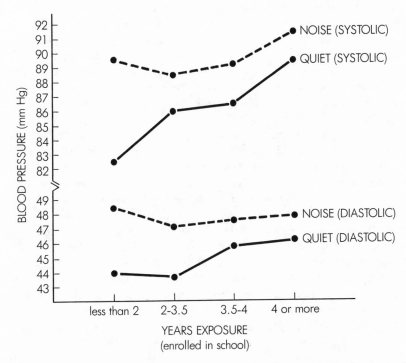

Figure 6.1. Systolic and diastolic blood pressure as a function of school noise level and duration of exposure. (Each period on the years-exposure coordinate on the figure represents approximately one quarter of the sample. For example, 25 percent of the sample had been enrolled in the present school less than 2 years.)

initiate new responses. Extreme effects of helplessness include fear, anxiety, depression, disease, and even death.

A number of researchers have induced helplessness effects in the laboratory by exposing subjects to uncontrollable bursts of noise (Hiroto 1974; Krantz, Glass, and Snyder 1974). Moreover, survey data reporting high levels of annoyance but low levels of complaints from noise-impacted populations have similarly been interpreted as reflecting a helplessnesslike state (Herridge 1974). This finding, however, is subject to a number of alternative explanations, and thus the helplessness interpretation is only suggestive.

Performance on a cognitive task preceded by a success or failure experience was used in the present study to examine the effect of noise on response to failure and on persistence on a difficult task. Response to failure is a standard measure of susceptibility to helplessness. Thus, if noise-school children were more susceptible to helplessness, they would show greater effects of a failure experience than their quiet-school counterparts would. A lack of persistence (or a "giving-up" syndrome) is considered a direct manifestation of the helpless state.

Each child was given a treatment puzzle to assemble after the tester demonstrated the task with another puzzle. All puzzles were based on the same nine pieces and required the child to fill in a template of a familiar shape. One half of the children received an insoluble (failure) puzzle, and one half received a soluble (success) puzzle. The soluble puzzle was a circle, and the insoluble puzzle was a triangle. Each child was allowed to work on the treatment puzzle for 2.5 minutes. After time was up on the first puzzle, the child was given a second, moderately difficult puzzle to solve. The second (test) puzzle was the same—a square—for all (success and failure) children. The child was allowed 4 minutes to solve the second puzzle. Whether or not the puzzle was solved, time to solution and the child's persisting or giving up before the 4 minutes had elapsed were used as measures of helplessness. We expected that children from noisy schools would be more susceptible to a failure (helplessness) manipulation than children from quiet schools would be, and thus would be less likely to solve the puzzle, slower to find the solution, and more likely to give up on the second puzzle following an insoluble (failure) treatment. Moreover, children from noisy schools, irrespective of their success-failure condition, were expected to give up more often than quiet-school children.

A large proportion (34 percent) of the children assigned to the success condition, and thus receiving a soluble treatment puzzle, failed to solve the treatment puzzle within the 2.5 minutes allowed. Since the puzzles were considered quite simple and had been pilot tested on children of the same age group, this result was quite unexpected. Although the fact that a number of children self-selected themselves into a failure condition makes interpretation of success-failure effects impossible, comparisons between the children from noise schools and those from quiet schools, irrespective of (controlling for) their pretreatment, are still valid. . . .

First, an examination of only those who were assigned to the success treatment condition indicates that children from noise schools were more likely to fail to solve the treatment puzzle (41 percent failed) than children from quiet schools were (23 percent failed). This effect, however, was only marginally significant . . . Second, there were similar effects of noise on the second puzzle, which occurred irrespective of whether the child received a success (solved or not) or failure treatment. As was the case with the first puzzle, noise-school children were more likely to fail the second puzzle (53 percent failed) than quiet-school children were (36 percent failed), . . . and were more likely to give up . . . than their quiet-school counterparts were. . . . As is apparent from figure 6.2, a marginal interaction between noise and months enrolled in school . . . suggests that the longer a child had attended a noise school, the slower he or she was in solving the puzzle . . .

Although the preceding analyses indicate that children from noise

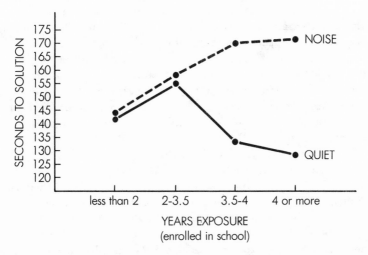

Figure 6.2. Performance on the second (test) puzzle as a function of school noise level and duration of exposure. (Each period on the years-exposure coordinate on the figure represents approximately one quarter of the sample. For example, 25 percent of the sample had been enrolled in the present school less than 2 years.)

schools are generally less capable of performing a cognitive task (at least puzzle solving) than children from quiet schools are, they provide only suggestive evidence that noise-school children feel or act as if they have less control over their outcomes. The strongest hint that failure on these puzzles on the part of noise-school children is related to helplessness is found in the data indicating that noise-school children were more likely to give up before their allotted time had elapsed than their quiet counterparts were. It is possible, however, that a constant proportion of children who failed on the second puzzle gave up. It would follow that the amount of giving up in the noise condition was inflated by the fact that there was a greater pool of failures. This interpretation suggests that increased giving up under the noise condition cannot necessarily be viewed as a sign of helplessness. A final analysis addresses this point. This analysis, which includes only those children who failed the second puzzle, indicates that the failures of noise-school children were associated with giving up (31 percent of those who failed gave up) more often than the failures of quiet-school children were (7 percent of those who failed gave up) . . . Thus, even though all of these children failed to solve the puzzle, noise-school children were less likely to persist than their quiet-school counterparts were.

Attentional Processes During Noise

Human performance studies report that noise often results in a restriction (or focusing) in one's breadth of attention (Broadbent 1971; Hockey

1970). Cues irrelevant to task performance are dropped out first, and then, if attention is further restricted, relevant task cues are eliminated. Performance improves under noise when discarded cues are those that are distracting or competing with primary task cues. Performance is adversely affected, however, when a task requires a wide breadth of attention and when focusing results in the neglect of relevant as well as irrelevant cues. Similarly, focusing can have a negative impact on interpersonal behavior when subtle social cues (e.g., another's look of distress) are dropped out, but can improve the quality of an interaction when the discarded cues are merely distracting (S. Cohen and Lezak 1977).

There is suggestive evidence that an attentional focusing strategy will persist even after noise is terminated. A number of studies have shown postnoise effects on performance and interpersonal behavior (e.g., Donnerstein and Wilson 1976; Glass and Singer 1972). These aftereffects of noise are consistent with what one would expect to occur when one uses a focusing strategy (S. Cohen 1978). As yet, however, there is no direct evidence that attentional focusing occurs following exposure to noise in either the laboratory or the field.[3]

Selective inattention. A strategy that is similar (and possibly identical) to attentional focusing has been proposed by Deutsch (1964) to account for the effect of community noise on the verbal abilities of children. Deutsch suggests that children reared in noisy environments become inattentive to acoustic cues. That is, they tune out their acoustic environment. (This could be viewed as their focusing their attention on other aspects of their environment.) Children who tune out their noisy environments are not likely to distinguish between speech-relevant and speech-irrelevant sounds. Thus, they lack experience with appropriate speech cues and generally show an inability to recognize relevant sounds and their referents. The inability to discriminate sound is presumed to account, in part, for subsequent problems in learning to read. Although recent research suggests that children living and attending school in noisy neighborhoods are poorer at making auditory discriminations and in reading (Bronzaft and McCarthy 1975; S. Cohen, Glass and Singer 1973), there is no direct evidence for the selective inattention mechanism. An alternative explanation is that noise masks parent and teacher speech, similarly resulting in a lack of experience with appropriate speech cues and, as a consequence, in reading deficits.

The present study attempts to assess the relation between environmental noise level and the selective inattention strategy in order (a) to determine the generality of noise-induced shifts in attention that occur in laboratory settings and (b) to test Deutsch's (1964) hypothesis. In line with the testing of the Deutsch hypothesis, the relation of the above-mentioned variables to auditory discrimination and reading achievement is also assessed.

Because children who are relatively inattentive to acoustic cues should be less affected by an auditory distractor, distractibility was used as a measure of selective inattention. Under both ambient and distracting conditions, the subjects performed a task consisting of crossing out the *e*'s in a two-page passage from a sixth-grade reader. They were instructed to move from left to right and from top to bottom of the page, as if they were reading, and to go as fast as they could without missing any *e*'s. Each subject worked on a short practice paragraph and then on the task for two minutes. Two versions (different samples of prose) were used.

In the distraction condition, the child worked on one of the versions of the task while a tape recording of a male voice read a story at a moderate volume. In the no-distraction condition, the alternative form of the task was completed under ambient sound conditions. The distraction and no-distraction tasks were administered on different testing days. Both the order of alternative versions of the task and the experimental conditions were counterbalanced. The criterion measure was performance (percentage of *e*'s found) on the distraction task after the scores were adjusted for no-distraction performance. It was expected that the children from noise schools would be less affected by distraction than the children from quiet schools. Since selective inattention is a strategy that develops over time, it was also predicted that this tuning-out strategy would increase with increased exposure (S. Cohen, Glass and Singer 1973).

Separate analyses examined the number of lines completed under distraction and the percentage of *e*'s in the completed lines that were found under distraction. No-distraction performance (number of lines in the first analysis and percentage of *e*'s in the second) was added as an additional control variable in order to equate the children on their ability to perform the task under quiet conditions. There were no differences between the noise group and the quiet group (nor was there an interaction) on the number of lines completed under distraction. There was, however, a significant interaction between noise-quiet and months enrolled in school . . . for the percentage-of-*e*'s-found measure. As is apparent from figure 6.3, the children in noise schools did better than the quiet group on the distraction task during the first two years of exposure and did worse after four years of exposure. Contrary to earlier evidence, this finding suggests that as the length of noise exposure increases, children are more, rather than less, disturbed by auditory distractors. One possible explanation for this effect is that at first, the children attempt (somewhat successfully) to cope with noise by tuning it out. Later, however, as they find that the strategy is not adequate, they give up. This interpretation is consistent with the helplessness data.

As suggested earlier, reading deficits in children from noisy neighborhoods have been attributed to noise-impacted children's selective filtering out of acoustic cues. Auditory discrimination and reading achievement were assessed in an attempt to replicate previous work and to determine whether there was an association between these measures and the children's attentional strategies. Standardized reading and math tests (administered during the second and third grades by the school system) were gathered from school files, and the Wepman Auditory

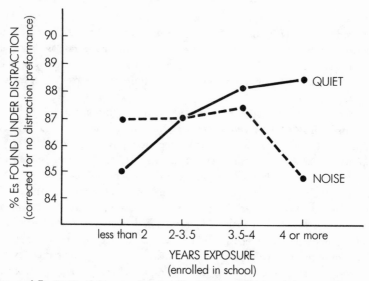

Figure 6.3. Distractibility as a function of school noise level and duration of exposure. (Each period on the years-exposure coordinate on the figure represents approximately one quarter of the sample. For example, 25 percent of the sample had been enrolled in the present school less than 2 years.)

Discrimination Test (Wepman 1958)[4] was administered individually to children in the soundproof van. The Wepman test consists of 40 pairs of words, some of which differ from each other in either initial or final sound, for example, *sick-thick* or *map-nap*. The pairs of words are recorded on tape and presented to each child through earphones. The child is instructed to report if the two words in each pair are the same or different. Control word pairs, in which the words are the same, allow for the elimination of children who have problems with same-different judgments or who are not attending to the task.

In order to roughly equate the noise and quiet conditions on the aptitude of the children at the time they entered school, the analyses of school achievement and auditory discrimination scores included an additional control for the mean cognitive abilities of the child's class on entering the first grade. None of the . . . analyses were significant for this cluster. Math, reading, and auditory discrimination were all unrelated to both noise and the Noise × Months Enrolled in School interaction.

Further analyses (Pearson correlations) suggest that the children who were better at auditory discriminations were also better on both the reading test . . . and the math test . . . There were, however, no significant relations between these variables and the selective inattention measure. The same analyses, including only noise-school children, and correlations partialing out control variables for both the entire sample and the noise sample yielded similar results. In summary, there is no evidence that aircraft noise affects reading and math skills, or that these skills are related to a selective inattention strategy.

. . . .

Quiet Homes and Noisy Schools

To determine whether or not living in a relatively quiet home (at least in terms of aircraft noise) would lessen the impact of school noise, we isolated the children living in the twenty quietest homes in the noise sample, that is, in homes with contour levels of less than 68 in terms of the Community Noise Equivalency Level (CNEL).[5] These children were then compared . . . with the remainder of the noise sample and with the entire quiet sample.[6] In no case was there a differnce between these quiet-home children and the remaining children of the noise sample. In a number of cases, however, even this small group of twenty showed the effects of noise reported earlier. Thus the noise-sample children from quiet homes were less likely to solve the first helplessness task puzzles than the quiet-sample controls were . . . The longer a child had attended a noisy school, the less likely he or she was to solve either the first puzzle . . . or the second puzzle. . . . Moreover, children from quiet homes but noisy schools were more likely to fail, . . . and to give up, . . . on the second puzzle than children from quiet schools were. . . . Further, their failures on the second puzzle were associated with giving up more often than the failures of quiet-school children were . . . Noise-school children from quiet homes also had both higher systolic blood pressure, . . . and higher diastolic blood pressure, . . . than children from quieter schools did . . . There were no effects, however, on the selective inattention task (crossing out e's under distraction condition), as reported for the entire sample.

These analyses suggest that living in a relatively quiet neighborhood did not lessen the cumulative impact of exposure to noise at school. The reason may be that the noise experienced during school attendance is sufficient to create noise effects.

AIR POLLUTION

A possible alternative explanation for differences between the noise and quiet samples is air pollution levels. Such an alternative is very unlikely. Sulfur dioxide was minimal at all the school sites, never exceeding the California standard (South

Coast Air Quality Management District, 1977; State of California, 1976).[7] Ozone and nitrogen dioxide standards were exceeded, but maximum levels were slightly higher at the control schools than at the airport schools. The maximum 1-hour rates in any school area for ozone (.21 parts per million) and NO_2 (.60 ppm) were below levels that generally show any effects on human behavior or health (Morrow 1975; National Academy of Sciences 1977).[8] Maximum carbon monoxide was slightly higher in the airport schools (30 vs. 27, 22 ppm), but average values were identical (6 ppm). The differences in maximum values of 8 ppm are negligible, and human effects from CO concentrations of less than 40 ppm are extremely rare (National Air Pollution Control Administration 1970). Note that we have used maximum values in arguing against an air pollution alternative, thus presenting a very conservative counterargument. Average values in all cases were considerably below established standards.

CONCLUSIONS

In general, the evidence presented in this article is consistent with laboratory work on physiological response to noise and on uncontrollable noise as a factor in helplessness. Thus children from noisy schools have higher blood pressure and are more likely to give up on a task than children from quiet schools are. The development of attentional strategies predicted from laboratory work and previous field research was, on the whole, not found. Contrary to prediction, increased years of exposure led to children's being more distractible rather than less. However, a general deficit in task performance on the puzzle task and increased distractibility do seem to support the more general hypothesis that prolonged noise exposure affects cognitive processes.

These data are most interesting, however, because of the tentative answers they provide concerning questions of adaptation to noise over time. One interpretation of the data is that they indicate some habituation of physiological stress response but show no signs of adaptation of cognitive and motivational effects. In fact, in a number of cases, increased length of exposure resulted in an increased negative impact of noise. First, the only evidence for an adaptation effect is provided by the systolic blood pressure data. On that measure, the greatest difference between the noise and quiet groups occurred during the first two years of exposure. As length of exposure increased, these differences leveled out but still remained substantial. Perceptions of noise and noise annoyance did not adapt. Thus children from noise schools and their parents reported more noise and being more bothered by noise. Parents, in fact, reported higher levels of noise as their length of residence in the noisy area increased. Neither the cognitive deficits on the helplessness puzzles (which actually increased over time) nor the giving-up syndrome of the children from noise schools lessened with increased length of exposure. Finally, although noise-school children were initially less affected by an auditory distractor, increased length of exposure (beyond four years) seemed to result in greater distractibility. Thus the preponderance of evidence suggests a lack of successful adaptation over time. The above interpretation, however, is only tentative. Although length-of-exposure differences may be due to increased exposure to noise, they may also be attributable to some unknown factors that differentiate between children who continue to live in the air corridor and those who move, or to some combination of exposure and these factors.

It should be noted that the failure of the present study to replicate the previously reported relation between community noise and reading ability (Bronzaft and McCarthy 1975; S. Cohen, Glass, and Singer 1973) may be attributable to an experimental design insensitive to noise-induced differences in school achievement. In both of the earlier studies, all the students attended the same school. Moreover, in the Cohen et al. study, students from both noisy and quiet apartments were taught in the same classrooms by the same teachers. In the present study, noise-sample children and quiet-sample children attended different schools, were in different classrooms, and had different teachers. It is likely that these factors add substantial error variance to the equation, making the detection of a small effect of noise quite difficult.

Can we conclude that community noise has effects that are similar to noise-induced effects reported in the laboratory literature? The similarity of our results to those reported in laboratory settings is striking. However, we still must be cautious. Replications of these results in other settings and with other populations are required before definitive conclusions are possible. To this end, our own research program includes an ongoing replication of this study, with a population exposed to traffic noise, as well as plans to collect longitudinal data on the children attending airport schools.

What conclusions can we make in regard to public policy? From a policy point of view, these data are valuable but not sufficient. At least 8 million people in this country are exposed to aircraft noise (U.S. Environmental Protection Agency 1974), and the vast majority of noise-impacted communities have racial and social class compositions more similar to the composition of the present sample than to that of the general population (U.S. Environmental Protection Agency, 1977).[9] In combination with the laboratory noise literature, these data clearly suggest lending additional weight to the possible impact of aircraft noise on psychological adjustment and on nonauditory aspects of health. Replications of these results, however, would substantially increase their potential influence in the realms of both science and social policy.

NOTES

1. This instrument is an electronic infrasonic device that records on a rotating paper disc. Measurements were taken with a rubber cuff entirely encircling the upper arm. The reliability of this device for blood pressure measurement in children has been established in previous work (Voors et al. 1976).

2. To investigate whether elevations in blood pressure occurred equally across races, separate regressions were calculated for whites, blacks, and Chicanos. Since the number of subjects in each of these regressions is small, only very substantial mean differences will reach statistically significant levels. Blacks and Chicanos attending noise schools had higher systolic ($<.05$ for blacks, $p<.25$ for Chicanos) and diastolic ($p<.25$ for blacks, $p<.10$ for Chicanos) pressure than their quiet-school counterparts did. For whites, there were no main effects of noise, but an interaction between noise and length of school enrollment indicated that an initial inflation of pressure for noise-school children disappeared as length of enrollment increased ($p<.01$ for both systolic and diastolic). These race differences will be pursued in a later paper.

3. The only study on the impact of chronic noise exposure on attentional focusing resulted in rather ambiguous findings, with children from noisy homes (as reported by parents) exhibiting general performance deficits but no focusing strategy (Heft 1979). A replication of the incidental memory task used in the Heft study was administered in the present study. Errors in administering the task, however, made the data uninterpretable.

4. J. Wepman, *Manual of Directions: Auditory Discrimination Test.* Chicago: Author, 1958.

5. CNEL is a measure of community noise giving more weight to noise occurring between 1900 and 2200 hours and the most weight to noise occurring between 2200 and 0700 hours (cf. Peterson and Gross 1972).

6. Noise was dummy coded. The two contrasts discussed in this section were used to determine the impact of noise. This is a conservative technique of doing the contrasts, since the error term for the entire sample is used in calculating the F.

7. South Coast Air Quality Management District. *Summary of air quality in South Coast Air Basin 1977* (ENP 78–1). Los Angeles: Author, 1977; State of California. *California Air Resources Board;: Technical Services Division,* Vol. 8 (2). Sacramento, Calif.: Author, 1976.

8. National Academy of Sciences. *Nitrogen Oxides.* Washington, D.C.: Author, 1977.

9. U.S. Environmental Protection Agency. *The urban noise survey (550–9–77–100).* Washington, D.C.: Author, 1977.

7

Mediating Influences of Social Support on Stress at Three Mile Island

RAYMOND FLEMING, ANDREW BAUM, MARTHA M. GISRIEL, AND ROBERT J. GATCHEL

The accident at Three Mile Island (TMI) was a dramatic and stressful event. Research on the psychological effects of the accident has indicated that area residents exhibited a number of stress symptoms immediately after the accident (Dohrenwend et al. 1979; Flynn and Chalmers 1980). The presidential commission investigating TMI concluded that psychological stress was among the principal consequences of the accident and research has found evidence of continuing stress among TMI area residents a year or more after the accident (Baum et al. 1981; Bromet 1980; Houts et al. 1980). However, even at the height of the accident, susceptibility to stress appeared to be selective; some residents were more profoundly affected than were others. The present study examines one explanation for differential response to stress at TMI—the mediating effects of social support.

It has long been suspected that interpersonal relationships play a significant role in determining the impact of stress in settings ranging from the battlefield to the delivery room (Nuckolls, Cassel, and Kaplan 1972; Shils and Janowitz 1948). One way of reviewing the protective function of social relationships has been in terms of the emotional support that people derive from others. Cobb (1976) defined this in terms of benefits associated with feeling loved and valued, and with being a member of a "network of communication and mutual

This research was partially supported by research grants from the National Science Foundation (BNS–81–12434) and from the Uniformed Services University of the Health Sciences.

obligation." In other words, the encouragement, opinion validation, and reassurance that people get from friends and family influence their response to stress and somehow make them more resistant to its effects. Research has indicated that under periods of stress or life change people manage better when they can derive support from social relationships (Cobb 1976; Cohen and McKay 1980; Kaplan, Cassel, and Gore 1977). It is less clear, however, whether social support affects people who are exposed to routine or low levels of stress. Research has not yet determined whether social support affects the impact of daily hassles and routine stressors that characterize daily life (Lazarus and Cohen 1977) or whether having little or no social support is a stressor on its own.

Two alternative perspectives on the effects of social support have evolved. The first, which we shall call the general "assets-benefits" hypothesis, holds that having little or no social support is stressful and that having high levels of support is beneficial whether stress is present or not. Loss of close friends or family can be a devastating negative event with significant health consequences (Bartrop et al. 1977; Holmes and Masuda 1974; Thomas and Duszynski 1974). Research has also indicated that general benefits such as longer life and better health are associated with higher levels of support (Berkman 1977; Cassel 1976).

The second perspective on social support is typically called the "stress buffering" hypothesis. It holds that having high levels of social support aids people in coping with stress but, in the absence of significant stress, it is neither helpful nor harmful. In other words, low levels of support are not stressful by themselves and place people at a relative disadvantage only under periods of unusual stress. Several studies have shown interactions between stress and support indicating that having social support is beneficial primarily when stress is relatively high (Andrews et al. 1978; Brown and Harris 1978; House and Wells 1977; Myers, Lindenthal, and Pepper 1975; Nuckolls, Cassel, and Kaplan 1972).

One aim of this study was to determine the extent to which differences in social support could account for variation in stress response among residents of the TMI area. We were also concerned with the relative utility of the general and buffering models in explaining stress responding under conditions of chronic threat. Finally, we were interested in the degree to which different aspects of stress (i.e., psychological, behavioral, and biochemical responding) are influenced by social support. This third aim was addressed by obtaining simultaneous measures of symptom reporting, task performance, and urinary catecholamine levels. Based on previous research, we expected to find an inverse relationship between stress and social support. If the general model of support proved to be most useful in explaining these effects, one would expect to find main effects of both stressors and level of support: TMI residents would exhibit greater stress than would control subjects, and supported individuals would exhibit less stress than would unsupported individuals. The buffering model, on the other hand, would be manifested as an interaction between stressor and support showing little, if any, difference between supported and unsupported control subjects, but large differences between supported and unsupported TMI residents.

METHOD

Subjects

A total of 109 subjects participated in this study. Of these, 35 were randomly sampled from an area within five miles of the TMI nuclear power station.[1] Although the sample size may be considered somewhat small and generalization to the entire TMI region may be somewhat limited, we felt that the TMI groups size would be sufficient to clearly demonstrate stress responding. In order to provide appropriate lower stress comparison groups and to control for possible effects of living near a power plant (whether damaged or not), three control groups were obtained. These groups were randomly sampled from demographically similar areas within five miles of an undamaged nuclear power plant, within five miles of an undamanged coal-fired power plant, and an area more than 15 miles from any type of power plant. Analyses of these groups indicated that there were not systematic differences among them on measures of stress.[2] As a result, these subjects were pooled into a single low stress control group. All subjects were paid for participating in the study.

Measurement of Social Support

A number of criticisms of social support assessments have been noted (Cohen and McKay 1980; Wallston et al. 1981). Primary among these have been (1) the confounding of emotional and instrumental support, and (2) whether or not measures of social support reflect the degree to which people believe that they have social support. As a result, a six-item scale measuring individual perceptions of the extent to which they had access to emotional support systems was used to classify subjects on this dimension.[3] Respondents were asked to indicate the degree to which they agreed or disagreed (on a 7-point scale) with the statements.

Measurement of Stress Response

Self-reported evidence of mood disturbance or psychological difficulty was obtained by considering the global symptom reporting index and several other subscales of the Symptom Checklist-90 (SCL-90; Derogatis, Rickels, and Rock 1976). The SCL-90 is a 90-item multidimensional symptom inventory that assesses the degree to which symptoms such as nausea, headache, loneliness, sadness, suspiciousness, and fear are experienced as bothersome. The global index reflects the number of different symptoms that were reported as being bothersome, and the subscales reflect distress associated with somatic sensations, anxiety, depression, alienation, suspiciousness, and orientation problems. The Beck Depression Inventory was also administered (Beck 1967).

Behavioral effects of stress were measured as performance on two tasks. The first, a proofreading task, was the same as was used by Glass and Singer (1972) in studying effects of exposure to noise stress. Subjects were given five minutes to proofread a brief passage taken from *The Death and Life of Great American Cities* (Jacobs 1961) into which a variety of errors had been systematically inserted. These errors included misspellings, grammatical mistakes, punctuation problems, and typographical errors. Subjects were told to read the passage carefully, marking any errors they found.

This measure of focusing or concentration ability was supplemented by a second task, a variant of an embedded figures task (Witkin, Goodenough, and Oltman 1979). The task consisted of eight complex geometric figures in which simpler "target" figures were hidden. Subjects were instructed to locate the target figure hidden within each complex figure.

Biochemical assessments of stress were obtained by measuring levels of catecholamines (epinephrine and norepinephrine) in subjects' urine. Subjects were asked to provide 15-hour urine samples—all urine voided from 6 p.m.– 9 P.M. on the sampling day was collected in special containers by subjects. These containers were kept refrigerated during the course of the sample collection and a noncaustic preservative was added at the outset to prevent deterioration of the samples. The samples were thoroughly stirred, measured for volume, and a smaller sample was saved and frozen. Subsequent assay of these samples for urinary catecholamine levels was done using COMT radioenzymatic procedures (Durrett and Ziegler 1980). Since a relatively constant fraction of the catecholamines secreted by the body is excreted as free epinephrine and norepinephrine (Beck 1967), estimation of these substances provides a good index of adrenal medullary activity and, hence, sympathetic arousal. Since stress has been shown to involve both adrenal medullary and general sympathetic activity, measurement of urinary catecholamines is an effective way of examining biochemical aspects of stress (Frankenhaeuser 1973).

These measures were selected for two reasons. First, they have been shown to vary with stress in a number of studies (Frankenhaeuser 1975a; Glass and Singer 1972; Singer, Lundberg and Frankenhaeuser 1978). Second, previous research at TMI has indicated that, a year and more after the accident at TMI, residents of the surrounding area differed from several control samples on almost all of these measures (Baum et al. 1981; Bromet 1980).

Procedures

Subjects were examined in their homes. The experimenter arrived at a prescheduled time, explaining the nature and requirements of the study. All subjects were provided with written descriptions of the study, and informed consent was obtained.

Each session began with a brief discussion of the project, at which time questions were answered. The embedded figures task was presented first, and subjects were allowed to work on it as long as they wished. Time spent on each item was recorded. Subjects were instructed to work on each item in order, and were told that once they had finished working on one, they could not go back to work on it again. They were allowed to attempt as many items as they wished. The number of attempts and the number of correct solutions were also recorded.

After completion of this task and a brief break, subjects were presented with the proofreading task. For this task, subjects were allowed only five minutes to find as many errors as they could. The number of errors correctly identified was recorded and expressed as a percentage of the total possible errors that could have been found.

Following the proofreading, the experimenter reviewed with the subject the written directions for the social support inventory, the SCL-90, and the Beck Inventory. In addition, complete written instructions for providing the urine sample were provided. An appointment was made for the following morning so that the urine sample could be picked up soon after it was completed.

RESULTS

Residents of all four areas under investigation were split by social support scores; and analyses of variance, crossing residence with level of perceived social support, were performed on the data. All data are expressed as means with larger values representing more of the dimension being measured. Post-hoc mean comparisons were performed according to procedures described by Tukey (Myers 1966).

Social Support

The six-item (each item scored on a 7-point scale) social support index yielded scores ranging from 14 to 42. The samples were split into approximately equal thirds according to their relative scores on this index. Among TMI residents, 13 were grouped into a low perceived social support group, 12 into a moderate level, and 11 into a high perceived social support group. Among control subjects, 23 fell into the low category while 27 fell into the middle and 24 into the high social support groups.

Symptom Reporting

The results of an ANOVA run on unequal n's, reflecting emotional distress are summarized in table 7.1. Although main effects for both residence and social support were significant for these measures, all were qualified by significant or near significant interactions between residence and social support. The general pattern of these data conformed to predictions based upon the buffering model: TMI residents reporting low levels of social support reported more symptoms, depression, anxiety, and alienation than did any other subjects (where interactions only approached significance, mean comparisons revealed the same pattern). TMI residents with moderate or high levels of social support did not differ from one another and were also comparable to control subjects. No differences were found among low stress control subjects as a function of social support ratings. Self-reported somatic distress (SCL-90) conformed to a pattern more like that associated with the general model. Residents of the TMI area reported greater somatic distress regardless of level of social support, $F(1,103) = 6.949$, $p < 0.1$. Further, subjects reporting lower levels of social support indicated greater somatic distress than did subjects with higher levels of support, regardless of where they lived, $F(2,103) = 3.110, p < .05$. These main effects of residence and support level were not qualified by an interaction.

Task Performance

Data for task performance also suggest the influence of a buffering effect of social support. TMI area residents reporting low levels of social support performed more poorly than did subjects in any other condition (see table 7.2). This was evident on both the proofreading and embedded figures tasks. TMI area residents reporting moderate and high levels of support did not differ from one another or from control subjects. Social support did not account for any differences in task performance among control subjects.

Urinary Catecholamines

The pattern of findings for biochemical response did not conform to the buffering model. Instead, they provided some support for a general effect of social support superimposed upon a general stress effect (see table 7.3). Regardless of reported level of social support, TMI residents exhibited higher levels of urinary epinephrine and norepinephrine $F(1,77) = 5.269, p < .09$; $F(1,77) = 10.496$, $p < .01$, respectively. Social support influenced norepinephrine levels indepen-

Table 7.1. Emotional Distress Measures

Social Support	Total Number of Symptoms (SCL-90)			Depression (Beck)			Anxiety (SCL-90)			Alienation (SCL-90)		
	Low	Moderate	High	Low	Moderate	High	Low	Moderate	High	Low	Moderate	High
TMI	44.2_a	17.3	15.7	11.5_a	2.8	1.7	0.8_a	0.3	0.2	0.9_a	0.1	0.1
Control	19.7	12.5	11.9	4.5	3.5	3.0	0.4	0.1	0.2	0.1	0.1	0.1
F TMI vs. control (1,103)	13.738, p < .001			4.507, p < .05			7.200, p < .01			7.119, p < .01		
F social support (2,103)	10.002, p < .001			11.048, p < .001			12.804, p < .001			7.821, p < .001		
F interaction (2,103)	4.470, p < .02			10.049, p < .001			2.229, p < .11			2.908, p < .06		

(Means with subscripts are significantly different from those without on each measure, p < .05)

Table 7.2. Performance Scores for Embedded Figures and Proofreading Tasks

Social Support	Embedded Figures (No. correct of 8)			Proofreading (% of errors found)		
	Low	Moderate	High	Low	Moderate	High
TMI	1.9_a	4.8	5.4	49_a	58_a	66
Control	5.1	4.9	5.7	78	76	73
F TMI vs. control (1,103)	4.363, p < .05			24.48, p < .001		
F social support (2,103)	2.685, p < .08			0.091, p < .5		
F interaction (2,103)	2.891, p < .06			2.898, p < .06		

(Means with subscripts are significantly different from those without, p < .05)

Table 7.3. Symptoms of Stress-Related Arousal

Social Support	Urinary Epinephrine (ng/ml)			Urinary Norepinephrine (ng/ml)		
	Low	Moderate	High	Low	Moderate	High
TMI	12.7	12.4	11.6	33.4	25.4	23.4
Control	9.4	7.2	6.9	22.6	14.2	15.7
F TMI vs. control (1,103)	5.3, p < .02			10.5, p < .002		
F social support (2,103)	.52, p < .5			3.7, p < .03		
F interaction (2,103)	.10, p < .5			.12, p < .5		

dently, $F(2,77) = 3.688, p < .05$. Epinephrine levels showed this same trend, but the main effect was not significant. Interactions between support and stress did not reach significance for either measure.

DISCUSSION

This study was concerned with several aspects of stress. Initially, it was designed to measure the degree to which residents of the TMI area continue to experience stress as a function of living near the damaged power plant more than a year after the accident. In addition, we were interested in the mediating influences of social support and the extent to which having support helped residents to cope with chronic stress. The results provided information on a number of levels. First, TMI residents exhibited greater evidence of stress across psychological, behavioral, and biochemical measures than did control subjects. Second, having little or no social support was associated with greater incidence of stress-relevant problems for TMI residents while having moderate or high levels of support was associated with fewer of these problems. However, the intervening influence of social support was not uniform across all three domains of measurement, suggesting that perceived support serves to facilitate coping rather than to protect people from stress. Each of these points will be considered in turn.

As expected, TMI residents exhibited greater evidence of stress than did control subjects. A year and a half after the accident, these residents continued to report greater symptom distress, including complaints about somatic problems, anxiety, and alienation, than did residents of areas near undamaged nuclear and coal plants or near no plant at all. These residents also exhibited poorer performance on tasks that have, in past research, shown deficits when subjects were exposed to stress. Finally, TMI residents had higher levels of urinary catecholamines than did control subjects. Although the sample size in this study was small, it was sufficient to demonstrate clear differences between TMI and control groups on major dependent measures. Across all three levels of measurement, then, TMI residents appeared to experience greater stress than did controls. Despite the fact that these levels suggested that TMI residents were experiencing mild stress (i.e., the intensity of these symptoms was, for the most part, subclinical), their chronicity suggests that the problems experienced by TMI residents are neither incidental nor minor. Rather, they seem to have had a significant impact on residents' lives.

As we noted earlier, TMI residents' responses to living near the plant are not uniform. Some residents exhibited greater stress than did others, and the primary purpose of this study was to examine a possible cause of this selective susceptibility. Perceived social support proved to be related to these variations in stress measures. TMI residents reporting moderate or high levels of social support reported less emotional distress than did TMI residents reporting little or no social support. Task performance was also better among TMI residents reporting higher levels of support. Since support did not affect response on these measures by control subjects, these findings are consistent with stress-buffering models of social support (Cohen and McKay 1980). While not particularly important in determining response under low stress conditions, social support appeared to be influenced when stress was greater. Under stressful conditions, having social support appeared to reduce psychological and behavioral consequences of stress.

Interestingly, biochemical measures of stress and self-reported somatic distress did not conform to this pattern (i.e., measures of stress responding buffered by higher levels of social support). Having social support at TMI reduced symptom and performance problems to levels comparable to control subjects', but TMI residents' catecholamine levels remained higher than controls', regardless of perceived social support. The same was true of somatic distress. While TMI residents having social support exhibited slightly lower catecholamine levels than did TMI residents reporting little or no support, this effect was weaker than the general elevation of catecholamines and somatic distress associated with living near TMI. Whatever aspect of social support was responsible for reducing the psychological and behavioral effects of stress among TMI residents was not particularly effective in reducing symptoms of physiological arousal associated with stress. Instead, main effects of social support for somatic distress and norepinephrine levels suggest a general arousal associated with lower levels of support. This main effect is taken as an indication that greater physiological arousal is associated with lower levels of perceived social support. In other words, the lack of support appears to enhance arousal, while greater levels of support do not necessarily reduce levels of arousal (Wallston et al. 1981).

The differences in the effects of social support on these different measures are striking. Catecholamine levels and somatic distress, which can be thought of as estimates of actual and perceived physiological arousal, all conform to one pattern (top graphs, figure 7.1). Task performance and symptom reporting of psychological distress, which may reflect effects of being stressed, conform to a different pattern (bottom graphs, figure 7.1). This may reflect the partial independence of physiological and psychological aspects of stress. Although we may expect these aspects of stress to overlap, they may very well tap different processes associated with a common event. The present data suggest that social support affects those processes involved in psychological and behaviorial aspects of stress but does not appreciably reduce arousal associated with stress.

If we view the stress response as a whole-body reaction (Mason 1975b) to appraisal of a situation as dangerous or threatening, we can begin to explain the differential impact of social support. Recognition of a stressor causes the body to mobilize through sympathetic arousal. At the same time, the individual evaluates the situation and his or her abilities to deal with it and begins to cope (Lazarus 1966). Successful coping, in turn, reduces effects of stress such as emotional problems and cognitive or motivational deficits. If this coping results in the termination of the stressor or in adaptation to it, arousal should also diminish. If, on the other hand, coping is sufficient to minimize some of the effects of stress but not eliminate it, the basic arousal characteristics of stress may not disappear. In this case, the individual will be forced to cope more or less continuously in order to suppress psychological problems and will remain in a state of arousal whenever resistance is necessary. Social support may bolster TMI residents' ability to cope and to minimize the aversiveness of stress, but the nature of the situation does not appear to allow either termination of stress or ready adaptation to it. Thus, TMI residents with moderate or high levels of social

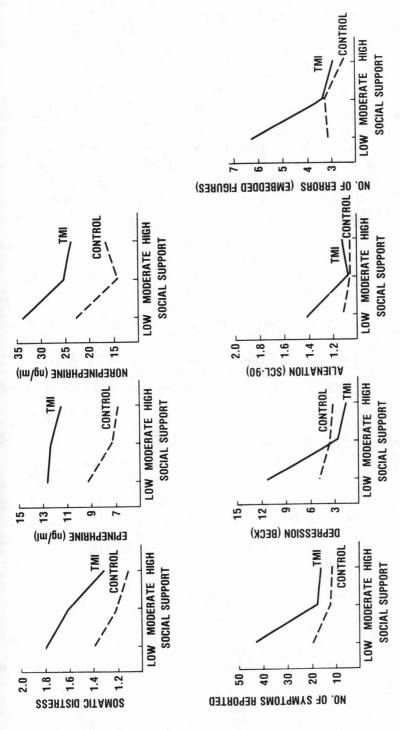

Figure 7.1. Summary of stress measures as influenced by social support. Somatic/physiological (top graphs) and psychological/behavioral (bottom graphs) measures show different patterns; the upper graphs show main effects of residence and support, while the lower graphs show interactions between them.

support may be better able to cope than are TMI residents with little or no support, but they can do no better in ending stress and reducing arousal.

This explanation is clearly speculative and will no doubt be refined and/or corrected by further research. Regardless, it suggests that the complexities of stress and the ways in which it is affected by an individual's social assets are far from simple. By simultaneously measuring psychological, behavioral, and physiological aspects of stress, some of this complexity was revealed. Thus, we have succeeded in doing more than providing further evidence of stress at TMI or of the beneficial aspects of social support or group membership. Future studies may provide additional information about the ways in which social support and stress are related.

NOTES

1. Streets were randomly selected within preselected neighborhoods. Residents were then randomly selected from these streets using an every-third-house sampling plan.

2. Analyses also indicated no systematic differences in demographic characteristics among any of the four groups. Correlations between demographic variables and outcome measures were very small, suggesting that prior background variation had little effect on our findings.

3. Previous use of this scale has indicated that it is a reliable instrument $(\alpha = .82$; test-retest reliability $= .70)$. In addition, the scale score has been significantly correlated with the distance one lives from one's family $(r = -.30)$. The items are:

    a. I often feel lonely, like I don't have anyone to reach out to.

    b. When I am unhappy or under stress, there are people I can turn to for support.

    c. I don't know anyone to confide in.

    d. I used to have close friends to talk to about things, but I don't anymore.

    e. When I am troubled, I keep things to myself.

    f. I am not a member of any social groups (such as church groups, clubs, teams, etc.).

8

The Psychological Stresses of Intensive Care Unit Nursing

DONALD HAY and DONALD OKEN

M uch has been written about the stressful psychological experience of being a patient in an Intensive Care (ICU) or other special care unit (Abram 1965; Bishop and Reichert 1969; DeMeyer 1967; Hackett, Cassem, and Wishnie 1969; Margolis 1967). Less well recognized, however, are the problems posed for those who work in an ICU that provides the complex nursing care required by critically ill, often dying, patients. Notable exceptions include the contributions of Vreeland and Ellis (1969) and of Gardam (1969).

The quality of a patient's care, and, hence, outcome, depends greatly upon the people providing that care, and the effectiveness of the latter is a function of their psychological state no less than of their technical expertise. This has special meaning for the ICU patient, whose very life hangs upon the care provided by the nursing staff. Yet, in this special environment, the psychological burdens imposed upon the nurse are extraordinary. Her situation resembles, in many ways, that of the soldier serving with an elite combat group.

Our understanding derives from the experience of one of us (DH) working directly as a member of the nursing staff of a 10-bed university hospital ICU over a period of approximately one year, plus multiple interviews and informal contacts with ICU nurses.[1] From these observations, we have developed some insights into the nature of the nurses' experience and the methods they develop to handle it. These, we believe, provide useful clues for lessening the stressful nature of the experience, and hence benefit the nurses and (through them) their patients.

A condensed version of this paper was delivered at the workshop "Psychiatric Contributions to Management of Intensive Care Units" at the Annual Meeting of the American Psychosomatic Society, Denver, Colorado, April 2, 1971.

The ICU Environment

A stranger entering an ICU is at once bombarded with a massive array of sensory stimuli (DeMeyer 1967), some emotionally neutral but many highly charged. Initially, the greatest impact comes from the intricate machinery, with its flashing lights, buzzing and beeping monitors, gurgling suction pumps, and whooshing respirators. Simultaneously, one sees many people rushing around busily performing lifesaving tasks. The atmosphere is not unlike that of the tension-charged strategic war bunker. With time, habituation occurs, but the ever-continuing stimuli decrease the overload threshold and contribute to stress at times of crisis.

As the newness and strangeness of the unit wears off, one increasingly becomes aware of a host of perceptions with specific stressful emotional significance. Desperately ill, sick, and injured human beings are hooked up to that machinery. And, in addition to mechanical stimuli, one can discern moaning, crying, screaming and the last gasps of life. Sights of blood, vomitus and excreta, exposed genitalia, mutilated wasting bodies, and unconscious and helpless people assault the sensibilities. Unceasingly, the ICU nurse must face these affect-laden stimuli with all the distress and conflict that they engender. As part of her daily routine, the nurse must reassure and comfort the man who is dying of cancer; she must change the dressings of a decomposing, gangrenous limb; she must calm the awakening disturbed "overdose" patient; she must bathe the genitalia of the helpless and comatose; she must wipe away the bloody stool of the gastrointestinal bleeder; she must comfort the anguished young wife who knows her husband is dying. It is hard to imagine any other situation that involves such intimacy with the frightening, repulsive, and forbidden. Stimuli are present to mobilize literally every conflictual area at every psychological developmental level.

But there is more: there is something uncanny about the picture the patients present. Many are neither alive nor dead. Most have "tubes in every orifice." Their sounds and actions (or inaction) are almost nonhuman. Bodily areas and organs, ordinarily unseen, are openly exposed or deformed by bandages. All of this directly challenges the definition of being human, one's most fundamental sense of ego integrity, for nurse as well as patient. Though consciously the nurse quickly learns to accept this surrealism, she is unremittingly exposed to these multiple threats to the stability of her body boundaries, her sense of self, and her feelings of humanity and reality.

To all this is added a repetitive contact with death. And, if exposure to death is merely frequent, that to dying is constant. The ICU nurse thus quickly becomes adept at identifying the signs and symptoms that foretell a downhill trend for her patient. This becomes an awesome addition to the burden of the nurse who has been caring for the patient and must *continue* to do so, knowing his outcome.

The Work Load and Its Demands

If the sense of drama and frightfulness is what most forcefully strikes the outsider, what the experienced nurse points to, paradoxically, is the incessant repetitive routine. For each patient, vital signs must be monitored, commonly at 15-minute intervals, sometimes more often. Central venous pressures must be measured, tracheas suctioned, urimeters emptied and measured, intravenous infusions changed, EKG monitor patterns interpreted, respirators checked, hypothermia blankets adjusted, etc. And every step must be charted. The nurse begins to feel like a hamster on a treadmill: she finishes the required tasks on one patient just in time to start them on another; and when these are completed she is already behind in doing the same tasks all over again on the first, constantly aware of her race with the clock. A paradox soon becomes apparent. Nowhere more than in the ICU is a *good* nurse expected to make observations about her patient's condition, to interpret subtle changes and use judgment to take appropriate action. But often, the ICU nurse is so unremittingly involved in collecting and charting information that she has little time to interpret it adequately.

The work load is formidable—even in periods of relative calm. Many tasks, which elsewhere would be performed by nurse's aides, require special care in the ICU and become the lot of the ICU nurse. Changing a bed in an ICU may require moving a desperately ill, comatose patient while watching EKG leads, respirator hoses, urinary and intravenous catheters, etc. Moreover, the nurse must maintain detailed records.

Night shifts, weekends, and holidays all mean less work on other floors. Only urgent or fundamental procedures are performed. But, in an ICU, emergency is routine: there is no surcease—no holidays. In fact, the regular recovery room in our hospital shuts down on weekends and holidays so that patients must be sent to the ICU after emergency surgery. It is not rare, on a weekend, to see several stretchers with these patients interposed between the fully occupied beds of the ICU, leaving the nurses with barely time enough to suction patients and keep them alive.

The quantity and variety of complex technical equipment poses tremendous demands on the knowledge and expertise of the nurse (Gardam 1969; Vreeland and Ellis 1969). Because of this and the nature of her tasks, temporarily floating in nurses from elsewhere when staff is short provides little in the way of help; indeed, this may even prove a hindrance. Yet, ICU nurses are fully able to fill in elsewhere when staff shortages occur; and they are not infrequently asked to do so, leaving the ICU understaffed.

The emergency situation provides added work. Although an ICU's routine is another floor's emergency, obviously there are frequent situations of acute crisis, such as cardiac arrest. These require the nurse's full attention and prevent her from continuing her regular tasks on her other patients. A few remaining nurses must watch and calm all other patients, complete as many of their regular observations and treatments as possible, and prevent other emergencies. Meanwhile, the nurses assisting at the emergency are called upon not only to do things rapidly but to make immediate and accurate decisions that oftentimes include determining the priority of several emergencies (Vreeland and Ellis 1969).

Habituation is both inevitable and necessary if the nurse is not to work in an exhausted state of chronic crisis. Yet, she must maintain an underlying alertness to discern and respond to cues which have special meaning. This is like the mother who hears the faint cry of her baby over the commotion of a party.

Nor is the work without its physical dangers, and the nurses know this. It is impossible to take fully adequate isolation precautions against infections because of time pressures and the bodily intimacy required to provide the needed level of care. Portable x-rays are sometimes taken with inadequately shielded nurses holding immobile patients in proper positioning. Heavy comatose patients must be lifted. Sharp needles, scalpels, etc., must be handled rapidly. Electric equipment must be moved, adjusted, and attached. Physical assaults on nurses by a delirious patient, though infrequent, can and do occur.

There are occasions also when distraught relatives misinterpret a situation, feel that their loved one is getting inadequate care and become verbally—and sometimes physically—abusive. The roots of these more dramatic misunderstandings lie in more general problems about visitors. On other floors, visiting hours occur daily at specified times, but in the ICU, there can be no such routinized schedule. Close relatives are allowed to see the patient at any time of the day or night. Though restricted to a brief (commonly 5-minute) period, their presence soon becomes a burden. In his constant inquiries about the patient's condition and prognosis, the relative is asking for more than information. He is seeking reassurance and support (Salter 1970; Vreeland and Ellis 1969). The nurse may wish to respond at this deeper level, but usually she cannot, because she has tasks that require more immediate attention. The relative, feeling rebuffed, begins to critically scrutinize the nurse's every action. With so much to be upset about, he is prone to jump to unwarranted conclusions. While many visitors see the nurses as "angels of mercy," others develop a projection of their worst fears. Seeing a nurse spend more time with another patient, he may feel his loved one is not getting adequate attention. Or, he may see blood, vomitus, or excreta soiling the patient's bed and misinterpret this as an indication of poor care, not appreciating the nurse's preoccupation with lifesaving activities. Moreover the nurse has little escape from hovering relatives: she has "no place to hide."

Doctors and Administrators

Visitors are not the only ones who cause problems. Some of the very people who might be expected to provide substantial support add to the stresses on the nurse. The potentially fatal outcome in the gravely ill ICU patients tends to stimulate feelings of frustration, self-doubt and guilt in their physicians. The ways he deals with these may have major consequences for the nurse. He may, for example, use projection and behave in a surly, querulous manner. He may bolster his self-esteem by becoming imperious and demand that the nurses "wait on" him.[2] He may also rely on avoidance as a way of distancing himself from his feelings about his seeming failure as a lifesaver. Though the nurse must remain on the unit for almost her entire shift, the physician can make good use of his prerogatives to move about freely. Especially at the time of a patient's death, the physician seems to have a way of not being present; the full burden of breaking the news and supporting the family through the acute grief reaction is left to the nurse to handle as best she can. Conversely, compensatory overzealousness may occur, and unnecessary heroic gestures be made to save someone beyond recovery. The physician may order special treatments and an unrealistic frequency of monitoring. The not uncommon incongruity of orders is especially revealing about this. A patient on "q15 minute" vital signs wil have nothing done—and correctly so—when these deteriorate. Or, the physician will recognize the inappropriateness of frequent monitoring, yet insist on fruitless *emergency* attempts at resuscitation (e.g., a pacemaker) when death supervenes. This not only increases the nurse's work load but adds to her frustration by diverting her energies from patients who could be saved. . . .

The Psychological Experience

We will now shift from a situational frame of reference to a psychological one and take a closer look at the concerns and feelings of ICU nurses. We will also examine the adaptive devices, individual and group, which they use to cope with their situation.

The work load, so great in its sheer quantity, is unusual also in its variety and the intricacy of its tasks as well as in the rapidity with which these must be performed. Great flexibility is required (which may partly explain why ICU nurses are predominantly in their early twenties).

Mistakes are, of course, inevitable. But, when every procedure is potentially lifesaving, any error may be life-endangering. Hence the ICU nurse lives chronically under a cloud of latent anxiety. The new nurse, particularly, begins to view the never-ending, life-dependent tasks as a specter of potential mistakes and their imagined dreadful sequelae. Some, of course, cannot shake this and soon arrange a transfer. The experienced nurse achieves a more realistic perspective, but a degree of residual uncertainty always remains, given the complexity of machines and procedures. Especially at times of stress, she too may become anxious. When this anxiety exceeds minimal levels, it reduces efficiency and decision-making capacity, inviting additional mistakes—the classic vicious circle.

When the inevitable error does occur, the nurse is in a dilemma. To make it public is likely to enhance her guilt and invite criticism. Moreover, it leads to the need to fill out an incident report, a further drain on her time and a potential blot on her record. Yet to fail to do so may compound the error by blocking corrective treatment. The experienced nurse develops a subtle adaptive compromise, reporting serious mistakes but fudging-over inconsequential ones. In either case, she must live with her guilt.

The ICU nurse has much in which she can take great pride. Yet her self-esteem takes an awful beating in many ways. Her awareness of her mistakes, both real and exaggerated, is one such factor. Another is her repeated "failure." The ultimate goal of the health professions is to save lives; yet, frequently, her patients die. Nor do the dying patients or mourning relatives provide much source of gratification, as do patients on other floors who go home well. (Even the ICU major successes are usually still seriously ill and are merely transferred.) On the bulletin boards of other units there are warm, sentimental cards and notes of appreciation. In the ICU, the cards are of a different and macabre quality. They say: "Thank you. You did all you could."

Further, the deaths provide a situation of repetitive object-loss, the intensity of which parallels the degree to which the nurse has cathected her patient. The intimacy afforded by the amount and frequency of direct personal contact, involving some of the most private aspects of life, promotes this attachment. This is further enhanced when the patient is conscious and verbal, since he is then so obviously human. Young patients are easily identified with friends and spouses— or with the self, stimulating anxiety about one's own vulnerability. In this country, with its cultural premium on youth, the death of a young patient tends to be regarded as inherently more tragic. Older patients may become transference objects of parental or grandparental figures.

All these warm personal attachments obviously provide great comfort for patients and family and make the job worthwhile. But they expose the nurse to a sense of loss when the patient dies. The balance is a delicate one. With comatose patients, it is easy to limit emotional involvement and subsequent grief. But here, paradoxically, one often sees the nurse project vital qualities into her patient.[3]

The threat of object-loss is pervasive. The nurse simply must protect herself—from grief, anxiety, guilt, rage, exhausted overcommitment, overstimulation, and the rest. She has no physical escape. But she can avoid, or at least attenuate, the meaning and emotional impact of her work (Rome 1969). For example, she may relate more to the machines than to the patient. And it comes as a surprise to an outsider to observe routinely some of the nurses in the ICU joking and laughing. Even whistling and singing may be observed, phenomena which are inexplicable and unforgivable to distraught relatives. Some of this ebullience arises as a natural product of the friendly behavior of young people working closely together. But a major aspect is gross denial as a defense against their stressful situation. Schizoid withdrawal or a no-nonsense businesslike manner (isolation) also are used, but cheerful denial is more common. The defensive and, at times, brittle nature of this response is especially evident at times of crisis. At a lull in procedures after a cardiac arrest, for example, giggling and outrageous joking of near hysterical proportion suddenly may supervene. Sometimes the blowup is in the form of anger. But, there are great constraints placed upon the expression of anger by the situation and the group.

The Group

The new ICU nurse experiences the trials of her early days on the job as the *rite de passage*. Some do not make it through. Those who do, learn that they have become members of a special, tightly knit group.[4] Naturally, they work together on a common job, sharing common experiences. But, there is far more to it than this. Most have volunteered. They have one of the most difficult jobs in the hospital. Nowhere else does a nurse so often literally save lives by her own direct actions. It stands to reason that nurses who operate special machines and perform special procedures for special patients must be special too! Rightfully, they take pride in their abilities and accomplishments. The very stressfulness of the job is a further source of pride, albeit with masochistic overtones. Like Commandos or Green Berets, they have the toughest, dirtiest, most dangerous assignment; and they "accomplish the impossible."

Further cementing group ties are the conditions of work. They carry on their duties in a common area, using common equipment (Vreeland and Ellis 1969). In emergency situations particularly, they share the responsibility for each other's patients. Even in nonemergency situations there is a general factor of enforced interdependency. Routinely, for example, one nurse must ask another to cover her patients when she goes for a meal. Here an unspoken but potent group norm becomes manifest. Refusal is impossible. Cooperation is absolutely essential for unit function. When a nurse returns from an absence, she may well find that only the most minimal monitoring has been carried out on her patient. No matter how justified its basis, she is likely to be irritated. Yet, group pressures for cooperation and the very fact that there is no time for anger on the job make it imperative to suppress or repress the hostility. These same forces inhibit the expressions of anger that arise inevitably during the course of everyday work when people are in regular close contact. In the total context, this ambivalent hostility serves to bind the group ties with still more intensity.

At the end of a shift of constant work and emotional turmoil, it is nearly impossible for the nurse to "turn it off" and return to normal pursuits.

She needs to unwind. To do so requires the understanding ear of someone who knows what she has been through. Who then is a more logical choice for an off-duty companion than another ICU nurse? Thus, one finds much group social activity: parties, showers, and just informal, off-duty get-togethers. While these might provide an opportunity to express interpersonal hostility, they more often result in "bull sessions" of shared experiences and problems. Similar discussions take place at lunch or coffee breaks, to which they go preferentially with coworkers. These shared feelings feed back to enhance group ties further.

External forces further define the group. The ICU is typically located in an area away from other nursing units. Frequently ICU nurses wear scrub gowns or other protective devices to decrease contamination and soiling; thus they have a distinctive uniform. Very significant is the attitude of other nurses through-out the hospital. Many tend to regard ICU nurses with considerable ambivalence in which envy and projection play a part, and react to being treated as outsiders by retaliatory disregard, isolating the group further.

Group cohesiveness is a logical solution to the multiple practical problems on the job and provides essential emotional support. Being a part of a special group is a major advantage in bolstering the nurse's pride and strength. However, there are not so desirable consequences. The force of the group and the extent of its activities can become all-encompassing, taking over the roles of family and friends. Thus, it can interfere with personal autonomy and outside social relationships. The pressures of the job and group activities may limit healthy introspection. (This may have temporary adaptive value for the woman beset with life problems, or tangled in inner conflict, allowing her to retrench while thus losing herself. But obviously, this can be seriously maladaptive if pursued as a long-term escape.) Absence from the group due to a concurrent social activity may be seen unconsciously as disloyal by both the nurse and the group, though inevitably the familial and social aspect of the group will wear thin for the woman who has achieved maturity and seeks a life of her own. Yet the nurse who fails to use the group may find herself taking out the tensions of work on her family. She may let off steam to a boyfriend, roommate, or husband. But soon, she learns that this can strain the relationship since the person on the receiving end cannot know what it is like to work in the ICU.

Group loyalty reinforces work pressure in stimulating guilt about any absence. The nurse with a minor illness (or one suffering from "combat exhaustion") cannot, in good conscience, stay away as she should. This would increase the work load for her peers. If she does stay home, she cannot "rest easy." Nor, as described above, can she say no to a request to cover another woman's patients, even if she is already working at peak load. This would violate the group norms and threaten the shared fantasy of omnipotence linked to the concept of being special and to the defensive denial of anxiety about mistakes.

This same mechanism can work also to the collective detriment of the group. Like the individual nurse, the group self-destructively cannot say no to situations where its total work load is unrealistic. Paradoxically, the individual almost never can get the group to support protests about realistic problems or unfair exploitation so that changes can be made. Intragroup competitiveness and rivalry may play a part in this. The nurse who will not tailor constructive criticism to the group norm finds she must leave. Since many such nurses will be thoughtful, aggressive people with good ideas, leadership potential is drained away. The whole situation lends itself to perpetuating the status quo and to no recourse but permanent flight (i.e., resignation) when the pressures on an individual build to the point of intolerability.

Some Possible Solutions

From the foregoing, it seems obvious that a constructive approach will capitalize on the many positive aspects of the group process, while attenuating its pathological features. One excellent way to accomplish this is through regular group meetings devoted to exploring the work experience, especially its stressful aspects (Kornfeld 1969b). These discussions can provide: (a) an avenue for ventilating suppressed intragroup hostilities as well as shared gripes; (b) a recognition that fears, doubts, guilt, and uncertainty are shared, acceptable feelings; (c) the abreaction and working through of feelings aroused at times of stress but which cannot be expressed due to work demands; (d) the sharing of innovative *ad hoc* techniques which individuals have found helpful in dealing with problems arising on the job; (e) recognition of realistic superior abilities and their delineation from masochistic fantasies of omnipotence; (f) a realization that minor mistakes are ubiquitous and inevitable, leading to the detoxification of guilt and shame; and (g) the development of constructive solutions for problems and effective suggestions for communication to administration. . . .

While this group process can enhance the appropriate sense of pride and "special-ness," more can be done to bolster self-esteem. Here, we have something to learn from studies of morale in combat troups (Grinker and Spiegel 1945). A distinctive uniform or an identifying patch may be helpful. A small pay differential, like that paid for special shifts, "hazardous duty pay," is an indication of special regard as well as a material reward. Periodic, brief, extra vacations (R and R—Rest and Recreation Leave) will do the same. Such periods might involve work on other nursing units rather than a true vacation, thereby providing education and communication for both staffs. One might consider also whether there should be a finite tour of duty on the ICU, with an enforced interval before a second tour. At the least, transfer to another unit should be made accessible and free from stigma; our experience suggests that often ICU nurses work past the point of "combat exhaustion" and then resign, sometimes with a sense of failure.

Another alternative might be to create a Unit Coordinator position through which the ICU nurses would periodically rotate. Freed from the regular nursing role and its duties, she could fulfill a number of important functions. In an emergency, she could help the head nurse organize the situation or provide an often crucial extra pair of hands. She could help orient new personnel. When consulting physicians arrive on the unit, she could familiarize them with its facilities and routine, thereby reducing their need for direct nursing assistance. She could serve as a major communication link with visitors, providing them with crucial emotional support, and keeping them "out of the hair" of others.

Competitive selection of nurses with superior skills appropriate for the job also will add to pride. In addition to technical expertise, applicants should be screened for psychological aptitude, perhaps by the liaison psychiatrist. In any event, an initial period of training and orientation (Boklage 1970) is essential, and should focus on job characteristics specific to the ICU. The group leader(s) should play a major role in this, so that the psychological aspects of the job experience are fully considered.

A sufficiently large nursing staff is necessary to allow coverage for vacations, weekends, and holidays without the use of outside "floating" assignees. The special characteristics of the unit should also be reflected in the assignment of other personnel. Insofar as the acuteness of its patients and the difficulty of their care are concerned, the ICU is highly specialized. In another sense, however, it is general: it provides care for almost every type of disease process. To provide the full range of treatment required, and to do so on a 24-hour, everyday basis, means that the ICU must be "a hospital within a hospital." Thus representatives of all relevant hospital services always must be at hand. Given a unit of sufficient size, a permanent pharmacist, inhalation therapist, x-ray technician, etc., may become a necessity as part of the regular ICU staff. At the very least, the person "on call" in each of these fields should be given the ICU as his regular assignment to ensure familiarity with the unit.

A *full-time* physician is an especial necessity, constantly and immediately available to examine patients, and as a source of information, advice, and support (Kornfeld 1969a). Whether a member of the attending or house staff, he must be delegated sufficient authority to be able to write new "orders" whenever indicated by the constantly changing condition of the patients, without necessarily consulting senior physicians of the speciality services to which the patients may be administratively assigned.

Conclusions

Perhaps it will seem as if we have been overly dramatic in our descriptions of the ICU as being so stressful. Most such units function very well. Other parts of the hospital (e.g., emergency and operating rooms) share many of the same stresses; and each deserves examination to understand its particular features. Moreover, nurses who work in the ICU do so by choice, suggesting that, for them, other assignments might be less gratifying or even more stressful. Yet, we believe that the seeming dramatization is, on careful scrutiny, an accurate portrayal and that the intensity and variety of the sources of stress in the ICU is somewhat unique. In any event, stress is there. Doubtless it is useful to an extent, enabling the nurses to maintain their critical alertness and ability to respond effectively to the needs of their patients. Yet there are many signs that its intensity goes well beyond this adaptive level. And since there are approaches to deal with this, it behooves us to utilize these for the benefit of both staff and patients.

NOTES

1. While our detailed observations were made on a single ICU, superficial contact with several other such units, which have many features in common, leads us to believe that our conclusions have significant generalizability. However, there may be some significant differences from other types of specialized units such as coronary care units, neurosurgical ICUs, transplant and dialysis units, etc.

2. Another factor in this overdemanding behavior may be his sense of inadequacy and self-doubt if he is unfamiliar with the unit and its highly organized functions (Kornfeld 1969b). This may be culminate in his issuing dictatorial orders and commands that are not commensurate with the realities of the situation.

3. Sometimes this mechanism backfires in an interesting way. The nurse begins to project specific attributes onto the comatose patient. When he recovers and asserts his real personality, especially if this has unpleasant characteristics, she feels a sense of disappointment and betrayal.

4. We have seen similar, though usually less intense, group formation among psychiatric nursing personnel, for some of the same reasons.

PART III

The Concept of Coping

Part III marks a transition from an emphasis on the nature of stress to the ways in which people handle stress, i.e., coping. The first selection, written by White (1974), makes several important theoretical distinctions among related concepts: adaptation, mastery, coping, and defense. As noted in our Introduction, White subsumes coping under the larger, more central concept of adaptation, and defines *coping* as adaptation under relatively difficult conditions. Using numerous illustrations involving animals, children, and adults, White clearly presents his argument that strategies of adaptation must simultaneously manage at least three functions or tasks if they are successfully to aid the individual's transactions with the environment: securing adequate information; maintaining satisfactory internal conditions; and keeping some degree of autonomy or freedom of movement. White's paper touches on many other important issues, such as the time dimension in adaptive behavior and the short- versus long-term value of defense mechanisms. This paper provides an excellent introduction to many of the issues currently dominating the stress and coping field.

The selection from Haan's 1977 book, *Coping and Defending,* is an important attempt to classify coping and to distinguish it from defense mechanisms. Haan argues that there are ten generic ego processes that may be expressed in three modes: coping, defense, or fragmentation. For example, one such ego process is restraint. The coping version of this process is suppression; the defense version is repression; and, the fragmentation version is depersonalization. What makes Haan's work so valuable and provocative is its clear value judgments regarding these properties. Haan believes, for example, that coping involves choice and is therefore flexible. Defense, on the other hand, turns away from choice and is, consequently, rigid. Coping is thus the preferred form of an ego process. As Haan has stated elsewhere:

I . . . have argued that coping is commonly understood to be a good way to handle problems; moreover, coping can be distinguished from defense. In *Webster's Third Unabridged Dictionary* coping means "to maintain a contest or combat, usually on equal terms or even with success . . . or to face, encounter . . . or overcome problems and difficulties." Concurring with clinical usage, *Webster's* supplies the following ideas about defense: "defendents' denial, answer, or plea opposing the truth of prosecutor's claims . . . fortification, justification . . . manner of self-protection." Thus, in common parlance, coping is not an action evoked solely by trauma, nor is coping a defense. Instead, it is an attempt to overcome difficulties on equal terms; it is an encounter wherein people reach out and within themselves for resources to come to terms with difficulties. *Defense* is unyielding fortification. (1982:255–256)

(You should compare Haan's point of view with that of White. Note that White actually discusses in his paper some of Haan's ideas, as formulated by Kroeber 1963).

Our next selection, by Lazarus (1983), stands in sharp contrast with the views of Haan and others in the mental health field who claim that the epitomy of positive mental health is accurate reality testing. Lazarus sees defense mechanisms (and self-deception in general) as ways of coping with stress, ways which under certain circumstances may be quite useful and healthy. Lazarus illustrates his point with numerous references to literary and psychological literature addressed to the concepts of *illusion* (false or optimistic beliefs about reality) and *denial* (refusing to face the facts). It is important to note that Lazarus is not suggesting that self-deception is always beneficial—it has its costs as well. He concludes his article with some principles concerning the costs and benefits of certain forms of self-deception. (For further information on this issue, see Lazarus 1979, and Taylor 1983).

The last selection in this section concerns coping and personality. Kobasa's (1979) article examines individual differences in response to life events (see Introduction). Why do some people experience high degrees of stress (i.e., many stressful life events) without becoming ill? According to Kobasa's research, personality variables help answer this important question. In her study of personality factors, which buffer some executives from stress-related illnesses, Kobasa found three significant characteristics: control, commitment, and challenge. Together, these three characteristics make up what Kobasa calls the "hardy personality." If Kobasa's findings prove to be reliable, it remains to be determined exactly how hardiness buffers a highly stressed individual from illness, and what hardy people actually do to cope with stress more effectively than others. Kobasa's research is a promising effort to identify the types of people who remain healthy in spite of life stress. (See also Kobasa, Maddi, and Kahn 1982; and Kobasa and Puccetti 1983).

9

Strategies of Adaptation: An Attempt at Systematic Description

ROBERT W. WHITE

A t the outset of this inquiry we are confronted by four commonly used words with overlapping claims upon the territory to be discussed. The words are *adaptation, mastery, coping,* and *defense.* No attempt at systematic description is likely to prosper if these words are left in a state of free competition, jostling for the thinly scattered grains of truth that might nourish their meaning. Their peaceful coexistence requires, as in any well-regulated hen yard, the establishment of some sort of pecking order that everyone observes and fully understands. The first step in this direction is simple: clearly the boss hen is *adaptation.* This is the master concept, the superordinate category, under which the other three words must accept restricted meanings. Descriptions of mastery, of defense, or of coping alone cannot be systematic in any large sense, but they can become part of a system if they are ordered under the heading of *strategies of adaptation.*

PRELUDE ON TERMINOLOGY

The concept of *defense,* to take it first, is an obvious one, signifying response to danger or attack, but it comes to use with a somewhat swollen meaning because of the position it has been given in psychoanalytic theory. Freud's genius as an observer, so apparent in his unveiling of sexual and aggressive inclinations, never burned more brightly than in his perception of what came to be called the *mechanisms of defense:* repression, projection, undoing, and the other devices whereby danger was parried and peace restored in the frightened psyche. Psychoanalytic therapists, following this lead, became expert at scenting anxiety in the free associations of their patients; expert, moreover, at unraveling the ramified operations whereby security was achieved. Presently these operations were seen to have worked over long periods of time, producing such complex results as character armor and the protective organization of personality. Unwary theorists even jumped to the generalization that development was a simple counterpoint between instinctual craving and defense. It became necessary after Freud's death for those who called themselves "ego psychologists" to restore explicitly the concept of adaptation and to confine defense to those instances of adaptation in which present danger and anxiety were of central importance.

The concept of *mastery,* perhaps an equally obvious concept, has never enjoyed the same vogue among psychologists. When used at all, it has generally been applied to behavior in which frustrations have been surmounted and adaptive efforts have come to a successful conclusion. The alternatives suggested by the word are not, as with defense, danger and safety, but something more like defeat and victory. This might imply a limiting definition, but in fact the concept of mastery has been used with no sense of limits. The English language, loved by poets for its flexibility, offers only pitfalls to the systematic thinker. There is nothing wrong with saying that danger and anxiety have to be mastered, which allows us to classify defense mechanisms as a form of mastery. It is equally correct to say that efforts at mastery serve as a defense against anxiety, which permits us to consider counteractive struggle a mechanism of defense. If mastery is to be used in any limited technical sense it should probably be confined to problems having a certain cognitive or manipulative complexity, but which at the same time are not heavily freighted with anxiety.

Where does the concept of *coping* stand? We can find out what we mean by it by noticing the kinds of situation chosen for studies of coping behavior. Sometimes these situations represent an acute dislocation of a person's life: serious crippling sickness, the death of close relatives, financial disaster, the necessity to live in a radically new environment. Sometimes the situation is less drastic, but it is still unusual in the subject's life: going to school for the first time, going to visit the child psychologist, or making the transition from high school to college. Nobody has chosen going to school for the sixty-third time as an occasion for coping. The freshman year at college, with all its new experience, clearly qualifies as coping, as does the sophomore year now that we are alert to the possibility of "sophomore slump" and dropping out, but nobody has yet detected any large-scale common problems that would justify choosing the junior year for an investigation of coping behavior. For "when the sea was calm," said Shakespeare, "all boats alike show'd mastership in floating"; only in a storm were they obliged to cope. It is clear that we tend to speak of coping when we have in mind a fairly drastic change or problem that defies familiar ways of behaving, requires the production of new behavior, and very likely gives rise to uncomfortable affects like anxiety, despair, guilt, shame, or grief, the relief of which forms part of the needed adaptation. Coping refers to adaptation under relatively difficult conditions.

This discussion of terms demonstrates the necessity of making *adaptation* the central concept. It may well be that in stressful situations things happen that have no counterpart in easier circumstances, but some of what happens is likely to come straight from the repertoire that is common to all adaptive behavior. There is a sense in which all behavior can be considered an attempt at adaptation. Even in the smoothest and easiest of times behavior will not be adequate in a purely mechanical or habitual way. Every day raises its little problems: what clothes to put on, how to plan a timesaving and step-saving series of errands, how to schedule the hours to get through the day's work, how to manage the cranky child, appease the short-tempered tradesman, and bring the long-winded acquaintance to the end of his communication. It is not advisable to tell a group of college students that they have no problems, nothing to cope with, during the happy and uneventful junior year. They will quickly tell you what it takes to get through that golden year, and as you listen to the frustrations, bewilderments, and sorrows as well as the triumphs and joys you will have a hard time conceptualizing it all as well-adapted reflexes or smoothly running habits. Life is tough, they will tell you, in case you have forgotten; life is a never-ending challenge. Every step of the way demands the solution of problems and every step must therefore be novel and creative, even the putting together of words and sentences to make you understand what it is like to cope with being a college junior.

Adaptation, then, is the only firm platform on which to build a systematic description. What is needed is an ordered account of *strategies of adaptation,* ranging from the simplest ways of dealing with minor problems and frustrations to the most complex fabric of adaptive and defensive devices that has ever been observed from the chair at the head of the psychoanalytic couch. If this can be done, the uses to be made of defense, mastery, and coping can be much more readily decided.

ADAPTATION AS COMPROMISE

There is another preliminary issue that is likely to get in the way if we do not deal with it at the start. Perhaps we can put a little blame on Freud for having started something that often crops up today as an unwitting tendency to think of adaptive behavior in a dichotomy of good and bad. Uncensorious as he was toward the neurotic behavior that circumstances and a repressive society had forced upon the patient, Freud was a stern and moral man who would not call a patient well until all neurotic anxieties were understood, all defense mechanisms abandoned, and all behavior brought under control of the clear-eyed ego that perceives everything exactly as it is. But this heroic perception was meant to apply only to neurotic anxieties, legacies of childhood that did not correspond to present dangers. The ideal patient, issuing from his analysis cleansed of all anxiety, was really cleansed only of defenses against dangers that no longer existed. So we must attach less blame to the fastidious Freud than to the careless popularizers of mental health wisdom who have communicated the thought, utterly bizarre in one of the most frightening periods of human history, that the mentally healthy person is free from all anxiety and meets life with radiant confidence. Of course we all know better than that when we stop to think, but in the psychological and psychiatric literature there lies a concealed assumption that dangers must be faced because they are not really there, that any delay, avoidance, retreat, or cognitive distortion of reality is in the end a reprehensible piece of cowardice. We must march forward, ever forward, facing our problems, overcoming all obstacles, masters of our fate, fit citizens of the brave new world. Foolish as it is, this unwitting assumption sufficiently pervades our professional literature so that we really do have to stop and think. What are the transactions that actually take place between a person and his environment?

In actuality, of course, there are many situations that can be met only by compromise or even resignation. Events may occur that require us to give in, relinquish things we would have liked, perhaps change direction or restrict the range of our activities. We may have no recourse but to accept a permanent impoverishment of our lives and try to make the best of it. Furthermore, when dangers are real and information incomplete it is in no sense adaptive to march boldly forward. History provides many examples, none better than General Braddock in our own colonial days, who marched his column of British regulars through the forests of Pennsylvania straight into a French and Indian ambush. Described not inappropriately in military metaphors, adaptation often calls for delay, strategic retreat, regrouping of forces, abandoning of untenable positions, seeking fresh intelligence, and deploying new weapons. And just as recuperation from serious illness is not the work of a day, even though in the end it may be completely accomplished, so recovery from a personal loss or disaster requires a long period of internal readjustment that may not be well served at the start by forceful action or total clarity of perception. Sometimes adaptation to a severely frustrating reality is possible only if full recognition of the bitter truth is for a long time postponed.

The element of compromise in adaptive behavior can be well illustrated from that rich storehouse of information provided by Lois Murphy (1962) in her study of young children in Topeka. She describes a number of three-year-olds brought for the first time from their homes to her study center, where the business of the day is to meet a psychologist and engage in some activities that constitute a test of intelligence. Her first two illustrations, boys named Brennie and Donald, present us at once with a striking contrast. Brennie appears to be confidence incarnate. He climbs happily into the car, alertly watches and comments upon the passing scene, charms everyone with his smile, walks into the testing room with perfect poise, accepts each proffered task with eager interest, makes conversation and asks for appropriate help from adults, and finally leaves the scene with a polite expression of thanks. Brennie might be judged a paragon of mental health, and any three-year-old so easy to deal with is certain to be a psychologist's delight. In contrast, the day of Donald's visit is a taxing one for the staff. The child comes accompanied by his mother, described as "warm and ample," and he utters not a word either during the ride, when entering the building, or for some time after he enters the psychologist's office. Invited to sit down, he stands resolutely beside his mother, his feet spread slightly apart. He will string beads only when his mother has done so first, and once embarked on this operation, he refuses to be diverted by the psychologist, who would like to get on with the test. Slowly he warms up enough to dispense with his mother's mediation and deal directly with the psychologist, but the testing still drags because Donald becomes involved in, for instance, building-block constructions of his own instead of those required for the test. The session ends with the assessment far from complete.

It is easy to imagine what Donald's session would look like in the records of a typical guidance agency. He has displayed two highly disquieting symptoms. He has a bad case of separation anxiety, clinging to his mother when he should be facing reality, and he also displays withdrawal and introversion by building with blocks according to his fantasy instead of responding properly to social stimulation. But before we hurry Donald into psychotherapy let us look at the situation from a child's point of view. As adults we know something that he does not know: we know that Mrs. Murphy and her staff are full of kindness and patience and that they will go to great lengths to keep discomfort and anxiety at a minimum. Donald can know only that he is being taken to a strange place for a purpose he cannot fathom. Many children by the age of three have been to the pediatrician's office, to the barber, and perhaps even to the dentist, and they may well have noticed a credibility gap between parental assurances and the discomforts actually experienced during these visits. Now they are being taken to play games with a nice lady—a likely story indeed! If such conditions existed for Donald, he exhibits commendable common sense in sticking close to his mother, the one familiar object, until he can figure out the nature of the racket. It is his good fortune that his principal observer, Mrs. Murphy, understands his position, perceives him not as anxiously dependent but as a "sturdy boy," and appreciates his strategy of adaptation. She says:

Over the years we have seen Donald, this pattern has continued: cautious, deliberate, watchful entrance into a new situation, keeping his distance at first, quietly, firmly maintaining his right to move at his own pace, to make his own choices, to set his own terms, to cooperate when he got ready. These tendencies persisted long after he became able to separate from his mother. (1962:32).

And what of the perfectly adjusted Brennie? In reviewing Mrs. Murphy's book, I likened Brennie to a genial cocker spaniel who welcomes friend and burglar with equal joy. He seems to trust everyone without discrimination. This is fine as long as he stays in a highly restricted circle consisting of family, nursery school teachers, and sympathetic psychological researchers, who support him lovingly and demand a minimum amount of compromise. But eventually Brennie is going to find out that life is not a rose garden. Before long he will be entering what Harry Stack Sullivan described as the "juvenile era," a time when crude competition and aggression among peers are only slowly brought under the control of ripening social understanding. He will find that there are adults who do not respect children and may even take advantage of them. In his teens some of his contemporaries will urge him not to trust anyone over thirty. It is easy to project his career line further into the still competitive adult world with the self-seeking, scandals, and rackets that fill the daily newspapers. By that time Brennie may have been badly burned for his innocent credulity and thus learned to be circumspect, but if we compare him with Donald at the age of three, we reach the painful conclusion that it is the cautious Donald who is better adapted to the average expectable human environment.

This is a long introduction to the main task of this paper, but it will not have been wasted if we now start that task with a clear realization of these points: (1) that the described phenomena of coping, mastery, and defense belong in the more general category of strategies of adaptation, as part of the whole tapestry of living; and (2) that adaptation does not mean either a total triumph over the environment or total surrender to it, but rather a striving toward acceptable compromise.

THE TREND TOWARD
INCREASED AUTONOMY

The point of departure for a systematic description of strategies of adaptation should be the broadest possible statement. Let us put it this way: adaptation is something that is done by living systems in interactions with their environments. It is important to emphasize both the noun *systems* and the adjective *living*. Our whole enterprise can founder at the very start if the basic image is allowed to be mechanical rather than organismic. It is characteristic of a system that there is interaction among its various parts, so that changes in one part are likely to have considerable consequences in at least several other parts. A system, furthermore, tends to maintain itself as intact as possible and thus displays more or less extensive rebalancing processes when injured or deformed. This much is true of inanimate systems as well as animate ones, which makes it necessary to qualify the systems under discussion here as *living*. For it is characteristic of living systems that they do something more than maintain themselves. Cannon's historic studies of homeostasis have familiarized us with the remarkable mechanisms whereby animal and human living systems maintain internal steady states, such as body temperature and fluid content, and restore such states when circumstances have forced a temporary departure. But Cannon was well aware that maintaining homeostasis was not the whole story; he saw it as a necessary basis from which living systems could get on with their more important business. This further business consists of growth and reproduction. Living systems do not stay the same size. They grow dramatically larger: the puppy that you once held in your hands becomes the big dog that you can no longer hold in your lap. This increase eventually reaches its limit in any one system, but not until arrangements have been made to start a whole fresh lot of tiny living systems on their way toward maximum growth.

The fundamental property of growth in living systems was well described in 1941 by Andras Angyal. Looking for "the general pattern which the organismic total process follows," Angyal pictured the living system as partially open to the environment and as constantly taking material from the environment to become a functioning part of itself:

It draws incessantly new material from the outside world, transforming alien objects into functional parts of its own. Thus the organism *expands* at the expense of its surroundings. The expansion may be a material one, as in the case of bodily growth, or a psychological one as in the case of the assimilation of experiences which result in mental growth, or a functional one as when one acquires skill, with a resulting increase of efficiency in dealing with the environment (1941:27–28).

Thus the life process necessarily entails expansion, but Angyal carried the matter further. Living systems, he pointed out, exhibit *autonomy*. They are in part governed from inside, and are thus to a degree resistant to forces that would govern them from the outside. If this were not true, the whole concept of adaptation would be impossible. Angyal then describes the direction of the organismic process as one toward an *increase of autonomy*.

Aggressiveness, combativeness, the urge for mastery, domination, or some equivalent urge or drive or trait is assumed probably by all students of personality. All these various concepts imply that the human being has a characteristic tendency toward self-determination, that is, a tendency to resist external influences and to subordinate the heteronomous forces of the physical and social environment to its own sphere of influence (1941:49).

It was an evil day, we may imagine, for the inanimate world when living systems first broke loose upon it. Conservative boulders doubtless shook their heads and predicted gloomily that if this subversive trend gained strength the day might come when living systems would overrun the earth. And this is indeed exactly what has happened. Most of the land surface is completely buried by living systems, and even the oceans are full of them. When we consider this outrageous imperialism it is small wonder that the expansion of peoples and of nations has been a besetting problem throughout human history. And even when we concentrate on strategies of adaptation, we must keep it in mind that human beings are rarely content with maintaining a personal homeostasis. Unless they are very old they are almost certain to be moving in the direction of increased autonomy. It can be a threat of disastrous proportions to discover in the midst of life that all avenues are blocked to further personal development.

Living creatures, in short, will constantly strive for an adaptive compromise that not only preserves them as they are, but also permits them to grow, to increase both their size and their autonomy. Consider an animal as it steps forth in the morning from where it has been sleeping and moves into its daytime environment. If all goes well, it will ingest a portion of that environment, maintain its visceral integrity by homeostatic processes and by eliminating waste material, add a tiny increment to its size, explore a little and thus process some fresh information about its environment, gain a bit in muscular strength and coordination, bask in the warm sunshine, and return at night to its den a little bigger, a little wiser, a little stronger, and a little more contented than it was in the morning. If the season is right, it may also have found an opportunity to set those processes in motion whereby a number of offspring will come into existence. A day like this can be described as one of maximum animal self-actualization. If all does not go well, the animal may return to the den hungry, cold, perhaps battered and bruised, yet still essentially intact as a living system, capable of recuperating during the night and setting forth again in the morning. Of course, it may have failed to keep itself intact or even alive, but we can be sure disaster occurred only because the animal's adaptive repertoire, employed with the utmost vigor, has not been equal to the circumstances. Animals try to go up; if they go down, they go down fighting.

SOME VARIABLES
OF ADAPTIVE BEHAVIOR

The adaptive capacities of any species of animal are to some extent represented in bodily structure, the product of natural selection. Protective coloring, great weight and strength, or such features as the rabbit's powerful hind legs that enable it to make bewildering hairpin turns in the course of its flight are part of the inherited equipment that favor certain styles of adapting. When we speak of strategies of adaptation, however, we are referring more particularly to the realm of behavior, the realm that is directly controlled by the nervous system and that is in various degrees open to learning through experience. This realm is traditionally broken down into receptive processes, central storage and organizing processes, and motor processes that lead to further sensory input. In the case of animals, whose inner experience, whatever its nature, remains forever closed to us, strategies of adaptation have to be described in behavioral language. They have to be described in terms of what can go on in a behavioral system of receptors, central structures, and effectors, not overlooking, of course, the contributions of the autonomic nervous system and the input of information from inside the body. How can we best describe the possibilities of adaptive control and regulation in an animal's behavioral system?

We could start with a flourish of analytic logic by talking sequentially about regulation in the sensory, the central, and the motor spheres. But this is a dangerous piece of abstraction; in actuality the whole thing operates not as a sequence but as a system. What happens when we surprise a squirrel feeding on the ground? There is a whisk of tail and before we know it, the animal has darted up a tree and is sitting on a branch chattering angrily at us. You might judge from a carelessly written mental health tract that the squirrel's behavior was neurotic and deplorable, inasmuch as it retreated instead of facing reality. But the squirrel is facing reality all right; it has simply elected to face it from a position of strength rather than from one of weakness. When you are on the cluttered ground and a huge creature is approaching, fear and flight are adaptive. When the cognitive field has thus been changed so that you are above the huge creature and have at your disposal all the escape routes provided by the branches of a tree, it is adaptive to sit down, be angry, and try the power of scolding. The squirrel has regulated the cognitive field, but has done so in large part by motor activity, and this is surely typical of adaptive strategies in the animal world.

Because the living animal is a system, adaptive behavior entails managing several different things at once. The repertoire by which this management is carried out can be conceptualized at this point in terms of action. One possibility is simply orientation with a minimum of locomotion. When locomotion is employed, it can consist of approach, avoidance while still observing the object of interest, or flight, and a final option is the complete immobility of hiding. Those are the possibilities stated in the most general terms. In order to behave adaptively the animal must use this repertoire to produce what prove to be, even in simple instances, fairly complex results. It seems to me that there are at least three variables that are regularly involved in the process, three aspects of the total situation no one of which can be neglected without great risk. If the animal is to conduct a successful transaction with the environment, perhaps leading to enhancement and growth, but in any event not resulting in injury or destruction, it must (1) keep securing adequate information about the environment; (2) maintain satisfactory internal conditions both for action and for processing information; and (3) maintain its autonomy or freedom of movement, freedom to use its repertoire in a flexible fashion.

I shall enlarge upon these three variables in a moment, but let us first place them in concrete form in order to secure the point that they must all be managed as well as possible at the same time. When a cat hears a strange noise in the nearby thicket, locomation stops, eyes and ears are pointed in the direction of sound, and the animal's whole being seems concentrated on obtaining cognitive clarity. But if this were the only consideration, the cat might now be expected to move straight into the thicket to see what is there; instead, it explores very slowly and with much circumspection, for it is combining the third variable with the first, maintaining a freedom of movement that would be lost in the thicket. If the noise turns out to have come from a strange cat intruding on the territory, and there ensues a battle of vocal and hair-raising threats leading to an exchange of blows, the second variable becomes decisive. We know from the work of the ecologists that animal battles rarely go on to the death. The animal that sustains injury, feels incompetent, or is slowed by fatigue, shifts its tactics from approach to flight, and wisely lives to fight another day. This result is more probable if the first and third variables have been sufficiently heeded so that the animal is not cornered and has kept escape routes open.

Information

Securing adequate information about the environment is an obvious necessity for adaptive behavior. Action can be carried on most successfully when the amount of information to be processed is neither too small nor too great. If the channels are underloaded, there will be no way to decide what to do, as we would express it in adult conscious experience. If the channels are overloaded, there will again be no way to decide what to do, this time because the number of possibilities creates confusion. Of course this is not just a quantitative matter; what really counts is the meaning of the information in terms of potential benefits and harms. With this modification, however, it is permissible to use a quantitative metaphor and say that there is a certain rate of information input that is conducive to unconfused, straightforward action, and that both higher rates and lower rates will tend, though for different reasons, to make action difficult. Adaptive behavior requires that the cognitive field have the right amount of information to serve as a guide to action. Depending on circumstances, then, adaptation may take the form either of seeking more information or of trying to cut down on the existing input. The cautiously exploring cat illustrates the former process, behaving as though it asked the question, "What is it?" But if the same cat is in the nursery and is exposed to the affection and curiosity of several children, it will try to get away from some of the overwhelming input and might be imagined to ask, "What is all this, anyway?"

Departure in either direction from the preferred level of information is illustrated in Murphy's descriptions of the Topeka three-year-olds. There is likely to be a shortage of information before the children arrive at the testing center, and this is not easily dispelled by adult explanations. Once they have arrived, however, the children are flooded by an input that, because of its newness, they cannot easily put in order. There is a new room, a psychologist, an observer, and a collection of more or less unfamiliar materials. We have already seen how the sturdy Donald dealt with this situation, standing close to his mother, surveying the scene with alert eyes, and consenting to take action only when he had structured the cognitive field sufficiently to isolate an activity he felt competent to undertake. Another of Murphy's procedures was to have groups of children come to her home for a party, a situation quite new, strange, and bewildering to them and possibly a little odd even to adult eyes, inasmuch as each child had an observer assigned to keep account of everything he did. Donald faced this situation with his characteristic determination to get the cognitive field straight. After a long silent survey, he discriminated a zone of likely competence in the toys in the garage and went there to examine them. Later, he picked out a safe entry into the social scene and ended the afternoon in fairly active participation. In this he was more daring than another boy who found his first manageable zone to be building blocks in a corner of the garage and stayed with it the whole afternoon.

Internal Organization

Working on the cognitive field alone will not guarantee adaptive behavior if the internal organization of the system gets too far out of balance. This is crudely obvious if an animal is injured in a fight, weakened by loss of blood, or exhausted in a long struggle. It is clear also in the lowered alertness, curiosity, and effort of children who are feeling sick. Even in young children it is possible to detect another form of internal disorganization that can seriously hamper adaptive behavior: the disorganization produced by strong unpleasant affects such as anxiety, grief, or shame. Some of the Topeka children confronted their first session with the psychologist with a degree of emotion that made it difficult for them to make use of the available information. One little girl, for instance, became tearful and inert, as if drained of energy. When able to try the tasks at all, she could scarcely muster enough force to attend, handle objects, or speak above a whisper, and her most characteristic movement was to push the materials gently away. The inhibition vanished magically when she started for home. A normally active boy showed the paralyzing effect of anxiety first by keeping close to his mother, avoiding contact with examiner and test materials, and then by tentative work on the tasks with quick giving up in the face of difficulties. He was able by these tactics to control the anxiety and work up to an active part in the testing. As his internal organization came back to its usual balance, he spoke more loudly, moved more vigorously, explored the materials more boldly, initiated conversation, and became increasingly master of the situation.

Autonomy

Even if the internal organization is in good balance and the cognitive field is being dealt with competently, adaptive behavior may come to grief if freedom of action is not to some extent maintained. Animals, we may suppose, often enough get trapped in situations from which they cannot escape, but to a remarkable extent they seem to avoid this mishap, as if they were constantly monitored by a small built-in superego reminding them to keep their escape routes open. Once when I kept hens, I was worried to see a large hawk circling high above the yard, but my neighbor reassured me that a hawk would go without its dinner rather than drop down into a narrow, high-fenced pen that might hamper its return to the realms of safe soaring; and, sure enough, no hens were taken. Preserving space in which to maneuver is always an important consideration in strategy.

Among the Topeka children Donald again comes to mind as one who kept initiative in his own hands by refusing to be drawn into situations until he had given them a thorough scrutiny. Tactics of delay and refusals to participate, frustrating as they may be to the psychologist and thus all too readily given a derogatory tag like "anxious avoidance" and "withdrawal," may actually be in the highest tradition of adaptive behavior, following the adage to "look before you leap." Especially adept at maintaining autonomy was a girl named Sheila, not quite three, who after looking at the test materials announced that she did not want to watch them and instead would play with the toys on the floor. There was no sign of anxiety, and very quickly she involved the examiner in her game with the toys. Momentarily intrigued by a performance test set up before her, Sheila began to play with it, but when gently pressed to follow the examiner's rules rather than her own, she returned to the floor, announcing, "I want to do *this*. We don't like the game we had." Murphy comments as follows:

Here we see a child who in the face of continuing and skillfully applied adult pressures maintained her own autonomy. And it was not merely a matter of refusing and rejecting; it was a matter of doing this without allowing the pressures to depress her mood or to restrict her freedom of movement. Instead, during most of the time, the pressures served to stimulate her to her own best efforts in structuring the situation and obtaining enjoyment from it and from the relationship with the adult (1962:82).

In adult life, Sheila possibly will become one of those who regard psychological tests as an invasion of privacy, and we should hesitate to criticize her for this because it may be part of a courageous career in the cause of civil rights.

Adaptive behavior, in short, involves the simultaneous management of at least three variables: securing adequate information, maintaining satisfactory internal conditions, and keeping up some degree of autonomy. Whatever the specific nature of the problem may be, those other considerations can never be safely neglected. But if we think in these terms, it becomes clear that strategies of adaptation typically have a considerable development over time. The temporal dimension is of the utmost importance for our problem.

THE TIME DIMENSION IN ADAPTIVE BEHAVIOR

I doubt if any serious student of behavior has thought about the adaptive process without considering it to be extended over time. Yet it seems to me quite common in clinical assessments to look for samples of such behavior, for instance the client's initial reaction to the examiner or the way inkblots are dealt with on first meeting, and then jump to the generalization that these are the client's characteristic ways of meeting his problems. Undoubtedly this is one of the reasons for the well-known fact that psychological assessments based on tests picture everyone, even the healthiest, as a clinical case needing some kind of improvement. The client's characteristic ways of meeting a problem the first time may not be how he meets them the second and third times, still less the twentieth time. On their first visits to the study center Donald and Sheila would not have been recorded as secure children; in neither case could the psychologist come anywhere near to completing the examination. Fortunately, they were studied over a long period of time, and we know that both are strong sturdy specimens of humanity with sense enough to take their own time and deal with things in their own way. Strategy is not created on the instant. It develops over time and is progressively modified in the course of time.

If illustration of this principle were needed, the Topeka children could again furnish us with vivid examples. There is the little girl at the party, physically slowed by a slight orthopedic defect, who at the outset cannot manage the jumping board even with help, and at the end jumps joyfully entirely by herself. There are the two sisters, age five and three, who have to accommodate themselves to the awesome prospect of moving to another city. Their strategies are traced through the months of anticipation and preparation, through the move itself, and through the first few weeks of finding security and satisfactions in the new environment (Murphy 1962:69–75, 168–70, 178–85). But if we think in terms of the three variables just discussed, the importance of the time dimension becomes self-evident. The values of the variables are not likely to stay long unchanged. Perhaps clearer cognition will reveal danger, increase fear, and precipitate flight, but a good many of the situations encountered by children are simply new. There is, of course, always a little risk in newness, so what is required is a cautious approach allowing time to assess both the risk and the possibility of benefits. The input of information may lead to sharper discrimination of the field, discovery of areas of likely competence and enjoyment, quieting of disturbing affects in favor of pleasurable excitement, and a lowering of the premium on maintaining strict autonomy. All such rebalancing of the variables implies processes of learning extended over time. A profitable familiarity with the cognitive field can be gained simply by protracted inspection with no motor involvement beyond moving the eyes and head. Closer familiarity requires the making of behavioral tests, discovering one's competence to deal with promising portions of the environment. There are great individual differences among children in the speed and apparent ease with which they deal with the newness of the world around them. Considering the many and varied adaptations that have to be made, we should not hastily conclude that the quickest strategies are necessarily the best.

HUMAN COMPLICATIONS
OF THE ADAPTIVE PROCESS

Up to this point we have described strategies of adaptation almost wholly in behaviorial terms. Illustrations have been confined to the behavior of animals and quite young children. The purpose of this maneuver has been to lay down a descriptive framework—one might say, a sort of biological grid—upon which to place the vastly more extensive strategies available to human adults. The human brain makes possible a transcendence of the immediate present that we do not suppose to exist in even the most intelligent subhuman primates. This is partly a matter of language and communication. As Alfred Kroeber memorably expressed it:

A bird's chirp, a lion's roar, a horse's scream, a man's moan express subjective conditions; they do not convey objective information. By objective information, we mean what is communicated in such statements as: "There are trees over the hill," "There is a single tree," "There are only bushes," "There were trees but are no longer," "If there are trees, he may be hiding in them," "Trees can be burned," and millions of others. All postinfantile, nondefective human beings can make and constantly do make such statements, though they may make them with quite different sounds according to what speech custom they happen to follow. But no subhuman animal makes *any* such statements. All the indications are that no subhuman animal even has any impulse to utter or convey such information (1948:41).

The result of this capacity to talk about and think about things that are not immediately present is in the end an immense extension of the human horizon. Asch describes this in the following words:

Men live in a field that extends into a distant past and into a far future; the past and the future are to them present realities to which they must constantly orient themselves; they think in terms of days, seasons, and epochs, of good and bad times. . . . Because they can look forward and backward and perceive causal relations, because they can anticipate the consequences of their actions in the future and view their relation to the past, their immediate needs exist in a field of other needs, present and future. Because they consciously relate the past with the future, they are capable of representing their goals to themselves, to aspire to fulfill them, to test them in imagination, and to plan their steps with a purpose.

    An integral part of man's extended horizon is the kind of object he becomes to himself. In the same way that he apprehends differentiated objects and their properties he becomes aware of himself as an individual with a specific character and fate; he becomes *self*-conscious. . . . Because he is conscious of himself and capable of reflecting on his experiences, he also takes up an attitude to himself and takes measures to control his own actions and tendencies. The consequence of having a self is that he takes his stand in the world as a person (1952:120–22).

It is in this vastly expanded world of experience that human beings must devise their strategies of adaptation.

    One's first thought may be that the ensuing complexities are certain to drown us. I believe, however, that we stand to gain by fitting strategies as far as possible into the three behaviorial variables deduced from animals and young children. Take first the second variable, the maintaining, and if possible the enhancing, of the system's internal organization. It is here that awareness of the remote, the past, and the future, and especially awareness of oneself as a person, most dramatically expand the meaning of the variable. Clearly there is much more to be maintained than bodily integrity and control over disruptive affects. One thing that must be enhanced if possible, and desperately maintained if necessary, is the level of self-esteem. In part this shows itself as a struggle to keep intact a satisfactory self-picture, in part as attempts to preserve a sense of competence, an inner assurance that one can do the things necessary for a satisfactory life. Wide are the ramifications of keeping up one's self-esteem. Almost any situation that is not completely familiar, even casual and superficial contacts with new people, even discussing the day's news, can touch off internal questions like: "What sort of impression am I making?" "How well am I dealing with this?" "What kind of a person am I showing myself to be?" When self-esteem is tender or when the situation is strongly challenging, such questions, even if only vaguely felt, can lead to anxiety, shame, or guilt with their threat of further disorganization. No adaptive strategy that is careless of the level of self-esteem is likely to be any good. We certainly regard it as rare, unusually mature, and uncommonly heroic when after an unfortunate happening that diminishes his importance or shows him to be wrong, a person quietly lowers his estimate of himself without making excuses or seeking to lodge the blame elsewhere.

Less dramatic but still important are the expanded meanings of the other two variables. Securing adequate information is no longer confined to the immediate cognitive field. Information about things absent assumes increasing significance, especially when it bears on courses of action that extend into the future. Resources for information are also much richer: other people can be asked, relevant reading matter can be sought, and in some cases it is possible to send friends, employees, or students out to increase the scope of one's informational net. The maintaining of autonomy similarly gains a future dimension and a wider meaning. Looking ahead into the future and frequently making plans of one kind or another, we soon learn to be at least somewhat careful about committing ourselves. We feel better if things can be left a little open, if there are options; if, for example, in taking a job we see room for varying its duties or believe that in any event it will be a good springboard toward other jobs. "If I take this job," so many have asked themselves, "with its demands for teaching or medical service, will I have time for my own research?" Preserving an acceptable level of freedom of movement continues to be an important consideration even when the present physical field of the exploring animal has expanded into the imagined future social field of the human adult.

ILLUSTRATIONS FROM RECENT RESEARCH

The understanding of strategies of adaptation can start from any one variable provided we bear in mind that the simultaneous management of all three variables is constantly involved. In one of the first psychiatric studies of severe life stress, Lindemann (1944) described the working-through of bereavement and grief in a way that includes all three. The need for information is important following bereavement because a great many established patterns of conduct both in the present and in the expected future have been fatally disrupted. As Lindemann put it, "the bereaved is surprised to find how large a part of his customary activity was done in some meaningful relationship to the deceased and has now lost its significance" (p. 142). New burdens will have to be assumed, new patterns of meaningful conduct discovered; how will all this be managed, and where will opportunities be found? Yet often enough the bereaved person is for some time unequal to contemplating the future, which would only emphasize the magnitude of the loss and increase painful and paralyzing grief. Internal organization cannot be maintained, thinking and action can hardly be carried forward at all, as long as this disruptive emotion remains strong. Self-esteem, too, is often put on trial, challenged by the intrusion of unexpected feelings of guilt. Lindemann notices how often "the bereaved searches the time before the death for evidence of failure to do right by the lost one; he accuses himself of negligence and exaggerates minor omissions" (p. 142). Considerations of autonomy, of preserving or opening up some sense of free movement, present themselves as soon as the immediate crisis has passed. Sometimes a death may be experienced as increasing the survivor's freedom, but typically a widowed spouse, especially if there is a family to bring up, looks into a future gravely constricted.

A few years ago, Hamburg and Adams (1967) reviewed a number of studies of behavior during major life transitions, putting a strong emphasis on the seeking and utilizing of information. They perceive the cognitive quest, however, in relation to the other two variables. Thus in patients with severe injuries that are bound to restrict their future activity the search for information is seen as serving the following purposes: "keeping distress within manageable limits; maintaining a sense of personal worth; restoring relations with significant other people; enhancing prospects for recovery of bodily functions; and increasing the likelihood of working out a personally valued and socially acceptable situation after maximum physical recovery has been attained" (p. 278). The time dimension proves to be significant in these cases. For a while, the depressing impact of the event must be controlled, and this is often accomplished by extensive denial of the seriousness of the illness. As time goes on, there is an increase of cognitive clarity, but this is usually achieved at the cost of an increase of depression, which now is better tolerated. The dismal truth is perceived only as rapidly as one can stand it. Similar processes of balance are revealed in studies of the parents of children suffering from leukemia. Again one can see delays in taking in the full meaning of the diagnosis and slow progress toward appreciation of the inevitable outcome. Again one can see the outcropping of guilt and the need of the parents to be reassured that more attention on their part to the early manifestations of the disease would not have changed the prognosis. In this situation, grief can be experienced in advance, and it was noticed that the more this was done, the less the parents were overwhelmed when the child's death finally occurred.

The use of strategies of adaptation in advance, in anticipation of problems that still lie ahead, would appear to be a peculiarly human attribute. It is unusually well exemplified in a study by Silber and colleagues (1961) of high-school seniors getting ready to enter college in the fall. The subjects were chosen because of their high level of competence in the more important aspects of adolescent life: their previous success gave them confidence, but did not exempt them from misgivings over the important step soon to be taken. The interviewers became aware of a large repertoire of adaptive strategies serving to increase information about college life, dampen anxiety, sustain and improve a self-image of adequacy, and provide reassurance that the new life would offer a variety of pathways to self-satisfaction. The students sought information by writing to their college, visiting the campus, and talking with the college students and graduates of their acquaintance. They filtered the information by selectively perceiving those aspects of their college that put it in the light of a benign, friendly, supportive environment. They sustained internal organization by the thought that worrying was normal, was shared by other prospective students—"Everybody feels this, everybody has to be a freshman once"—and might even have a useful function in preparing for eventualities. They further reminded themselves of previous analogous situations successfully dealt with, such as the transition from junior to senior high school, identified themselves as part of a group well prepared for college, and lowered their levels of aspiration with respect to academic performance and social prominence during the freshman year. Particularly significant was the building of a sense of competence by a process of role rehearsal during the spring and summer. The students began to read books they thought would be required at college, to exert themselves in courses considered to be on a college level, and to take special pains with term papers, understood by them to be of great importance in college performance. Anticipating their increased independence, some of them began buying their new clothes and practiced more careful budgeting of their time. In their choice of summer jobs they veered away from those associated with adolescent status, like baby-sitting and mowing lawns, looking instead for work that would put them in competition with adults and would increase their experience in dealing with adults on an equal level. With respect to autonomy, they rehearsed in fantasy the different things they might do to secure help, win popularity, and find avenues for their individual skills and interests. And if worse came to the worst, as one of them expressed it, "If I want to go home, I'll be able to."

It is worth noticing that the strategies of adaptation pursued by these prospective college students accomplished more than could reasonably be implied by the words *defense* and *protection*. I wonder if they do not imply more than most people have in mind when they use the word *coping*, which according to my desk dictionary means contending, striving, opposing, or resisting "on equal terms." The limits of definition are at this point shadowy, but we must be sure not to overlook what these young people actually accomplished while dealing with the problems of transition. The men and women who walked on to their respective campuses in September were not quite the same people who received news of their admittance the previous spring. Whatever distortions and defensive operations may have crept into their college-oriented behavior, these were greatly overbalanced by substantial increases in realistic information, in realistic expectations, and in actual competence through role rehearsal and through summer jobs. They had grown, they had matured, they had exhibited Angyal's trend toward increased autonomy, and as human beings they stood taller than the high-school adolescents they had been six months before. One of the great advantages of research on coping is that it brings back into the psychological and psychiatric literature the persistence, the will to live, the courage, and indeed the heroism that are as much a part of human nature as the retreats, evasions, and petty impulse gratifications that bulk so large in our thinking about psychopathology. Let us be sure that the concept of coping does not shrink in its meaning so that we lose this great advance over our constricted past and forget that strategies of adaptation lead not just to equilibrium but to development.

A CLOSING NOTE
ON DEFENSE MECHANISMS

I shall now bring defense mechanisms back into the discussion. You may have thought that I was angry with them, but I am angry only with the overweening part they have been accorded in the understanding of personality. The mechanisms of defense, the ten of them listed by Anna Freud (1937), or whatever the number may be, have a legitimate place among strategies of adaptation. They *are* strategies of adaptation, and we can assume that in the course of human history they have relieved untold millions of people of anxiety that would otherwise have been overwhelming. Possibly when it comes to actual process, the defense mechanisms are not even very different in kind from other adaptive processes. Theodore Kroeber (1963) has pointed out the impressive continuities between defense mechanisms and estimable adaptive devices. Repression has a counterpart in suppression, reaction formation in substitution, and rationalization in the most strenuous and disciplined logical analysis. According to this way of thinking, defense mechanisms can be seen as adaptive devices gone wrong, and the way in which they have gone wrong is in failing to maintain a balance among the three variables I have been discussing. Presumably because the threat to internal organization is acute—the anxiety unbearable—obtaining further information is sacrificed, and the cognitive field is either partially blacked out or subjected to a major interpretative distortion. As far as our knowledge of defense mechanisms goes, derived largely from psychoanalytic treatment, they work for the time being; in short range they are adaptive. They cause trouble in the long run because they contain no provision, so to speak, for learning anything new about sources of danger. Closing the cognitive field is a static solution, guaranteeing that dangers will not be reexamined and may, therefore, retain their original power to precipitate anxiety. Thus defense mechanisms can be considered poor devices, the work of which must sometimes be undone for the sake of psychological health, but they cannot be denied their place as a class of strategies of adaptation.

WHAT DIFFERENCE DOES IT MAKE?

The question "What difference does it make?" is often asked by laymen about our technical and theoretical discussions and is, I believe, one which we should always ask ourselves. What value can we anticipate from imposing a grid of three very general variables upon the seemingly endless phenomena of adaptive processes? What good is accomplished by distributing the phenomena into categories labeled: (1) securing adequate information about the environment; (2) maintaining satisfactory internal conditions both for action and for processing information; and (3) maintaining autonomy or freedom of movement? What practical virtue is there in asserting that strategies of adaptation in order to be reasonably successful require the simultaneous management of these three considerations, the holding of some sort of balance among them?

I do not for a moment think that this descriptive maneuver illuminates all our difficulties or contains inherent advice for mental health practices. The variables may not be the best ones, and they may be too big. The second one, for example, which might be called maintaining and enhancing the inner structure and functional capacity of the system as a whole, contains in the human case aspects as disparate as controlling disruptive affects and maintaining a satisfying self-picture. For practical purposes a breakdown into separate subvariables would certainly be necessary. But whatever may be the shortcomings of the description offered in this essay, however small the step that has been taken, I am going to close with the claim that it is a step in the right direction.

As a profession—and here I mean to include psychiatrists, psychologists, social workers, and all others who work in the domain broadly called mental health—we have been for a long time heavily concerned with how people feel, not so much with what they do. It has been our faith that if people could be made to feel right inside, to experience trust, to feel loved and valued, to relinquish their jealousies and competitive aggression toward the members of the family circle, then only could we expect their behavior to change; then only could we confidently leave them to their own devices. So we have been tempted to concentrate on these inner states, trying to influence them directly through the power of insight and the efficacy of a relationship in which the most regularly described element is warmth. Yet increasingly we have been confronted by the painful fact that this method of getting at the roots of the difficulty is, after all, something short of a startling success, even though many have benefited greatly from it, and that in any event it is likely to take quite a long time. Now comes the movement for community mental health, with its ideal of making our services available to all segments of the population. Whatever reservations we may have about so vast an aspiration, it is inevitable that a democratic society should try it, just as in the last century it was inevitable that an education through high school should come to be considered the right of every child regardless of economic circumstances. Community mental health may not work, but there is no doubt in my mind that we are going to try it.

It would be good, therefore, if it *did* work, but its working will certainly require astonishing economies of professional time. We are forced to think about doing things faster. And I submit that one way to do this is to concentrate more carefully on what clients do, or on what they can be encouraged to do by advice or a suitable arrangement of circumstances. There has never been doubt that action is capable of changing feeling. The most telling example is the gain in confidence and the reduction of anxiety that follow the successful performance of some act that has been the object of misgivings. Giving instruction and advice, offering explanations and suggestions to parents, suggesting changes in the environment—these have always been part of the helping strategy. The medical profession, always quick to erect polysyllabic defenses, has lately reasserted its claim to stay on top of these activities by calling them "paramedical," while the psychologists, equally jealous, have attacked the whole disease model of behavior disorders and pinned on psychotherapy the new label of "behavior change." As a pacifist with respect to professional prestige quarrels, I argue only that we may find, if we try it modestly but persistently, using our best insight and taking care to evaluate our results, that fairly simple and direct methods of influencing behavior can produce a good deal better results than we have been taught to suppose. But our best insights will not be enough if they all have to do with inner states, defense mechanisms, and the precipitates of interpersonal relations. There must be a new sensitivity to potentialities for action, to what the client might just be capable of doing for himself with a little encouragement, and to what he might be able to do if he knew that it was important and would help him with his problems. Into this we can have insight only if we are thoroughly familiar with strategies of adaptation as they occur in everyday life.

To emphasize the point, let us suppose that in that high school where the competent adolescents were studied there is a less competent boy, admitted to college like the others, but facing the prospect with far less spirit. His parents notice that he seems preoccupied and worried, complains of not sleeping, looks thinner, and acts less inclined to seek the company of his friends. He announces that he feels tired and will spend the summer at home, mowing the lawn, rather than looking for a summer job. The parents, wanting their boy to have everything of the best, send him to an expensive psychiatrist. What will happen? My hope would be that the psychiatrist, aware of the wide range of strategies of adaptation shown by other boys in this situation, would use his influence chiefly to persuade his patients to try some of them. The boy may be afraid of the total experience, but he may not be afraid to visit the campus, obtain literature, talk to college students he knows, buy some clothes alone, write school essays as if they were college essays, and apply for a man-size summer job. And if these can be managed, even if only with encouragement and one at a time, he has already moved along the path toward college and will make the final transition with less difficulty. But one can imagine that the talks might settle on the boy's passive-dependent tendencies, which he certainly has, and perhaps on resentment against the parents who seem willing to let him leave home, which he may also have. He can be shown that he is a passive-dependent spiteful little brat, but he can also be shown, without mentioning this, how he can become a man. It seems to me the path of wisdom to try the latter first. If it works, there is a solid victory that will probably fortify the patient somewhat against future difficulties. We all know that it may not work without change in archaic anxieties and wishes that have become preemptive, and this would call for a second and different strategy of therapeutic intervention. In community mental health work, however, there will rarely be time and staff to provide this second chance. What is tried first will generally be all that is tried.

A paper written several years ago bears on this issue in a rather amusing way. It is probably tactless to speak of it because it deals with the delicate topic of giving up smoking. In their research the authors (Leventhal, Watts, and Pagano 1967) exposed their subjects, cigarette smokers all, to a variety of urgings to stop smoking, including a somewhat alarming film, and in some cases an extremely disquieting one, that showed in color the surgical removal of a blackened lung. In contrast to a control group, these measures produced marked effects in the form of fear, determination to stop smoking, and an actual reduction in number of cigarettes smoked during the following week. The subjects were also divided another way: part of them received instructions on how to stop smoking, and part of them did not. The instructions were taken from a booklet used in antismoking clinics and were highly detailed. They dealt with avoiding conditions conducive to smoking, with the preparation beforehand of excuses for declining cigarettes, with tricks like carrying gum, not carrying matches, and taking deep breaths when the urge to smoke became strong. They also advocated a heightening of awareness by writing down the reasons for smoking and for stopping. At the end of the first week, the instructed and the uninstructed groups had both smoked much less, there being little difference between them. But when questioned after a month, and again after three months, the instructed subjects were holding their gains nicely, while the curve for the uninstructed group was moving suspiciously back in the direction of the original level of cigarette consumption. Would we have expected this result? Should it not have been that the subjects who experienced the most fear would make the greatest change in their smoking behavior? Apparently not: in this situation the effects of fear could easily peter out, whereas lasting effects occurred in those who knew what to do, who were equipped with instrumental acts that gave them a strategy of adaptation to carry out their intention.

There are many influences today that make us reluctant to tell people what to do. Partly, no doubt, it is the effect of the contemporary culture that has become so extravagantly negative to anything that smacks of direction and authority. Partly it comes from our profound absorption of Freud's image of man, based on neurotic man in whom an enfeebled and compromised ego opposes in vain the vast powers of unconscious id and superego. But partly, I think, the trouble is that we do not know what to say. Knowing so much about the ways in which common sense, realism, inventiveness, and courage can be spoiled, we have dismissed them rather than studying how they still work. Herein lies the importance of the study of strategies of adaptation. We all need to become paramedical experts, widely familiar with behavior change, keenly aware of the whole range of strategies of adaptation. At this point, our democratic society needs community mental health. What we professionals need to do to make it work is to rediscover at a new level of sophistication the homely wisdom of the past.

10

Conceptualizations of Ego: Processes, Functions, Regulations

NORMA HAAN

TAXONOMY

The model of ego processes described here first included coping and defense functions proposed by Haan (1963) and Kroeber (1963), and later elaboration (Haan 1969) added ego fragmentations to the array. Its taxonomy is composed of ten generic processes, each having three possible modes of expression—coping, defense, or fragmentation (see table 10.1 for the organization of the array . . .). The three modes of coping, defense, and fragmentation are distinguished one from another by a set of formal properties which are shown in table 10.2. Coping involves purpose, choice, and flexible shift, adheres to intersubjective reality and logic, and allows and enhances proportionate affective expression; defensiveness is compelled, negating, rigid, distorting of intersubjective reality and logic, allows covert impulse expression, and embodies the expectancy that anxiety can be relieved without directly addressing the problem; fragmentation is automated, ritualistic, privatistically formulated, affectively directed, and irrationally expressed in the sense that intersubjective reality is clearly violated. In effect, coping processes continue an open system, defenses produce particular closures of the system, and fragmentations signal temporary or more enduring dysfunctions that reject intersubjective realities that contradict important private formulations.

As an example of a generic process and its three modalities, the model is so structured that a coping function like *empathy*, a defense function like *projection*, and a fragmenting reaction like *delusional ideation*, comprise a trio with the quintessential, generic meaning of interpersonal *sensitivity*, that is, behavior that is attuned to formulating and understanding another's unexpressed or par-

Table 10.1. Taxonomy of Ego Processes

Generic processes	Modes		
	Coping	Defense	Fragmentation
	Cognitive functions		
1. Discrimination	Objectivity	Isolation	Concretism
2. Detachment	Intellectuality	Intellectualizing	Word salads, neologisms
3. Means–end symbolization	Logical analysis	Rationalization	Confabulation
	Reflexive-intraceptive functions		
4. Delayed response	Tolerance of ambiguity	Doubt	Immobilization
5. Sensitivity	Empathy	Projection	Delusional
6. Time reversion	Regression-ego	Regression	Decompensation
	Attention-focusing functions		
7. Selective awareness	Concentration	Denial	Distraction, fixation
	Affective-impulse regulations		
8. Diversion	Sublimation	Displacement	Affective preoccupation
9. Transformation	Substitution	Reaction formation	Unstable alternation
10. Restraint	Suppression	Repression	Depersonalization, amnesic

tially expressed thoughts and feelings, however accurately this might be done. These three modes of *sensitivity* may be distinguished one from another in terms of the properties shown in table 10.2.

The model and its taxonomy were designed with a number of considerations in mind. Kroeber and I thought there was clear need to represent the rational, logical, productive, wise, civil, loving, playful, and sensual aspects of people's ego actions. Such formulations needed to be more direct and parsimonious than various psychoanalytic concepts that had already been proposed to deal with such considerations: (1) the convoluted and long road whereby id eventually becomes neutralized to produce the secondary autonomy of the conflict-free ego sphere (Hartmann 1958); (2) other formulations whereby a "good" ego energy is added, but as a lesser power, to those representing the primitive id (White 1963);

Table 10.2. Properties of Ego Processes

Coping processes	Defense processes	Fragmentary processes
1. Appears to involve choice and is therefore flexible, purposive behavior.	1. Turns away from choice and is therefore rigid and channeled.	1. Appears repetitive, ritualistic, and automated.
2. Is pulled toward the future and takes account of the needs of the present.	2. Is pushed from the past.	2. Operations on assumptions which are privatistically based.
3. Oriented to the reality requirements of present situation.	3. Distorts aspects of present requirements.	3. Closes system and is non-responsive to present requirements.
4. Involves differentiated process thinking that integrates conscious and pre-conscious elements.	4. Involves undifferentiated thinking and includes elements that do not seem part of the situation.	4. Primarily and unadulteratedly determined by affect needs.
5. Operates with the organism's necessity of "metering" the experiencing of disturbing affects.	5. Operates with assumption that it is possible to magically remove disturbing feelings.	5. Floods person with affect.
6. Allows various forms of affective satisfaction in open, ordered and tempered way.	6. Allows gratification by subterfuge.	6. Allows unmodulated gratification of some impulses.

(3) the necessity that the single ego mechanism of sublimation carry the entire burden of expressing civilized impulses (Fenichel 1945); (4) the undeveloped notion of primary autonomy, which supposed that people's effectiveness was basically due to constitutional factors (Hartmann 1958; Murphy 1962).

Since all the classical definitions of the defenses included some element of negating intersubjective truth and reality, Kroeber and I reasoned that additional forms of ego actions, which do not negate truth and reality, were needed to describe human functioning. To illustrate, in the commonly used language of the clinic, the following denotations are made: isolation negates the logically indicated connecting relationships among things; intellectualization negates the same relationships, but more particularly the affective concomitants of cognitive propositions; rationalization negates the reality of a chain of causal events; doubt negates the person's necessities and capacities to make decisions; projection negates the person's own evaluation of himself; regression negates the reality of the person's age and time within his own life span; denial negates the perceptual reality of the person's present circumstances; displacement negates the object or the situation of his affective reactions; reaction formation negates his socially uncivil reactions; and repression negates the reality of his affective reactions by erasing their cognitive representations.

Despite clinicians' sensitivity to the distortions of reality and logic wrought by defensive functions, they seem to be reluctant to raise the questions about what ego functioning would be like if it were not defensive. A corollary question follows: does negation of intersubjective and intrasubjective reality and logic typify only the defensive functions of people seeking psychological help, or is it more widespread? The unsatisfying answer seems to be that the successfully analyzed become well defended, but patients and other people frequently negate reality and distort logic.

To deal with these problems, a short step was taken beyond the defensive processes. The coping functions were constructed in accordance with the assumption that the defenses represent just one *mode* or facet of generic processes that people use to solve their general problems of living. With this assumption in hand, the generic processes as well as their coping modes could be identified. Thus the defensive intents of the ten classical mechanisms lead by logical extension first to the identification of the generic and coping processes and later to the fragmenting functions, which were derived in the same manner and on the same grounds after these various clinical terms, often used to describe psychotics, were also seen to be processes (Haan 1969).

Although coping-defense-fragmentation trios were constructed on the rational grounds just described, their intraassociation can be empirically examined. Alker (1967) studied the cooccurrence of defensive projection and coping empathy, as Powers and Alker (1968) did for coping suppression and defensive repression. Both studies lend support to the postulate that there are basic generic processes (in at least these instances), with either coping or defensive modes becoming manifest in immediate transactions.

The ego model is divided into four sectors according to functions that are primarily cognitive, reflexive-intraceptive, attention-focusing, or affective-impulse regulating. These divisions are conceptual conveniences, which cannot actually exist as pure forms given the psychological unity of the person. Obviously, cognition is always informed by affective reactions even at the purest of logical situations, just as affective reactions must be informed and represented by cognitive formulations and symbolizations. Still their separation represents a partial reality, and empirically attained results in various studies utilizing this model suggest that the distinctions are useful and practical.

The cognitive sector generally represents the active, outer-directed, instrumental aspects of man's problem-solving efforts and involves extensive extrapsychic accommodation. Three generic and general strategies are included: discrimination, detachment, and means–end symbolization. Conceivably all three can be brought to bear on any one problem, but people approach problems with different and preferred patterns of strategies. The generic affective regulations are also three in number and represent the supposition that when feelings and emotions are not directly and primitively expressed, which they almost never are except by the infant, they can only be accommodated by diversion, restraint, and transformation. The reflexive-intraceptive and attention-focusing sectors probably bear more explanation. None of the generic reflexive-intraceptive functions of delayed response, sensitivity, and time reversion represent people's activities as moving forward and intending to accomplish some end. Instead they reflect the person's assimilatory engagement with his own thoughts, feelings, and intuitions. Although the attention-focusing characteristics of concentration are probably self-evident, some clinicians may be surprised by the definition of denial as a process of focusing attention. However, careful analysis of denial will probably convince the reader that its ineffectiveness results from the person's selective focusing of attention rather than from some more efficient and complex means of negation. Denial is a way for the person to say, very simply, that a troublesome or unpleasant perception is not there, so that he need not take further action. He may focus instead on the pleasant side of the matter—the cloud's silver lining. Since nothing much is definitively changed by denial, either in the person's formulations or in his external situation, he may very well be plagued again if the problematic condition persists.

Most of the coping functions are represented by commonplace ideas (with the exception of substitution and regression in the service of the ego, or ego regression, as it will be called for short). All the defensive and fragmenting processes are well known to clinicians. However their individual meanings and arrangements need further emphasis. In the listing below the generic processes are generally defined, while various direct comments that might occur in a conversation are given for each of the individual processes. Affective regulations are not often represented by succinct verbal statements because they represent patterns of action, so general descriptions are given for these processes.

Cognitive Functions

Discrimination: Separates idea from feeling, idea from idea, feeling from feeling

Objectivity:	"I am of two minds about this problem."
Isolation:	"I can't see the forest for the trees."
Tangential concretisms:	"This tree is the only one; there is no forest."

Detachment: Lets mind roam freely and irreverently, speculates, analyzes

Intellectuality:	"My past economic insecurities have led me to a degree of petty stinginess."
Intellectualizing:	"My stinginess can be explained by my anal character."
Neologisms, word salads:	"An anality is the site of the parallel."

Means–end symbolization: Analyzes causal texture of experiences and problems

Logical analysis:	"Let's start at the beginning and figure out what happened."
Rationalization:	"I was trying at first, but then one thing after another happened."
Confabulation:	"The atmosphere spread and debilitated the family."

Reflexive-Intraceptive Functions

Delayed response: Holds up decisions in complex, uncertain situations

Tolerance of ambiguity:	"There are some matters that can't be resolved when you want them to be."
Doubt:	"It's the decisions that get me; I don't know what will happen if I choose to do it."
Immobilization:	(under pressure from questioner) "I just can't move."

Sensitivity: Apprehends others' reactions and feelings

Empathy:	"I think I know how you feel" (second person agrees that first speaker does).
Projection:	"Don't think I don't know what you have in mind" (second person surprised and mildly guilty).
Delusional:	"You'd be surprised if you knew what plan I have prepared for you" (grandiosity).
	"You want to do me in; I can see it in your eyes" (persecution).

Time reversion: Recaptures and replays past experiences—cognitive, affective, social

Regression–ego: "Let's brainstorm this for a while."
Regression: "I just can't deal with such situations; I'll just have to give up."
Decompensation: (Person acts out his helplessness, incompetency, harmlessness more than he speaks about it)

Selective awareness:

Attention-Focusing Functions

Concentration: "I intend to work on this job now, and I'll worry about that later."
Denial: "Since every cloud has a silver lining, it's best to pay attention to that."
Fixation, distraction: "I listen only to the one true voice in the world" (or person's attention flits from one intense matter to another).

Affective-Impulse Regulations

Diversion: Affectivity expressed in diverse ways and situations

Sublimation: Person expresses affectivity, both positive and negative, toward objects, people, and activities in relevant and understood ways
Displacement: Person displaces his affective reactions from the instigating situation to express them in another situation of greater safety, for example, taking it out on his dog, sexualizing children, animals, or great concern for a body part.
Preoccupation: Person reacts affectively and intensely to a random assortment of people, situations, and objects.

Transformation: Primitive affectivity transformed to more complicated forms

Substitution: Person appears to have thoroughly and comfortably transformed uncivil feelings into their socialized forms.
Reaction formation: Person's reactions are so socialized that they seem strained, excessive, and brittle.
Unstable alternation: Person vacillates back and forth between the most uncivil, primitive expressions of feelings and the most excessive civilities.

Restraint: Affectivity restrained

Suppression: Person restrains his affective-cognitive reactions when their expression would be dysfunctional, but he knows what he feels and what he is doing.

Repression: Person curtails his cognitive knowledge and
                               reactions, irrespective of his condition and the
                               situation, but his affectivity is free-floating.
Depersonalization, amnesic: Person restrains his affective reactions to the
                               point that he loses track of where he is cog-
                               nitively and has little sense of who he is.

Although this taxonomy includes most of the commonly used ego
processes, it is likely not complete and may even be wrong in some ways. For
instance, the defensive function of undoing, its likely coping counterpart of rep-
aration, and its fragmentary form of restorative ritualisms have not been included
in most presentations because it is difficult to observe these processes in most
research settings. The actual application of this model to a person's ongoing ego
processing leads to observations of various patterns of ego functions. Most people
move up (or down) a hierarchy of preferred or situationally indicated functions to
deal with knotty problems; moreover under close scrutiny most people are seen
to be neither wholly defensive or wholly coping. Various combinations and patterns of ego functions also account for complex chains of ego actions. As an
example, take the clinically complex phenomenon of counterphobia: first, denial
is invoked as a simple negation of the original fear; second, projection leads to
the secret supposition that it is another, rather than the self, who is afraid; third,
displacement permits the negated reaction to be expressed and lived out.

The unusual features of the taxonomy are its overall organization of
previously disparate ideas, its attempt to distinguish the three modes of ego
processes within a single genre, and its specification of the various sectors of
functioning—cognitive, intraceptive-reflexive, attentional, and affective. As was
previously understood and commonly agreed with respect to the defensive processes, none of the functions is necessarily conscious or unconscious; rather their
operation is best regarded as "silent" or preconscious. They are known by their
actions, and if they are "unconscious," it is not an insurmountable task to help
their users to become aware (as in psychotherapy) that they persistently employ
particular methods to solve problems.

ORGANIZATION

The processes are not in themselves organizations, but their most general purpose
is that of facilitating the person's momentary and lifelong organizations. Several
features of the present ego model make this work possible. First, there is the
attempted comprehensiveness of the ego taxonomy itself which includes cognitive,
reflexive-intraceptive, attentional, and affective functions. Although we are im-

mediately concerned at this point with the person as a self-actional system, all of the processes are expressed in interpersonal as well as intrapersonal contexts. Second, and in parallel to the first point, is the fact that various situations instigate complementary intrapersonal hierarchical organizations of ego actions, however short-lived or mild the circumstances might be. More enduring contexts, such as a research career in physics, facilitate special, more durable kinds of organization. Third, and more separately, is the proposition that the person's everyday organizing attempts imply his larger, single enterprise of making self-consistent sense to himself. Fourth, the three general modes—coping, defensive, and fragmentary—form another kind of hierarchical organization. They represent a utilitarian hierarchy. The person will cope if he can, defend if he must, and fragment if he is forced, but whichever mode he uses, it is still in the service of his attempt to maintain organization. Whether he copes, defends, or fragments depends on his possibilities for maintaining a degree of equilibrium with the aid of his internal resources vis-à-vis the demands of a particular situation or a series of life situations. His coping does not insure his situational success nor do his defending or fragmenting entail his failure. Whatever mode he employs or whatever outcome he achieves depends on the nature of his situations; some may actually encourage defending or fragmenting reactions, for example, the so-called schizogenic family.

Many personality theories depend on sources external to ego processes to provide whatever organizational push is deemed necessary, as was noted in the last chapter. Psychoanalysis depends on the thrust of the id or superego, and behaviorism, on the effects of consistent external reinforcements from parents and the world. In the present formulation ego functions are the vehicles whereby organization is enacted, but the cause for synthesis lies in man's need for a degree of self-consistency. If there is merit in this proposal, the model of ego functioning does not need stipulations of physiological drive, id instincts, and perhaps not even traditional motives to explain most instances of dynamic, consistent functioning, and development. Instead, plans, intents, and enterprises may be sufficient to describe people's coherencies.

If this description of the nature of people's organizational efforts should prove wrong, it creates no great problem for the model. Its focus on ego processes makes it catholic in regard to motivation since all such thrusts must still be filtered through processes of ego decision. The model is also catholic with respect to terminal achievements, such as competence, self-actualization, or principled moral judgment, since whatever the outcome, ego processes are the midwives. Its coping mode makes it hospitable to the "new" stimulus-seeking motivations. Curiosity, exploration, intrinsic motivation, and the like are all intents of open systems that are experience-seeking, self-exposing, and information-gathering. All of these activities must be processed as well. Its defensive and fragmentation modes could be seen as simple intents to reduce the tension of drives in unbearable situations. If motivations to seek stimuli or to reduce drive tension turn out not to be literal or separate from ego plans themselves, these kinds of behaviors can then be ascribed, as they are here, to the intrinsic activity of men wishing to maintain a degree of togetherness as evolving beings. Altogether, diversity and complex individuation in both motivation and outcome are permitted by the present formulation since commonality is sought in processes. Just as there are alternative ego manifestations of the same drive, the same outcome can be achieved by diverse ego routes and for different reasons.

11

The Costs and Benefits of Denial

RICHARD S. LAZARUS

S ome years ago, to be sophisticated meant accepting *accurate reality testing* as the hallmark of mental health (Erikson 1950; Jahoda 1958; Maslow 1954; Menninger 1963). Everyone knew that self-deception was tantamount to mental disorder. If one wished to manage life successfully, it was not only necessary to know the truth, however painful, but to revel in it and even drown in it if need be. One recent form this doctrine has taken is that we must always be "in touch with our feelings" and absolutely honest about them with others. This outlook about reality is still dominant today (Haan 1977; Vaillant 1977). However, I no longer believe such a thesis is sound; one can argue, in fact, that illusion is necessary to positive mental health.

Clearly, illusion and self-deception are closely related concepts. To have an illusion is to believe something that is not so; therefore, assuming that there is an adequate basis for assessing reality (an assumption often unwarranted), it is a self-deception. But if we were to equate having illusions with being crazy (as Freud did with the defense mechanism of denial), most or all of us would have to be condemned to asylums. We have collective illusions, for example, that our society is free, moral, just; that successful people work harder, are smarter, more favored by God than others, and so on. We believe in a God (which we capitalize to express the reification), just as the Greeks believed in many gods. And we believe that our God is the true one while someone else's is not, or that there is no god. We also believe, to some degree, in personal immortality; Becker (1973) has argued that all our striving and products stem from a single, powerful psychological force—the denial of death. True, these notions may be only partly

This paper was supported in part by a research grant from the National Institute on Aging (AG 00799).

Constructive criticisms of an earlier draft by Professor Gerald A. Mendelsohn and members of my research group are appreciatively acknowledged.

illusory "working assumptions," but the line separating a working assumption from an illusion is indeed difficult to draw.

People not only have systems of belief that they share with others in their culture and social groups, but also maintain their own idiosyncratic set of beliefs about themselves and the world in which they live (Bem 1970). Many of these beliefs are passed down from forebears and may never be challenged or examined; they are what Rokeach (1968) calls "primitive" beliefs. Other beliefs and belief systems are forged out of the experiences of living. Some are implicit and barely accessible to awareness; others are formal and fully conscious, and form central personal themes affecting expectations and commitments. Some run counter to accepted wisdom, while others fit in comfortably with those shared by peers.

In any case, one finds a genuinely unsettling discrepancy between the way most mental health professionals view reality testing and self-deception, and the outlook of many writers of fiction and poetry who maintain that life is intolerable without illusion. It is instructive to consider how these fiction writers have treated the issue.

ILLUSION AND REALITY IN FICTION

The idea that illusion is essential to life is the core theme of Eugene O'Neill's *The Iceman Cometh*. The protagonist of the play, Hickey, who has unmasked himself and zealously wants to free the other blighted denizens of a saloon from their self-deceptions, destroys one man in the process and severely distresses all the others. An acceptable mode of living does not return until reality testing is abandoned in favor of illusion.

Henrik Ibsen's play *The Wild Duck* is built on the same theme that one must protect and nurture illusions, or in Ibsen's terms, "the saving lie." As with O'Neill's character Hickey, Ibsen creates the personage of Gregers, a neurotic moralist who presses his own destructive truths on a young peer, shattering the latter's illusions about his past and present, inadvertently encouraging the suicide of his 14-year-old daughter, and shattering his family's happiness and morale.

In *Man of La Mancha*, author Dale Wassermann tells us that instead of writing a cynical commentary on the remarkable human capacity for self-deception, his musical adaptation of Miguel de Cervantes' *Don Quixote* is a plea for illusion as an important and powerful sustaining force in life. We are urged to "dream the impossible dream," "fight the unbeatable foe." "Facts," says Wassermann's Don Quixote, "are the enemy of truth."

Consider also the vignette below from Allen Wheelis' (1966) *The Illusionless Man,* which clearly implies that without illusions our lives are empty. Speaking of the wedding to his bride-to-be, Lorabelle, for whom illusion is all, Henry, the illlusionless man, says:

God won't be there, honey; the women will be weeping for their own lost youth and innocence, the men wanting to have you in bed; and the priest standing slightly above us will be looking down your cleavage as his mouth goes dry; and the whole thing will be a primitive and preposterous attempt to invest copulation with dignity and permanence, to enforce responsibility for children by the authority of a myth no longer credible even to a child. (p. 17)

At the end of the story, when Henry and Lorabelle are near the end of their lives, Wheelis clearly tells us that illusion is the only workable way of life:

. . . he could see himself striving toward a condition of beauty or truth or goodness or love that did not exist, but whereas earlier in his life he had always said, "It's an illusion," and turned away, now he said, "There isn't anything else," and stayed with it; and though it cannot be said that they lived happily, exactly, and certainly not ever after, they did live. They lived—for a while—with ups and downs, good days and bad, and when it came time to die Lorabelle said, "Now we'll never be parted," and Henry smiled and kissed her and said to himself, "There isn't anything else," and they died. (p. 44)

Friedrich Dürrenmatt's powerful play *The Visit* is another illustration of how writers have often treated illusion and reality. The setting is a post-World War II town in Italy that has neither vitality nor economic viability. The townsfolk see hope in the anticipated return visit of an aging millionairess who had grown up there in poverty. They hope she will give them financial aid. As part of her offer of a huge sum, however, she stipulates a terrible condition, namely, the execution of her lover whose treachery had eventuated in the death of her child, imprisonment, and her ultimate banishment from the community. She now wants retribution, or "justice," as she puts it. At first the town leaders seem reluctant to accept the immoral bargain, but gradually it becomes apparent that everyone has been living on the anticipated windfall. The climax comes with the acceptance and formal celebration of the evil bargain and the execution of the lover. The town now thrives economically and socially. The mayor emphasizes that the money is not being accepted for its own sake, but for justice, and the townsfolk cheer. Dürrenmatt offers two social messages here: first, that prosperity and social vitality generally rest on evil; second, that evil is denied and disguised in the cloak of justice. In effect, he is saying that our most cherished social values depend on self-deception; they are illusions, little better than sugar-coated distortions of social reality, which is at root evil.

Perhaps the most celebrated modern literary figure to deal with illusion and reality and make it his trademark was Pirandello, whose plays offer multiple and complex variations on social- and self-deception. For example, *Henry IV* deals with a man who lives out the fantasy of being a long-dead monarch with hired retainers, advisors and the like, but who confuses all participants and on-lookers about whether he is really insane or merely play-acting. *It Is So! (If You Think So)* concerns the efforts of a townspeople to decipher the relationships of three people, a husband, a wife and her mother, each of whom has a very different conception of himself and the others. Not only do the husband and his mother-in-law view reality in diametrically opposed ways, but the wife, knowing that her spouse and mother cannot manage without their own self-deceptions, adapts herself to both simultaneously; thus, through a social deception, she engages in a humanitarian act toward those she loves. One of the townsfolk, who has insight into what is going on and probably speaks for the author, argues that each set of illusions is as real as any other. It is, therefore, impossible to know external reality without viewing it through the eyes of the individual person.

Summarizing Pirandello's outlook on illusion and reality in the play *Liolà,* Bentley states:

The play is about appearance and reality and shows, in what readers have always regarded as Pirandello's characteristically tricky fashion, that reality is not more real than appearance. Further, there are real appearances and merely apparent appearances. And just as appearances may be more real than reality, so merely apparent appearance may be more real than real appearance.

. . . for Uncle Simone, to appear to be a father is enough: appearance will establish his paternity more surely than actually having done the deed. However, strictly speaking, he does *not* appear to be a father; for the whole town knows the truth. He only appears to appear to be the father. That he appears to be the father is a kind of social pact or legal fiction. (1952:xiii)

Pirandello himself puts it as follows:

The harder the struggle for life and the more one's weakness is felt, the greater becomes the need for mutual deception. The simulation of force, honesty, sympathy, prudence, in short, of every virtue, and of that greatest virtue veracity, is a form of adjustment, an effective instrument of struggle. The "humorist" at once picks out such various simulations; amuses himself by unmasking them; is not indignant about them—he simply is that way!

And while the sociologist describes social life as it presents itself to external observation, the humorist, being a man of exceptional intuition, shows—nay, reveals—that appearances are one thing and the consciousness of the people concerned, in its inner essence, another. And yet people "lie psychologically" even as they "lie socially." And this lying to ourselves—living as we do, on the surface and not in the depths of our being—is a result of the social lying. The mind that gives back its own reflection is a solitary mind, but our internal solitude is never so great that suggestions from the communal life do not break in upon it with all the fictions and transferences which characterize them. (Bentley 1952:xiv)

In a vigorous assault on the concept of reality, *How Real Is Real?* communications psychologist Paul Watzlawick (1976) cites Fyodor Dostoevski and Franz Kafka as particularly good literary examplars of the "dissolution of reality." He observes Hermann Hesse's suggestion that Prince Myshkin in Dostoevski's *The Idiot* "does not break the Tablets of the Law, he simply turns them round and shows the contrary to them is written on the other side." Moreover, Watzlawick considers the metaphysical argument between Alyosha and Ivan in *The Brothers Karamazov* as the supreme literary example of this dissolution of reality. Ivan speaks of the imaginary confrontation between the Grand Inquisitor and Jesus, whom he has arrested after the latter's descent once again to earth. In the Inquisitor's view of reality, Jesus has betrayed humankind by wanting people to be free to choose, by rejecting miracles, and by refusing to rule the world as one unanimous and harmonious "ant heap." These three ideological positions have made the lot of humans miserable. On the other hand, the organized Church, says the Grand Inquisitor, keeps people happy by providing miracles, mystery, and authority. Thus we see two diametrically opposite views of reality—Jesus versus the Grand Inquisitor, in which the same virtue, humanitarianism, leads to quite logically opposite conclusions.

Thus, the importance of illusions may well be, as Bentley (1952:viii) has observed, "the main theme of literature in general."

ILLUSION AND REALITY
IN PSYCHOLOGICAL THOUGHT

Despite the longstanding dominant view of psychiatry and clinical psychology that accurate perception of reality is a hallmark of mental health, there have been numerous voices expressing the constructivist view that people create their own realities. The New Look movement of the 1950s also emphasized individual differences in the way events are perceived and cognized (Folkman, Schaefer, and Lazarus 1979; Lazarus 1978).

Some psychologists, such as Frankl (1955), have built entire psychological and therapeutic systems on the need for meaning in our lives, and have emphasized the devastating effects of the loss of such meaning. In a recent study of stress and coping in concentration camp survivors, my colleagues and I (Benner, Roskies, and Lazarus 1980) also suggested that such meaning served as a coping resource during the Holocaust, and that its loss helps to account for the troubled pattern of adjustment among survivors. This also seems to be a time in the industrialized Western world characterized by widespread loss of meanings that once served as anchors in people's lives, although the concept of alienation, which includes meaninglessness as a core concept (Kanungo 1979), was important in sociological thought before the turn of the century.

The important point, however, is that the kinds of beliefs on which people depend have an uncertain reality basis regardless of the fixity with which they may be held. One person's beliefs can be another's delusions. From a communications theory perspective, Watzlawick writes:

The reader will have noticed that I have been unable to avoid the use of terms like "really," "actually," "actual fact," and thus have apparently contradicted the main thesis of the book: that there is no absolute reality but only subjective and often contradictory conceptions of reality.

Very frequently, especially in psychiatry where the degree of an individual's "reality adaptation" plays a special role as the indicator of his normalcy, there is a confusion between two very different aspects of what we call reality. The first has to do with the purely physical, objectively discernible properties of things and is intimately linked with correct sensory perception, with questions of so-called common sense or with objective, repeatable, scientific verification. The second aspect is the attribution of meaning and value to these things and is based on communication.

This domain of reality, however, says nothing about the meaning and value of its contents. A small child may perceive a red traffic light just as clearly as an adult, but may not know that it means "do not cross the street now." The first-order reality of gold—that is, its physical properties—is known and can be verified at any time. But the role that gold has played since the dawn of human history, especially the fact that its value is determined twice daily by five men in a small office in the City of London and that this ascription of value profoundly influences many other aspects of our everyday reality, has very little, if anything, to do with the physical properties of gold. But it is this second reality of gold which may turn us into millionaires or lead us into bankruptcy. . . .

It is a delusion to believe that there is a "real" second-order reality and that "sane" people are more aware of it than "madmen." (1976:140–42)

Yet, in spite of the ambiguities in judging reality, strip us of beliefs in which we are heavily invested and we are deeply threatened, alienated, and perhaps even seriously disrupted in our life course and capacity for involvement and satisfaction. In effect, we pilot our lives by virtue of illusions that give meaning and substance to living. Life cannot easily be lived and enjoyed without a set of both shared deceptions and self-deceptions, that is, without beliefs that have no necessary relationship with reality.

Alfred Adler's concept of "fictional finalism" (see Ansbacher and Ansbacher 1956), which suggests that human actions are pulled by future considerations rather than pushed from the past, and which draws on Hans Vaihinger's (1911) *The Philosophy of "As If,"* is relevant here. Vaihinger argued that we live by fictional ideas that have no necessary connection with reality, for example, that "all men are created equal," "honesty is the best policy," and "the end justifies the means" (see also Hall and Lindsey 1957, on Alfred Adler).

That living "as if" could be a workable strategy in the real world is not surprising when we realize that from early childhood on we are treated to two alternative and simultaneous modes of thought: fairy tales and magic on the one hand, and the "real world" on the other. Yet both modes seem capable of residing comfortably together, and even of being fused. In his theory of cognitive dissonance, not only did Festinger (1957) fail to help us understand and predict which of many dissonance-resolving strategies people use, but I think he was wrong in presuming that it is always urgent for people to resolve dissonances. Quite the contrary, though some of us are more sensitive to self-contradictions than others, we tolerate them very easily, and much of the time do not even notice when we or others engage in them. Moreover, as Freud emphasized, humans have a great capacity for rationalizing or dispelling apparent contradictions.

Rather than equating the use of illusion with pathology, a more appropriate and interesting conclusion would be that mental health *requires* some self-deception. Otto Rank has also adopted this position by suggesting that the problem of the neurotic person is that he or she senses the truth, but cannot deal with it. Rank wrote:

With the truth, one cannot live. To be able to live one needs illusions, not only outer illusions such as art, religion, philosophy, science and love afford, but inner illusions which first condition the outer [i.e., a secure sense of one's active powers and of being able to count on the powers of others]. The more a man can take reality as truth, appearance as essence, the sounder, the better adjusted, the happier will he be . . . this constantly effective process of self-deceiving, pretending and blundering, is no psychopathological mechanism. (1936:251–52)

We must somehow face the seeming paradox that illusion or self-deception can be both adaptationally sound *and* capable of eliciting a heavy price. The paradox is: How is it possible for self-deception to be at once healthy and pathogenic? The paradox can be resolved by shifting to the more sophisticated question: What kinds and degrees of self-deceptions are damaging or constructive, and under what conditions, or as Becker has put it, "On what level of illusion does one live?" (1973:189). Alternatively, perhaps some illusions work better than others.

THE DENIAL PROCESS
AS A FORM OF SELF-DECEPTION

Denial is the negation of something in word or act, or more properly, both, since thoughts and actions are apt to be conjoined in any defense process. Logically speaking, the negation can be either of an impulse, feeling or thought, or of an external demand or reality; but, as we shall see, both Sigmund and Anna Freud distinguished denial from repression as being focused on external rather than internal conditions. Examples of denial in the larger sense include: I am not angry; I do not love you; I am not distressed; I am not seriously ill, dying or facing extinction; I am not in danger; he doesn't mean any harm; she is not a competitor, etc. Some of these denials refer to environmental realities, others to intrapsychic forces.

In speaking of the denial process, one is immediately faced with multiple ambiguities. One of the most common sources of confusion is the equation of denial with *avoidance*. Behaviorally speaking, for example, one may exhibit denial by not paying attention to or not speaking of the threatening connotation of events. Thus, if we wish to deny that we are mortally ill, we will also avoid this idea in thought, deed or word. This is what Anna Freud seems to have meant by denial "in word and act." Therefore, it is not an illogical presumption that a cancer patient who does not mention the terminal nature of the illness, particularly when there is provocation, is denying the imminence of death. Although the presumption is not unreasonable, it is incomplete. A terminal patient may know full well that he or she is dying, but prefer not to think or talk about it. This is not denial, but avoidance; there is a world of difference between the two.

Another source of ambiguity is that one cannot deny what is not *known*. Therefore, if physicians have evaded communicating the diagnosis and prognosis, or have pussyfooted about it or been excessively subtle with a person who is not particularly perceptive, then the impression that this person is denying may be incorrect. Here, what is being revealed is ignorance rather than denial. There is a considerable difference between shading things a bit, and a full-fledged process of denying what clearly should be known and acknowledged. Only very careful, in-depth exploration is capable of providing the empirical basis for this distinction.

In saying this I have accepted the idea, at least provisionally, that there are "realities" to be denied, although we must be extremely careful about how we deal with this idea. Put differently, if we could not take this position, there would be no basis for speaking about denial or for doing research on it. We cannot become completely hamstrung by the mataphysical problems. Thus, while subject to the usual diagnostic reservations, a rapidly developing carcinoma or a clogged coronary artery offers reasonable (realistic) bases for an appraisal that one's life is threatened. Similarly, the death of a loved one involves a reality that needs to be taken into account in living and for which a grief process would be appropriate. Whether the absence of grief is inappropriate is somewhat more difficult to assess.

Still another important source of confusion has to do with the extent to which the process of denial is tentative or well-entrenched, or as clinicians used to say, *well-consolidated*. A well-consolidated denial is presumably unshakeable. Many, perhaps most, denials are tentative constructions, responsive to this or that bit of information, mood, or whatever. Many patients who seem not to "know" they are dying really do know at some level of awareness, perhaps only dimly; this idea is expressed in the concept of "middle knowledge" (Weisman 1972b). Somehow, their declining physical fortunes, leakage from what has been said to them, contradictions in word and fact, all conspire to give the patient a sense, however slight, of what is happening. As Oken (1961) has put it, "A patient who is sick enough to die knows it without being told," although he or she must often play along with the reassuring, denial-focused statements of physicians, friends and relatives (Hackett and Weisman 1964). What is called denial in such cases may be, at best, only a *partial* denial process that depends on social circumstances to sustain it. A partial denial involves the capacity to bring the denied "reality" into awareness, or to act on the denied knowledge when it is necessary. It is not a full-fledged self-deception but only a tentative "suspension of belief."

In his treatment of denial in terminal cancer patients, Weisman (1972b) also addresses the question, "What is being denied?" He describes first-order denial as a denial of *facts,* for example, that a loved one has died, that one has cancer, or that manifest symptoms imply an important life-threatening illness. Such denial is usually tentative because the facts in a life-threatening or progressive disease ultimately make the first-order denial process untenable. In second-order denial, the potentially damaging or threatening primary facts are accepted, but the worst *implications* are denied. The distinction here is very much like that made by Watzlawick (1976) of first- and second-order realities, noted earlier. After all, it is the ultimate meaning of the facts for one's well-being that constitutes the threat. Third-order denial refers to the refusal to accept the further implications of one's extinction or personal death.

We have had the unfortunate habit in the past of treating the processes of coping as static states of mind, as fixed cognitive achievements (or traits), expressing the idea that the person has arrived at a stable interpretation (or defense). A better way of thinking is that, except for relatively rare instances of consolidated defenses, people are constantly seeking a way to comprehend what is happening to them; this *ongoing process* of construing reality is a constantly changing one, depending on many variables within and outside of the person. Thus, when we consider denial, or any other kind of self-deception or illusion, we are dealing with flux, and we must always be aware of the slippery nature of the event we are trying to understand (Lazarus 1978).

Consider the following excerpt of an interview from my own research on coping with stressful encounters, specifically the threat of being electrocuted:

There I was alone vacuuming up this water near all the exposed wiring . . . I hoped I wouldn't get electrocuted. But then I thought: "Well, this thing is made to take water and I have on rubber soles," and so I felt I wouldn't get electrocuted and kept on doing it but made sure I didn't touch anything. As soon as Bernie came back I said, "You're sure this is safe: I'm not going to get electrocuted doing this?" And he said, "I hope not; I don't think so." I know he was kidding. At least I hope he was. And he had been doing it before I arrived. He has a lot of common sense about these things so I shook off most of the fear and just ran the vacuum.

Then we drank our wine and laughed at each other and just let it go . . knowing we had to face it again tomorrow. We changed the situation by working on it together. I got over my anxiety about the wires by being very careful and knowing that Bernie wouldn't have me do something dangerous. The glass of wine really made me feel better. What else can you do? I don't like to get all upset. That was the first time we'd had a glass of wine at work. After all, life is just a game. It wasn't severe anxiety and I moved to a safer spot and everything was okay. I just let go of the fear. I did it by concentrating on what I was doing. I am just glad I was wearing crepe soles.

Many things seem to be happening here, including recognition of the danger, and efforts to bring the fear under control by bravado and avoidance. Still, the coping process seems also to contain denial-like elements, including the effort to accept Bernie's reassurance ("He has a lot of common sense" and "Bernie wouldn't have me do something dangerous"). To anyone (an observer) aware of the danger of standing in water near exposed wiring, to be convinced so easily and reassured by the crepe soles seems to involve a tremendous degree of denial. Yet how can we assess the actual sense of danger the person speaking could have experienced on the basis of what she saw and knew?

Another lesson of importance is that denial is not a single act, but a highly *diverse set of processes* that respond to different external and internal conditions, and that are inferred with varying degrees of confidence on the part of the observer. There can be no satisfactory answer to the question of the adaptational outcomes of denial without there also being a sound basis for identifying, describing and measuring the defensive process itself. Hasty and superficial measurement is hardly the way to undertake research on the problem (see Horowitz et al. 1975 . . . for examples of an in-depth process measurement approach).

A thorough exposition of the concept of denial in theoretical terms is impossible to undertake here. It would go back to Freud, follow his shifting conceptions of defense in general, and proceed to subsequent psychoanalytic writers. Such an account is currently available in a book by Sjöbäck (1973), who gives considerable space to the history of thought about denial. As was noted earlier, Freud actually saw denial as a "disavowal" (to use his term) of external reality. It was also assumed to occur only in psychosis. He and others, including Anna Freud (1937) and Otto Fenichel (1945), continued this conception in later writing. On the one hand, Anna Freud may have changed her view of the matter much later, and, at least by implication appeared to regard denial as capable of having positive clinical significance. In a book by Bergmann, on which Anna Freud collaborated, a case is reported of a child with polio whose father's very strong denial was said to have potentiated remarkable feats of physical function in the sick child. About this, Bergmann wrote:

> It is interesting to realize that the physical and medical evaluation could not explain how this child managed to walk so well with or without the cane because tests of muscle strength revealed quite insufficient power for such an accomplishment. With Carl it was evidently a case of "mind over matter." What had also to be taken into account was the father's denial of the facts, his unfaltering belief that everything was going to be all right again. Actually, it must have been the influence of the father's unrealistic attitude (and not my sensible advice) which contributed to Carl's amazingly successful recovery, the degree of which could not be explained in physical terms. (1958:111)

Still others (Jacobson 1957) later extended the concept of denial to mean a defense against intrapsychic forces (i.e., instinctual fantasies, wishes and impulses). Such an enlargement of the concept, however, has produced confusion. For example, if denial is a defense against intrapsychic processes as well as external reality, how is it to be distinguished from repression? The problem has never been resolved satisfactorily, and is part of the continuing uncertainty and confusion about definition and measurement (Fine, Joseph, and Waldhorn 1969; Lipowski 1970). Whether it is more useful to distinguish among many types of denial, as I do here, as well as among related processes such as avoidance, or to speak of a generalized process, a family of denial, as it were, that includes a large range of specific patterns, remains at issue.

What then is the resolution of the seeming paradox, stated earlier, that the use of denial is both harmful and beneficial; that although we venerate reality testing as a hallmark of mental health, life is intolerable without illusion? The resolution takes two forms. First, we must recognize that denial consists of many diverse forms, some of which are disavowals of clear realities, and others merely implications of avoidance. The latter merges with affirmations or positive thinking in the face of ambiguous circumstances; in short, it is what we mean by illusion. By carefully making such distinctions, both definitionally and in assessment, we can ultimately justify the seemingly contradictory assertion that sometimes denial-related processes have positive outcomes and other times negative. Second, we can recognize that the costs and benefits of denial and denial-like coping processes depend on the context in which the processes occur. That is, the adaptational outcome must be considered in relation to the situational demands and constraints on action, and the resources available to the person, in short, the coping alternatives. In the section that follows, some of these contextual variables play important roles in producing positive or negative outcomes.

RESEARCH ON DENIAL-LIKE PROCESSES
AND THEIR CONSEQUENCES

The definitional and conceptual confusion that surrounds denial, as it does most other defensive processes, makes the problem of evaluating its outcomes even more difficult. For example, although there are a substantial number of research studies of denial-like processes, it is difficult to compare them because of variations in the way the coping process is understood and measured.

In this connection, it is instructive to consider a rating scale designed by Hackett and Cassem (1974) to measure denial in coronary care patients; it is based on Anna Freud's concept that denial is a general psychological goal that can be achieved in many diverse ways. Hackett and Cassem's scale includes some items that express denial explicitly in words, and others in which the denial is implicit, as in the item, "The patient avoids talking about the disability." We have already seen that combining alternative tactics such as avoidance and denial in word under the same general rubric, risks confusion about which process is actually being used by the person. It may be a much better research strategy to carefully differentiate diverse denial-like processes so that their impact on adaptational outcome can also be distinguished.

Nevertheless, it is worth trying to wade into some of this research in an effort to extract whatever hypothetical principles we can, recognizing that they must be tentative at best. To undertake this I have chosen the device of examining two types of studies: those in which denial seems to have damaging adaptational outcomes, and those having constructive ones. In making this categorization I have had to overlook some definitional and measurement problems. This is why I have used the term "denial-like processes" in all headings in place of "denial" per se. The studies cited below vary greatly in their methods of assessing the coping process, although the word "denial" is used in all. Strictly speaking, one cannot treat them as studies of denial without evading the very definitional issues I raised earlier.

No attempt has been made to provide a thorough review of all research; the citations were chosen to be illustrative. However, a fuller list of studies has been offered previously (Wortman and Dunkel-Schetter 1979).

Studies of Denial-Like Processes with Damaging Outcomes

An important line of thought about denial has come from the work of Lindemann (1944) and Bowlby (1961) on grieving. Lindemann found denial of pain and distress a common feature of the grief process among the bereaved. Other observers have suggested a similar pattern among those sustaining an incapacitating loss such as spinal cord injury (Dembo, Leviton, and Wright 1956;

McDaniel and Sexton 1970; Wright 1960). Implicit in Lindemann's concept of "grief work" was the notion that if the bereaved person was prevented by processes such as denial and avoidance from grieving fully, it would result in failure to negotiate the bereavement crisis; the latter requires emancipation from the emotional bondage to the deceased and the formation of new relationships.

A parallel theme was also stated later by Janis (1958, 1974) in the concept of the "work of worrying." Janis found that low fear prior to surgery was associated with high distress and behavioral difficulties during the later recovery period; this was consistent with the view that denial of threat prevented the patient from realistically anticipating and working through the post-surgical discomforts. Although there was no direct measure of denial, and the findings on which this concept was based have not been replicated, the concept has had good staying power because of its ring of truth and supportive findings from other types of investigations (Cohen and Lazarus 1979).

In his more recent writings about decision-making (Janis and Mann 1977), vigilance continues to be viewed as desirable because it potentiates a search for information and the weighing of alternative coping strategies in the face of threat. Research by Horowitz (1975) makes use of an idea similar to the "work of worrying," namely, the tendency for unresolved threats (in the form of thoughts and images) to enter into awareness as unwanted intrusions (see also Freud's concept of repetition compulsion). Breger's (1967) treatment of dreams as efforts by the person to cope cognitively with unresolved conflicts also clearly falls within the same conceptual tradition.

Another direct descendant of this line of thought is the series of studies generated and reviewed by Goldstein (1973), which uses a sentence completion test measure of vigilance (or sensitization) and avoidance (repression) as the opposite extremes of a coping continuum. Vigilants are those who accept and elaborate fully on the threatening meaning conveyed by incomplete sentence stems. (To the stem "I hate," they write: "my parents," "nosey people," "anyone who is smarter than me," etc.) Avoiders seem to evade or deny what the researcher presumes is the threatening content. (To the stem "I hate," they write: "to be caught in the rain without an umbrella," "no one.") Nonspecific defenders fall into neither extreme category, and are said to adapt their form of coping flexibly to the circumstances. To oversimplify this research (Andrew 1970; DeLong 1970), avoiders do not do well in anticipatory threat situations or when they are exposed to repeated threats (e.g., when they are shown the same stressful movie more than once). The assumption is that their characteristic mode of coping prevents coming to terms with the threat. Avoiders and vigilants also seem to be differentially benefited by diverse interventions in anticipatory stress situations—avoiders do better when left alone; vigilants respond best to detailed preparation. Although the data are more complicated and unclear than one would wish, they seem consistent with the concepts of grief work and the work of worrying, and point to avoidance or denial as processes that can interfere with successful mastery by preventing appropriate cognitive coping prior to a stressful confrontation.

A recent study of asthmatic patients (Staudenmayer et al. 1979) further supports the above ideas, but adds an important behavioral dimension. Asthmatics were divided into those who respond to symptoms with vigilance and those who disregard them. When the slightest sign of a developing attack is noticed, the former grow fearful and vigilant; the latter evade or deny the seriousness of the symptom and wait out the situation, expecting or hoping that the attack will not materialize and the symptoms will disappear. These authors found that the high-fear, vigilance patients were far less likely to be rehospitalized over a six-month period than the low-fear, denial-oriented patients. The former tended to take action quickly when breathing difficulties ensued, while the latter tended to disregard these difficulties, and hence allowed the attack to progress too far to treat short of hospitalization. Here too we see the value of vigilance and the high cost of avoidance and/or denial in a medical outcome; in this case the denial-like coping process leads to the failure to act in one's own best interest.

An oft-cited and even clearer demonstration of the theme that denial may interfere with actions necessary to survival may be found in the research of Katz et al. (1970) with women who discovered a breast lump. Denial, mixed with rationalization, was reported to have been the most common form of coping employed, being used by 11 out of 30 subjects. They found that there was often considerable delay in getting medical attention, which in the event the lump was malignant, added greatly to the danger of metastasis and reduced the chances for surgical care. Delays in seeking medical help for a heart attack have also been reported. Von Kugelgen (1975) and Hackett and Cassem (1975) cite cases of men who, while undergoing such an attack, did vigorous pushups or climbed flights of stairs to convince themselves that what they were experiencing was not a heart attack.

Studies of Denial-Like Processes with Constructive Outcomes

In recent years, clinical thought has shifted considerably from an emphasis on intrapsychic conflict to environmental conditions, such as catastrophic illness, as factors in adaptational crises in ordinary people (Lipowski 1970). In all likelihood, this shift in part reflects the positive mental health movement and a retreat from a preoccupation solely with inner dynamics and pathology. A series of studies influenced by the research and theorizing of Roy Grinker, Sr. (Offer and Freedman 1972) has been particularly influential in the growing acceptance of the idea that denial-like processes could have positive as well as negative adaptational consequences. Defensive processes are not treated as the exclusive property of "sick" minds, but as an integral feature of healthy coping as well.

Included in this research are studies of the victims of severe and incapacitating burns (Hamburg, Hamburg, and deGoza 1953), of paralytic polio (Visotsky et al. 1961), and other life crises, summarized analytically by Hamburg and Adams. A major thesis has been that self-deception, for example, by denial of the seriousness of the problem, is often a valuable initial form of coping, occurring at a time when the person is confused and weakened and therefore unable to act constructively and realistically. In a severe and sudden crisis, "time for 'preparation' is likely to be bought by temporary self-deception, in such a way as to make recognition of threatening elements gradual and manageable" (1967:283). Davis (1963) too has observed that denial of the gravity of the illness (polio) and its damaging implications permits the parents to have a longer time perspective about their child's recovery, and to be able to accept as milestones comparatively small steps toward recovery, such as being fitted with leg braces. And in writing about the atomic holocaust at Hiroshima, Lifton has suggested that early denial might facilitate ultimate adjustment by allowing the survivors to engage in a "psychic closing off" from "the threat [of psychosis] posed by the overwhelming evidence of actual physical death" (1964:208). The above, then, offers a stage-related concept of denial in which the "disavowal" of reality is temporary and helps the person to get through the devastating early period of loss and threat; it sets the stage for later acknowledgment (Kübler-Ross 1969) of the situation and the mobilization of more realistic coping efforts.

A number of research studies have suggested that there is a high incidence of denial-like coping processes in severe, incapacitating illness, and that these coping activities can have positive adaptational consequences. Denial of the danger and its imminence has been reported as common in cancer (Cobb et al. 1954), with denial inferred from retrospective depth interviews and identified to some degree in 90 percent of a sample of 840 patients. In patients with spinal cord injuries, Dinardo (1971) used the Byrne questionnaire scale of repression-sensitization, a dimension akin theoretically to Goldstein's (1973) sentence completion measure; he found that repressors displayed greater self-esteem than sensitizers; moreover the latter type of injured persons were significantly less happy. Dinardo also obtained ratings of adjustment from physical therapists, occupational therapists and nurses, and found that repressors seemed to do better, although the difference was not statistically significant. In considering this type of evidence, we must be wary of the measure itself (see also Lefcourt 1966). First, the Byrne scale is a trait rather than process measure. Second, it can be as readily regarded as a measure of anxiety as a coping process, though these concepts are quite interdependent. Third, there appears to be no correlation among the three diverse trait measures of presumably the same process (Lazarus, Averill and Opton 1974).

Stern, Pascale, and McLoone (1976), on the other hand, used interview techniques to assess the coping process following acute myocardial infarction. What are called "deniers" by the authors (representing 25 percent of the sample) were more generally optimistic, did very well in returning to work and sexual functioning, and suffered less from post-coronary depression and anxiety. This finding is consistent with Hackett, Cassem, and Wishnie's (1968) claim that denial of the danger of death may be associated with decreased mortality and better post-coronary adjustment in the coronary care unit.

Cohen and Lazarus (1973) have reported a study of vigilance and avoidance of relevant information by patients the night before surgery. Patients who avoided such information showed a more rapid recovery post-surgically, fewer minor complications, and less distress than vigilant patients, a finding quite opposite to that of Janis. The process measure did not correlate at all with a trait measure of repression-sensitization (similar to Byrne's), which in turn failed to correlate with outcome. The authors offer both an institutional and psychological interpretation. With respect to the former, it is possible that physicians were guided in their decision to send patients home by virtue of their manifest attitude; pollyanna avoider-deniers would seem better candidates for early dismissal than worried, complaining vigilants. As to the psychological interpretation, a hospital environment encourages passivity and conformity, which would make vigilance a useless coping strategy since little or nothing one does will affect one's actual fate.

More equivocal concerning the outcome of denial is the research of Wolff et al (1964) with the parents of children dying of leukemia. This well-known study found that parents who were "well-defended" (largely through denial-like forms of cognitive coping) showed lower levels of corticosteroid secretion during the child's illness than those who were poorly defended. Thus, to the extent that lowered stress levels can be considered a positive consequence, denial-like coping had positive adaptational value. On the other hand, a follow-up study with the same parents (Hofer et al. 1972) obtained data suggestive of a later reversal: Those who had high secretion levels prior to the child's death showed lower levels many months after; alternatively, those who had low prior levels had higher ones later.

If this finding turns out to be solid and does not merely represent regression to the mean, it also points up the idea that one must be time-oriented in evaluating adaptational outcomes of coping. One might say, for example, that the well-defended parents benefited *during* the illness, but were more vulnerable *after* the child's death because they failed to do "grief work"; in contrast, those who continued consciously to struggle with the impending tragedy were better off later because of the anticipatory coping. To complicate matters further, a later study by Townes, Wold, and Holmes (1974) suggests that fathers did the work of grieving prior to the child's death while mothers did not, so that subsequent mourning was sustained and more intense for the latter. Although such data as these are suggestive (the difference did not reach statistical significance in the study by Townes et al.), none of the studies cited in this research arena is capable of clearly settling the issue of denial and the passage of time. Nevertheless, they are consistent with the concepts of anticipatory coping and with the antithetical role denial might play in it. We are still left with the possibility that denial may be helpful only in a limited time frame, and might exact a price later on.

Recent observations by Levine and Zigler (1975) on denial in stroke victims may also be considered here. Measuring denial idiosyncratically by examining their real- versus ideal-self disparity, stroke victims were found to have the greatest use of denial (i.e., showed a larger discrepancy between presumed loss of function and how it was appraised) compared with two other handicapped groups, namely, victims of lung cancer and heart disease. Denial, assessed in this way, appeared to produce a comparative state of emotional equanimity in the stroke patients despite the fact that they actually suffered the greatest damage to functioning among the three disorders. One could argue, moreover, that a more realistic self-assessment by the stroke victims would have had little value, adaptationally speaking, since little or nothing more could have been done about their deficits even with a more realistic appraisal. Perhaps it could be said in such an instance that ignorance is more functional than the bitter truth.

Before leaving studies in which denial has proved constructive, it is worth noting a recent neurohumoral discovery that, with a small leap of the imagination, seems to have a bearing. Biochemists (Guillemin et al. 1977) have discovered that, simultaneous with the secretion under stress of ACTH by the pituitary gland, another hormone called endorphin-B is also secreted. ACTH stimulates secretion of corticosteroids by the adrenals; endorphin-B seems to affect morphine-sensitive brain tissue, presumably acting like an analgesic and psychedelic. A severely wounded animal, or a badly frightened or enraged one, might well be expected to produce not only corticosteroids (as in Selye's GAS stage of resistance), but also this morphine-like substance. This may help explain why Beecher (1957) and others have observed a remarkable absence of pain in wounded soldiers, or why in battle men sometimes throw themselves into combat seemingly oblivious of the consequences. It may not be altogether fanciful to suggest that chemicals such as endorphin-B could be the neurohumoral analogue of denial and other comforting cognitions (Mechanic 1978b) or, as I have elsewhere referred to them, palliative forms of coping. The analogy could be reassuring to those who take seriously the thesis that palliative forms of coping, denial among them, might play a valuable part in the overall human armamentarium of coping.

PRINCIPLES CONCERNING COSTS AND BENEFITS OF DENIAL-LIKE COPING PROCESSES

In accordance with these analyses and the research cited above, a useful summary of the adaptational consequences of denial-like processes is offered, which contains four principles:

(1) The first is a version of an old truth, namely, that circumstances alter cases. Put more pedantically, denial can have positive value under certain conditions and negative value under others. Specifically, if direct action to change the damaging or threatening person-environment transaction is adaptationally essential or useful, the family of processes called denial (when they undermine such action by avoiding or disavowing the threat or danger) will be destructive. On the other hand, when direct action is irrelevant to the adaptational outcome, then denial-like processes have no necessarily damaging consequences, and could even be of value by reducing distress and allowing the person to get on with other matters.

This principle also allows us to extrapolate to other damaging circumstances, for example, illnesses such as kidney failure and diabetes. Control of these illnesses depends on vigilant attention to diet and exercise, and to behavioral and bodily signals of the need for dialysis or insulin. To the extent that successful denial of fact or damaging implications pushes the person to overlook such signals and therefore to evade suitable actions, it is counterproductive and could even be fatal. However, depression and disengagement are also enemies of efforts to stay alive and functioning well, and to mobilize the necessary vigilance over a long time requires relatively good morale and the feeling of hope. It could be argued, therefore, that some positive thinking in the face of a severe hardship might also prove of value and even be necessary.

The distinction implied in principle one is between what my colleagues and I have been calling *problem-focused coping* and *emotion-focused coping,* and which I had earlier spoken of as direct action and palliation (Lazarus and Launier 1978). They represent two of the most important functions of coping, namely, that of changing a damaging or threatening relationship between person and environment (problem-focused) and regulating the emotional distress produced by that relationship (emotion-focused). In current research in my laboratory, Folkman and Lazarus (1980) found that in every complex stressful encounter people use a mixture of both kinds of coping. Moreover, when an encounter is appraised as permitting little or nothing to be done, there is a pull toward emotion-focused coping; and when it is appraised as permitting constructive actions, the shift is to problem-focused modes. Folkman also found that work pulls for more problem-focused modes, and illness pulls for emotion-focused ones. Denial clearly falls within the emotion-focused function, and as noted below in principle four, when denial is partial, tentative or minimal in scope, it does not necessarily undermine the *simultaneous* use of problem-focused forms of coping when these might have relevance to the person's plight.

(2) The second principle is that when a given type of stress must be encountered again and again, then denial (which could keep up morale and

keep down distress) will prevent ultimate mastery. In effect, there are *time-related* implications in the use of denial.

(3) The third principle is also *time-related*. Denial can have positive value at an early stage of coping when the person's resources are insufficient to cope in a more problem-focused way. Severely injured patients gain from denial when their life hangs in balance, when they are too weak or shocked to act constructively and so need to be supported by others. Thus, the patient with spinal cord injury is helped for a while by believing that bodily functions that have been lost will return, or that the incapacitation is not as severe as it seems. Only later will the person be strong enough to come to terms with the reality of the condition and ultimately struggle to cope in a practical, problem-focused sense. There is no contradiction between principles two and three. Both agree that denial is valuable, but only in an early stage. Principle two concerns the price of denial for later similar encounters, while principle three treats denial as a temporary preservative before more problem-focused forms of coping can be brought to bear.

(4) Principle four is that some *kinds* of denial are more or less fruitless and dangerous, while others may have considerable value. For example, of two objects of denial, emotional distress and the harm or threat inherent in some encounter, the former has less utility because it provides little reason for the person actually to feel better—while denying, the person still feels upset. On the other hand, if we can believe that we are not seriously ill, or not in some danger, there is no reason to be upset; the threat has been shortcircuited (Lazarus and Alfert 1964; Lazarus et al. 1965). Furthermore, logically it would seem to be far more dangerous to deny what is clear and unambiguous than to deny what cannot be known for certain. The most obvious example is the difference between denial of *fact* and denial of *implication*. The fact that one is sick is harder to deny successfully than the implication that one is going to die soon, and still harder to deny than the notion that one will in some sense live on after death. There is an insightful joke that wherever one goes after death can't be such a bad place since no one has ever returned to complain about it. If one denies what is ambiguous, the fiction is more easily sustained and is apt to be less pernicious adaptationally.

The last principle above also concerns instances in which denial is partial, tentative, or minimal in scope (as in Lipowski's, [1970], term "minimization"). Then it should be far less pernicious, and often quite useful. I started by noting some of the self-deceptions or illusions people live by and how important they are for mental health. It is useful to remember that these self-deceptions are not usually challenged by evidence, nor do we even try to test them by the methods of science. This kind of denial is closer to the sense of "as if," to illusion in the more literary usage, or to working fictions or assumptions.

Moreover, throughout human history such working fictions have been regarded as useful not only in maintaining morale, but in aiding effective adaptation. An example from stress and coping theory is the distinction between two ways in which the same demanding or troubling event can be appraised. One person is *threatened* by it, the other *challenged* (e.g., Lazarus 1978; Lazarus and Launier 1978; Lazarus et al. 1980). Some people appear to have the happy faculty of viewing harsh experiences in a positive, challenging light while others seem constantly to view them dourly as threats. There is even reason to think that the former persons feel better and perform more effectively in the face of adversity than the latter. It is an important and practical research issue.

The discussion of threat and challenge above might remind us of a popular inspirational book of several decades past, Norman Vincent Peale's *The Power of Positive Thinking,* which exhorted the reader to think positively even about life's travails and setbacks as the most serviceable way of life. To propose that it is better to appraise a stressful encounter as a challenge than as a threat is not very different from arguing that we would all lead happier, more productive lives if we could learn to think positively. Such an outlook is nicely expressed in the Hebrew expression common to Israelis, *yiheyeh beseder* (it will be all right). The problem with Peale's inspirational message is not that he was altogether wrong about this, but, as in the case of all advice and inspirational messages, those who need them most are least able to use them effectively.

12

Stressful Life Events, Personality, and Health: An Inquiry Into Hardiness

SUZANNE C. KOBASA

An exceptional number of studies in the last twenty years (cf. Dohrenwend and Dohrenwend 1974; Gunderson and Rahe 1974) have suggested that stressful life events precipitate somatic and psychological disease. This article considers the importance of personality as a conditioner of the illness-provoking effects of stress.

During the last decade, investigators have shown that the recent life histories of hospitalized persons contain significantly more frequent and serious stressful events than do histories of matched controls from the general population (e.g., Paykel 1974) and that Navy personnel who begin a cruise with high stress scores suffer more illness episodes during the months at sea than do sailors who start out with low stress scores (Rahe 1974). But the possibility of a causal connection between stress and illness is hardly a new idea. Physicians, philosophers, and persons simply concerned about staying healthy have long wondered about the etiological significance of life events. The distinctiveness of recent research lies in its attempt to define and measure stress.

In the current studies, a life event is defined as stressful if it causes changes in, and demands readjustment of, an *average person's normal routine*. This definition of stress has relied upon the empirical demonstration (Holmes and

This article is based on the author's doctoral dissertation (Kobasa 1977), submitted to the Department of Behavioral Sciences at the University of Chicago. The preparation of this manuscript was supported in part by Public Health Service Grant MH-28839-01 from the National Institute of Mental Health. The author wishes to thank Robert R. J. Hilker, James Kennedy, and all of the executives who participated in the study. Special appreciation is extended to Salvatore R. Maddi who supervised the project. Chase P. Kimball, David E. Orlinsky, and Marvin Zonis contributed many useful suggestions as dissertation committee members.

Masuda 1974; Holmes and Rahe 1967b) that there is a general consensus about the degree to which specific life occurrences involve change and require readjustment. This consensus emerged from the ratings of stressfulness of a long list of events made by thousands of subjects varying in age, sex, socioeconomic status, race, cultural background, education, and religion. From this consensus, stressfulness weights for the life events were obtained.

Deriving from this research is the Schedule of Recent Life Events (Holmes and Rahe, 1967b), which contains positive (e.g., marriage), negative (e.g., illness of a family member), frequent (e.g., minor traffic violation), and rare (e.g., death of a child) occurrences. The associated Social Readjustment Rating Scale (Rahe et al. 1971) gives the consensual weights for these events (e.g., on a scale from 1 to 100, divorce gets a mean score of 73 and vacation, a score of 13). The stressfulness of a particular person's life is measured in this procedure by finding out what events he or she has encountered and scoring the occurrences according to their consensually quantified weights.

This consensual approach to stress as measurable environmental input has allowed easy collection of large amounts of data and uncomplicated analysis of the statistical relationship between stressful life events and illness onset. The findings of stress research have had dramatic impact in both professional journals and popular magazines. In the journals (e.g., Rabkin and Struening 1976), one usually finds some caution urged about too quickly concluding a causal relationship between stress and illness on the basis of correlational and methodologically weak studies. This warning is mitigated, however, by a sense of optimism that there is something to this stress and illness connection and a wish for studies that are more sophisticated in design and methods of analysis. But in the popular literature (e.g., Wolfe 1972), final conclusions have already been drawn. Readers are provided with a self-administered stress test and told the likelihood of illness associated with each total stress score (e.g., a score above 300 means an 80 percent chance of getting sick). Readers whose stress scores are high are warned that if they wish to remain healthy they should avoid additional stressful encounters, even to the point of shunning such everyday necessities as driving on the Los Angeles Freeway.

This advice seems inadequate, insofar as modern life can be characterized as inherently stressful (Brodsky 1977; Toffler 1970). A person might indeed be able to keep from getting married or taking on a new mortgage, but how can one prevent the effects of pollution and overcrowding or of being assigned to a different job when his or her company signs a new contract? Further, increasing levels of stress tend to coincide with increasing opportunities and potential resources (Kobasa, Hilker, and Maddi 1977).[1] By avoiding stress, modern persons may be turning away from a chance to better their lives.

Before deciding to avoid stressful life at any cost, one should consider the actual magnitude of the relationship between stress and illness. Although correlations range from .20 to .78, the majority fall below .30, and in Rahe's naval data, the correlations are consistently around .12 (Rabkin and Struening 1976). Many stress and illness researchers, in their preoccupation with group means, have failed to question the distribution of their data. Variability of both stress and illness scores within groups has been observed to be extreme in several studies (Wershow and Reinhart 1974). One likely explanation for these data is the presence of subjects with high stress scores who are not getting sick. Oddly, such subjects have been overlooked in the popular and professional literature on stress and illness.

Studying Stressed
but Healthy Persons

In contrast, the present study considers how highly stressed subjects who remain healthy differ from those who show illness along with high stress. Studying the individual who undergoes high degrees of stress without falling ill amounts to inquiring about the mediating factors that affect the way one reacts to stress. Holmes and Masuda (1974) and the majority of other stress investigators attempt to draw a direct causal link between the occurrence of stressful life events and the onset of illness by reference to the physiological model of a stress reaction formulated by Hans Selye (1956). Stressful life events are said to evoke "adaptive efforts by the human organism that are faulty in kind or duration, lower 'bodily resistance' and enhance the probability of disease occurrence" (Holmes and Masuda 1974: 68). Holmes and others, however, fail to take into account what Selye goes on to say about individual differences and the stress reaction. In the study described in this article, the more subtle points in Selye's work are referred to, in the attempt to consider factors in the stress reaction that serve to deflect the negative impact of stressful events. Mediators of the stress and illness connection, which probably include physiological predisposition, early childhood experiences, and social resources, as well as the mediator emphasized here, personality, are together responsible for what Selye calls the distinctive way in which each individual "takes to" stressful life occurrences.

The proposition of this study is that persons who experience high degrees of stress without falling ill have a personality structure differentiating them from persons who become sick under stress. This personality difference is best characterized by the term *hardiness*. The conceptual source of the supposition, in contrast to the passive and reactive view of humankind found in most stress and illness work, is a set of approaches to human behavior that Maddi (1976), in his categorization of the major personality theories, calls fulfillment theories. The hardy personality type formulated here builds upon the theorizing of existential psychologists (Kobasa and Maddi 1977; Maddi 1975) on the strenuousness of authentic living, White (1959) on competence, Allport (1955) on propriate striving, and Fromm (1947) on the productive orientation. Hardy persons are considered to possess three general characteristics: (a) the belief that they can control or influence the events of their experience; (b) an ability to feel deeply involved in or committed to the activities of their lives, and (c) the anticipation of change as an exciting challenge to further development. Much research has already shown the advantages in behavior of control (e.g., Lefcourt 1973; Rodin and Langer 1977; Rotter, Seeman and Liverant 1962; Seligman 1975), commitment (e.g., Antonovsky 1974; Kobasa and Maddi 1977; Lazarus 1966; Lazarus, Averill and Opton 1974; Moss 1973), and challenge (Fiske and Maddi 1961; Maddi 1967). In discussing the hypotheses presented below, the implications of theory and research concerning these three general characteristics are extended to considerations of health and illness.

Hypothesis 1. *Among persons under stress, those who have a greater sense of control over what occurs in their lives will remain healthier than those who feel powerless in the face of external forces.* Following the model proposed by Averill (1973) to explain his laboratory observation that some organisms are not debilitated by stressful stimuli, the highly stressed but healthy person is hypothesized to have (a) decisional control, or the capability of autonomously choosing among various courses of action to handle the stress; (b) cognitive control, or the ability to interpret, appraise, and incorporate various sorts of stressful events into an ongoing life plan and, thereby, deactivate their jarring effects; and (c) coping skill, or a greater repertory of suitable responses to stress developed through a characteristic motivation to achieve across all situations. In contrast, the highly stressed persons who become ill are powerless, nihilistic, and low in motivation for achievement. When stress occurs, they are without recourse for its resolution, give up what little control they do possess, and succumb to the incapacity of illness.

Hypothesis 2. *Among persons under stress, those who feel committed to the various areas of their lives will remain healthier than those who are alienated.* Committed persons have a belief system that minimizes the perceived threat of any given stressful life event. The encounter with a stressful environment is mitigated by a sense of purpose that prevents giving up on one's social context and oneself in times of great pressure. Committed persons feel an involvement with others that serves as a generalized resistance resource against the impact of stress (Antonovsky 1974). Committed persons have both a reason to and an ability to turn to others for assistance in times demanding readjustment.

Although commitment to all areas of life—work, social institutions, interpersonal relationships, family, and self—should be characteristic of highly stressed persons who do not fall ill, one area is singled out as particularly important for health. Staying healthy under stress is critically dependent upon a strong sense of commitment to self. An ability to recognize one's distinctive values, goals, and priorities and an appreciation of one's capacity to have purpose and to make decisions support the internal balance and structure that White and other theorists (cf. Coelho, Hamburg, and Adams 1974) deem essential for the accurate assessment of the threat posed by a particular life situation and for the competent handling of it.

Hypothesis 3. Among persons under stress, those who view change as a challenge will remain healthier than those who view it as a threat. Persons who feel positively about change are catalysts in their environment and are well practiced at responding to the unexpected. Because they value a life filled with interesting experiences, change seekers have well explored their environment and know where to turn for resources to aid them in coping with stress. They have a predisposition to be cognitively flexible, which allows them to integrate and effectively appraise the threat of new situations. Their basic motivation for endurance allows them to persist even when the new information is exceedingly incongruous and, thereby, maximally provoking of strain and illness (Moss 1973).

Given the characterization of hardiness contained in the first two hypotheses, it should be clear that the highly stressed but healthy individual is not engaging in irresponsible adventurousness. At the core of the search for novelty and challenge are fundamental life goals that have become, in adulthood, increasingly integrated in a widening diversity of situations (Henry 1968; Neugarten 1974).

Although personality is the primary concern of the study reported here, other kinds of variables may well differentiate the highly stressed and healthy from those who have fallen ill under stress. These would include a variety of psychological, social, physiological, and environmental mediators. In order to increase understanding of those who fall ill and stay healthy under high stress, the present study included information concerning various demographic characteristics and perceptions of stressfulness of events.

METHOD

Overview

The first task was the identification of high stress/low illness and high stress/high illness groups. For this purpose, all members (N = 837) of a large subject pool were mailed a stress and illness questionnaire. They were asked to report, by month and year, which of a list of stressful life events and illness episodes they had experienced in the previous three years. A total stress score and a total illness score were obtained for each subject by the standard procedure of noting the items checked and multiplying these by their frequencies and consensually defined weights. Subjects were then assigned to one of the two groups or put aside. Assigned to the high stress/low illness and high stress/high illness groups were 126 subjects above the median for total stress and below the median for total illness and 200 subjects above the median for total stress and above the median for total illness, respectively. Discarded subjects included 322 low-stress cases and 22, or all, of the female subjects. In further group refinement, 40 high stress/high illness cases whose peak illness score preceded rather than followed their peak stress score and 10 borderline cases from each of the two groups were put aside. Finally, because of a request from the company for which all of the subjects worked that the sample to be administered personality questionnaires be kept at a workable minimum, a set of 100 subjects was randomly selected from the 116 remaining high stress/low illness cases and 100 randomly selected from the 150 remaining high stress/high illness subjects.

Within three months of the stress and illness testing, the two groups were mailed another questionnaire. This questionnaire contained several personality tests, along with questions about demographics and perception of life stressfulness.

The data from approximately half of each group were used to test hypotheses concerning group differences in hardiness. Data from the remaining cases in each group were used to cross-validate the results. The division of the groups into test and cross-validation cases was necessitated by the statistical technique relied upon in the study, discriminant function analysis, which has been characterized in previous research by problems of generalizability due to instability of results (cf. Huberty 1975). Although powerful as a tool for looking at group differences, discriminant function analysis, like regression analysis, has not always provided results that hold up in the making of inferences from sample results to some population, and over repeated samplings. Until a replication of the study is possible, the use of a "holdout sample" must be relied upon for an accurate test of the adequacy of the derived discriminant function that defines group differences.

Subjects

This study required a subject pool both large and stressed enough to obtain sufficiently large groups for study. All of the middle and upper level executives of a large public utility served as the pool from which groups were selected. This utility, in the year prior to the onset of the study, had entertained serious discussion (in executive seminars, company publications, and consultations with the medical department) of the increasing numbers of stressful events faced by executives. These events consisted of changes instituted by the utility itself, like a program of job evaluations that led to some promotions and many more demotions, as well as requirements for readjustment from external sources, such as the federal government's affirmative action demands. These changes, coupled with the expected usual range of personal and family stresses, suggested that stress scores for the subject pool would be generally high.

Demographically, the pool was quite homogeneous. The modal characteristics of the subjects were (a) male gender; (b) 40 to 49 years of age; (c) married, with two children; (d) on the third or middle management level, and having been there for 6 years or more; (e) possessing at least a college degree; (f) wife not working outside the home; (g) usually Protestant, and attending religious services very or fairly often.

Measurement of Stress and Illness

The most frequently used scales in stress and illness research, the Schedule of Recent Life Events and the Social Readjustment Rating Scale (Holmes and Rahe 1967b), were employed in this study. Additions to these scales were made on the basis of pilot testing. The majority of additions were more detailed specifications of the original items, modeled after suggestions from other adapters of the test (Hough, Fairbank, and Garcia 1976; Paykel 1974). Each of the most ambiguous events was replaced by two events, one presenting the positive form of the Holmes and Rahe item and the other, the negative version. "Change in financial state," for example, was translated into "improvements in financial state" and "worsening of financial state." These specifications were given the seriousness weights of the items from which they were derived. Other additions to the Holmes and Rahe list were based on a pilot use of the test with 50 randomly selected executives. In response to the question "What other events have you experienced during the past 3 years?", these subjects reported 15 events not found on the original list. Most of these referred to occurrences at work. Seriousness weights were assigned to these additions by the investigator and 20 other judges using the ratio scale judgment procedure of Holmes and Rahe (1967b).

The illness items in the stress and illness questionnaire were taken from the Wyler, Masuda, and Holmes (1968) Seriousness of Illness Survey. After consultation with the medical director of the executives' company, 118 of the diseases listed in this survey were chosen as applicable to the pool being tested. Each illness item is characterized by a seriousness weight based on a consensual agreement of numerous and diverse judges (both medical and lay) and is obtained in a manner similar to the derivation of the Social Readjustment Rating Scale. The reliability and validity of this scale as a complete listing of disease syndromes in a form accessible to both laypersons and physicians, and as an accurate set of evaluations of the general seriousness of various distinct illnesses, has been established (cf. Wyler, Masuda, and Holmes 1970).

Measurement of Personality,
Demographic, and Perception Variables

A composite questionnaire, made up of all or parts of four standardized and two newly constructed instruments, was designed to test the three personality hypotheses. The standardized tests were chosen for their theoretical relevance and empirical reliability and validity. All of the instruments are appropriate for use with a sample of executives (i.e., a group of well-educated adult professionals who are relatively free of gross psychopathology).

The *control* dimension was measured through four different instruments. What has been called decisional control or autonomy was measured through the Internal-External Locus of Control Scale (Lefcourt 1973; Rotter, Seeman, and Liverant 1962), and the Powerlessness versus Personal Control scale of the Alienation Test (Maddi, Kobasa, and Hoover 1978).[2] The latter instrument also provided a way of measuring cognitive control (i.e., the ability to find meaning in stressful life events) in its Nihilism versus Meaningfulness scale. Coping skill (i.e., the availability of responses with which to deal with stressful life events) was measured through the Achievement scale of the Personality Research Form (Jackson 1974; Wiggins 1973).

The question of whether these forms of control are accompanied by a need to dominate the behavior of others was addressed through administration of the Leadership Orientation scale of the California Life Goals Evaluation Schedules (Hahn 1966) and the Dominance scale of the Personality Research Form (Jackson 1974).

The *commitment* dimension was measured by the Alienation Test (Maddi 1978). Of relevance here are the alienation versus commitment scores this test yields in five areas of functioning (work, social institutions, interpersonal relationships, family, and self). The degree of consistency across a subject's different forms of involvement was also tested. This was done through the Role Consistency Test, adapted from the Gergen and Morse (1967) Self-Consistency Test to measure the compatibility among the subject's reported five most important life roles.

Measurement of the orientation to *challenge* required the administration of several tests. The degree to which the executive sought out rather than avoided stimulation from his environment was measured through the Preference for Interesting Experiences scale of the Hahn (1966) test and the Vegetativeness versus Vigorousness scale of the Alienation Test. The executive's ability to seek challenge even in the face of potential psychological, social, and biological threat was indexed by Hahn's scale of Security Orientation. Cognitive flexibility versus cognitive rigidity was measured through the Need for Cognitive Structure scale of the Personality Research Form and the ability to persist even in the most challenging environment, through the Need for Endurance scale of the same instrument. Finally, the degree to which an orientation toward challenge was characterized by a general sense of responsibility toward life's demands was measured through the Adventurousness versus Responsibility scale of the Alienation Test.

Subjects were asked about three demographic characteristics: age, job level (third, fourth, fifth, and officer), and number of years spent at current level. Executives were also asked to rate on a scale of 1 (not at all stressful) to 7 (extremely stressful) how stressful they usually think each of the following areas of life is: work, financial concerns, social/community involvements, interpersonal relationships, family, and personal or inner-life concerns.

RESULTS

Stress and Illness Scores

Of the 837 executives who were contacted by mail, 670 (80 percent) returned completed stress and illness questionnaires. The mean stress score was 399, with a standard deviation of 162, a range from 0 to 2,239, and a median of 306. The mean illness score was 913, with a standard deviation of 1,115, a range from 0 to 6,900, and a median of 550. Comparison of these executives' scores with norms available in the literature (Holmes and Masuda 1974; Wyler et al. 1968, 1970) indicates that on the average, they had experienced a moderate amount of illness (comparable to the threat of life and discomfort associated with having a peptic ulcer or high blood pressure) in the previous 3 years. During this period, they had, on the average, also encountered sufficient change and demands for readjustment in their lives to constitute major life crisis (what Holmes has associated with an 80 percent likelihood of getting seriously ill in the near future).

A Pearson product-moment correlation of .24 ($p < .025$) was obtained between the total stress and total illness scores. Canonical correlations were also run to determine whether a stronger relationship might be obtained. Stress scores—both the standard weighted scores and simple frequencies—for various areas of life (work, home, community, etc.) were used as the predictor, and illness scores—both weighted and frequencies—for various body systems (cardiovascular, respiratory, etc.) were used as the criterion set. Neither analysis of unweighted stress events and illnesses nor correlations of selected types of stress with selected types of illness, however, significantly strengthened the statistical relationship between stress and illness. The weak, but significant, correlation of .24 is consistent with most of the available research reports (Rabkin and Struening 1976).

Testing of Group Differences

Completed personality questionnaires were returned by 86 percent of the high stress/low illness and 75 percent of the high stress/high illness subjects. Forty "test" subjects were randomly selected from each group for analysis of differences across personality, demographic, and perception variables, and 81 subjects were put aside for cross-validation purposes.

Mean differences between the test subjects of the two groups were evaluated by *t* test. None of the demographic variables and only one of the perception variables yielded significant differences, whereas several of the personality variables did so. Further evaluation of group differences was achieved by a discriminant function analysis done on all the personality variables plus the one perception variable that yielded a significant *t* score. After all data are transformed into standard scores, discriminant function analysis computes a discriminant equation, or a linear combination of weighted variables that produces the greatest statistically derivable distance between the two groups. The larger the weighting or discriminant coefficient of a variable, the more powerful it is as a group discriminator.

Table 12.1 presents all variables submitted to discriminant function analysis and their summary statistics, including significance of difference between groups established by *t* test. The results demonstrate that high stress/low illness executives can be distinguished from high stress/high illness subjects. The 11 variables for which a standardized discriminant function coefficient is provided in the table combine to form a significant function, with a Wilks's Lambda of .64, significant at the .001 level, and a canonical correlation of .60. The Wilks's Lambda (see Huberty 1975) is a measure of the original variable's discriminant power, before it is removed by the discriminant function. The canonical correlation is a measure of the association between the single discriminant function and the set of dummy variables that defines the two group memberships. Given the composition of this function, the general position concerning hardiness is confirmed. High stress/low illness executives are, at least in some ways, more in control, more committed, and more oriented to challenge than are high stress/high illness executives. Looking at the variables that make the most significant contribution to the discriminant equation and that are also responsible for significant mean differences, the high stress/low illness executives are distinguished by their sense of commitment to (or lack of alienation from) self, their sense of vigorousness (as opposed to vegetativeness) about life, their sense of meaningfulness (as opposed to nihilism), and their internal (as opposed to external) locus of control. One perception-of-stress variable joins the important personality discriminators—high stress/low illness executives find the personal sphere of their lives significantly less stressful than do the high stress/high illness subjects.

Several personality variables appear to contribute to the discriminant equation even though they do not yield significant mean differences by *t* test. Although it is risky to interpret the discriminant coefficient of these variables, it is worth noting that the direction of mean difference is in general consistent with the hypotheses concerning hardiness as an insulation against illness.

Along with their analytic function, the discriminant coefficients also

Table 12.1. Differences Between High Stress/Low Illness and High Stress/High Illness Executives

Variable	High stress/ low illness[a]		High stress/ high illness[a]		t value	Standardized discriminant function coefficient
	M	SD	M	SD		
Control						
Nihilism	196.05	133.61	281.02	169.86	2.49**	.73
External locus of control	5.92	4.10	7.90	4.61	2.03*	.22
Powerlessness	301.15	188.93	388.47	188.44	2.11*	—
Achievement	16.50	2.10	15.12	3.20	−1.20	—
Dominance	14.60	3.26	13.85	4.46	.86	—
Leadership	33.47	7.34	34.63	6.80	.73	.43
Commitment						
Alienation from self	102.35	117.24	219.15	185.77	3.36**	1.04
Alienation from work	181.67	122.04	223.73	175.09	1.22	.43
Alienation from interpersonal	256.02	162.76	316.10	165.24	1.64	—
Alienation from family	158.47	139.02	198.72	144.33	1.27	—
Alienation from social	202.15	100.21	226.95	133.93	.94	—
Role consistency	29.22	6.42	29.50	6.44	.19	.30
Challenge						
Vegetativeness	155.50	140.24	216.27	160.94	1.98*	.99
Security	21.11	6.33	22.19	8.60	.34	.35
Cognitive structure	13.35	2.81	14.10	2.85	1.10	.21
Adventurousness	269.00	164.58	337.54	174.95	1.78*	—
Endurance	15.97	2.35	14.37	3.19	−.96	—
Interesting experiences	34.97	6.83	32.52	7.02	−.92	—
Perception of personal stress	3.00	1.21	3.83	1.73	2.46**	.43

Note. For all variables, the higher the number, the greater the degree of the variable observed. Superior hardiness is indicated by higher scores on achievement, role consistency, endurance, and interesting experiences, and lower scores on nihilism, external locus, powerlessness, dominance, leadership, alienation (from self, work, social institutions, interpersonal relationships, and family), vegetativeness, security, cognitive structure, and adventurousness. A subject's scores on all areas of alienation, measured by the Alienation Test, have a possible range of 0 to 1,200. Vegetativeness, nihilism, powerlessness, and adventurousness scores, also from the Alienation Test, may range from 0 to 1,500. External locus has a low of 0 and an upper limit of 23. The scales taken from the Jackson test—achievement, dominance, cognitive structure, and endurance—have a minimum value of 0 and a maximum of 20. The California Life Goals scale—leadership, security, and interesting experiences—may range from 0 to 60. Role consistency has a low of 0 and a high of 40; perception of personal stress can range from 0 to 7.

[a]N = 40.
*p < .05.
**p < .01.

serve a classificatory and validation purpose. Multiplying a subject's scores on the discriminating variables by the associated coefficients allows one to predict the likelihood of the subject's membership in each of the groups. As a test of the classificatory power of the derived discriminant equation, its coefficients are (a) reapplied to the test subjects used to derive the equation and (b) applied to the scores of the "holdout" cases. The discriminant function presented in table 12.1 shows predictive capability both internally and externally. Applying the unstandardized versions of the discriminant function coefficients to the raw scores used to derive the function, 78 percent of the "test" cases are correctly classified (80 percent of the high stress/low illness executives and 75 percent of the high stress/high illness subjects). This significantly correct ($p < .025$) classification is matched in the external cross-validation. Using the unstandardized coefficients on the raw data from the "holdout" subjects, 35 hits (77 percent) and 21 hits (60 percent) in the high stress/low illness and high stress/high illness groups, respectively, are realized ($p < .05$).

These cross-validation results offer support for the stability and generalizibility of the results obtained through discriminant function analysis. An examination of the statistics for the entire sample (test cases plus holdouts), which are notably similar to those of the test cases in table 12.1, illustrates the strength of the discriminant analysis. Table 12.2 presents the mean values, standard deviations, and t values for the full high stress/low illness and high stress/high illness groups.

DISCUSSION

This study of persons who do not fall ill despite considerable stress suggests that personality may have something to do with staying healthy. Using the five most significant discriminators of the high stress/low illness executives (i.e., the variables that contribute to the discriminant equation and produce significant ts) one can speculate on what happens when the hardy individuals meet a stressful life event—how they evaluate the threat posed by the event and cope with it.

A male executive having to deal with a job transfer will serve as an example. Whether hardy or not, the executive will anticipate and experience the changes that the transfer will bring about—learning to cope with new subordinates and supervisors, finding a new home, helping children and wife with a new school and neighborhood, learning new job skills, and so on. The hardy executive will approach the necessary readjustments in his life with (a) a clear sense of his values, goals, and capabilities, and a belief in their importance (*commitment* to rather than *alienation* from *self*) and (b) a strong tendency toward active involvement with his environment (*vigorousness* rather than *vegetativeness*). Hence, the hardy executive does more than passively acquiesce to the job transfer. Rather, he

Table 12.2. Differences Between All High Stress/Low Illness and All High Stress/High Illness Executives

Variable	High stress/ low illness[a]		High stress/ high illness[b]		t value
	M	SD	M	SD	
Control					
Nihilism	217.01	141.03	262.23	161.77	1.82*
External locus of control	5.38	3.90	7.51	4.60	2.05*
Powerlessness	314.95	190.65	364.20	189.50	1.82*
Achievement	16.40	2.35	15.95	3.03	−1.02
Dominance	14.35	3.38	14.27	4.19	−.13
Leadership	33.89	6.56	34.53	6.29	.54
Commitment					
Alienation from self	113.87	122.66	180.56	150.65	2.97**
Alienation from work	180.61	129.22	201.68	159.69	.89
Alienation from interpersonal	276.53	159.95	309.64	151.54	1.30
Alienation from family	168.93	145.83	200.99	144.62	1.35
Alienation from social	205.39	98.37	219.28	123.45	.76
Role consistency	28.80	6.78	29.59	6.84	.71
Challenge					
Vegetativeness	160.04	133.34	215.26	153.54	1.82*
Security	21.52	6.83	22.63	7.43	.95
Cognitive structure	13.16	2.77	13.75	2.94	1.26
Adventurousness	276.88	165.58	330.84	158.91	1.78*
Endurance	15.01	2.95	14.53	3.15	−.96
Interesting experiences	34.29	6.31	32.80	7.00	−1.37
Perception of personal stress	2.72	1.31	3.61	1.79	3.48**

[a]N = 86.
[b]N = 75.
*p < .05.
**p < .01.

throws himself actively into the new situation, utilizing his inner resources to make it his own. Another important characteristic of the hardy executive is an unshakable sense of meaningfulness and ability to evaluate the impact of a transfer in terms of a general life plan with its established priorities (*meaningfulness* rather than *nihilism*). For him, the job transfer means a change that can be transformed into a potential step in the right direction in his overarching career plan and also provide his family with a developmentally stimulating change. An *internal* (rather than *external*) locus of control allows the hardy executive to greet the transfer with the recognition that although it may have been initiated in an office above him, the actual course it takes is dependent upon how he handles it. For all these reasons, he is not just a victim of a threatening change but an active determinant of the consequences it brings about. In contrast, the executive low in hardiness will react to the transfer with less sense of personal resource, more acquiescence, more encroachments of meaninglessness, and a conviction that the change has been externally determined with no possibility of control on his part. In this context, it is understandable that the hardy executive will also tend to perceive the transfer as less personally stressful than his less hardy counterpart.

The mechanism whereby stressful life events produce illness is presumably physiological. Whatever this physiological response is, the personality characteristics of hardiness may cut into it, decreasing the likelihood of breakdown into illness. Needless to say, description of the actual nature of physiological mechanisms and their links to personality and stressful occurrences will have to wait for more sophisticated stress research. Until then, however, two alternative explanations of the present results should be considered.

It could be argued that there is a spurious factor at work in the subjects' completion of questionnaires, one that determines what they say about personality, stress levels, and illness experience. Mechanic (1976) has discussed the possible distortion of stress data by a variable that he calls illness behavior. From Mechanic's perspective, one could suggest that the high stress/high illness executives have not really undergone any physiological breakdown but that they simply want to act and be treated as if they are sick and thereby withdraw from a life situation experienced as too stressful. The best evaluation of this position would come from a study that employs physiological rather than self-report measures of illness and monitors physiological states before and after the occurrence of a stressful life event. Until such studies are available, reliance must be placed on data already collected. Mechanic's explanation seems much more likely to apply to the self-report of mild, vague symptoms than to report of more serious illness. For example, headaches and indigestion might well be reported by subjects engaging in illness behavior. But it seems unlikely that definite illnesses requiring medical diagnosis, such as heart attack, cancer, detached retina, and even hypertension would be erroneously reported. Illnesses of the latter sort are responsible for high illness scores on the self-report instrument used in the present study. It is therefore not likely that the results obtained can be explained completely by the concept of illness behavior.

Another alternative explanation would suggest that the observed personality differences between the high stress/low illness and the high stress/high illness executives result from the latter group having experienced illness. Presumably, the high stress/high illness executives were not more alienated, external in beliefs concerning locus of control, and uninterested in change before the illnesses occurred. Their responses to the personality questionnaire may reflect the psychologically debilitating effects of illness. A prospective, longitudinal study in which stress and personality scores at Time 1 are used to predict illness scores at Time 2 is obviously necessary. But the present study provides some basis for regarding the alternative explanation as less likely than that offered here. Although not discussed in this report, subjects found to be low in stress and high in illness showed personality scores midway between the high stress/low illness and high stress/high illness groups (Kobasa 1977). It is of specific relevance to the alternative explanation that the low stress/high illness subjects were lower on nihilism, alienation from self, vegetativeness, and external locus of control than were high stress/high illness subjects. This finding indicates that personality questionnaire responses indicative of lack of hardiness are not merely a response to illness.

Continued work in the area of stress is essential. There is still much to be learned about the role of personality and other mediators in the connection between stressful life events and illness or health. Should studies incorporating physiological measures and employing prospective designs confirm the present findings, then instead of merely warning persons to avoid stressful lives, social scientists will be able to illuminate ways of developing the personality character-istics that can aid in a productive and healthy life led in the full complexity of modern, urbanized, industrialized societies.

NOTES

1. S. C. Kobasa, R. R. J. Hilker, and S. R. Maddi. *Remaining healthy in the encounter with stress.* Paper presented at the meeting of the American Medical Associa-tion Congress on Occupational Health, St. Louis, Missouri, September 1977.

2. S. R. Maddi, S. C. Kobasa, and M. Hoover. *The Alienation Test: A Struc-tured Measure of a Multidimensional Subjective State.* Manuscript submitted for publi-cation, 1978.

Part IV

Coping with
the Stresses of Living

Readings in Part IV center on coping with stress in a variety of life contexts, such as within the family, work, and military settings. A significant issue highlighted by these selections has to do with the many determinants of coping behavior. In particular, note how cultural, situational, and personality factors appear to operate in complex ways to influence the manner in which individuals or groups handle threatening circumstances.

Pearlin's (1980) article describes a fascinating bit of research and theory focusing on psychological distress among adults and how it relates to "life strains." Life strains refer to types of circumstances that have the capacity to elicit emotional distress. Pearlin mentions three such life strains: slow-to-change problems of daily life (e.g., conflict); scheduled events in the life cycle (e.g., getting married); and, nonscheduled events (e.g., being fired or laid-off). How adults cope with these life strains in their occupations and families is discussed at length by Pearlin. Throughout his article, Pearlin emphasizes the importance of society and its organization in eliciting distress as well as in helping people to cope with it. For example, social status affects the availability of informal and formal helping agents—that is, of social supports—as well as the nature of the social and economic hardships one might face. As Pearlin (1980:176) states: "Social organization is both a wellspring of many life strains and, paradoxically, of the resources capable of moderating the negative effects of the strains." (Also see Coehlo, Hamburg, and Adams 1974, for further discussions of the importance of social organization in stress and coping.)

Mechanic (1978b) has argued that there are basically two components of adaptation, namely, one dealing directly with the situation ("coping"), and another dealing with one's feelings about the situation ("defense"). The amount of stress one experiences is therefore dependent upon the effectiveness of, and available means for, coping and defense. In a classic naturalistic investigation of graduate students studying for a major examination, Mechanic carefully observed and interviewed students and their families for three months prior to and one month following the exam. The brief selection included here emphasizes "defensive" modes (such as joking and humor) used by students anticipating their examinations. Mechanic found that older and very anxious students found little about their plights to joke about and that, among all students, joking tended to occur most frequently at certain points in time (e.g., just prior to the examination week). Moreover, as the exams became imminent, the nature of the jokes changed from that of tension-release (i.e., poking fun at the study material) to "avoidance—banter" (i.e., humor which permitted avoidance of the anxiety-provoking material); as time was running out, the switch to the latter type of joking was "adaptive" in that it protected students from being confronted with new and potentially stressful ideas. Mechanic's study is one of the more thorough and wideranging naturalistic studies of stress and coping, and the reader may want to examine his book, *Students Under Stress,* in its entirety.

Hazardous occupations provide excellent opportunities for studying coping processes, especially in times of disaster. Lucas (1969) reports a series of interviews obtained from coal miners following their rescue from a coal mine disaster, examining in detail the social and psychological forces operating while the men were trapped underground. One of their most pressing problems was a dwindling water supply and they quickly had to find an adequate solution. The men eventually decided they would have to drink their urine in order to survive but, before this could be initiated, severe inhibitions against the act had to be overcome. The social forces eventually legitimizing this normally repugnant act were complex, and Lucas' reconstruction and analysis of these forces provide penetrating insights into the cultural and social dynamics shaping coping behavior under life-threatening circumstances.

The final selection in this section deals with the difficult psychological adjustments experienced by many Vietnam veterans. Horowitz and Solomon (1975) have written a prophetic and influential paper in which they expected to see increasing numbers of veterans with *delayed stress response syndromes*—a group of experiences and reactions which may include, among other things, nightmares, painful moods and emotional storms, impaired social relationships, aggressive and/or self-destructive behaviors, and a fear of losing control over one's hostile impulses. Their predictions were based on a number of clinical, field, and experimental studies which suggested that when faced with severe stress, individuals have a tendency to cope cognitively by alternating between periods of intrusiveness and denial—that is, they tend psychologically to go back and forth between a compulsive repetition of the stressful events and their associated emotions and a denial of those events. This form of coping may last for decades in extreme instances.

Because of the way the combat experience was structured in Vietnam (e.g., frequent rotations to safety), soldiers often engaged in denial-numbing tendencies, at least until they finally reached the safety of the United States following their tour of duty. Then, as defenses were allowed to relax, many would begin to experience intrusive-repetitive tendencies—though this might not occur for a year or more after returning home. Thus, apparently well-adjusted Vietnam veterans might not begin to show signs of difficulty (as evidenced by delayed stress reactions) until considerable time had elapsed following their battle experiences.

Horowitz and Solomon also address treatment difficulties and strategies with this population as these veterans present the typical therapist with some unusual problems and characteristics. For example, unlike the neurotic who fears that he or she will inflict harm onto others (but has not), the veteran often *has* engaged in violent activities, or at least has witnessed them. (For more information on stress disorders among Vietnam veterans, see Figley 1978.)

13

Life Strains and Psychological Distress Among Adults

LEONARD I. PEARLIN

In recent years my colleagues and I have sought to draw out the complex linkages between the social circumstances of adults and the emotional distress they experience. Although this work is far from being either definitive or complete, it has brought into view a number of general features of the adult portion of life. For example, we see adulthood as a period in which newness is more commonplace than stability. Adulthood is not a quiescent stretch interspersed with occasional change; it is a time in which change is continuous, interspersed with occasional quiescent interludes.

It has become similarly apparent from our work that adults are responsive to life circumstances and to fluctuations in these circumstances. This means, as Bernice Neugarten (1969) has observed, that adulthood is much more than that part of life in which people simply act out feelings and dispositions acquired from childhood experience. Thus, a satisfactory explanation of levels of emotional distress among adults cannot rely only on personality characteristics formed early in life, but must also take into account current experience and ongoing change. Furthermore, the results of our work indicate that no single phase of adulthood seems to have a monopoly on change. There may be distinctive constellations of problems that are especially likely to converge at particular periods, such as the transitions of middle age (Levinson 1977), but people have to confront severe challenges at other times of their lives as well.

Although much of our analysis has emphasized variations in psychological distress, we recognize that there are many ways in which lives can take on new directions. Values, beliefs, ideologies, interactional patterns, interests, and activities—indeed, the entire range of dispositions and behaviors—are subject to modification as one moves across the life span. However, these kinds of changes, which may give the appearance of being removed from and unrelated to distress, often find expression in anxiety and depression, for such feelings represent the emotional summation of important circumstances in the lives of people. In addition, of course, distress is important in its own right. It is an unpleasant condition that can come to dominate our awareness and from which we actively seek relief. Thus emotional distress both signals important life changes that are under way and, at the same time, constitutes a state against which people are likely to launch a barrage of coping responses. In either case, psychological distress is a central element in life changes, though certainly not the sole element.

The search for conditions affecting the emotional states of people necessarily leads to the larger society and its organization. Inevitably, the study of adult development entails more than the study of adults: it must also seek to identify those elements of social structure that are intertwined with and give direction to the lives of people. There are at least three ways in which societies and their organization are implicated in the emotional development of their members. First, they may be the source of the forces that have the capacity to adversely (and beneficially, too) affect the well-being of people. Even stressful situations that appear to stem from the confluence of chance conditions, as in marital conflict, are often traceable to fundamental social arrangements (Pearlin 1975b). But the most convincing indication of the contributory role of basic social organization is that many stress-provoking circumstances are unequally distributed among people having different social positions and statuses (Pearlin and Lieberman 1979). The different life strains among the rich and the poor, for example, or among men and women, or among the married and unmarried provide a clue that strains do not result from the chance experience of individuals but that they derive from the locations of people within the broader societal organization. Thus, in studying adult development in general and psychological distress in particular, a foremost task is to determine the difference in vulnerability to stressful circumstances of different groups within the society.

Second, while exposure to stressful circumstances varies with the social characteristics of people, it is also true that identical circumstances may have very different effects on individuals within a group if they occur in different social contexts. For example, retirement may result in chronic depression for the person who is separated from the sole source of activities he loved, but may be the source of elation for another to whom retirement is an escape from dreaded labor. Giving birth can be a blessed event for the mother having her first child, or an event leading to depression for the mother who already has several young children (Pearlin 1975a). There are many events and circumstances, then, that do not by themselves move people along a particular course of emotional change or development; instead, the consequences of these circumstances are given meaning by the context or situation in which people are embedded at the time.

A third general mode of social influence on adult development is represented in the coping resources people possess. Some of these resources are represented by the informal and formal helping agents to whom one can look for aid. Because the availability of these resources varies for different social groups, people do not necessarily have equal access to important social supports. There are also psychological resources that one draws upon from within oneself, and the distribution of these, too, may follow lines of social demarcation. For example, among the psychological coping resources of adults, self-esteem and mastery are most effective (Pearlin and Schooler 1978), and the likelihood of having these important elements of personality increases with one's position in the socioeconomic system (Rosenberg and Pearlin 1978). Status within the broader society, therefore, helps to determine access to crucial coping resources. And these are indeed resources to be prized, for they are instrumental in helping people withstand some of the deleterious effects of severe social and economic hardships.

Thus, societies have a dominant part in influencing individual change and adaptation by being the source of challenges and hardships, by providing the contexts that give meaning to and determine the consequences of these hardships, and by allocating resources—both social and psychological—that help people fend off the harmful emotional distress that may otherwise result. Social organization is both a wellspring of many life strains and, paradoxically, of the resources capable of moderating the negative effects of the strains. I point out these different contributions for two reasons. First, I wish to underscore that adult development does not go on apart from surrounding social circumstances, as though it simply involves the acting out of a preexisting scenario. Second, in calling attention to the different modes of social contributions to adult development, I seek to emphasize that development should not be construed as a single course universally followed by all people. It would perhaps fit reality better if we were to assume that there are many developmental patterns, each shaped and channeled by the confluence of the social characteristics of adults, their standing in the social order, the problematic experiences to which they must adapt, the social contexts and situations in which they are embedded, and the coping resources with which they are equipped. Simply knowing that most adults get married, have children, enter occupational life, and retire does not come close to providing us the information we need to examine properly the processes of adult development.

In our own work we are far from having evaluated all of these considerations as they relate to psychological distress, but we do have information that cuts across some of the issues. For much of this information I shall rely largely on research in which I and several collaborators have been engaged in recent years. For this reason, it would be useful to provide some of the background and perspectives of our work.

The aim of this research, which began several years ago, was to explore the relationships between persistent hardships threaded through daily life and psychological distress. We first conducted unstructured exploratory interviews with about 100 people, asking them to discuss the problems they faced as workers, breadwinners, wives and husbands, fathers and mothers. From these discussions several recurring themes concerning the problems people face in their occupational and family life were identified. Through a series of pre-tests these themes were gradually transformed into standardized questions that, in 1972, were asked in scheduled interviews with a sample of 2,300 people between the ages of eighteen and sixty-five representative of the adult population of the Chicago urban area. The detailed and lengthy enumeration of the problems about which people were queried and the batteries of questions used to measure them are partially reproduced in Pearlin and Schooler (1978). Here I shall provide only a general description.

With regard to the occupational arena, first of all, we assessed the presence and intensity of a range of problems, such as the noxiousness of the work setting (the existence of dirt, dust, noise, or danger); estrangement from and conflicts with both fellow workers and authorities; and various work pressures and overloads. Next, information was gathered indicative of three types of marital problems and conflicts: the lack of reciprocity, or inequalities in give and take between husbands and wives; the failure of one's spouse to fulfill a variety of role expectations, such as affection, sexual partnership, and provider-homemaker duties; and, third, the lack of recognition and acceptance by one's spouse of one's own "real," quintessential self. Finally, in the parental area, the problems about which we inquired concerned children's violations of parents' standards of general conduct; deviations from long-range parental aspirations and goals; failure to accept parental definitions of morality; and lack of consideration or respect for parents. Much of the inquiry, then, sought to evaluate the extent to which the lives of individuals are invaded by a host of conflicts and hardships arising from work and economic life, marriage and child rearing—indeed, from labor and love.

In addition to measures of these relatively persistent role problems, information was gathered regarding a large array of devices people employ to cope with the problems. As in the case of the role problems, coping behavior was first identified in the early, unstructured interviews; questions were then systematically developed and standardized for use in the sample survey. Still another body of questions was intended to provide measures of various manifestations of psychological distress. For this purpose we employed scales that had been developed from presenting symptoms of patients diagnosed as suffering from such emotional ailments as anxiety and depression (Derogatis et al. 1971; Lipman et al. 1969).

Overall, then, the range of information gathered by the research conducted in 1972 has made it possible to examine a network of connections between the social characteristics of people, the persistent problems that pervade their daily experiences in major social roles, their patterns of coping with such experiences, and the psychological outcomes that emerge from the confluence of these factors.

During 1976 we returned to Chicago and reinterviewed a subsample of our respondents. [1] We repeated virtually all of the questions about role problems, coping responses, and symptomatologies of emotional distress, thus providing the opportunity to assess changes that may have occurred in these domains between 1972 and 1976. However, in concentrating on persistent role problems, the initial survey omitted from consideration other key sources of psychological distress. In particular, it did not include the many crucial life events that have the potentiality for arousing psychological disturbance. While the persistent role problems are likely to surface so insidiously that their onset may be difficult to recognize, life is liberally sprinkled, too, with events that have discrete temporal origins, are difficult to ignore, and require accelerated adjustments. The follow-up survey was designed to capture these events.

A good deal of attention has been given in recent years to life events and their effects (Myers et al. 1972; Paykel, Prusoff, and Uhlenhuth 1971), much of it based on Social Readjustment Rating Scale developed by Holmes and Rahe (1967b). Considerable criticism has been leveled at this scale on methodological grounds (Brown 1974; Rabkin and Struening 1976), but the conceptual deficiencies of the instrument are equally outstanding. On the positive side, the scale does succeed in identifying a number of apparently potent events. Unfortunately, it does not differentiate among events in ways that permit the reconstruction of an individual's experience as he traverses time and space. Instead, it treats important life events as haphazard and interchangeable occurrences, thus obscuring the variations in patterns of events among people with different social status, the anchoring of these patterns in different social roles, and the emergence of events at different stages of adult life. It was our goal to distinguish among events in a manner that goes beyond the simple compilation of undifferentiated occurrences.

Pivotal to our efforts in this direction is the distinction between scheduled and nonscheduled events. [2] Scheduled events involve those transitions into and out of roles and statuses that are normally experienced in the course of the life cycle. Because they are so closely tied to the life cycle, they usually have a high predictability. We refer to them as scheduled events in order to underscore the regularity of their unfolding in the lives of people. Thus, whereas the enduring role problems entail the chronic frustrations, conflicts, and hardships people encounter within existing roles and statuses, transitional events focus on the scheduled yielding and acquiring of those roles and statuses attendant upon life-cycle changes.

Our follow-up interview inquired into a number of such events within each role area. In occupation we considered the following to represent events of this type: entry into the labor market; withdrawal from occupation in order to have and care for a family; and retirement because of age. Being newly married and experiencing "timely" widowhood are the two transitional events in the marital area. The parental role is somewhat unique because, strictly speaking, one can only acquire the role of parent but not lose it. However, we do treat as scheduled events a number of critical junctures which serve as benchmarks in the child's progress toward eventual independence. These include such transitions as the child's entry into school, completion of school, departure from the parental household, and marriage of the adult child. At each of these steps the parental role, although it is retained, undergoes some transformation.

The second type of event about which we inquired in our follow-up survey involves crises, eruptive circumstances, and other unexpected occurrences that are not the consequence of life-cycle transitions—the nonscheduled events. Although events of this order may be widespread, people typically do not count on them occurring within their own lives. Such exigencies may be no less common than problems woven into the fabric of day-to-day roles or those that emerge in the course of scheduled transitions, but they are ordinarily not among the occurrences that people expect to experience personally. Events of this type in the occupational arena are being fired, laid-off, or demoted, having to give up work because of illness, and—more desirable—being promoted and leaving one job for a better one. Divorce, separation, and the illness or premature death of a spouse are events within marriage that, while widespread, do not have the scheduled regularity of transitional events. And finally, the illness or death of a child represents such events in the parental arena.

Underlying our research, then, are a few simple perspectives. We hold, first, that adult emotional development does not represent the gradual surfacing of conditions that happen to reside within individuals. Instead, we see it as a continuing process of adjustment to external circumstances, many of them rooted in the organization of the larger society and therefore distributed unequally across the population. We have identified three types of circumstances that have the capacity to arouse emotional distress; we refer to these collectively as life strains. This category includes the dogged, slow-to-change problems of daily life; the highly predictable, scheduled regular events that are attached to the life cycle; and the less expected and often (though not always) undesirable eruptive events. Because many of these vicissitudes are anchored to major social roles, they vary in space as people move among their multiple roles, as well as through time as the roles they occupy undergo change. The configuration of life strains may differ from one stage of adulthood to another, but the process of adjustment and change goes on through the entirety of life.

Although these are the guiding considerations and perspectives of our research into psychological distress among adults, we have only begun to discern the outlines of the vast web of interrelationships among the issues. In the following pages I shall describe some of our empirical findings, looking first at the periods of life when different life strains are likely to surface, the effects of the strains on psychological distress, and then how people cope with them.

AGE DISTRIBUTION AND THE EMOTIONAL IMPACT
OF LIFE STRAINS

Many of the life strains we have delineated for study have previously been shown
to occur unequally across important groups in the society (Pearlin and Lieberman
1979). The distribution of the strains among people of different age levels is
especially germane to developmental concerns. There is no simple way to summarize this distribution, for the persistent problems, the scheduled transitional
events, and the nonscheduled events each have somewhat distinctive associations
with age. Furthermore, the strains rooted in the world of work are related to age
in a different fashion than are the strains involving the more expressive worlds of
marriage and parenthood. Thus, the relationships of life strains to age vary both
with the type of strain and with the role from which the strains arise. The data
are somewhat complex, therefore, but it is this very complexity and richness, so
often overlooked in research into psychological well-being, that we seek to capture
in conceptually distinguishing different types of circumstances and events as they
present themselves within major social roles.

　　　Within the occupational arena we find that the younger the worker
is, the more likely it is that he will be exposed to most of the strains included
in our study. With regard to the relatively persistent problems, for example,
younger workers are somewhat more apt than older workers to feel job pressures
and overloads and to have depersonalizing and separating experiences with fellow
workers and authorities. Even more powerful associations with age are found for
those strains represented by scheduled life events. Thus, people leaving the work
force to have or to care for families are usually young (and almost always women).
It is typically the younger, too, who are either entering or re-entering the job
market. The only predictable transition more commonly found among older than
younger workers is, of course, retirement from work for reasons of age. Finally,
the nonscheduled events, such as being fired, laid-off, or demoted are almost
exclusively the experiences of younger workers, as are promotion and movement
between jobs. The only nonscheduled event occurring with disproportionate frequency among older people is retirement from work because of ill health. Overall,
there is a very clear picture of younger workers more often having to confront the
changes associated with the establishment, interruption, or advancement of career,
of being vulnerable to occupational insecurities and disruptions, and of facing the
more continuing and persistent problems of work. These findings suggest that
the world of labor may become gentler with age.

　　　Some of this picture changes when we examine marital strains, for
these are somewhat more evenly distributed across the age span. As in occupation,
the relatively persistent problems of marriage tend to be found among the younger
wives and husbands. Thus, it is the younger married men and women who are

particularly likely to see their spouses as failing to fulfill ordinary role expectations; they are also less likely to feel accepted by their spouses in a fashion that supports the valued elements of their self-image. The two scheduled transitions, being newly married and being widowed, are divided between extreme age groups, the first being predominantly an experience of the younger and the latter, of course, of the older. There is a similar age split involving, on the one hand, divorce and separation and, on the other, illness and disability, the former, expectedly, being mainly an experience of younger people and the latter of older people. In the parental area, we find that the persistent problems of child rearing are primarily confronted by younger parents. However, the transitional events occur across a wide age range, for they closely follow life-cycle developments. Thus, it is younger people who are becoming parents and seeing their children off to school and then through adolescence. But it is the older parents who see the departure of children from the household and into marriage.

An overview of the age distribution of the life strains described above reveals several patterns. Young adults simultaneously face the formidable tasks of having to establish themselves in their occupations, having to accommodate to marital relations that probably are not yet crystallized, and having to take responsibility for young children who of necessity are heavily dependent on them. Thus, chronic hardships and conflicts that can be found within these major social roles are much more likely to invade the lives of young adults, and to have been reconciled or left behind by the older adults. Some of the more undesirable nonscheduled events are also more common at younger ages, particularly those involving the loss of jobs and the termination of marriage by divorce and separation. By contrast, a number of the scheduled transitions are events experienced later in life, especially such life-cycle transitions as retirement, the loss of a spouse because of death, or the departure from the household of the last child.

Younger people, then, have more life strains to contend with, but they are frequently of a sort that dissipate with time. The strains faced by older people, although perhaps fewer in number, are more irreversible in their character. These differences make it difficult to judge on which group the greatest demands for adjustment fall. There is one matter of which we can be quite certain, however: as the adult part of the life span unfolds, people are exposed to a continuous, although shifting, flow of circumstances that challenge their adjustive capacities and have the potential for creating intense psychological distress. The study of adults, therefore, is to a large extent the study of conditions of work and of expressive relations as these engage people at different segments of the adult period of life, setting the stage for further psychological development.

Let us turn from the age distribution of the various life strains to a consideration of their emotional impact. The problems and vicissitudes that people encounter are not equal in their potential to arouse distress. On the contrary, we have observed considerable difference among them in this regard (Pearlin and

Lieberman 1979). In the world of work, for example, it is the nonscheduled loss of job or job status that is most likely to result in anxiety and depression, emotional states that we have combined into a composite measure of distress. Thus those who have been fired or laid off in the four-year period between 1972 and 1976 are considerably more apt than those whose occupational life has been stable to experience distress. The coefficient of association for this relationship (gamma) is .31. Being demoted produces an even closer relationship (gamma = .41), and having to give up work because of poor physical health is most closely associated of all (gamma = .74). Somewhat surprising, retirement from work because of age has no appreciable consequence for emotional distress, but giving up work in order to have or care for a family does have fairly substantial consequences for distress (gamma = .30). Promotion and changes in place of employment, despite their being apparently desired events, still have significant positive (although quite modest) relationships (.14 and .22, respectively). Finally, each of the more persistent problems of work (with the exception of working in noise, dirt, or other noxious environmental conditions) has distressful effects, the most notable among them being problems with fellow workers and authorities (gamma = .32). It is noteworthy that those circumstances and events in the work world that are most emotionally painful are also those most likely to impinge on younger people.

Marital strains are somewhat different from those in occupation, for in this domain it is the more durable strains encountered in everyday marital relations that exert the greatest impact, not the scheduled or nonscheduled events. Thus the coefficient of association for the relationship of distress to divorce and separation is .23, and that of distress to widowhood, .31. By contrast, perceived failure of spouses to fulfill role expectations, to exercise reciprocities in the relationship, and to recognize and accept their partners as they want to be seen have coefficients of association with distress of .40, .34, and .40, respectively. Where marriage is concerned, therefore, it is evidently psychologically less disturbing to have the relationship terminated than to live out the relationship under conditions of frustration and conflict. New marriages have some special interest in this context. From one perspective they represent a transition to a new role whose importance persumably makes it capable of producing distress. Yet, from another perspective, being newly married means that the more chronic strains may not have had the opportunity to appear or become crystallized, thus minimizing psychological distress. The latter effect apparently prevails, for being newly wed has no statistically discernible deleterious psychological effects.

From the very few cases in our sample where the death of a child has occurred, it is evident that for parents to outlive a child is probably the most severe hardship that people can endure. On the other hand, there are a number of more common events of parenthood linked to the life cycle which, although often viewed as emotionally difficult, are not at all inimical to well-being. I refer to such events as the last child's entrance into school, or completion of school, or of his departure from the parental home. Indeed, the marriage of a last child is to a notable extent negatively associated with emotional distress (gamma $= -.21$). The surge of well-being associated with seeing one's children married and out of the house may result not only from contemplating the delights of the empty nest but also from knowing that a succeeding generation is in the process of creating its own nests. Perhaps the caring for and commitment to succeeding generations, what Erik Erikson refers to as generativity (1950), extends beyond one's children to embrace one's grandchildren as well. Whatever the reason, the confrontation by parents of the daily problems of child care and training is considerably more distressful than those transitional events signaling the growing independence of children and their final departure from the household.

These, then, are some of the principal relationships between life strains and psychological distress. But regardless of how well we succeed in identifying pivotal events and persistent problems in the various role sectors of adulthood, our ability to predict their emotional consequences will be limited if we do not also take into consideration how people cope with them.

COPING

It is fair to state that interest in coping far exceeds our knowledge about it. Because it has been approached from a variety of perspectives by scholars representing a variety of disciplines, the growth of our understanding of coping has not been cumulative. Our work differs from that of most others in that it emphasizes those elements of coping that are learned from and shared with the groups to which one belongs, ignoring the more idiosyncratic individual coping styles. But despite differences in their perspectives, all students of coping are in agreement, at least implicitly, that people are not merely passive targets of problems that arise in their lives, but that they actively respond to them in an effort to avoid being harmed by them. Largely because of these responses, emotional distress cannot be explained solely in terms of impinging life strains, for the manner in which people cope mediates the psychological consequnces of the strains.

Although much remains to be discovered, a great deal has already been learned about coping from the 1972 data (Pearlin and Schooler 1978), more than can be presented in detail here. I shall confine myself to discussing the connections between the coping dispositions of individuals and the value system of the surrounding society. To understand these connections, it must be recognized that the most common mode of response to life strains is the employment of a large inventory of perceptual and cognitive devices enabling one to view one's problems as relatively innocuous. Essentially this entails defining a situation or problem in a manner that reduces its threat and consequently minimizes its stressful impact. This type of coping does not eradicate the problem itself; it controls and shapes the meaning that the problem has for the individual so that its stressful effects are buffered.

The control of meaning typically relies heavily on the selective use of socially valued goals and activities. Many illustrations can serve to explicate this statement. If a man is exposed to intense strain in his work, he may avoid distress by relegating work to a marginal place in his life, committing himself instead, for example, to being a good husband or father. Thus, adults not infrequently will move those roles in which there is painful experience to the periphery of importance, making more central those that are comparatively free of hardship. In rearranging their priorities, people temper stress by demeaning the importance of areas in which failure and conflict are occurring. This selective commitment to different areas of life is possible, first, because there is a temporal and spatial segregation of important roles, and, second, because societies offer a veritable smorgasbord of values to their members. It is the plethora of equally acceptable desiderata, each congenial to society's ideals, that makes it a simple matter to substitute one commitment for another. One doesn't *have* to be a dedicated worker; he will still be conforming to the cherished values of the society if he chooses instead to be a devoted father. And this option may save him a great deal of pain.

The rearrangement of priorities may take place within roles as well as between roles. A woman reports, for example, that when her husband drinks to excess, which is frequently, he becomes abusive toward her. When asked how she deals with this problem, she replies that she pays no attention to it, for in the things that really matter—being a steady worker and a good earner—he is a prince. One can predict what she would prize if he were an inadequate breadwinner but a considerate husband. And if the situation were reversed so that she did esteem her husband for his kindness and ignored his failure as a breadwinner, she would be no less adhering to social values.

The selective use of valued goals and activities to mold the meaning of circumstances is an easily available coping tool, commonly used and quite efficacious. But whereas this strategy functions to limit the intensity of emotional distress, other devices function more as strategies for enduring distress. The coping strategies of this type help people live with and manage distress without being overwhelmed by it. There are many devices that potentially serve this function, such as immersing oneself in television viewing (Pearlin 1959) or drinking for the relief of anxiety (Pearlin and Radabaugh 1976). Here, however, I shall focus on those distress management techniques that make use of widespread beliefs and precepts. Many of these find expression in commonly used and easily recognized adages that represent prescriptions for surviving stress. Some, for example, seem to promote a passive forebearance in the face of adversity with a promise of better things to come: "things always work out for the best," "time heals all wounds," and so on. Others urge that we "look on the positive side," or that we "count our blessings." Sometimes it is the problems of others that make us aware of our blessings. This is powerfully illustrated in Betty Rollin's account of her intense effort to adjust to her mastectomy. She relates that some weeks after her surgery a friend called and recited a litany of domestic problems. Rollin became involved in her friend's travails and describes how, following the telephone conversation, "it occurred to me that I was doing something I hadn't done for a long time. I was worrying about someone else. At last, I thought" (1976:188). Other people's miseries can lighten our own.

Other beliefs indicate that our suffering is an inherent part of the design of life, perhaps even a manifestation of higher purpose. Commonly used exhortations to "take the bad with the good," or that "it is meant to be" suggest that people attempt to cope with hardships by seeing them as preordained, part of a divine plan. This theme is poignantly expressed by miners' wives in interviews that are being conducted as part of an investigation into the ways people cope with this perilous occupation.[3] One woman whose husband was killed in a mine accident, for example, tells us that when she is depressed and asking herself why her husband died, she tells herself: "You know God doesn't make mistakes, you know that, so why are you acting like an idiot." She states: "Talking out loud to myself . . . does help." Societies, then, offer a potpourri of beliefs, and their selective use enables people not only to survive distress but to make a moral virtue of it. As might be guessed, coping at this level is more commonly found among older than younger adults.

There is a possibility that changes in adults' lives resulting from scheduled role transitions and those stemming from nonscheduled crises bring forth different coping modes. We have little empirical information to go on at this time, but there is reason to believe that the different types of life strains evoke coping efforts particularly suited to their nature. Thus the salient feature of role transitions is the predictability of their emergence; scheduled changes can be anticipated far in advance of their actual occurrence. We know about retirement before we receive our gold watches; we know something about marriage before the wedding ceremony. Because such role transitions are built into the life cycle, we begin learning about some of the changes they entail far ahead of the events themselves. Our adjustments to the conditions imposed by the loss and gain of roles thus depend to some extent on how accurately or with what distortions we foresee what we will later encounter. Effective coping with role transitions, therefore, would seem to depend on the role rehearsals that we conduct in our imaginations, the selection and use of role models, and other techniques that enable us to estimate how well present dispositions will fit with future demands. Where there is a perceived lack of congeniality between the present and the future, we engage in anticipatory adjustments. The success or failure of coping with transitions is very likely predetermined by the authenticity of the preparatory learning and the anticipatory adjustments people begin to make prior to the actual change.

Neither the selective use of values and beliefs to control meaning or to control distress itself—the reponses I described earlier—nor the anticipatory role rehearsals used to contend with scheduled transitions would appear to be well-suited to coping with more sudden and eruptive life changes. Events of this sort lack the persistence needed for the crystallization of perceptual and cognitive adjustments; and because they also lack the predictability of the scheduled transitions, anticipatory preparation for the event is more difficult. How, then, do adults cope with eruptive conditions? It is in dealing with events having a crisis quality, perhaps, that people are most likely to engage in help-seeking behavior. The nature of the particular crisis, of course, has a great deal to do with what help people want and from whom they may seek it. To deal with some kinds of nonscheduled events, people, without necessarily being aware of it, may seek only subtle emotional support within an informal network of friends or family; for other problems they may turn to experts in the hope of receiving from them information or prescriptions for ameliorative actions. In any event, it is likely that seeking help, as in the case of other coping modes, is selectively invoked by adults in dealing with different kinds of exigencies and crises.

The adult portion of the life span, then, is peppered with socially generated life strains that differ with regard to their persistence and predictability. Many life strains may have their roots in the fundamental arrangements of society; but societies are at the same time also the source of many efficacious devices people use to withstand the full impact of the strains. Indeed, as varied as the life strains are, the ways of responding to them are richer yet. One learns from his experiences, from his membership groups, and from his culture a vast array of acceptable modes of anticipating, appraising, and meeting challenge. If these modes fail him, either because of their inherent lack of coping efficacy or because the challenging circumstances are not amenable to individual coping efforts, then he becomes vulnerable to psychic distress. But if one copes effectively, as people typically appear to do, then life strains may even have a positive contribution to one's development through the adult portion of the life span. Although much is still conjectural, we can be quite certain that to understand the well-being of adults, we need to observe the unfolding of the circumstances and events they experience, the meaning of the experience for them, and their attempts to avoid being harmed by it.

I have to this point deliberately omitted certain complexities so as to delineate more clearly the main currents of our work. One of these omissions concerns the reciprocity between the circumstances and events of life and psychological distress. Although I have talked of distress solely as following from life strains, there is a distinct possibility that distress, in addition to being an effect of life strains, is also an antecedent of strains. Even with the availability of longitudinal data such as ours, a great deal of care and rigor is required before the causal ordering of important social and psychological phenomena can be established. However, certain of our data, especially the discrete events that occurred in the lives of respondents in the four-year period between interviews, give some ready indication of what is causing what. By their very nature particular events can be considered as relatively impervious to influence by preexisting psychological dispositions. Being widowed may be taken as a suitable case in point. The coefficient of association (gamma) between the 1972 psychological distress level and subsequent widowhood is .19, but the coefficient between widowhood and the later, 1976 identical measure of distress is .32. It is remotely possible that preexisting distress could contribute to the demise of a spouse, but it is clearer, both because of the nature of the event and the magnitude of the associations, that the spouse's death is an antecedent condition for distress. Virtually all of the preliminary examinations made along these lines, including those of events that are less clearly susceptible to influence from prior distress, indicate a similar asymmetry of influence. Psychological distress, although it may very well contribute to future events, is more likely to result from conditions of life than to give shape to these conditions. However, it is clear that new methodologies are needed in order to reconstruct with confidence the processes by which social forces and events affect people, and by which people may come to affect the forces and events that play upon their lives.

Under special conditions, some events may lose their scheduled or nonscheduled distinctiveness; that is, many of the events that are ordinarily highly predictable may, in a given set of circumstances, lose their predictability. Consider a woman who, after years of trying to have children, becomes pregnant at the age of forty. Not only is she outside the remarkably clear timing norms for this kind of event (Neugarten, Moore, and Lowe 1965), but she may also feel that she is at some special risk. Consequently, an event easily anticipated and prepared for under usual circumstances can, under unusual circumstances of timing and meaning, become cloaked in uncertainty and doubt. Correspondingly, other events that are usually considered as eruptive crises may acquire the features of highly regular occurrences. Thus, a miner's wife relates that she anticipates that after ten years of work her husband will become ill with black lung disease. She is not merely engaging in gloomy guesswork in making this prediction, for this is what happened to her father and two uncles. A limiting illness at the age of about forty is, in these circumstances, a predictive event tied to a patterned occupational career. Where the meaning and nature of events is altered by special conditions, the effects of these events and the coping responses they evoke will probably also be altered.

Underlying many of the relationships that I have talked about is a question that merits consideration if we are better to understand adult development and change: what is it about events that creates anxiety and depression? One possible answer might hold that it is the undesirability of many events that explains their exacerbation of psychological distress. This does not stand up, however, for even events that are patently desirable, such as being promoted, are nonetheless still associated with distress. Another explanation might emphasize the loss entailed by certain events, that being separated from something that was once part of ourselves leads to emotional disturbances. This argument may have some merit, for several of the events most powerfully related to distress do involve the loss of role or status. Nevertheless, there are some losses—for example, those represented in the departure of children from the home or in retirement—that do not have deleterious effects. And if loss is painful, it could be reasoned that gain should be beneficial. But this is not the case, for there are some acquisitions, such as entering into a new occupation, that are capable of generating distress. A third explanation would assert that events impose an alteration in a delicate balance within us. Disequilibrium among our inner psychic forces, in turn, is an inherently intolerable condition that produces tension and other symptoms of distress that are likely to persist until a new equilibrium is established. This explanation, however, fails to explain the low level of distress following some quite dramatic changes, such as retirement or the emptying of the nest.

There is yet another possible explanation, one that we tested empirically. Events may not affect adults because they are unwanted, or invoke loss, or because they throw the organism out of delicate psychic balance. Instead, events promote emotional distress when they adversely alter the more durable conditions of life with which people have to contend. The effects of events, we suggest, are channeled through the structured circumstances that people have to grapple with over time. Considerable support for this interpretation emerged from the analysis of our data. Thus, in looking at certain events involving role loss, such as retirement, divorce, or widowhood, the loss itself matters far less to psychological well-being than the quality of experience one has in being newly retired, divorced, or widowed. For example, if retirees who are free of economic hardships and who enjoy ties to social networks are compared with those who have limited economic resources and are relatively isolated, it is only the latter who are found to possess the symptoms of distress. The same is true for those who are newly single, whether because of the death of a spouse or divorce: when the durable conditions of singlehood are benign, the yielding of the marital role does not arouse distress. Where newly single persons experience hardships, on the other hand, they are very likely to suffer intense distress. The injurious psychological effects of events entailing the movement from one role to another, therefore, appear to depend not on the loss or transition per se but almost entirely on conditions people live with at the end of their role passage. Change by itself does not affect emotional well-being; change that leads to hardships in basic, enduring economic and social conditions of life, on the other hand, does. Even those transitions brought about voluntarily may result in pain when they lead to negative conditions that are beyond one's ameliorative control.

In mulling over what we have learned from observing the distressful effects of life strains, we have addressed a question that is a fundamental concern of this book: Do problems in labor and in love intrude upon each other? More concretely, can one confront hardships in one's occupation without these eventually leading to strife in one's family relations; can one suffer frustration and conflict as a husband or wife, father or mother, without experiencing increased strains as a worker? On the one hand, people are whole, and it is difficult to think of important experiences occurring in one part of life without influencing the other parts. But on the other hand, there is a structural separation of social roles that enables people to segregate painful experiences arising in one role from the experiences arising within other roles. Our efforts to find the answers to this question are hardly final, but from evidence at hand it appears that disruptions of labor and love are indeed somewhat independent. Thus the intensity of strain a person experiences in his occupation bears relatively little relationship to those he experiences as a spouse or parent. To an appreciable extent adults apparently do contain strains and stresses in time and space; and this, in turn, says a great deal about the organization of coping behavior.

NOTES

1. This time in collaboration with Morton A. Lieberman of the Committee on Human Development at the University of Chicago.

2. I am grateful to Neil Smelser for suggesting these conceptual labels.

3. These are currently being conducted in collaboration with Nancy Datan and Carol Giesen of the Department of Psychology at West Virginia University.

14

Some Modes
of Adaptation: Defense

DAVID MECHANIC

A s we see it, a person's behavior represents a more or less consistent pattern of response—what we call his *personality.* He attempts to maintain cognitive integration by controlling the information that enters the cognitive system and by making it congruent with his views and needs (Festinger 1957).

Organizing his behavior around attitudes of the self and the relations of the self to the external world, he deals not only with objective situations, but also with perceived subjective threats. The information that enters the cognitive system may be relevant or irrelevant, important or unimportant to the task at hand or to the attitudes the person holds about himself in relation to the task. In instances where relevant information does enter the system, the individual either may integrate it into his cognitive orientation or attempt to reject it. In doing this he seeks various kinds of support from others in the communication structure of which he is a part and from cues which he finds in his environment.

The system of defenses described by the classical psychoanalytic theorists attempts to indicate *what* occurs, but tells us little that is clear as to *how* this occurs. Thus, whereas the descriptions of behavior—repression, denial, projection, intellectualization, and so on—sensitize us to these happenings, the conditions under which these distortions occur and how they develop remain unclear.

A step in the direction of solving this problem has been provided by some interesting studies by David Hamburg and his associates (Hamburg, Hamburg, and deGoza 1953). Studying the adaptive processes of badly burned soldiers, they observed that many of the adaptive processes were social—that these processes involved communication as well as cognition, and that cognitive defenses were associated with environmental cues. These insightful papers suggested that perhaps we might learn a good deal more if we would attempt to understand the social and social-psychological contexts within which defense occurs.

THE NEED FOR DEFENSE

The students under study most definitely saw stress as a major factor in the challenge of passing the examinations. Many of them believed that if they could defend adequately and maintain their anxiety at some comfortable level, they would be adequate in their performance. Both students and faculty were asked to indicate the importance of the ability to remain relaxed and the ability to work under pressure for students taking preliminary examinations. The difference in perception of stress as a factor was quite considerable when viewed through the eyes of students and faculty in table 14.1

Since students do find that preparation is a major factor in reducing anxiety, tasks that keep them from working on examination preparation were likely to raise their anxiety level. We expected, therefore, that students would think it more important than faculty to put aside everything for their studies in order to pass the examinations. And, as analysis of table 14.2 shows, they did just this.

COMFORTING COGNITIONS
AND FAVORABLE SOCIAL COMPARISON

The most consistently observed defense device used by the students under study was that of seeking comforting information from the environment that was consistent with the attitudes and hopes the student held about the examinations.

Table 14.1. Perceived Importance of Defending Against Stress by Students and Faculty

Items	Percent of Students Responding Very or Fairly Important (N-22)	Percent of Faculty Responding Very or Fairly Important (N-21)
Ability to remain relaxed	68	29
Ability to work under pressure	100	76

Table 14.2. Rated Importance of the Ability to Put Aside Everything for Studies by Students and Faculty

	Percent Responding Very or Fairly Important
Students (N-22)	91
Faculty (N-21)	38

Often these comforting cognitions were made on the basis of comparing oneself favorably with others, or by finding cues in the environment that made the person more confident about his situation. A number of these comforting cognitions have already been pointed to in preceding chapters. For example: "most students who had failed preliminary examinations in the past had had difficult personalities"; "the faculty expects less from this year's group as compared with earlier ones because most of the people in the present group have been here for only two years."

This is not to say that what is necessarily comforting for one student is comforting for all. But in general the persons who most often verbalized these attitudes were those for whom they were most comforting as measured by other criteria. For example, as we have pointed out, the attitude concerning the faculty expecting less of second-year students was developed and communicated by second-year students. It is true that one or two of the older students also accepted this idea, but these students had little to lose by its acceptance. In addition, the fact that a belief may be accurate does not invalidate it as a defense; on the contrary, accurate beliefs are valuable as defenses because they do have environmental support. Thus, while the inaccurate defenses may be more striking to the observer, they are probably more likely to lead to later problems of adaptation. The student who can draw satisfaction from the fact that he is competent and that others think him competent is in a better position than the student who holds this as an illusion.

A number of comforting thoughts, verbalized in early interviews with the students, were included in the questionnaire administered to students. They were asked to indicate how often they had felt, thought, said, or done each of a number of things (see table 14.3).

The assurance that occurred most frequently resulted from favorable social comparison—a student compared himself with other students who had taken examinations in prior years and passed, and told himself that he was as knowledgeable or more so than the student with whom he was comparing himself. Others *drew on past experience,* and, by reassuring themselves of their competence in the past, they felt more competent in the present: "I wouldn't have gotten this far unless I knew something," "I've handled situations in the past," and other such similar statements. Still others saw themselves as well liked, and almost all of the students believed to some extent that if you were liked, your chances of having a good outcome on the examinations were better. Others sought to externalize responsibility: "If I am doing all I can, what's the use of worrying?" Let us take some examples from the interviews to illustrate how the student verbalized these comforting comparisons and cognitions.

I think I'll pass because I think that if decisions have been made previously, that I'm one who will pass rather than fail. . . . So I'll really have to botch up

Table 14.3. Students' Reported Use of Comforting Cognitions

Comforting Cognitions	Percent of Students	
	Who Report Using This Cognition Very or Fairly Often	Who Report Using These Cognitions With any Frequency
I'm as bright and knowledgeable as other students who have passed these examinations	64	91
I've handled test situations in the past—there's no good reason why not now	59	86
I am doing all I can to prepare—the rest is not up to me	50	86
I wouldn't have gotten this far unless I knew something	50	86
I'm well liked in this department	45	77
I've already demonstrated my competence on past work, they will pass me	26	77
You can't fail these examinations unless you really mess up	23	73
They wouldn't fail me—they've already decided I'm going to pass	18	30
This is a test of stress; I can deal with that	14	59
If I'm not cut out for the field, it's best that I know it now	14	55

writtens to get them to alter their opinion of me. . . . I evaluate the people on the faculty as being reasonable people . . . who should make reasonable demands for performance on writtens which I should be able to meet.

[I was saying] that we are pretty scared of the questions that were asked on the old examinations and yet we haven't seen the answers that people have given to these questions to see what they were like; to see the quality of the answers—the answers which were acceptable in terms of passage. Perhaps, if we were able to see some of the answers that have been acceptable, we would feel a little better. I don't feel that we are significantly more defective than other people who have passed these . . . or that we worked any less. From this standpoint, it would seem that our chances of passing are just as good as those who passed.

I was afraid that reading so few books wouldn't be enough. Then I found out that other people were reading these and felt secure with them. Now I feel better.

It seems that people pass [the examinations] pretty easily.

I have a much better memory than most people.

[I tell] myself how clever I am. . . . I usually have done better. I think it contributes to my normal state of well-being.

Considering the people who passed previously, I think my chances are at least even.

Hundreds of such statements came up in the interviews with students. The examples took many forms, and enumerating them would be unnecessary for our argument. What is important to recognize is that these beliefs arose in the interaction process; they were exchanged back and forth among students, and many were held commonly and were consensually validated.

This is not to suggest that all social comparisons are favorable. As we indicated earlier, social comparison often aroused anxiety. It is through social comparison processes that the individual attempts to ascertain both his strengths and his weaknesses, and to evaluate what soft spots need plugging. The student who fails to take part in this type of social comparison can lose considerable information about the examinations and possible modes of preparation, although as a result he may be able to keep his anxiety at a lower level. This was especially true of two, low-anxiety, isolated students who were not comparing themselves to others, and who had little idea how much others were studying. Both of these students studied considerably less than the rest of the group, and both performed at a level below the expectations of faculty. One of these two students had communicated and compared himself so little with others, that he had no idea that other students were aiming to pass at the Ph.D. level. All along, he prepared casually, feeling that he would be satisfied attaining an M.A. pass. After the examinations the student became considerably agitated about his performance, knowing that had he set his expectations higher he might have performed better and closer to the expectations others had of him. The reactions of these two low-anxiety persons were somewhat similar to the reactions that Grinker and Spiegel (1945: 128) observed among some soldiers: "One sometimes sees men who err in the opposite direction and fail to interpret danger when they should. As a consequence, they are protected against developing subjective anxiety. . . . The defect in discrimination gives them the appearance of being unrealistic and slap-happy, illustrating the maxim that fools walk where angels fear to tread."

It is thus the process of social comparison that allows the student to pace himself. For example, one student decided a few weeks prior to examinations to postpone them until the following fall. Notice how social comparison was a prime influence in this decision.

I think, to a great degree, interacting with people like you who keep asking me what I am doing and other people who are doing things, sort of hearing that certain people are reading this, that, and the other, has kind of gotten me to the point of feeling that I'm not preparing for them like other people are. I really don't have a chance to. Maybe it would be best that I didn't take them at all rather than take them and not do so well. . . . I talked to a couple of people, [student X] and [student Y], in Central Building, and I've heard some from my office partner who knows [students A, B, and C] who are taking them and he related some of the things that they are doing. I feel, myself, that I would like to do some of these things . . . I don't have the time this semester. . . . So these sorts of things have gotten me to think that I'm not preparing too well. And I think that it would be best that I don't take them at all.

JOKING AND HUMOR

Joking as a useful form of defense has been given considerable attention by philosophers, psychologists, and humorists, but only in recent years have its social functions been noted to any significant degree. In recent studies by Coser (1959), Fox (1959), and Hamburg and associates (Hamburg, Hamburg and deGoza 1953) on the hospital ward, some of the social functions of joking under stress have been pointed out.

Four weeks prior to examinations students were asked to indicate how much they joked about examinations. Every student indicated that he had joked to some extent.

Table 14.4. The Extent of Student Joking About Examinations

Extent of Joking	Percent of Students (N-22)
Joked a great deal	23
Joked some	54
Joked not very much	23
Joked none	—

The older students who were more anxious and more upset about examinations seemed to find it more difficult to find humor in the examination situation.

Table 14.5. Student Status and Joking

	Percent of Students Who Joked		
	A Great Deal	Some	Not Very Much
Older students (N-8)	—	62	38
Second-year students (N-14)	36	50	14

Since joking is an interpersonal event and may serve as an avoidance device in interaction, we would expect that joking about examinations would be more likely to arise among the second-year students, who are more centrally located in the communication structure, than among those more isolated. Table 14.6 confirms this.

It appears that joking occurred primarily among those who were high-moderate and moderate-anxiety types. Students who were very anxious, with some exceptions, did not see the examinations as humorous as did some of the moderate-anxiety students. This was true especially of the older students who felt that they had suffered considerably in going through the process; yet it did appear that humor was an important mode of anxiety reduction. Also it seemed that joking occurred most frequently at certain points in time. For example, it seemed to increase in intensity just prior to the week of examinations, and the form that it took also seemed to change. Well before examinations, joking consisted mainly of poking fun at the material—a form of tension release. As examinations approached, however, tension-release humor still was present, but avoidance banter seemed to increase in significant quantity. A possible explanation for the change in the kind of joking forms was that as the examinations approached, time pressures increased and students became aware that time for future coping effort was limited. Therefore, a useful defense would allow for avoidance of serious discussion about examinations and avoidance of the kinds of anxiety stimuli that were discussed in an earlier chapter. For example, a few days prior to examinations, it would be of little use for a student to discover that five important textbooks had been read by others while he had spent his time on less significant details. Joking as an avoidance technique allowed for keeping further information that might have been disruptive out of one's frame of reference.

Before going on to describe and give some examples of the kinds of humor that developed, the reader should be warned that he might not find student humor terribly humorous. Humor is highly situational, and often specific to those sharing a common frame of reference. Regardless of how the jokes appear to the reader, they were in fact funny from the student's perspective.

Joking as a form of tension release. Joking is a useful device to reduce tensions resulting from uncertainty. One of the more common problems for stu-

Table 14.6. Joking Among Second-Year Students and Centrality in the Communication Structure*

	Percent of Students Who Joked		
Degree of Centrality	A Great Deal	Some	Not Very Much
Three or more communication links (N-6)	67	33	—
Less than three communication links (N-8)	12	63	25

*This relationship did not hold among older students. Having three or more communication links was atypical of older students.

dents in dealing with examinations is the uncertainty they feel as to which questions or areas will appear on examinations and the sampling used in choosing these questions. Students feel that it is conceivable that one can know an area well yet encounter an examination where he cannot answer the questions. Put in another way, students believe that an element of chance is operating, that the student may be lucky or unlucky in the questions he encounters. In the student story that follows, the uncertainty in the examination process was made to appear ludicrous.

I heard a cute story the other day about the manner in which certain people go around assigning questions for the examinations. . . . He grabs down a great big book and goes thumbing through it and happens to pick up one little area, one little section in the bottom of the page in the middle of the volume. And he says: "Hmmmm, this strikes my fancy. I've never seen this before. I think I'll put this on the examinations and see what they could tell me about this."

One of the situations found most amusing by the students concerned a discussion about a possible question on examinations. As the reader will remember, most of the students felt that if you do not know the answer to a question, you still should attempt to write something. The situation described below deals with a discussion of this strategy.

When I walked into the Monday class, everyone was joking around . . . [student D] was telling us his point of view of what he would do if he didn't know a question. . . . He would give another answer to it. . . . The other fellows said, "Okay, we'll test you out. What is the [Spencer] hypothesis?" or some obscure thing I never heard of. And so [student D] sort of laughed and said, "Well, I never heard of that but I'm sure getting familiar with the [Zipp] effect."
[Later student D] came in and said, "Okay, I found out what [Spencer] is." And [student A], who doesn't take our other course, said, "WHAT???" And everybody said, "You better be sure you know that, that's very important." And someone said it was such and such and such. And somebody else turned around and said, "What is its present status?" and everybody laughed.

Here again, the question, "What is its present status?" was experienced by the group as a humorous remark. This is probably due to the fact that many of the questions on doctoral examinations ask students to discuss the development and present status of various concepts. In a sense the group was having a good laugh over the examinations and, to some extent, over the stereotyped forms the questions sometimes take.

Another source of humor was the obscure items that students often pick up in their reading for examinations, that they then go around and jokingly ask other students about. In a sense this represents a take-off on the anxiety-arousing effect students have on one another, and also is sometimes used as a device to hide one's own anxiety about examinations. Below are some examples:

Generally we joke about things that don't mean too much . . . and obscure things. [Student F] said something like, did I know that the average visual acuity of an eight-year-old elephant was the same as a female horse?

He came across a little bit about Meyer, the photosensitive crab. So this seemed like a particular bit of nonsensical information which he passed all over the department. "You got to know about Meyer." It has kind of been the joke of the week.

One of the students who participated a great deal in joking described what he perceived to be the function of joking about examinations.

All of this doesn't mean anything. It's not going to be useful in preparing for the writtens . . . but I think it's a tension-reducing mechanism. It keeps you from getting too serious about them, in a sense, letting the thing get the better of you, which I'm sure has happened to some people in the past, and I'm sure it has had an adverse effect.

Students also made seemingly silly comments to one another, or thought of funny comments they might make. Apparently this made the whole process seem a little more unreal, a little less serious.

I was thinking about walking in on the first examination and yelling, "Hey, I thought this was going to be multiple choice."

"Sick" Humor. This type of humor is represented by jokes about failing. Usually these jokes involve saying, "I'm going to fail, ha, ha, ha," or "We'll fail and then we can go out and kill ourselves." By attaching an absurdity to the situation, the student seemed to make the real situation and the threat it presented more remote and more impossible.

Another kind of "sick" humor pertained to what the student should do should he fail. Once again the same function was apparent. By making the possibilities absurd, failure seemed more remote.

[Student C] said, "Next year at this time, I'll be getting ready to get out of this place, and I'll be looking for a job." And I said, "Yeah, next year at this time I might be selling shoes." Someone else said, "Yeah, if it weren't for these writtens."

We got into a discussion, you know, how I always wanted to sell shoes. . . . A lot of talk is this sort of humorous thing about it.

Whether the jokes were concerned with selling shoes or picking cotton, their intent was the same: to debunk the seriousness of the possible outcomes. This could take various forms; for example, one student usually referred to the examinations as the "spring quizzes."

Joking as an Avoidance Device. Joking is one of the most effective methods for avoiding a serious discussion. Certainly anyone who has ever tried to have a serious discussion with a person who insists on being jovial will realize how effective humor may be as an avoidance device. It allows an individual to fend others off in a friendly but effective fashion, and it makes them keep their distance. It also can be used as a form of attack on others, and should they object, one always can have the recourse to "I was only joking." It is this ambiguous function of joking that allows one to attempt attack and avoidance without making himself too vulnerable to being charged with his offense. One student explained how joking might be utilized in this fashion:

When [student X] comes in, he wants to talk seriously about the examinations. But I don't want to talk seriously about them because I feel that I'm not going to pass and that isn't very funny. Another thing is that I don't want to tell him that I don't think I'm going to pass. . . . [Student X], he's pretty serious and I tease him. He comes in and asks, "What are you studying for statistics?" And I spend the next five minutes reeling off all this nonsense (laughs), and he's getting more and more anxious. He just bothers most people more because he is serious. He's pretty anxious really. . . . Everybody is just real childish and real silly. It's easier to be funny than to be serious.

The joking playfulness one can observe here combined teasing, hostility, and anxiety avoidance. One student, for example, related how he became very anxious after he had found a question he could not answer on an old examination. After asking another student if he knew the answer, he reported that the other student also became anxious, and, feeling that he had done his duty, he went to bed. Another student, from the viewpoint of the recipient of the communication, related a somewhat similar situation:

When I try to study in the office, somebody will come up to me and say, "What are you studying? What are you studying?" When I tell them, they say, "Oh, you don't want to study that. What do you want to study that for?" And they'll go on. It makes me angry. They're doing it because they feel threatened sort of. . . . Everyone wants to be sure that nobody knows anything more than they do. . . . So instead you tease.

One student who generated considerable anxiety, and who a number of students were avoiding, was sometimes heavily sanctioned by names. This was done to discourage his serious attitude toward examinations, which made the other students anxious.

Students also did a considerable bit of clowning.

[Student B] was on a jag a couple of weeks ago. Every time someone walked into the room, he asked them, "Why are you so hostile to me?". . . . It's just easier to keep laughing. It doesn't bother you as much to joke about it.

This kind of joking, especially among one of the cliques, continued until writtens began, and then to some extent seemingly subsided. At any rate, there was an apparent decrease in the hostile jabbing that had taken place just before the examinations. Once examinations started, however, students became more genuinely friendly to one another and supported one another more than they had at any prior period. It would appear that once the examinations had begun, and some of the tension was reduced, the competitive jockeying was no longer necessary. The clearly defined threat now was not other students but the examinations themselves. And the group seemed to unite against this threat.

. . . .

A DYNAMIC VIEW OF FEELINGS
AND BEHAVIOR AS EXAMINATIONS APPROACH

As the examinations approached and as student anxiety increased, various changes occurred in behavior. Joking increased, and, while students still sought social support and talked a great deal about examinations, they began specifically to avoid certain people who aroused their anxiety. Stomach-aches, asthma, and a general feeling of weariness became common complaints, and other psychosomatic symptoms appeared. The use of tranquilizers and sleeping pills became more frequent.

For those who had started studying intensively at an early date, exhaustion crept in and they lost their desire and motivation to study.

I just don't seem to be picking up things. You know, like I'll look over stuff and I just don't seem to get it. It's very depressing to spend time and not feel it's doing any good. . . . I just wish they would get them over with. It's just bugging me. . . . I'm getting tired of sitting at that desk. I have all sorts of psychosomatic complaints. My back hurts and so forth. . . . I wish they were over. They're so awful. . . . I was about ready to turn myself into [the psychiatric ward] but now I'm taking antidepressant pills.

A number of other students also complained of an inability to concentrate on their studies:

My minute-to-minute motivation seems to have gone down. When I started, I was a real eager beaver but now it seems, the last week or so, I've had a little trouble. If I have a half hour off, I'll sit in the social room rather than study for that half hour.

Lately I've been feeling depressed. I don't feel that I know anything. I just feel so mentally defective, like what I have done goes into one ear and out the other. . . . Instead of putting in a last-ditch effort, I can't. I'm just sort of tired of the whole business. I'm tired of studying. I'm tired of school. I'm just tired.

While the student feels saturated with study, he still is acutely aware of the short time available for further preparation. Thus he is torn between the feeling that he must study and his inability to concentrate and study effectively, which leads to considerable anxiety, self-doubt, and disgust. As anxiety reaches a high level, students come to agreements not to discuss examinations, but as the saliency of examinations is too great these agreements are rarely maintained. Also, the excessive concern about examinations is reflected in dreams about them. Unreality is another common feeling, the "this isn't happening to me" effect.

As examinations approach, the most common feeling is one of unpreparedness and impending disaster, although these reports of impending doom usually are disqualified in some way. The student, for example, will predict doom and then declare that he must be pretty stupid to say something as silly as that. Listed below are some of the indications students gave that failure was imminent.

I feel now, rather unrealistically, I think, that I can't remember any names. I can't remember this. I can't remember that. I feel unprepared for this.

I spoke to [student C] . . . about how depressed we were. . . . The main thing he hopes is that they'll let him take them again. He keeps saying this over and over because he's now in one of these stages which I think we all go through, where you just feel that there's no possibility of passing and that you are a failure.

I kept having the feeling like I'm going to fail and that I don't know anything.

When the examinations are nearly upon the student, anxiety is very high, even for those rated as low-anxiety persons, although students do fluctuate between confidence and anxiety. Since studying is difficult, the student questions his motivation, interest, and ability in the field. He reassures himself that he does not care how well he does—that all he really wants out of the process is the Ph.D. degree. Even four weeks prior to examinations 82 percent of the students reported that they had said to themselves, "All I really want from this process is the Ph.D. degree." They attempted to defend against their feelings by behaving in a silly, manic way, and avoidance joking became very prevalent. Expectation levels were set lower and lower, and many of the students jokingly talked about what they were going to do after they failed or how they were going to prepare for examinations the next time they took them. It appears that for the student supreme confidence at this point was considered not only presumptuous, but sacrilegious. Under these conditions the group became very cohesive and individuals became supportive of one another and exclusive of younger students in the department.

. . . . .

15

The Management
of Abhorrent Behavior—
Survival Period

REX A. LUCAS

This [discussion] is concerned with the way in which men make social adjustments. Specifically, we will examine a situation in which men took action
which was abhorrent to them—the drinking of urine. The extreme conditions
draw attention to steps in social adjustment and to process and mechanisms that
pass unnoticed in day-to-day living.

It hardly need be established that the drinking of urine is a taboo
in our society, a taboo so strong that few would even think of consuming it. This
is not surprising because during the socialization of the child, the behavior patterns surrounding urination are carefully disassociated from sexual activities and
from liquid intake required by the body. Urination is separated spatially and
socially from eating, drinking, and other social activities. The widespread pro-
hibition of drinking urine is so strongly held and so remote from everyday life
that few entertain the thought of it. Among many, urination is associated with
rinsing of hands, which suggests dirt or germs. Urine is usually thought of as a
liquid waste from the body; the implications are that urine contains at best
impurities and at worst poison.[1]

. . . .

During the escape period the men defined their position as one from
which escape was highly likely, so their free use of water was appropriate to this
definition. No one took seriously a rather tentative warning about the depletion
of the water supply. After unsuccessful attempts to make their way to the main
shaft, their definition of the situation was modified somewhat—they thought that
immediate escape was not too likely. At this point, their concern about water was
not great. It was not until the lights failed and further exploration was ruled out,

when the men defined their situation as one from which escape was impossible, that they became concerned about the water supply. At this point the men checked the water supply, searched for additional water, and instituted rationing. They shifted their goals and activities from escape to survival.

WATER SUBSTITUTES

[Finally,] the six miners [reached] the point when the last of their water had been used and they sat in the dark, intensely thirsty, and without liquid.

> DICK: There wasn't much we could do but set and wait . . . what we listened for mostly was the rescue group, and we knew we could last a few days there if the gas didn't get us.

The men, intensely conscious of their need for water, explored possible substitutes and alternatives. They chewed bark, sucked coal, and chewed tobacco in an attempt to keep their mouths and throats moistened. While these alternatives did not provide liquid, they artificially excited the saliva glands, thus modifying the discomfort associated with thirst. Eventually even this comfort was no longer possible:

> FRED: I chewed bark, but I couldn't get no moisture out of it. It was just dry and I spit it out. I tried chewing tobacco, but I couldn't get no juice out of it. See, you don't have any wet in your mouth at all.

The men realized that their new situation was perilous; the use of bark, coal, and tobacco neither contributed moisture nor stimulated the saliva glands. Each man had a dry parched tongue and throat, cracking lips, and an intense thirst. Beyond these discomforts, all six wished to live as long as possible,[2] in case they were found by rescuers. In other words, each man was aware of his own physiological needs, shared a similar definition of the situation, and sought some immediate action. In the words of A. K. Cohen, "the crucial condition for the emergence of new cultural forms . . . is the effective interaction with one another of a number of actors with similar problems of adjustment" (1955:59). At this point, the men considered the drinking of urine as a substitute for water.

THE INITIAL GESTURES

The emerging action took place in an extreme context, for the environmental conditions forced the men to consider a course of activity which was unthinkable. In this analysis every word concerned with the phenomenon in the accounts of all six men will be utilized. In this way we can follow the process with some precision and guard against any possible biased selection of material.

The initial gestures were reported in this fashion:

> BOB: Our water was all gone, so I said, "Well, boys, we're going to have to drink our pee," and they kind of laughed. Then Ed said, "The more you drink it, the more it'll go through your system, and it will keep us going for a while."
>
> ED: Harry said, "Well, we won't drink it, we will just rinse our mouths out with it."
>
> BOB: So, all at once, I hear somebody up streaming their can, and then after we was all doing it.

This account will be examined sentence by sentence so that we can follow the sequence carefully. Bob made the initial gesture suggesting a new course of action, "Well, boys, we're going to have to drink our pee." As an innovator, he provided the initial gesture which might elicit responses, suggesting the receptivity of the others. Such an initial gesture often takes the form of a tentative and ambiguous suggestion[3] so as to permit the speaker to retreat, if necessary, to save face; in this case, the gesture was presented, not as a suggestion, but as a tentative statement of future inevitability—"we're going to have to . . ." Thus there was little personal identification with the recommendation of an abhorrent act. But the idea had been made explicit and a potential behavior pattern had been socially born, so to speak.

This initial gesture was motivated by tensions and discomforts common to all the men, so we may well anticipate that the resolution of the problem was carried out through a process of mutual exploration and joint elaboration (Lippett, Watson, and Westley 1958). Novel social action, and, for that matter, a culture itself, emerges out of social interaction. In this instance, the proposed solution of the miners' problem could not be carried out within the cultural tradition because the suggested action had no embodiment in the miners' action model. For this reason the responses of the other five miners were of prime importance as indicators of the social feasibility of the suggestion. The responses of the five provided the feedback on the acceptability of the suggestion.[4]

The response to the initial gesture was "and they kind of laughed." This response indicated uncertainty rather than amusement. There was no immediate overt acceptance of the idea; on the other hand, there was no outright rejection, no ridicule, no one said "no," nor prophetically, "I'd rather die than drink that stuff." The initial response was merely a "kind of" laughter.

The mutual exploration of the proposed action continued. Ed said, "The more you drink it, the more it'll go through your system, and it will keep us going for a while." In his statement Ed supported the suggestion, expanded and legitimated it. He pointed to the legitimacy of the intake of urine in terms of satisfying biological "needs" of survival, in the Sumner sense, to "keep us going for a while." His statement that drinking urine would sustain life supported the suggestion with strong affect. He also implied that in terms of liquid each man could become a self-contained, self-perpetuating unit—"the more you drink, the more you will have."

THE EXPRESSIVE QUALITIES OF THE ACT

So far, then, we have noted the original exploratory suggestion—uncertainty, laughter, but no rebukes—followed by a statement of approval and further commitment based on the utility of the suggestion.

Next, Harry contributed to the growing social product, "Well, we won't drink it, we will just rinse our mouth [sic] out with it." On the face of it, this statement seems to be most inappropriate—six miners faced death by thirst, yet one man suggested that they do not drink, but merely "rinse our mouth out with it." This requires further analysis.

Until this point we have considered thirst in terms of liquid intake and the drinking of urine in terms of functional requirements of biological or instrumental needs. It is important to remember that the interaction concerns the drinking of *urine,* which is considered repugnant in our society. The proposed social action, as we have seen, was shaped by the men's present situation, their present need, and the present definition of the situation, but it was also affected by preexisting experience. The miners' prior social experience was responsible for their view of urine drinking as abhorrent.

Bales (1951:8), Parsons (1951:79–88), Hare (1963:12),[5] and others have postulated that analytically every act may be viewed simultaneously as both expressive and instrumental. Acts differ in terms of primacy given to one aspect or the other, but they all involve both. Every word or gesture carries with it at least two kinds of information, task and social-emotional, on at least two kinds of levels, group and individual. First, a gesture has implications for the task of the group in that it affects the decision-making process; second, it has implications for the relative evaluation of members as well as the emotional attachments among members (Hare 1963:63). Third, on the individual level, every gesture affects individual decision-making and goal achievement, but, fourth, at the same time the gesture affects the internal expressive or social-emotional life of the individual. Again, these four types of implication of any individual act are analytical in nature; in real life it is difficult to distinguish one without talking about the others.

The examination of the interaction leading to urine drinking is important, analytically speaking, because it draws our attention to the expressive aspect of the action. In this instance, the men attached conscious urgency to *both* the instrumental and expressive qualities of the proposed act. The comment of Ed legitimated the instrumental qualities of the act on both an individual and group level: "it will keep us going for a while." On the other hand, Harry made due recognition of and allowance for the expressive qualities. He picked up the cue provided by the laughter which greeted the original gesture. He shared the expressive uneasiness made explicit through this laughter and suggested a preliminary mechanism for the management of sentiments and tensions.

The statement took into account that the emergence of the new instrumentally essential action simultaneously evoked a revulsion in all the men. (When emerging actions do not involve heavily emotion-laden preexisting attitudes, we often forget that the actions constitute innovations or deviant behavior.) As an aid in overcoming this revulsion, Harry stated that if the men could not bring themselves to drink body waste, they would do no harm if they merely rinsed out their mouths to relieve secondary thirst symptoms. The statement suggested that on an individual level the miner would be merely rinsing his mouth and need not face the abhorrence of drinking urine, thus supplying a way of handling individual expressive difficulties. Harry's statement, which went unchallenged, also had expressive implications on a group level. He announced that the individual would not lose face; his prestige would not be affected because he carried out this type of harmless behavior.

At this point, one of the men took an important step, the first preliminary action on the original suggestion. "So all at once, I heard somebody up streaming their can, and then after we was all doing it." "We was all doing it"—once begun, each man took the initial step of saving his urine in his water or lunch can. What had been put forward as a tentative statement by Bob was translated, by this time, into initial action. Step by step each man had become progressively involved, and this was a crucial first physical symbol of action and commitment.

SOCIAL LEGITIMATION OF THE ACT

When the process reached this point, a long discussion and exchange of views occurred—interaction about which we have only suggestions rather than an account. This conversation aided the men in getting used to the idea. It is clear from their accounts that an important factor in this exchange was that one of the miners had heard of or "known fellows who had drunk their own [urine]." Although urine drinking was not within the experience of the miners, this established it as within the realm of human experience. Urine drinking, then, was possible and not unprecedented, although it ran contrary to the workaday mores of the miners themselves:

> ED: When the water ran out, one of the fellows spoke. He said he had known fellows who had drunk their own—that was the argument. Well, each fellow did [drink]. We had our water cans and I had my bottle.
>
> FRED: Bob suggested drinking urine. I never thought of that, you know. Every time we had to go to make our urine, we just saved it in the can.
>
> HARRY: Well, I don't know how we come to mention it. Someone said, "Let's drink our urine." Well, we made up our mind that we should drink it. We was all talking there. We used our own water cans and we used our own urine. I never thought of this before. When we were trapped in the mine explosion [two years previously] we had lots of water.
>
> DICK: My buddy Bob mentioned drinking urine. He hadn't drunk his, but the water was all drunk up and I was so dry. He kept talking about it first.

The citing of the precedent was of great importance because, as the comments clearly document, urine drinking was a novel idea to all but one of the men. Although they all suffered similar discomfort and fear, the particular suggestion put forward by Bob was not concurrently held by the other men. They were not simply waiting for someone to make explicit a shared inward plan of action. The novelty of the suggestion is not surprising considering the lack of a cultural model for such behavior; for five of the miners urine drinking had not been embodied in thought, not to mention action.

The statements of the men indicate that the original suggestion initiated a process of mutual exploration and joint elaboration. The move was not accepted or legitimated on the basis of prestige or status of the person who made the suggestion. The very anonymity of references to Bob, in terms of "one of the fellows," "someone said," supports this contention.

The statements "He said he had known fellows who had drunk their own—that was the argument,"[6] "He kept talking about it first," and "We was all talking there" suggest the considerable discussion, justification, and redefinition of the situation that was in progress. The conversation was directed mainly to the expressive aspects of urine drinking. Each miner was contributing to the process of making urine drinking socially permissible.

The six men had come a long way from their first definition that escape was at hand and the copious drinking of water which was appropriate to this assumption. Within three days they defined their situation as one from which escape was impossible, rescue questionable, and they had taken the first action toward drinking urine.

SUMMARY OF MAIN POINTS

The miners became aware of their need for liquid and began to search for alternatives. They sucked and chewed coal, bark, and tobacco. Step by step the next moves were as follows:

1. An initial gesture suggesting urine consumption as a water substitute was put forward.
2. None of the men rejected the suggestion.
3. A response was made approving and enlarging upon the initial gesture, adding legitimation on instrumental grounds.
4. A response was made approving and enlarging upon the initial gesture, adding further legitimation on expressive grounds.
5. A social action translated the original suggestion into the first stage of execution. This move initiated action, and through it, reinforced social support for the idea.
6. A long period of discussion characterized by elaboration and justification of the action in expressive terms followed.

This sequence constituted the social legitimation of action which a day previously was unthinkable. Through the sharing of a similar concern, redefinitions of the situation, and a process of mutual conversion, the beginning of a new action pattern emerged on a group level so that, as one miner put it, "we made up our mind that we should drink it." This social decision is an important one for, as Lewin (1947:35) has pointed out, "it is usually easier to change individuals formed into a group than to change any one of them separately."

INDIVIDUAL EMOTIONAL QUALITIES OF THE ACT

At this point we might anticipate the verification of Freud's suggestion that first we discuss it and then we do it. However, despite instrumental urgency and social permissibility, not a single miner was able to drink:

FRED: It gagged me, you know.
DICK: It came up at first.
ED: It was a while before I decided to take mine.
BOB: You've got to go kind of easy because if you don't, you might throw up. I only threw up once.

The involuntary gagging, vomiting, and avoidance were physiological manifestations of strong emotional feeling. These manifestations persisted despite the urgent individual physiological requirements for liquid and the social permissiveness of urine drinking on both instrumental and expressive grounds. The shared abhorrence of urine drinking was so deeply internalized, so much a part of each man's normative system, that each still had to deal *individually* with the emotional nature of the new socially approved behavior. As one man said: "It was just the thought—it was not real water. If somebody had passed it to us in the dark and told us that it was something else, it would have been different, but, of course, we knew what it was."

It is quite apparent that an additional step lies between the achievement of social permissiveness and subsequent individual action. That step involves coming to terms with the expressive aspects of emerging action on an individual basis. Perhaps interracial contact involves similar problems. Although interracial contact may be socially permissible and legally mandatory, to some individuals the implications are so repugnant that personal contact is impossible. Somehow the individual must personally come to terms with the emotional nature of the activity. In the case of the miners, some process or technique was necessary to permit activity, normally repugnant, to become personally acceptable in order to avoid physiological reaction. Each had to overcome his involuntary inability to drink.

All of this is instructive, as it directs our attention to the individual and his relation to emerging action. The emergence of action in a group is usually recognized as an original "need," an innovation, and social acceptance, but the fact that the innovator himself has to come to terms with the innovation is often overlooked. In the case of the miners, this "coming to terms" is clear because of the strong emotional overtones surrounding the nature of the action.

Cohen considers this same process in slightly different terminology:

We may think of this process as one of mutual conversion. The important thing to remember is that we do not first convert ourselves and then others. The acceptability of an idea to oneself depends upon its acceptability to others. Converting the other is part of the process of converting oneself. (1955:61)

This is a neat statement of part of the process under examination. We noted the gestures leading to mutual conversion. But we also saw that, once the drinking of urine became acceptable and group-supported, each individual still had a long way to go before he was able actually to drink. It is clear that social acceptability is an important step toward the emergence of new action, but social acceptability is not individual acceptability. Converting the others is the first part of the process of converting oneself. But once behavior has become socially approved, the next step is the process through which each individual somehow makes this behavior personally acceptable. This is the second part of the process of converting oneself.

.   .   .   .

TECHNIQUES FOR EXPRESSIVE ADAPTATION

Each man went through behavior routines which permitted him to become "used to the idea." These processes permitted activity normally repugnant to become acceptable in order to reduce the physiological inhibition toward drinking. We now return to the men's accounts:

> BOB: We was all rinsing our mouth out and taking a sup. Your mouth gets so dry and you rinse your mouth out—quite bitter. Well, you just force yourself; you got to take it. You've got to go kind of easy because if you don't you might throw up. I only threw up once. I washed my mouth out once, sometimes twice, before I drank. We saved our own urine.
>
> ED: It was a while before I decided to take mine. Well, at first I would rinse out my mouth. You rinse out your mouth several times first, and then eventually you would take a little swallow, and after a while, it wasn't so bad as you thought it was. Sipping every half hour perhaps, some a little sooner, some a little further away.
>
> FRED: But the first two or three drinks, you know, well, I didn't drink it; it gagged me, you know. I would rinse me mouth out, and then a little would trickle down—but, oh, I would near throw it up. . . . I didn't though.
>
> TOM: After the water ran out, I started to drink urine—my urine. I started wetting my lips and then hold my breath and wash my mouth out.
>
> HARRY: For a day or so I just put a little in my mouth and rinsed my mouth and spit it out. Then we started swallowing a little wee bit.
>
> DICK: Everybody started drinking it. I waited as long as I could, but I had to drink it. I never drank too much all the time I was there, I drank about a glassful maybe. I started wetting my lips, then washed my mouth out, and I drank about four or five hours later. It came up first.

The six men all used similar techniques to come to terms with the expressive implications of the act. For instance, all the men used internal conversation, in part a continuation of the conversation which had already taken place on an interpersonal level. This involved comments such as, "Well, you just force yourself; you got to take it."

All the men gradually retrained their senses. The men did more than "get used to the idea," they also got used to the reality. Each man removed the secondary thirst symptoms by wetting cracked lips and parched mouth before spitting. In doing so, the miners used a well-recognized social technique of experimenting without irretrievably committing themselves. It will be remembered that, early in the exchange, it was established that just rinsing out the mouth was innocent behavior and did not constitute highly repugnant action. After a span of time manifestly experimenting and latently retraining the senses and emotional reactions, "then we started swallowing a little wee bit," and "after a while, it wasn't as bad as you thought it was."

From this it was not far to a subtle technique. It began with the miner experimenting without irretrievably committing himself. While participating in what he could convince himself was the innocent behavior of mouth rinsing, accidentally on purpose "a little would trickle down." In this technique rather than gradually training the senses, the man was out to deceive his sentiments. By accidentally swallowing a little while he wasn't looking, as it were, he was attempting to bypass the physical manifestations of repugnance.[7] A detailed and systematic discussion of these techniques and mechanisms will be made shortly.

SOCIAL ELABORATION OF THE ACT

Once initial repugnance was overcome, but still a part of this same process of coming to terms with the urine, further social redefinitions and refinements ensued. Joint social elaboration was carried on—the six men literally exchanged recipes. Available flavors were restricted to bark and coal. Two practices began to emerge; the first involved the flavoring of the urine in its container by adding bark or coal, and in the second procedure, the flavor was added in the mouth, by chewing either bark or coal and "juicing it up" by a swallow of urine. But again the men speak for themselves:

> BOB: We put bark in it. I think Dick put bark in it, and I put bark in it. We put some coal in it. I said, "Dick, coal is good for our heartburn, why wouldn't it be good to eat? So we started eating coal. Dick and I did and I think the rest tried it too.

ED: I ground up a little coal, and we had some bark. They would say, "Got a piece of bark there?" and I said, "It is a dry piece," but I chewed it and chewed it and chewed it, and I said, "Boys, you want to do it like that—chew it fine to get the juice." I don't imagine it did any good. Anyway, we would chew it until our mouth got so dry, and once in a while, we would take a swallow of water to juice it up a bit—improvised water.

FRED: We got so dry it was beginning to taste good, you know, I would rinse my mouth out about a couple of times a day, maybe a couple times through the night, I would imagine. Then I got to the stage I could swallow.

HARRY: We chewed some bark, we would take a mouthful of bark and chew that for a while and then take a little drink of water.

BOB: I chewed bark; it was dry getting down, but I took a little bit of my water and I kind of washed it down and I felt better.

Once the problem of drinking had been solved on an individual level, the continuing process returned to the level of interaction for elaboration and refinement. These accounts bring three points to our attention: in the first place, the exchanges of recipes aided individuals in controlling their emotional behavior by pooling techniques. Literally the men are saying, This is how I do it, and it works, so you try it too. In the second place, it was probably helpful to each individual to know that others, by implication at least, were having emotional difficulties in drinking. The very fact that urine drinking itself and the difficulties involved were the subject of long and occasionally bantering exchanges tended to give each man some social support in dealing with his shared, but essentially private problem. In the third place, we should note that through these exchanges a further redefinition emerged. The word "urine" moved from "urine" to "it" to "water," or more delicately, "improvised water."

THE COMPLETION OF THE ACT

. . . Urine was called water, it was being flavored, and once these new patterns were legitimated by the group and each individual in both expressive and instrumental aspects, urine drinking, repugnant under ordinary circumstances, posed few problems. Once the action was firmly established, it became expected and approved behavior within the particular setting:

BOB: I had no trouble at all, once I started to drink.

FRED: I didn't mind the end of it. I was taking gulps of it down, but it would only take that dryness away for maybe five or ten minutes and then you would be just as dry as ever.

TOM: Eventually, I drank as much as I wanted, but I don't think I drank too much. I never felt like vomiting.

HARRY: At the last of it, we were just drinking it. We did worry a bit about it.

DICK: One fellow down there—I thought he was drinking beer. He seemed to be at the can all the time.

Although urine drinking had become a legitimate and accepted action, not all doubts were removed. The comments, "I don't think I drank too much," or "We did worry a bit about it," suggest nagging questions regarding the long-term physiological effects of urine drinking which relate to the notion that urine is harmful if not poisonous. There was some irritation at the inefficiency of the urine because it did not seem to quench the thirst for any great length of time.

The important implication of this urine drinking pattern was that each miner became a self-sustaining, self-priming unit in relation to liquid output and input. Although the new pattern was social in its development, and, once accepted, socially supported, each individual carried on independently.[8]

. . . .

NOTES

1. These statements are valid in a general sense despite a wide range of notable exceptions, even in North American culture. The family physician, for instance, often dipped his finger in a medical urine sample and touched it to his tongue as a quick test for diabetes. Other people recall traditional folk remedies brought from Eastern Europe which incorporated the patient's urine. Despite the taboo, it is probable that many people are able to describe the taste of urine.

2. ". . . thirst depends less on the absolute water content of the body than on its water content *relative* to certain solid constituents, notably salts" (Wolf 1956:71).

The length of time it is possible for man to survive without water depends upon the heat, humidity, and other environmental conditions. Murray (1960:71) suggests, "Water is one of the essential requirements for human life. . . . Death occurs about four or five days after total water deprivation, depending on other factors such as environmental temperature." Wolf states: "A rat curiously may survive longer (13 days) with food and no water than with water and no food (8.5 days). This is not true generally of larger animals such as the dog or man. . . . How long one can survive depends on the conditions. . . . It is estimated that a man cannot survive when he has lost water amounting to 20 percent of his body weight (1956:73). Mariott suggests, "Death occurs when the loss reaches approximately 15 percent of body weight or 20 to 22 percent of body water in about 7 to 10 days" (1950:13).

3. For a discussion of this process, see Cohen 1955:60–65.

4. For a discussion on feedback, see Bales (1951, 1954); Cohen (1955:61); Homans (1950:153–55, 273–76).

5. This analytical distinction between instrumental and expressive aspects of behavior is a common one, often appearing as "task-oriented" (instrumental-adaptive) and "emotional-oriented" (expressive-integrative). Hare, for instance, uses the term *task behavior* to include categories of observing, hypothesizing, and formulating action and the term *social-emotional* to include categories of control and affection. The term *expressive,* always polar to *instrumental* or *adaptive* behavior, has a long history in psychology: see Allport and Vernon (1933), or Wolff (1943). The dichotomy, however named, is a gross one. "Expressive," however, should not be equated with "emotional" because the concept subsumes the expression of the individual idiosyncratic personality in cognitive style, emotional style, motor acts, as well as affect. In a technical sense, "expressive" may be used instead of "feeling," "emotion," or "affect," but certainly, "emotional" cannot be used as a substitute for "expressive." When "expressive" is used in this study, it includes both affect and the idiosyncratic aspects of behavior. The terms *affect, feeling,* and *emotion* are used when there is no doubt that we are considering that aspect of behavior exclusively.

6. As we shall see, under certain conditions it is preferable to drink someone else's.

7. There is no suggestion in the reports that the men perceived any alternative method of drinking urine other than saving it in containers and then drinking. There is no indication that they knew that urine is sterile while in the body; lone trappers and woodsmen in the North immediately urinate on a cut, using the urine for its sterile qualities before binding the wound. It is only when the urine makes contact with the oxygen in the atmosphere that it immediately begins to decompose and the process of decomposition produces the rank and characteristic odor of urine. The whole problem of gagging from this distasteful stimulus could have been circumvented by drinking urine without allowing it to make contact with the air. This method, however, would have involved the breaking of another set of deeply internalized norms. The revulsion related to urine drinking without the liquid contacting the air was probably even greater than that involved in attempting to drink rank-smelling urine from an open container.

8. Compared with the preoccupation with water and thirst, there were very few comments on food and hunger. Only seven of the eighteen men [these six, plus twelve from another study] mentioned the subject of food in their account of the entrapment. The following comments are typical:

ED: We had very little to eat.
DAN: My stomach never bothered me . . . except for a little gnawing hunger.

This lack of discussion of hunger and food seems to reflect the findings of authorities on the importance of food in relation to water in terms of discomfort and survival. "It is generally agreed that healthy persons can fast for two weeks . . . without undue suffering or adverse physiological effects as long as water is available" (Olsen 1960:167). This view is supported by Brown, "Food is not very important in a desert emergency nor is it desired by thirsty men" (1947:158) "Thirsty food" was particularly unwelcome by the miners:

FRED: The boys found a chocolate bar. We split that up. Well, I had a piece the first time; well, it made me worse—the chocolate made me thirsty. When it came time around for me to go and get my chocolate, I said, "No. You fellows go ahead. Take it. I don't want it," because it was just making me thirsty.

16

A Prediction of Delayed Stress Response Syndromes in Vietnam Veterans

MARDI J. HOROWITZ and
GEORGE F. SOLOMON

M ilitary psychiatrists in Vietnam (Bourne 1970) did not encounter the frequency of major stress response syndromes noted during World War II (Grinker and Spiegel 1945), but stress response syndromes often begin only after termination of real environmental stress events and after a latency period of apparent relief. We expect that civilian mental health professionals will see stress response syndromes in Vietnam veterans over the next few years, will tend to overlook the etiological importance of their military history, and will encounter difficulties in establishing effective treatment for such persons. Because this topic is so important, we have attempted to formulate here our initial observations of psychopathology and treatment difficulties on the basis of case reports and in the absence of formal survey or research quantification and control. These assertions, therefore, must be regarded as preliminary and speculative.

BACKGROUND

In World War II it was the custom to keep fighting personnel at the front line for long periods of time and psychiatric disability often increased in direct proportion to the length of time in combat. In air crews with repeated combat missions, 50 percent or more of those involved (Grinker and Spiegel 1945) might eventually have severe symptoms of combat neuroses. Similar statistics were accumulated for those in ground forces (Lewis and Engel 1954). In the Korean War and again in the Vietnam War, military psychiatrists were prepared for numerous psychiatric casualties by the experiences of World War II. In the Vietnamese conflict fewer psychiatric casualties than expected were reported (Bourne 1970) and, of special note, there were fewer signs and symptoms of traumatic neuroses than anticipated.

An important background to present considerations is found in the consistent data from clinical, field, and experimental studies of stress response syndromes. Breuer and Freud (1895/1955) in their study of hysterical neuroses, then felt to be a posttraumatic syndrome, documented the intrusion of "warded off" ideas, the compulsive repetition of trauma-related behavior, and the recurrent attacks of trauma-related emotional sensations. They also documented the interrelated but seemingly opposite syndrome constellation of denial, repression, and emotional avoidance. Subsequent psychoanalytic studies (as recently summarized by Furst 1967) have indicated the generality of such tendencies after stress. Field studies, especially those which have investigated concentration camp victims, confirm these observations. Persons exposed to severe stress, perhaps not until after an extended period of relief or latency, will have (a) recurrent intrusive dreams, nightmares, daytime images, and waves of painful emotional reexperience, and (b) ideational denial, emotional numbing, and behavioral constriction (Krystal 1968; Lifton 1970; Niederland 1968; Oswald and Bittner 1968). Such syndromes may continue for decades (Matussek and Mantell 1971; Nefzger 1970). Experimental studies also confirm the generality of these tendencies across persons who vary in predisposition (Horowitz 1969, 1970; Horowitz and Becker 1972).

Stated briefly, these coherent and convincing studies indicate two main aspects of stress response: an intrusive-repetitive tendency and a denial-numbing tendency. It is believed that the former tendency is an automatic property of mental information processing which serves the functions of assimilation and accommodation, a kind of "completion tendency" (Freud 1920/1953; Horowitz and Becker 1972). The denial-numbing tendency is thought to be a defensive function that interrupts repetition-to-completion in order to ward off intolerable ideas and emotions. The intrusive-repetition symptoms usually lead to the diagnosis of stress response syndrome; the signs of denial and numbing may go unobserved.

Special Characteristics of the Vietnam Experience

The Vietnam experience, especially for those involved in combat, differed from experiences in World War II. Combat experiences in Vietnam were shorter and relieved by rotations to relative safety. These rotations affected men rather than units. Fidelity to a small group or a leader was thus sometimes limited. Wide availability of drugs made emotional withdrawal or self treatment for fear possible. Varied attitudes towards the Vietnam War prevailed and the opposition of military and civilian populations was relatively frequent. The purposes of the war were unclear and often stated in terms of killing rather than liberation of territory as a goal.

In World War II, persons under great stress might initially go into a period of denial and numbing. They would be retained at the front line. Stress would mount. Signs and experiences characteristic of intrusive and repetitive feelings, ideas, and behaviors developed when stress exceeded the person's capacity to maintain denial. In Vietnam, because of repeated periods of safety, it would be relatively more possible for the soldier to enter and remain in the denial and numbing phase of stress response syndromes; the lower pace of accumulating stressful perceptions allowed maintenance of defenses. This denial and numbing might be fostered by the availability of drugs (Lifton 1973). The lack of group fidelity would also contribute to a state in which the person felt alienated, reacted with depersonalization, and isolated the experience from other events in the past and future.

Then the veteran would return to the United States. At this time he would experience a period of relief, a latency period in which there was a feeling of well-being and relatively good functioning. The denial and numbing, the alienation, compartmentalization, and isolation of the experience from everyday life would continue for awhile. Paradoxically, it might only be with the vision of continued safety, with the permissible relaxation of defensive and coping operations, that the person might then enter a phase in which intrusive recollections of the experience were reemergent.

For instance, a returning veteran might ostensibly adapt quite well and establish a marriage, engage in a satisfactory employment situation, or return to school, only to experience the emergence of such symptoms as nightmares, daytime intrusive images, or emotional attacks related to his Vietnam experience. This is paradoxical in that it would be opposite to what is commonly assumed in clinical practice. The common assumption is that compulsive repetitions of past traumas occur when they are related to or precipitated by more current stresses. The emergence of such symptoms might occur as late as a year or more after release from the stressful experience. This emergence, of course, could also be precipitated by arousal of new conflicts and damage to defensive-adaptive fantasies about the patriotic purposiveness of his war work or wonderful anticipations of what homecoming would be.

Preliminary Observations

In 1969 a series of consultations was begun by the authors with staff members at two different Veterans Administration hospitals. One of the more typical patient contacts, quite frustrating to all staff members, would involve a young veteran with a history of current and past usage of drugs such as LSD, speed, and heroin. The overt reason for the contact was usually a request for sleeping pills and tranquilizers. The veteran would be seen for only one or two visits and then would drop out, failing to establish or maintain a treatment contract. In one hospital, veterans identifying themselves as having served in Vietnam were rare. At the other hospital, white Vietnam veterans were seen but black Vietnam veterans rarely came for treatment. After a reaching out, at both hospitals, Vietnam veterans of various races entered the treatment program. The earlier "absence" of cases was due, we felt, to distrust on the part of Vietnam veterans for any facility attached to the government.

A second observation was then made, a negative one: According to the staff, stress response syndromes were not spontaneously reported by the population of Vietnam veterans. In spite of reports of a low incidence of such syndromes in the combat zone, we expected that delayed responses would occur in the population returned to civilian life. We suspect that these veterans not only wished to hold back their experiences in Vietnam but might not spontaneously report the relevant symptoms. Episodes such as intrusive thought are not only difficult to describe, but suggest to the subject a loss of control which is embarrassing to describe.

Correspondingly an educational program was undertaken to review for the psychiatric staffs both the intrusive-repetitive and denial-numbness aspects of common stress response syndromes. This included theoretical discussions supplemented by bringing in a representative of a veteran's organization and showing the film, "Winter Soldier," which evokes many of the psychodynamic issues as they are experienced subjectively by veterans.

As a result of these efforts, new cases of stress response syndromes in Vietnam veterans began to be reported in each subsequent case conference. It seemed that these patients were now being found in the existing case load because therapists were alert to the possible presenting symptoms and could ask for them in spite of the weakness of the therapeutic alliance and the tendency of the patients to present only details related to their immediate requests, as for sleeping pills.

As these new case vignettes were presented, classical stress response syndromes were noted. These are similar to those reported by other investigators (Borus 1973; Fox 1972; Shatan 1974; Solomon et al. 1971).

A typical case can be composited as follows:

The person has been back from Vietnam for about 1½ years. He did ostensibly well, was able to get a job and to marry. He felt somewhat estranged from his peers at work and did not discuss combat experiences with them. Recently he has begun to have difficulty sleeping, has intrusive daytime images and some nightmares of combat scenes although not necessarily one repetitive "story."

These scenes commonly involve atrocities whether or not he was involved in committing them himself.

During the daytime he is often suspicious and, when frustrated or in fear-arousing situations, feels that he is in great danger of losing control over his hostile and aggressive impulses. With growing hostility and suspicion he may conceal firearms to protect himself. There is also fear of going crazy and guilt over his own pleasurable responses to his intrusive ideas of committing severe physical violence to others. There may be startle reactions, psychosomatic syndromes, anxiety attacks, loss of motivation, and depression.

The person often turns to drugs such as heroin or sedatives because they temporarily relieve the depressive, anxious, fearful, and hostile mood states. Interpersonal difficulties may supervene because of the person's continued and uncontrollable suspicions, moodiness, surly behavior, or excessive demands that he be taken care of. Threats by the person are frequent and will also alienate interested others. The person wants to ward off any reminders that may create intrusive and repetitive experiences and will tend to be defensive in any inquiry by others as to his past experiences.

He thus becomes progressively more isolated and develops secondary syndromes ranging from neurosis to psychosis.

PREDICTIONS

On the basis of the above formulations and observations one may predict that, after a latency period characterized by relief and relatively good functioning, typical stress response symptoms may appear. These symptoms might include nightmares, painful moods and emotional storms, direct or symbolic behavioral repetitions, and concomitant secondary signs such as impaired social relationships, aggressive and/or self-destructive behavior, and fear of loss of control over hostile impulses. Many veterans will find it difficult to integrate the memory and associated fantasies of their Vietnam experiences with their life schemata of the past, present, and future. This inability to assimilate a time of life into an ongoing schemata will lead to impaired self-concepts, tendencies to depersonalization, depression, shame, frustration and reactive rage, and psychosocial disabilities.

Such veterans are unlikely to seek help from ordinary psychotherapeutic facilities, especially those associated with the government. If and when they do appear they may conceal their Vietnam experiences and reactive signs and symptoms. Even if patients develop trust in a treatment facility, perhaps due to the good reports of their peers, they may nonetheless experience unusual difficulties in establishing a therapeutic relationship.

Some Treatment Difficulties

As indicated above, establishment of a therapeutic relationship is difficult for these patients. They distrust any agency affiliated with the government and the "establishment." This difficulty is related to both their experiences with a war in which the issues were unclear and, upon their return, feelings of estrangement from contemporary society. Their demeanor is suspicious and fearful or a defensive stance of hostility and arrogance, or both.

They are fearful of their own mood states and hostile impulses. They fear they cannot control them and do not believe that the therapist can help with this. They know that many of their experiences are beyond the realm of the experience of the therapist and may conflict with his value judgments.

Such veterans are afraid of authority figures. If they reveal their current impulses toward aggressive and destructive acts, they imagine they might be committed to hospitals or revealed to legal authorities. While this fear is usually a projective fantasy, in some cases it has rational components. The person may know he has acted illegally or violently or may be close to doing so. He may not know the infrequency of involuntary commitment or the ethics of confidentiality.

One of the great misfortunes and difficulties in the treatment of such patients is that their fear of committing violence is based on historical reality, not fantasy. Contrast their situation with that of obsessional neurotics. Obsessional neurotics may have similar recurrent intrusive thoughts of doing harm to other persons. In their past, however, they have not done the degree of physical harm that they imagine. In contrast, some Vietnam veterans will have witnessed such violence and may have participated in it. They know not only that such violence is really possible since they have committed it, but also that it may be pleasurable as well as guilt-provoking. The obsessional patient usually has available the reassurance that he has never acted on his fantasy. Some Vietnam veterans may have the damaging knowledge that they have acted violently in the past and this leads to a blurred distinction between what is current fantasy, past reality, or current and future possibility. In other words, there has been a shortening of the conceptual distance between impulse and act, fantasy and reality so that conditioned inhibitions to destructive behavior have been reduced and are difficult to reimpose.

The presence of reduction in inhibitory capacity and increased fears of loss of control does not mesh well with the existing technical procedures familiar to most psychotherapists. Many maneuvers in dynamic psychotherapies are designed to counteract defenses and reduce inhibition in general. Maneuvers designed to increase control capacities and to separate realms of fantasy and real action are less familiar. The therapist may add his own uncertainty to the equation. Further, the therapist may fear the patient's potential for violence, a fear that is readily transmitted to the patient through nonverbal communications. The unhappy synergy of the fears of patient and therapist impairs the therapeutic relationship.

Another treatment difficulty is related to the observation of impaired self-concept frequently found in such veterans. This may be due not only to the nature of this particular war but to the life phase in which many of the veterans find themselves afterward. They have often gone into the military service from situations in which they were relatively dependent on peer group or family (Morris 1970). They have been separated relatively abruptly from the military service and catapulted back into adult civilian life. This happens at a time when cultural values are indistinct and blurred, when there are multiple routes to life, many of which are blocked to them because of their race or their lack of skills or appropriate credentials (Borus 1973).

The ready availability of drugs in Vietnam and the possible adaptational use of such drugs (although self-administered) may lead them again into this route to a sense of well-being. The use of such drugs, especially those that induce daydreaming, fantasies, or pleasant altered states of consciousness, further blurs distinctions between reality and fantasy and promotes grandiose self-images. Such grandiose fantasies provide restitution for feelings of defect in self-esteem, self-values, or self-peer and self-society commitments.

The compensatory grandiosity alluded to above is sensed by the person to be fantasy and not reality and, hence, is a secret. Were this secret revealed there is danger of appearing contemptible in the eyes of those who would not share the fantasy belief system. Such patients are generally shy or they isolate specific areas from communication because they fear that their grandiosity might be revealed to the therapist or to peers (Kaplan 1972). The need to avoid shame intensifies the problems of balancing realistic self-appraisals with idealized hopes. To avoid shame, humiliation, or identity diffusion, such patients often maintain a third attitude which is one of distance, arrogance, superiority, suspiciousness, and disdain toward therapists. This defensive attitude may intermix with a realistic lack of rapport with some therapists who cannot fully empathize with the Vietnam experience.

These focal difficulties, when present, add to the everyday problems of beginning and continuing a useful therapeutic situation. Some strategies for surmounting such difficulties are considered below.

TREATMENT STRATEGIES

Shatan (1972) and Lifton (1973) emphasize the unique aspects of the problems of Vietnam veterans. While not in disagreement, we are predicting general and delayed stress response syndromes as are not uncommon in civilian populations. These syndromes, we expect, will be appropriately treated by the conventional techniques and arts of individual and group psychotherapy (Horowtiz 1973,

1976). Nonetheless, special features are expected to complicate these treatments. Discussion of the common practices of psychotherapy is beyond the scope of this paper, but we can describe some approaches to the treatment difficulties described in the previous section. The combination of contempt, distrust, and fear of authority figures with impaired self-concepts and fear of loss of self-control makes the therapeutic relationship especially hard to establish. This becomes the first hurdle of treatment.

Ideally the aim is to help the patient develop a very clear idea of what his current problems are and what can be done to help him with them. Toward this end, a pitfall must be sidestepped—the pitfall of assuming a kind of governmental commitment often implied by the organizational relationship between the veteran and an agency such as the Veterans Administration. This pitfall is hard to skirt, however, because of the complex tangles of legality, reparations, and financial aid to the disabled. In spite of these complex issues, the therapist must center with the patient on some focal concerns that cause current subjective pain. The issue of loss of control is of extreme importance and vital to the therapeutic alliance; it should be explored early.

Part of this exploration includes asking the patient about fears of loss of control in a direct, simple, and calm manner. Any possible episodes of loss of control should be described in detail. It is especially important that the therapist ask for what has helped the patient to regain control, however brittle or fragmentary this control may have been.

The conceptual labeling of experience that occurs during this process is already a step in the direction of gaining control. This step toward gaining of control by establishment of conceptual labels and explanations is sometimes called intellectualization and then, in an unclear manner, regarded as a defense mechanism to ward off emotional experience. But intellectualization and rationalization are high order adaptive maneuvers as well as defenses. One wants to help the patient to use these operations before emotional explorations in order to keep emotional recollections within tolerable limits. Premature interpretation of intellectualization and rationalization as defensive maneuvers is therefore an error.

Given the vulnerability of these patients to narcissistic injury, inquiring about their difficulties in self-control must be done in a tactful manner. Many of the controlling efforts introduced by patients into their lives will themselves appear to be symptoms of psychopathology and thus patients will also be reluctant to discuss them. For example, one patient moved from one chair to another during therapeutic interviews, a procedure which was also followed at home while talking with friends. This maneuver had become a ritual which he used to terminate intrusive thoughts of an aggressive nature. The moving from one chair to another appeared to be a compulsion and the patient had to disguise it with some excuse such as "going to the bathroom" or "looking for an ashtray." When this behavior was noted in therapy the patient was quite embarrassed, but, with a tactful approach and intellectual scaffolding provided by the therapist, he was able to discuss the purpose of the movements, intrusive thoughts, and his fear of loss of control over violent impulses.

The distrust and withdrawal of some Vietnam veterans from therapists is not to be attributed only to internal psychological conflicts. Many of these patients have been through a different order of experience from that of most therapists. This may give both participants a continued aura which one therapist aptly called "spooky." When this problem occurs, a professional, paraprofessional, or lay co-therapist with Vietnam experience may be useful in firming a tenuous therapeutic relationship, as suggested by Shatan (1972) and Lifton (1973) in their attempts to explain the effectiveness of self-help groups organized by veterans organizations.

Dealing with Impairments in Control of Violent Impulses

The establishment of a therapeutic relationship and the inquiry into the patient's own methods of control is in and of itself a step toward improving control capacity. This first step can be called conceptual labeling; it increases the power of problem-solving thought as a tool for conflict reduction. This process is continued in attempts to find routes that the patient may take when he is in danger of being triggered into explosive aggressive actions. The relationship with the therapist is already one such route, since patients commonly use an introject of the therapist as a quasipresence during a potentially explosive situation. That is, the patient talks to himself "as if" he were the therapist, or he tells himself during the tense moment that he will tell the therapist about this episode later. This possibility of discourse with the therapist provides one route out of a dangerous interpersonal situation because there is a sense that something can be done about it.

Even in a phase of therapy focused on control of violent impulses there is an interrelationship between at least three factors: (a) the felt commitments that compose the therapeutic relationship, (b) the internalizations and externalizations that flow into and around the relationship, and (c) the cognitive and emotional processing of ideas and feelings. Ordinarily there will be gradual exposure of warded-off components of real memories and fantasies of the past, present, and future. The therapist will help the patient preserve a sense of safety and tolerable exposure by interpretation, clarification, suggestion, "presence," or direction.

Psychotherapists are most familiar with interventions designed to unfreeze responsivity. They try to promote the cognitive and emotional processes that lead to assimilation of the implications of stressful events and accommodation of the self to a changed situational configuration. Part of this process involves what has been called abreaction and catharsis. At times, in efforts to subvert defensive functions and evoke abreactions, forced role playing, hypnosis, or chemical hypnosis have been used. A potential error is premature use of such procedures. The recollections and emotional storms are often beyond the current capacity of the patient to assimilate. The therapist may gain information about stressful events and associations to these events but the patient may, in effect, receive an overdose of his own repressed memories and fantasies. A gradual procedure of cognitive and emotional working-through with repair of impaired control capacities is, in our opinion, preferable.

Problems of control over violent impulses are complicated whenever real violence has occurred, whenever human beings are dehumanized or devalued, and whenever reality and fantasy images are fused. In some instances, the patterns of impulsive violent behavior are so marked that experimental approaches to treatment are indicated. One such approach is described below. It has been tried in only two cases and was found to be useful in both. It can only be presented as a speculation for the consideration of other therapists.

Let us presume a patient who is preoccupied with impulses and fears of conducting a murderous physical attack on another human. When the patient is in a state of discontrol, he may be unable to prevent himself from doing some violent physical act. Unfortunately, insight into the sources of frustration, fear, and aggression do not always provide adequate mitigation of impulses or increases of controls. One approach to such patients is what could be called the establishment of hierarchical routes of behavior. The act of physical bodily assault is placed as number one on this hierarchy. The hierarchy thus starts from the "worst possible outcome" and reduces the severity of behavior patterns progressively. The next place on the hierarchy is developed in further discussions with the patient. He is asked this type of question: If he is in a period of explosive arousal, one in which control is not possible for him, what could he do which would be almost equivalent to the physical assault on another but, in his own mind, not quite as destructive to another? The patient may offer the idea that he thinks he could slam his fist into a wall instead of into a face. The third place on the hierarchy of actions is developed by discussing what might be almost as "good" a discharge as slamming his fist into the wall but would be somewhat less destructive to him. The answer might be to walk away from the argument or upsetting confrontation. The dangerous action, murderous assault, is thus gradually worked down until it is of lesser order.

In the patients on whom this method was tried, the incremental steps seemed possible even during the explosive state. That is, it was at first possible to avoid physical assault by wall striking but not by retreat. Later it was possible to move from wall striking to retreat. Finally it was possible to move to verbal but not physical aggression.

This type of talk with patients also accomplishes the steps described as approaches to problems of control: (a) increase in the hope and trust of a therapeutic relationship, (b) development of conceptual labels which allow ratio-nalization and intellectualization as adaptive maneuvers, (c) establishment and practice of new routes of behavioral expression, and (d) reestablishment of controls that have been deconditioned by warfare.

Dealing with Guilt

Another special feature germane to the treatment of stress response syndromes in Vietnam veterans is the nature of their guilt and shame responses. As with control of violent impulses, the unusual feature may be the reality and indelibility of the relevant memories. Unlike guilt from childhood neuroses re-volving around the fantasies of oedipal and preoedipal configurations, realistic shame and guilt cannot be relieved simply by clear expression and rational work-ing-through.

Lifton (1973) has dealt at length with these issues and we agree with his principle of the need to convert static guilt to animated guilt. That is, maneuvers in addition to insight are necessary to balance the stress-related mem-ories (and fantasies) with enduring self-images and values. What is helpful is not novel; it can be briefly summarized as clarification, atonement or penance, and restitution.

Clarification consists of the usual psychotherapeutic maneuvers for clear expression. The therapist may route the patient with questions: Who is he now? How powerful or how weak is he now? How responsible was he and is he now? How responsible were others and society in general? How much atonement and penance is necessary and sufficient to relieve his sense of guilt? Atonement and penance are of course the classical maneuvers of the Catholic church for the reduction of guilt. The maneuvers are classical because they work comparatively well. Confession, a period of emotional pain, and self-accusation are included in this concept. Unfortunately, self-destructive behavior is also included. Again, clarification with the patient of how much self-impairment he must inflict on himself is important. Otherwise there will be endless and repetitive episodes of self-destructive behavior such as job loss, object loss, or self-lacerations. In some instances, plans for symbolic restitution provide a route away from self-destructive patterns and toward life-affirming strategies. By symbolic restitutions we mean actions which heal people or the environment.

SUMMARY

The Vietnam situation led to the kinds of events that predispose participants to a denial-numbing type of stress response while in military service. Discharge may be associated with relief and ostensible readaptation to civilian life. Unresolved stress will, however, lead to intrusive-repetitive type responses even months or years after situational exits. We therefore predict delayed stress response syndromes in Vietnam veterans that may surface during the coming years. In addition, all the usual therapy problems and solutions relevant to the treatment of stress response syndromes are expected to prevail. Special treatment consideration should be given to problems in the establishment of the therapeutic relationship, in imposing controls over violent impulses, and in reducing the effects of shame and guilt.

PART V

Coping with Death and Dying

Perhaps no topic had enjoyed as much growth of interest among students in recent years as that of death and dying. The mysterious cloak which has traditionally surrounded the concept of death seems to have lifted and we now find ourselves bombarded with an array of books, seminars, and encounter groups all geared to explore this once feared topic. The readings in Part V reflect this new appeal. They are concerned for the most part with how people cope with their own death or with the loss of beloved ones. Although much remains to be unraveled, psychiatrists, psychologists, and sociologists interested in "thanatology" (i.e., the study of death) are making progress in our understanding of the psychological aspects of one's own death as well as of coping with the loss of another.

The "fear of death" is looked at in our first selection. Hackett and Weisman (1964) observed that patients suffering from myocardial infarction or incurable cancer often deny the threat of imminent death. Yet the effectiveness of the denial process may be undermined by what the authors call "middle knowledge," i.e., the dying patient's dim awareness of his or her own imminent death. This knowledge is just "below the surface" of the denial, manifesting itself in subtle behavioral signs like slips of the tongue, threatening dreams, etc. Its manifestations vary depending on the dying patient's interpersonal relationships. For example, persons visiting cancer patients tend to withdraw from them psychologically, in a subtle manner, and to feel anxious when the illness, or death, are discussed. As a result, visitors exude optimism seeking to generate a false mood of hope. The patient senses all this, feels alienated and depressed about it, but plays along because to do otherwise would threaten the continuation of these relationships. Thus, he or she not only has to face dying, but also the loss of communication with friends and loved ones along the way. Hackett and Weisman point out, too, how the objective and interpersonal situations differ between the myocardial infarction patient who can maintain hope and the terminal cancer patient who cannot anticipate recovery.

Friedman, Chodoff, Mason, and Hamburg (1963) present a detailed clinical description of the stresses experienced by parents of children dying of leukemia and the characteristic coping devices used by these parents to help them deal with their anticipated loss. The reader will be struck by the seemingly endless and often contradictory pressures felt by the parents and the numerous coping mechanisms (such as intellectualization and denial) used to handle their distress as well as to manage their dying child. Friedman et al. remind us again (see also, for example, Hackett and Weisman 1964; Lucas 1969) that social factors can have considerable impact on stress and its resolution. For example, Friedman et al. note that relatives, typically the grandparents, frequently displayed more denial than the parents, thus often making it more difficult for the parents to accept fully the reality of their child's condition. Social forces, however, seemed also to help the parents in that many learned how to cope with their distress by observing other parents in the study successfully go through similar experiences. In short, the observations provided by Friedman et al. offer crucial insights into various psychological and sociological processes often inherent in the struggle to survive and manage the anticipated loss of a beloved one from a terminal illness.

Thoughts of death and dying do not occur just to the ailing person or the wounded soldier. Death and dying are possible at all times and places and affect all of us to some degree or another. As Feifel has stated:

It is becoming clear that death is for all seasons. It is not the restricted domain of the dying patient, elderly person, combat soldier, or suicidal individual. Children as young as two years of age are already contending with the idea of death. We have disabused ourselves of the fancy that sex is a happening that comes to life at puberty, as a kind of full-bodied Minerva emerging from Jupiter's head. In a similar vein, it is fitting that we now recognize the psychological presence of death in ourselves from infancy on (1977:6).

In our next selection, Shneidman (1977) examines death and dying from the perspective of the college student. While the thought of bright, gifted, college-aged individuals having to deal with death and dying is not a pleasant one for many, the realities—as suggested by Feifel's quotation—are nevertheless quite clear: Death touches the lives of this population too.

Some of Shneidman's conclusions are most interesting. For example, he reports that college students are both in awe of death and attracted to it, believe that psychological factors can influence or cause death, and do not think about death more often than most. Shneidman provides touching case histories to illustrate the dying process in college students (primarily from an emotional, psychological perspective) and also how college students handle bereavement. Of interest, too, is Shneidman's discussion of the college student as thanatologist, as a helper to those who are in the process of dying. Courses in thanatology are beneficial, according to Shneidman, because they can often help students wrestle with notions of death and even help them make career decisions, such as whether or not to enter the "helping" professions.

A number of selections in our anthology have made reference to the "broken heart" notion, namely, that the death of an individual may make emotionally close suvivors highly susceptible to illness and even death (e.g., see Cohen 1981; Shneidman 1977). Our next selection, by Stroebe, Stroebe, Gergen, and Gergen (1982), is a fascinating (and statistically oriented) look at mortality rates among widowed individuals. To what extent do data support the "loss" effect? According to Stroebe et al., there is ample evidence that people die of a "broken heart." More specifically, it seems the risk of death is especially high following the loss of one's spouse—this is particularly true for widowers during the first six months of bereavement. Many of the causes of death among the widowed appear to be psychologically influenced (e.g., heart diseases and suicide) and Stroebe et al. devote a considerable portion of their article to discussions of *hopelessness* and its causes. Their social-psychological approach to understanding hopelessness and its effects on mortality is enlightening.

Several points about the Stroebe et al. article should be made here. First, as the authors note, there are methodological difficulties with many of the studies and thus the findings must be viewed with caution. Moreover, in parts of their paper not presented here, Stroebe et al. point out possible alternative explanations (in contrast to the psychological one) for the "loss" effect. For example, they mention the possibility that if like tend to marry like, then healthy (unhealthy) individuals will marry healthy (unhealthy) others. Thus, the fact that spouses die at about the same time or ages is due to marrying a similar other (known technically as "homogamy"). Another explanation for the proximity of deaths among spouses is that they shared unfavorable environments. That is, sharing harmful living conditions—harmful enough to cause death—would be reason enough to find both spouses dying at similar times (and from similar causes). A final major point to be made is that Stroebe et al. devote considerable space in their original article to "cognitive" approaches to understanding the causes of hopelessness. They emphasize theories dealing with *feelings of having lost control* over one's environment—see the works of Mandler (e.g., 1975) and Seligman (e.g., 1975). The reader will want to consult the original version, edited here because of space limitations, to get a richer sense of the theoretical possibilities for understanding the effects of bereavement on mortality.

17

Reactions to the Imminence of Death

THOMAS P. HACKETT and AVERY D. WEISMAN

In a large general hospital, where numerous deaths occur in the course of a day, it is almost impossible to find a dying patient who is allowed to respond to the imminence of death in his own way. By the time he reaches his deathbed, the attitudes and fixed opinions of physicians and relatives have been thrust upon him. With the "best interest" of the patient at heart they encourage and offer hope even before the patient expresses a desire for such reassurance. The healthy human being assumes that the threat of death eclipses all other fears and does not realize that the dying patient may not share this point of view. Although the prospect of death is awesome and fearful to those about to die, it does not necessarily exclude other concerns.

This presentation deals with two groups of people: (1) terminal cancer patients who are facing certain death, and (2) patients with severe myocardial disease who have a chance of survival, but who are threatened with the possibility of imminent death. It will be shown that both groups react to the death threat by denying it in various ways, some effective and some not. The effectiveness of this denial (Engel 1962; Freud 1937; Lewin 1950), we feel, depends to a large extent upon the way in which it is handled by those who care for the patient. We define denial as the repudiation of part or all of the available meaning of an event for the purpose of minimizing fear and anxiety.

ATTITUDES OF OTHERS

The importance of the attitudes of others and their influence on the way in which a patient reacts to the threat of his death became apparent to us a few years ago when we began to investigate the emotional responses of 28 patients in the terminal stages of cancer (Hackett and Weisman 1962; Weisman and Hackett 1962). Each was seen approximately four times a week until he died. Relatives were interviewed when possible, and close communication existed between the psychiatrist and the surgeon or internist in charge of the case. All these patients had been told they had cancer, but none had been informed that he would die within a short time.

From our interviews with patients, families, nurses, and physicians we found two seemingly incongruous patterns. Relatives, nurses, and doctors substantiated what most of us believe to be true of the dying patient—that he is an expert at denying that he is dying. On the other hand, when the tape recordings of these interviews were examined in detail, we found quite obvious references to impending death. Threatening dreams, nightmares, slips of the tongue, references to loneliness and grief, and the tendency to recount stories of fatal illnesses they had witnessed in friends or relatives documented our suspicion that these patients were deeply concerned about the true nature of their disease. Hesitant and indirect questions about what could be expected of the future offered the investigators the opportunity to share the fears of their patients. Such inquiries were generally so unobtrusive that the physician could easily disregard them if he chose. Not all 28 patients disclosed their fears to the same degree. Some directed their concern to continuing symptoms, especially to physical pain, rather than to death itself; but all revealed more about themselves as a result of having a receptive listener.

Because the attitude of the visitor so often determined the type of communication, it was possible for two people to come away from separate visits to a sickroom, each maintaining an opposite point of view. The first might say the patient was untroubled and confident, the other that the patient was deeply concerned about his immediate fate. More often than not, the visitor, intent on encouraging optimism, heard only what he wanted to hear. The fear of death was not openly expressed. Instead, the patient would complain of symptoms without inquiring about the reasons for their persistence. He would often speak tentatively about the distant future when he would be well. Such a remark offered an ideal chance for the optimist to join in the planning. If this were done, the patient appeared to be animated and pleased. Should the visitor refrain, the patient usually became silent and somber. All of the 28 patients were aware of false optimism. Yet, at the same time, they gave every appearance of being susceptible, grasping and clinging to the flimsiest of hopes. It was as though their ability to deal consistently with the reality of their illness was determined in large part by the attitude of their visitors.

It is difficult for most people to succeed in deceiving those who know them well. The husband of a patient in the terminal phase of carcinoma of the cervix said, "I couldn't tell her with a straight face she'd get better. She'd see right through me." With this man deception would impose a telltale strain. His wife might be heartened to receive good news, but would, at the same time, be aware of the way it was imparted. The doctor faces a similar scrutiny, even though he may be a stranger to the patient. Often, it is not what he says, but the manner in which he expresses it, that alerts the patient. Sixteen of the 28 patients complained that their doctors told them too little and tended to generalize in the answers they did give. On the other hand, the patient's questions were usually asked in such a way that a generalization would supply a seemingly adequate reply. In only one instance did a patient ask her doctor whether she was going to die soon. The direct question is more often put to individuals who are not in a position to answer it, such as ward attendants and student nurses, whose discomfiture adds to the patient's sense of alarm.

ATTITUDES OF THE PATIENT

As a result of a change in the attitudes of those around him, a change based largely upon the desire to generate false hope, the patient comes to know that he is dying. It is a peculiar kind of knowledge because it seems to violate everything he most wants to believe or everything that people think he wants to believe. We have used the term "middle knowledge" (Hackett and Weisman 1962; Weisman and Hackett 1961, 1962) to describe the dying patient's awareness of his imminent death. He is between knowing that what his body tells him means death and what those around him deny is death. He yields to their encouragement because to do otherwise would risk the loss of human contact—a loss as genuinely threatening as death itself. His ability to reject selectively the significance of symptoms increases at times so that he can actually experience transient hope. But always underneath is the gnawing fear that a hoax is being perpetrated on him. He is truly in the middle of knowing and not knowing. Hinton (1963), in his study of 102 dying patients, observed that "at least three-quarters of the patients here studied became aware that they were probably dying." He goes on to say, "If a patient sincerely wanted to know his possible fate, and was met by prevarication or empty reassurance, he felt lonely and mistrustful."

The most agonizing and intolerable threat to the dying is loneliness—the feeling of being apart from the lives of others. The loneliness is compounded by a perceptible change which occurs in those who care for them. The living tend to draw away from the dying. Sometimes it is an obvious withdrawal, more often a subtle sense of growing estrangement. Anyone who has been through a deathwatch appreciates the difficulty of being a helpless observer when someone's life is dwindling away. Much of this hardship can be alleviated for the visitor if he encourages the patient to think about an eventual recovery and a return to health. This type of myth-making is largely for the benefit of the visitor. The patient soon comes to find that when he does hint at wanting to know more and when he is skeptical of what the doctors tell him, his inquiries are met with awkward silences, scoldings about losing faith, or broad blandishments of hope. He learns that to pursue his doubts by asking questions seldom yields more than uneasiness between himself and those upon whom he depends for companionship. Therefore he stops asking and becomes a player in the deathbed drama in which optimism is the theme. For the terminal patient the effectiveness of denial is sharply undercut by "middle knowledge," which is the product of both the patient's ability to assess the reality of the facts of his illness and his capacity for gauging the honesty of others.

Since the treatment of the terminal patient is not the major concern of this paper, the reader is referred to the principal contributors in this field (Eissler 1955; Feifel 1959; Worcester 1940). The most controversial issue in therapy always revolves about the amount of information the patient should be given. Those who believe that the patient should be encouraged to deny focus their therapy on ways of judiciously supplementing the patient's use of denial. The others, who feel that many patients have less capacity to use denial than is commonly thought, direct their attention toward minimizing those factors, among which denial is a frequent offender, which augment the feeling of isolation and loneliness in the dying. They believe that being the victim of a silent conspiracy between doctors and relatives imposes as much pain upon the patient as the facts of his illness. If there is a way of preparing the dying for death, it will have as its foundation the affirmation of warmth and affection between the patient and those who are about to be bereft.

In contrast to the person dying of cancer, the patient who has sustained a myocardial infarction appears to derive more benefit from denial. Our work with the cardiac patient began with an investigation of 23 patients placed on the monitor cardiac pacemaker (Browne and Hackett, unpublished data). This group was chosen because it consisted of people facing a death threat in a setting which we felt might accentuate fear. As a rule, one of every two patients requiring pacemaker assistance succumbs. The appearance of the instrument was not designed to comfort the patient. It consists of an oscillograph which makes a continuous recording of the patient's EKG and an audible bleep which accompanies the pulse. The bleep, which sounds like the nagging peep of a newly hatched chick, alerts the nurse to cardiac irregularities. Should the heart stop, an alarm bell rings and an automatic shocking device sends jolts of electricity to stimulate the myocardium. This device is at the patient's bedside. We predicted that our patients would prefer having the apparatus out of their rooms, monitored at some central point where they could not hear the bleep or see the tracing. This was not the case—another reflection of how often the healthy fail in their attempts to empathize with the sick and dying.

Of the 23 patients, 4 were in semicoma, 5 were delirious and 14 were alert and responsive. Only one of the 14 was frightened by the machine. The remaining 13 patients regarded it as a friendly protector. This attitude was enhanced by the nurse who admitted them to the ward. She, with providential wisdom, introduced the pacemaker as a "mechanical guardian angel" without, of course, mentioning that its capacity for salvaging failing hearts was limited (Craffey 1960). Even those patients who experienced the painful shocks did not mind having the pacemaker in the room. Instead of being apprehensive at having to listen to the bleep which accompanied every heartbeat, 12 patients interpreted the sound as a reassurance that everything was all right. One patient was annoyed by the sound but wanted the machine in his room despite it. The most common fantasy was that as long as they were attached to the machine their hearts could not stop. It was not unusual for these patients to experience anxiety when being weaned from the pacemaker. The majority chose to regard the machine as an ally and to reject the recognition that it also vividly presented evidence of their precarious condition.

Along with concentrating on the salutary aspect of the pacemaker, these same 13 patients consistently denied that their hearts were severely damaged and that they feared death. This type of denial can be separated into two groups which we may call major and partial denial. The group of major deniers consisted of 7 males, all of whom denied having any fear or worry about their illness. Each believed that too much attention was being given his heart. Even though 3 of them had suffered from previous coronaries, and 2 others had been shocked by the pacemaker, they denied concern about the possibility of dying or even of being unable to return to their old manner of life and work. Their life histories were filled with situations in which the death stress was met with denial. For example, one who had been the victim of a bandit had charged the gunman, was wounded three times, and afterwards asserted that he had never considered the possibility of being killed before, during, or after this incident. Another had spent three weeks on a life raft in the Pacific, never doubting that he would be rescued. All had histories of anginal pain for which help was never sought. Characteristically, when the symptoms of the myocardial infarction began, these patients ignored them until others noticed their distress and insisted on their seeking hospital attention. Illness they considered a weakness, and those who allowed themselves to acknowledge it, weaklings. They all shared what could best be described as an exaggerated Victorian concept of manly behavior. They believed that a true man did not feel fear or if he felt it, never admitted that he did.

The 6 patients in the category of partial deniers were similar to the major deniers, except that, upon closer questioning, they admitted having experienced fear as a reaction to their illness even while they tended to minimize it. Their pasts were not as florid with examples of stoicism in the face of adversity as were the others'. They tended to rationalize the symptoms of their heart attacks as "indigestion" or "muscle strain" rather than to attempt to ignore the symptoms altogether. One patient, a man in his late twenties with an extensive family history of coronary disease, experienced severe precordial pain following his participation in a wrestling match. He immediately thought that he was having a heart attack but felt that his age was against it. In order to decide the issue he determined to run up five flights of stairs to his apartment, thinking that if it was his heart he would die; if not, he would live. He made the effort, almost perishing on the way, and fell into bed gasping, but happy in the knowledge that his distress was not "coronary trouble." Even after he had been admitted to the hospital and diagnosed as having a massive myocardial infarction, he tended to doubt the diagnosis as the result of his experiment with the stairs. Nevertheless, he submitted to the restrictions placed upon him and behaved as though he fully believed what he had been told by his doctor. Like all other patients in the category of partial deniers, he spoke of the future as though it would in no way be altered by his illness.

Both the major and the partial deniers displayed emotions entirely consistent with what they said. Anxiety and depression were not in evidence. No patient required tranquillizers. However, as we analyzed the tape recorded interviews, there were inconsistencies, contradictions, and slips of the tongue which readily demonstrated the presence of "middle knowledge." It was not, however, as undermining or as minatory as the "middle knowledge" of the cancer patient. One reason for the difference, we feel, is that the cardiac patient's tendency to minimize or deny was honestly augmented by the attitude of those who attended him. There was no silent conspiracy between doctor and relatives because everyone was in agreement that hope was of paramount importance. The cardiac patient did not have to be deceived. The encouragement offered him stemmed from the knowledge that legitimate hope existed. He could indeed pull through this episode and live out a considerable span of years. Death, although a genuine possibility, was not an imminent certainty. Relatives, as well as hospital personnel, did not have to pretend or act out an optimism which had no basis in fact. Although the cardiac patient was more concerned about his heart and future than he would directly admit, he did not suffer the alien and lonely fear of being deceived. While it is true that he selectively denied many grim aspects of his illness and converted the pacemaker into an ally without recognizing its more sinister meaning, the cardiac patient's denial could honestly be bolstered by those who were responsible for his health.

Whereas the terminal cancer patient often has a legitimate basis for complaining that he had been deserted by his doctors and nurses, the critical cardiac patient was constantly looked after. None spoke of being lonely. On the contrary, their most frequent complaint was of receiving too much attention for what they considered a minor condition. Their denial was never challenged directly or inadvertently. The close attention they received was in marked contrast to the situation of the patient dying from a malignancy. When the latter is pronounced incurable, the physician often asks the chaplain to make regular visits and concomitantly withdraws his presence. At the same time that he substitutes the chaplain's visits for his own, the doctor frequently increases the amount of narcotics administered to the patient who has been declared terminal. This is especially obvious when the doctor has judiciously limited the narcotic intake over long periods against the patient's will. When this change is abrupt and unexplained, the patient invariably interprets it as a sign that nothing more can be done for him.

The tendency of the human being exposed to the threat of death to negate or alter the meaning of the threat along less stressful lines is further illustrated in another study of cardiac patients (Olin and Hackett, unpublished data). Thirty-two randomly selected cases of acute myocardial infarction were interviewed very shortly after admission to the hospital. None appeared anxious or overly concerned about his condition. Reassurance about prognosis and the future was not requested. All denied being frightened. The initial symptom in each case was chest pain, which was severe in 27 cases. The average duration of the pain from its onset to the time active measures were taken to obtain medical help was 5.2 hours. This delay in seeking help is explained by the patient's attempts to rationalize the cause of his discomfort. Fifteen patients believed they had severe indigestion and sought relief through antacids and other self-administered medications. Four thought they were coming down with a lung condition such as pneumonia. Nine diagnosed themselves as possibly having heart trouble and the remaining 4 attributed the pain respectively to cancer, a cold, an ulcer, and fatigue. The 9 who correctly diagnosed their condition as "coronary" delayed obtaining medical help an average of 10.3 hours (twice that of the others), indicating that suspecting a diagnosis does not always result in appropriate action. In fact, the longest period of delay in the group (60 hours) was endured by one of these 9. All 32 patients responded to the pain as though they were determined to avoid, at all costs, acknowledging its true significance. This came to light as the data revealed that 24 patients were familiar with coronary disease either through having had anginal attacks, a previous myocardial infarction, or through witnessing it in a relative or close friend. Thirteen of the 24 patients had histories of anginal attacks and of these, 4 had been hospitalized with previous myocardial infarctions. Obtaining a past history of symptoms suggesting coronary disease in either the patient or his relatives was not always a simple matter. Four patients in this series denied having had anginal attacks and 6 others gave a negative family history. Whereas subsequent interviews with relatives tended to substantiate the patient's account of his present illness, they also revealed alarming gaps in memory for significant past events. The wife of one man said that he had been troubled by severe attacks of precordial pain for a number of years before his present admission. Upon being confronted by this he minimized these spells as "acute indigestion." "They always went away when I burped or took sodium bicarb." When he was told that the "spells," as described by his wife, often occurred when he was working vigorously, he replied, "Yeah, that's why you sweat, to get the acid out. It builds up in your stomach and you get pain. My father had the same thing." It turned out that his father, who he said had died of a "shock" had complained for years of "indigestion" and then dropped dead suddenly. A check with the family doctor disclosed that the patient's father had been taking nitroglycerine tablets regularly, not antacids as the patient had remembered. In taking the history of the coronary patient, one must remember to verify the absence of symptoms with a relative.

For the groups of patients studied, denial was the common response to the stress of imminent death. The defense of denial is always accompanied by a "middle knowledge" which indicates underlying doubts antipathetic to the goal of denial. The power or extent of the "middle knowledge" depends in large part upon the patient's interpersonal relationships. Its effectiveness depends in large part on the way it is dealt with in an interpersonal setting. If the other party honestly endorses the optimism he offers the patient, which seems to be so with our cardiac cases, "middle knowledge" does not undermine the effectiveness of denial. When, however, the other party cannot genuinely reciprocate hopefulness and must rely upon myth-making to create an aura of optimism, the flaws of the deception do not escape the terminal cancer patient. "Middle knowledge" undercuts the usefulness of their denial whether it is experienced as open doubt or as vague uneasiness. In treating any critically ill patient one must always assume that he harbors many unspoken questions. The physician should not offer unsolicited answers for these questions but should develop a relationship in which the patient is free to raise whatever issues he chooses.

18

Behavioral Observations on Parents Anticipating the Death of a Child

STANFORD B. FRIEDMAN, PAUL CHODOFF,
JOHN W. MASON, and DAVID A. HAMBURG

There are few tasks in the practice of medicine as difficult as trying to help the parents of a child afflicted with a disease which is invariably fatal. Since the physician cannot change the reality of the tragic situation, he frequently feels totally unable to lessen the parental suffering. However, understanding the nature of the stress as experienced by the parents and appreciating that there are characteristic ways in which they cope with the situation should enable the physician to offer helpful support in a majority of cases.

Forty-six parents of children with neo-plastic disease were involved at the National Institutes of Health (NIH) in a study of the adrenal cortical response under conditions of chronic psychological stress, and this work has been reported elsewhere (Friedman, Mason, and Hamburg 1963). The present paper

The authors are deeply indebted to the parents who participated in this project, and to the Clinical Associates who cared for their children on Ward 2-East. Dr. Myron Karon of the Medicine Branch of the National Cancer Institute offered his continuous support and facilitated many aspects of this study. We also gratefully acknowledge the encouragement and support given by Drs. C. Gordon Zubrod, Emil Frei, III, and Emil J. Freireich of the National Cancer Institute. Mr. Paul C. Hartsough tabulated much of the data, and Mrs. Joanna Kieffer, Miss Susan Rusinow, and Mrs. Martha Mantel were responsible for the office and secretarial work. The authors are also indebted to Mrs. Mary Miller and her nursing staff on the "normal volunteer" ward and to Mr. Lawrence Burke of the Social Service Department. Drs. George Engel, Arthur Schmale, and Gilbert Forbes were kind enough to critically review the manuscript.

is concerned with the clinical impressions gained over a two-year period while this study was in progress and the implication of these findings to physicians caring for children with similar diseases, adding to what is presently in the literature (Bierman 1956; Bozeman, Orbach and Sutherland 1955; Greene and Miller 1958; Knudson and Natterson 1960; Natterson and Knudson 1960; Orbach, Sutherland, and Bozeman 1955; Richmond and Waisman 1955).

SUBJECTS AND GENERAL METHOD OF STUDY

The 46 subjects represented one or both parents of 27 children, all of whom had been referred for treatment with chemotherapeutic agents to the Medicine Branch of the National Cancer Institute. In all cases, the child had previously been hospitalized elsewhere for clinical evaluation, and the suggestion for referral was most frequently made by a physician at the time he communicated the diagnosis to the parents. In a minority of cases, the matter of referral was initiated at a time later in the child's clinical course. Within 24 hours of each child's admission to NIH, the parents were informed of this study by the principal investigator and invited to participate. During a ten-month period in 1960–61, a total of 36 children (including 2 siblings) were admitted for the first time to the pediatric ward of the National Cancer Institute. Of these, the parents of one child did not wish to participate in the study, while the parents of seven other children were unavailable for formal inclusion, though most could be interviewed occasionally.

The median age of the 26 mothers was 33 years, and that of the 20 fathers, 35 years. As seen in table 18.1, there was a broad representation of socioeconomic level, though the majority of parents were high school graduates and from families where the estimated annual income was $4,500 or more. Approximately two-thirds of the parents lived in an urban or suburban environment, and a majority professed the Protestant faith. One mother and three fathers were married for the second time.

Nineteen of the 27 children, including the 2 who were siblings, had acute lymphocytic leukemia, 1 had acute myelogenous leukemia, 6 had metastatic "solid" tumors, and 1 child was found to have a benign lesion following an erroneous referral diagnosis of leukemia. The median time from when the parents learned the child's diagnosis from the referring physician and admission to the National Cancer Institute was two and five weeks for the children with leukemia and "solid" tumors, respectively. The group of children with leukemia appeared to experience a clinical course consistent with a recent review of this disease by Freireich et al. (1961), though somewhat modified by the constant development of new therapeutic techniques. All the children with "solid" tumors had widely

Table 18.1. Descriptive Data on the 26 Mothers and 20 Fathers

	Mothers		Fathers	
Data	No.	%	No.	%
Age				
Range	23–49	—	25–49	—
Mean	33.4	—	36.0	—
Median	33.0	—	35.3	—
Education				
< High school	8	31	7	35
High school	12	46	7	35
> High school	6	23	6	30
Income (est.)				
< $4,500	6	23	5	25
$4,500–$7,500	16	62	12	60
> $7,500	4	15	3	15
Environment				
Urban	15	58	13	65
Suburban	3	12	1	5
Rural	8	31	6	30
Religion				
Protestant	23	88	17	85
Catholic	3	12	3	15

metastatic lesions and were referred for systemic chemotherapy. The sex distribution, age at the time admitted, and the average number of siblings for this group of children is shown in table 18.2.

Thirty-five parents, 20 mothers and 15 fathers, lived some distance from NIH and were admitted to a ward of the National Institute of Mental Health, where they resided during all or a portion of the time their children were hospitalized. Eleven parents, 6 mothers and 5 fathers, who lived in the immediate vicinity of NIH were available for study to a lesser extent and were seen on what we have considered an "outpatient" basis.

The period of observation for the parents living on the ward ranged from approximately one week to eight months; two months was the median time for the mothers and one month for the fathers. The parents spending a total of four to eight months on this ward had their stay interspersed with periods at home when their children were ambulatory.

The ward for the parents was two stories above the children's ward and was designated as a "normal volunteer" floor. There were generally 6 to 8 parents staying on this ward at any given time, and the floor was arranged so that each couple, or two mothers, could have a single room with an adjoining bathroom. The parents were usually on the pediatric floor with their children during visiting hours (11 A.M. to 1 P.M., and 3 P.M. to 8 P.M.), but spent most

Table 18.2. Descriptive Data on the 27 Children

	Diagnostic Group			
Data	Leukemia (N= 20)	"Solid" Tumor (N= 6)	Benign Lesion (N= 1)	All Groups (N= 27)
Sex				
Male	12	2	—	14
Female	8	4	1	13
Age (in years)				
Range	1.5–16.0	2.0–7.5	—	1.5–16.0
Mean	7.0	5.0	—	6.5
Median	5.3	4.5	4.0	5.0
Siblings				
Average number	2.4[a]	1.7[b]	—	2.2
Patient only child	11	—	—	1
Patient oldest child	4	2	—	6
Patient youngest child	9	3	1	13

[a] Includes three stepchildren in one family; two in a second family.
[b] Patient and sibling adopted in one family.

of the remaining hours on their own "normal volunteer" ward, though they were entirely free to leave the Clinical Center at any time.

The parents studied in the ward setting were interviewed by one of the investigators (S.B.F.) in his office at least once a week and were seen on the ward almost daily. In addition to these interviews and observational notes, the nurses on the "normal volunteer" ward made and recorded observations, and each morning the parents filled out a brief questionnaire regarding their activities during the previous 24 hours. The parents seen on an "outpatient" basis were interviewed approximately once every two weeks when their children were hospitalized, and there was the additional opportunity to see these parents during periods when their children were in remission and living at home. All parents were also observed interacting with their children on the pediatric ward, though no systematic attempt was made to study the children.

The interviews were primarily concerned with each parent's perception of his child's illness and clinical course, the defenses utilized by the parent to protect him from the impact of the stressful situation and the threatened loss, and the individual's ways of dealing with the many problems that arise when caring for a seriously ill child. Further information was obtained at weekly group sessions open to all the parents and led by one of the investigators (S.B.F.); this investigator was also in frequent contact with the ward physicians,[1] the nurses caring for the children, and with the social worker assigned to the pediatric ward.

Although the parents of the children with leukemia and metastatic tumors faced many of the same problems and shared similar experiences, this paper will primarily discuss the parents of the children with leukemia. An attempt will be made to generalize from our observations, with an emphasis on the findings that are most relevant to the problems of clinical management. No claim is made that the psychodynamics underlying the observed behavior have been fully described; data regarding the specific symbolic meaning of the threatened and actual loss for each of the parents were generally not available.

In cases where we contrast our findings with those of others, we would like to emphasize that differences probably existed in the populations under study and the unique setting in which our study was conducted. However, though the parents living on the "normal volunteer" ward were in a somewhat artificial setting, the general applicability of our findings is supported by the similarity of behavior observed both in the parents studied on the ward and in those studied while they continued to live at home.

EARLY REACTIONS OF PARENTS

Learning the Diagnosis

In general, the parents stated that they had some prior knowledge about leukemia and therefore suspected their child might have this disease before actually hearing it from a doctor, and, in this sense, they somewhat anticipated the news. However, without exception, the parents recalled a feeling of "shock" or of being "stunned" when hearing the definitive diagnosis. Only an occasional parent reported a concomitant feeling of disbelief, though in retrospect most parents feel that it took some days before the meaning of the diagnosis "sank in." Thus, in this study, the majority of parents appeared to intellectually accept the diagnosis and its implication, rather than to manifest the degree of disbelief (Knudson and Natterson 1960; Natterson and Knudson 1960) and marked denial (Bozeman, Orbach, and Sutherland 1955) described by others. Only later did they consciously begin to hope that the diagnosis might be in error.

In cases where the referring doctor discussed leukemia and its clinical course in detail, the parents later realized that little of this general information was comprehended at the time. Certain immediate decisions had to be made, particularly whether the child was to be referred to NIH, and only that information which aided the parents in handling this immediate situation appeared meaningful. The fathers generally took the major responsibility for such decisions at this time, and also tended to offer emotional support to their wives.

Upon arrival at NIH, there was a tendency to be overwhelmingly impressed, and this was associated with revived hope, expressed by statements such as: "If any place can save my child, it will be here." During the period of this study, this reaction was anticipated by the ward physicians who pointed out shortly after the child's admission the realistic aspects of the situation and the present limitations of the chemotherapy.

These statements by the ward physician that NIH was not omnipotent often invoked an immediate reaction of hostility, sometimes expressed by saying that "*only* God could decide" their child's future. However, after a period of a few days to a few weeks, all but a minority of the parents then praised the ward physician for having taken this approach. They felt that they had "now heard the worst," and no longer had to contend with the dread that there was some unknown, even more devastating news, yet to come. Our impression was that this direct approach gave the parents confidence in their ability to master subsequent developments, and tended to discourage unrealistic and maladaptive behavior patterns.

Three fathers, two of whom were not formally included in this study, reported a marked hostile component during their early reaction to learning the diagnosis. One confessed to an immediate urge to "blow up the world," another overtly threatened to attack his child's physicians, and a third partially succumbed to the impulse to injure others by deliberate recklessness while driving. All three of these fathers had a history of significant psychiatric problems, two in the form of overt paranoid behavior. Though it was not unusual for a parent to show evidence of hostility directed towards others, the open frank expression of such thoughts and impulses always reflected psychopathology in our experience.

Guilt

Once the diagnosis of leukemia was made, the parents would, almost without exception, initially blame themselves for not having paid more attention to the early nonspecific manifestations of the disease. They wondered whether the child would not have had a better chance of responding to therapy if the diagnosis had been made sooner. Although such reactions of guilt were extremely common, and the deep emotional basis of such feelings has been emphasized by others (Richmond and Waisman 1955), most parents in this study readily accepted assurance from the physician that they had not neglected their child. Particularly reassuring to the parents was the information that the long-term prognosis in most cases of childhood leukemia is essentially the same no matter when the diagnosis is made.

Thus, in the majority of parents, guilt was not manifested by prolonged and exaggerated feelings of wrong-doing, but was more characteristically a transient phenomenon. The various etiologic possibilities which were considered included genetic and controllable environmental factors, but most parents did not dwell on their own possible contribution to the development of the disease and were able to minimize their feelings of guilt. However, we are aware that the degree of guilt reported in a study such as this is dependent upon the intensity with which each subject is studied, the depth of interpretation by the investigator, and the definition of the term itself.

Notwithstanding the above qualifications, a minority of parents did display obvious indications of guilt that were more than transient, and which appeared as persistent self-blame for the child's illness. As one mother said, "It is God's way of punishing me for my sins." More often, a parent would blame himself for not having been more appreciative of the child before his illness. Things had not been done together, the buying of toys had been postponed, or perhaps the child had been disciplined too severely. This attitude frequently led to over-indulging and over-protecting the now ill child, with no limits put on his behavior. The ward physician would sometimes comment on such extreme practices, but this paternal pattern, to the extent that it was generated by underlying guilt, was exceedingly resistant to change.

Seeking Information

The ward physician had at least one lengthy interview with the parents shortly after each child was admitted and, later, periodically discussed the child's condition with the parents and was readily available to answer any further questions. The parents were generally aware of and appreciative of these efforts, but there remained what appeared to be an insatiable need to know *everything* about the disease. For many weeks, there was, characteristically, an extensive search for additional information, especially about therapeutic developments.

This search took many forms, but most noticeable, at least to the medical and nursing staffs, was the exchange of information among parents on the floor solarium which served as a waiting room for the parents between the morning and afternoon visiting hours. Here the "new" parents would glean information from the group, not only about leukemia and its therapy, but also regarding hospital policies and organization. Information from the three ward physicians and the nurses would be pooled and minutely evaluated for consistency. However, it was inevitable that a parent would not be completely objective in relaying information, and an individual's fears, defenses, neurotic tendencies, and lack of a general medical background would not infrequently lead to misinterpretations and overgeneralizations; limitations that most parents recognized in this mutual sharing of information.

Friends and relatives served as an abundant source of "information" about leukemia, often given with the intent of cheering up the parents. For instance, a parent might be told of a patient who lived for years with leukemia, the informant failing to say that the patient had been an elderly man with a chronic type of the disease. This kind of "information" was of little practical use to the parents and contributed to their tendency to deny the disease, a point which will be discussed later.

Newspaper and magazine articles were read many times if they were even remotely related to leukemia or childhood cancer, and relatives, friends, and acquaintances from all parts of the country would send such clippings. Furthermore, particular attention was paid to *where* the reported work had been done, with parents openly inquiring whether the doctors at NIH were aware of a "latest development." There were repeated requests for written authoritative information about leukemia, as it was recognized by the parents, particularly the mothers who usually had the responsibility of keeping their husbands informed, that there was a limitation on how much could be accurately retained after talking with a doctor.

It was noted that parents would become confused and anxious whenever they perceived divergent "facts" or opinions regarding their child's condition, even if the differences were negligible or imaginary. For instance, one couple became quite agitated when a doctor said their child had a bacteremia and then a second physician referred to the same process as septicemia. Similarly, the parents would perceive minor or major variations in degrees of pessimism or optimism at any given time among the doctors.

The seeking of information can be understood partly as a realistic attempt to learn as much as possible about leukemia in order to better master the situation and care for the ill child. However, the process of learning about leukemia appeared constructive only up to a point, and a sudden upsurge of parental questions often reflected increased anxiety or conflict, which could not be resolved by the acquisition of more detailed information about the disease.

PSYCHOLOGICAL MANAGEMENT
OF THE ILL CHILD

The Hospitalized Child

An almost universal concern of the parents was the question of how much the children knew, or should know, regarding their diagnosis. Anxiety about this problem was considerable, although obviously influenced by the particular parents involved, the age of the child, and the help received in this area from the physician. The majority of parents, even those who realistically accepted the nature of the tragedy, shielded their children from ever hearing the word "leukemia," though in the hospital setting this was at times all but impossible. Our impression is that *some* acknowledgment of the illness is often helpful, especially in the older child, in preventing the child from feeling isolated, from believing that others are not aware of what he is experiencing, or from feeling that his disease is "too awful" to talk about. Unfortunately we have no data which clearly help answer the question of how best to inform children of their illness, but others (Dameshek and Gunz 1958; Hoerr 1963; Rothenberg 1961) have suggested approaches, though primarily applicable to the adult with a fatal disease, and Marmor (1963) further comments on the difficulty of the physician's task in deciding what to tell the cancer patient and his family.

Another common problem was that the younger children with leukemia frequently openly rejected their parents, making such statements as, "I hate you and I don't ever want to see you again," with the result that the parents would feel that they had, in some way, failed their child. This pattern of behavior appeared most commonly after the children had been ill for some time, and seemed in part related to the parents' inability to prevent painful procedures and prolonged hospitalization with consequent damage to the usual childhood faith in parental omnipotence. Furthermore, we have speculated that the children sensed their dependence on the medical and nursing staff and were therefore fearful of expressing hostility directly toward these individuals.

This ability of even young children to perceive the transfer of authority from their parents to the professional staff manifested itself in many ways. Within a remarkably short time, the children would, for instance, directly ask the nurses and doctors for permission to deviate from their diet or to partake in various recreational activities. The parents were accordingly bypassed and would often feel that they were no longer important to their children. Even when the children developed symptoms at home, they might ask the parents to call "my doctor," again reflecting their awareness that the parents' ability to help them was limited.

Diagnostic and therapeutic procedures were painful to the parents as well as to the children. Parents differed on whether or not they desired to be with their children during such procedures, although they usually would not express their wishes unless explicitly asked. Some parents were markedly relieved when they were not expected to be present at such times; others became less anxious if they were allowed to stay with their children and comfort them.

Parents of the younger children often mentioned the difficulty they experienced each evening when they had to leave a child crying in protest or despair. The parents would generally make an effort to continue the usual routine of putting their child to bed, usually with the help of a favorite toy or doll, and within a week or two most children accepted the fact that the parents had to leave each evening. However, a minority of children and parents never appeared to tolerate this daily separation.

The Child in Remission

Parents would eagerly look forward to the time that their child would go into remission and be discharged from the hospital, but their pleasurable anticipation of this event was frequently tempered by considerable concern regarding the necessity of again assuming the major responsibility for the child's care. They feared that without warning some acute medical problem would arise, and any past feelings of inadequacy associated with failure to recognize the original symptoms were reawakened.

Discipline was a common problem when the child returned home, especially if the parents hesitated to set reasonable limits on the child's behavior. The over-indulged child would increase his demands on the family until rather belated disciplinary measures had to be instituted, sometimes only after the other children in the family had grown openly resentful of the special favors received by their apparently well sibling.

Over-protection usually accompanied the over-indulgence, with activities such as swimming and bicycle riding being prohibited as they might "tire" the child. Ecchymoses resulting from normal activities created anxiety in the parents who associated the bruises with leukemia, and in many cases, this anxiety may have unconsciously led to unnecessary curtailment of the child's physical activity. Furthermore, the fear that the child might overhear his diagnosis sometimes led to discouraging attendance at school and other activities. Thus, returning home for some children meant living a rather isolated and restricted life, and the added strain for the parents led a few of them to be aware of longing for the relative security of the hospital.

DEFENSE PATTERNS
AND COPING MECHANISMS

Coping Behavior

Coping behavior is a term that has been used (Hamburg, Hamburg, and deGoza 1953; Visotsky et al. 1961) to denote all of the mechanisms utilized by an individual to meet a significant threat to his psychological stability and to enable him to function effectively. Such behavior would consist of the responses to environmental factors that help the individual master the situation, as well as the intrapsychic processes which contribute to the successful adaptation to a psychologic stress. The stressful episode in this study, evoking such adaptive and defensive reactions, has been defined as the totality of events associated with being the parents of a child with a fatal disease, and includes both the external events and the associated inner conflicts, impulses, and guilt.

The success or failure of this coping behavior may be evaluated in at least two ways. The observer may judge whether the behavior allows the individual to carry out certain personal and socially defined goals. In the setting of this study, one frame of reference was the relative ability of the parent to participate in the care of the ill child and fulfill other family responsibilities. Though value judgments on the part of the observer are constantly invoked when using such criteria, this area is certainly of major concern to the physician caring for the child with leukemia.

The effectiveness of coping behavior may also be evaluated in terms of the individual parent's ability to tolerate the stressful situation without disruptive anxiety or depression, regardless of whether the behavior is socially desirable. Such judgments were made in studying the parents' hormonal response (Friedman, Mason, and Hamburg 1963; Wolff et al. 1963), where it was found that pathological as well as socially desirable coping patterns were associated with stable 17-hydroxycorticosteroid excretion rates, if such behavior was effective in protecting the individual from anxiety and depression. Optimally then, coping behavior not only enables the parent to deal effectively with the reality situation, but also serves the protective function of keeping anxiety and other emotional distress within tolerable limits.

The "shock" of learning the diagnosis and the associated lack of emotional experience has already been mentioned, and this may conveniently be classified as an extreme degree of isolation of affect, a mechanism by which the apparent intellectual recognition of a painful event is not associated with a concomitant intolerable emotional response. Only after a few hours or days was there profound emotional feeling and expression associated with the intellectual awareness of what had happened, this usually occurring only after the necessary arrangements had been made for the child's immediate treatment. This lack of affective experience continued to be a conspicuous defense, and enabled parents to talk realistically about their children's condition and prognosis with relatively little evidence of emotional involvement. Thus, the parents were frequently described by the medical and nursing staffs as being "strong," though occasionally this behavior was interpreted as reflecting a "coldness" or lack of sincere concern. The parents were also often aware of this paucity of emotional feeling, frequently explaining it on the grounds that they "could not break down" in the presence of the children or their physicians. However, that there was some uneasiness about their apparent lack of emotional expression was suggested by the fact that parents would occasionally verbalize their confusion and even guilt over not feeling worse.

In an occasional parent, the process of intellectualization was extreme, as if the parent was trying to master the situation through complete understanding. Here, there was not only the usual desire for medical knowledge, but a persistent tendency to discuss leukemia in a detached and highly intellectualized manner, at times clearly identifying with the physicians. For instance, the parent might wish to examine a peripheral blood smear, since he "always wondered how our body works."

Over a period of time the parents became increasingly knowledgeable about leukemia, and would often request rather detailed information regarding their child's condition, especially about laboratory results. Inquiries about a hemoglobin level or leukocyte count were common, and in addition, occasionally such data would spontaneously be given by a doctor in order to help explain the more general situation. This led to attempts, generally unsuccessful, on the part of some parents to predict what therapy their child should receive next, with confusion and suspicion when their "medical judgment" disagreed with that of the physician. Having once received such detailed information, the parents tended to expect a daily briefing, and would exhibit at first disappointment, then anger, when this routine was interrupted. Such concern over details did serve a defense function by allowing the parents, as well as the doctors, to avoid the more general, but also the more tragic and threatening aspects of the case. However, our impression was that, over-all, more anxiety was generated than dissipated by this practice.

Another defense, less ubiquitous than isolation of affect, but also generally present in greater or lesser degree, was the mechanism of denial, by which is meant the intellectual disclaiming of a painful event or feeling. A few parents openly denied the seriousness of the illness and prognosis; in these individuals there was always a history of a similar defense pattern during past episodes of stress. Such parents did not seem to "understand" the importance of various procedures and therapeutic plans, and were therefore prone to direct hostility towards the physicians.

Motor activity also appeared to often serve a coping function, the parent usually being partially aware of the motivation behind such activity. Thus, one mother realized that when her child was acutely ill, she would markedly increase the amount of time she spent sewing and knitting. This intermittent activity served to physically remove this mother from the threatening situation and to give her "something else to do and think about."

The mothers readily participated in the overall care of their children, and the importance of such activity to the parents, such as allaying existing guilt, has been emphasized by others (Bierman 1956; Knudson and Natterson 1960; Orbach, Sutherland, and Bozeman 1955; Richmond and Waisman 1955). This type of activity appeared most supportive to the mothers who, in contrast to their spouses, found the nursing role consistent with their past experiences and self-image.

It should be emphasized that defensive activity does not always, by any means, interfere with adequate and effective behavior. Rather, there appears to be an optimal range of defending or "buffering" oneself from the impact of having a child with a fatal disease. Deviation from this range in one direction, by denying reality, interferes with optimal participation in the care of the child by not allowing the parent to fully meet the responsibilities and demands associated with the situation. On the other hand, when a parent lacks adequate defense patterns applicable to these circumstances, his ability to care effectively for his child is also significantly hampered. This latter situation was vividly illustrated by one father who wanted to stay by his boy's bedside, but found it intolerable to do so because he would be preoccupied with thoughts of the boy ultimately dying. The only way this father could decrease his own anxiety was to stay away from the Children's Ward, leaving his boy alone for relatively long periods of time.

Social Influences

As has been discussed, the adjustment seen in most of the parents characteristically included a relatively high degree of intellectual acceptance of the diagnosis and prognosis. Realistic arrangements, including those directly related to the care of the ill child, were therefore facilitated. However, this acceptance was not easy to achieve and came about only after a good deal of emotional struggle, expressed as "We had to convince ourselves of the diagnosis." It is therefore pertinent that relatives and friends did not usually help in this process, but rather, were more likely to hinder the realization of the child's condition.

Typically, the children's grandparents tended to be less accepting of the diagnosis than the parents, with more distant relatives and friends challenging reality even more frequently. The tendency for the degree of reality-distortion to increase with the remoteness of its source from the immediate family almost made it appear that some of the parents were surrounded by "concentric circles of disbelief." Friends and relatives would question the parents as to whether the doctors were *sure* of the diagnosis and prognosis, and might suggest that the parents seek additional medical opinion. Comments would be made that the ill child, especially if he was in remission, could not possibly have leukemia as he looked too well or did not have the "right symptoms." Individuals cured of "leukemia" would be cited, and in a few cases, faith healers and pseudomedical practitioners were recommended.

Although parents generally perceived most of these statements and suggestions as attempts to "cheer us up and give us hope," they found themselves in the uncomfortable position of having to "defend" their child's diagnosis and prognosis, sometimes experiencing the feeling that others thought they were therefore "condemning" their own child. Thus, the parents were not allowed to express any feelings of hopelessness, yet, as will be discussed later, they were paradoxically expected to appear grief-stricken.

Grandparents not only displayed more denial than the parents, but often appeared more vulnerable to the threatened loss of the loved child. Therefore, many of the parents felt that they had to give emotional support to the grandparents, at a time when it was most difficult for them to assume this supportive role. Our impression is that this marked degree of emotional involvement on the part of the grandparents helps explain the observations of Bozeman, Orbach, and

Sutherland (1955), who noted that the mothers in their study did not often turn to their own mothers for support or guidance. In spite of this, grandparents generally were informed of the diagnosis almost immediately, though parents would occasionally first tell "people we hardly knew . . . just to make sure that we could get through it."

Though society did not allow the parents to give up the hope that their children might survive, it also assumed that they would be grief-stricken. Therefore, the parents were not expected to take part in normal social activities, or be interested in any form of entertainment. The relatively long course of leukemia made this expectation not only unrealistic, but also undesirable in that some diversion appears necessary in allowing the parents to function effectively in the care of the ill child. Illustrative of this area of conflict was the experience of one mother, whose child had had leukemia for one year. She gave a birthday party for one of her other children and was immediately challenged by relatives who "could not understand how my family could have a party *at a time like this.*" Such remarks often produced anxiety, guilt, or confusion in a parent, leading this same mother to remark "that being a parent of a leukemic child is hard, but not as hard as other people make it."

An additional problem was that friends and relatives often besieged the parents with requests for information about their child. Parents would have to repeatedly describe each new development, listening by the hour to repetitive expressions of encouragement and sympathy, and occasionally having to reassure others that the disease was not contagious. This arduous task was ameliorated in the cases where a semiformal system evolved where some one individual, often a close friend or a minister, would be kept up to date so that he in turn could answer the multitude of questions.

Although it was clear that friends and relatives sometimes aggravated the parents' distress, they also provided significant emotional support in the form of tactful and sympathetic listening and by offering to be of service, as has been described in detail by Bozeman, Orbach, and Sutherland (1955). The major source of emotional support for most parents during the period of hospitalization appeared to be the other parents of similarly afflicted children, with the feeling that "we are all in it together" and with concern for the distress experienced by the other parents, a mode of adjustment discussed in detail by Greene (1958). The parents learned from each other, and could profit by observing the coping behavior manifested by others in the group. Thus, the common fear of "going to pieces" when their child would become terminally ill was greatly alleviated by watching others successfully, albeit painfully, go through the experience.

Search for Meaning

The parents generally found it intolerable to think of their child's leukemia as a "chance" or meaningless event. Therefore, they tried to construct an explanation for it, displaying a certain amount of urgency until one appropriate to their particular frame of reference could be accepted.

A few parents were content with what might be termed a "deferred explanation"; that is, they accepted and appeared satisfied with the knowledge that it would be some years before a scientifically accurate answer was available to tell them why *their* child had acquired leukemia. Parents in this category were all relatively well-educated and were able to evaluate the current thoughts regarding the etiology of leukemia, coming to the *conclusion* that definitive proof of causation was still lacking. However, this did not constitute an acceptance of leukemia as a "chance" phenomenon, but rather implied an ability to wait for the accumulation of more knowledge regarding the etiology of the disease.

A greater number of parents appeared to need a more immediate and definitive answer. They would eagerly and unconditionally accept one of the more recent theories concerning the etiology of leukemia, such as the "viral theory," with some additional explanation as to why it was *this* particular child, rather than some other child, who developed the disease. Most parents constructed an explanation which was a composite of scientific facts, elements from the parent's past experiences, and fantasies. Though in the majority of cases their concept of etiology served to partially resolve any feelings of being responsible for the child's illness, the synthesis sometimes appeared to reflect parental self-blame. In these instances the guilt appeared to be less anxiety-provoking than the total lack of a suitable cause for the leukemia, and therefore guilt may at times be thought of as serving a defense function for the individual (Chodoff 1959).

Religion

The attempt of parents to attribute meaning to the fact that their child developed leukemia was inseparable from their religious beliefs and orientation. Most parents expressed the sentiment that religion was of comfort to them, occasionally making such statements as "It helps us be more accepting" and "At least we know he will be in Heaven and not suffering." These statements seemed to be sincere reflections of the help that the parents received from their religious beliefs, though these same parents did not characteristically discuss the child's prognosis in religious terms, nor were topics of religion often brought up spontaneously in the interview situation. In contrast, a few individuals primarily thought about their child's illness in a religious context, with statements made that "This is the Lord's way of protecting him from an even worse fate." In these parents, there was a tendency to accept the illness as God's will, with the acknowledgment that one could not expect to fully understand His ways.

Although a strong religious orientation made the illness more understandable for some parents, having a child with leukemia caused other parents to doubt their previously unquestioned religious faith and these doubts sometimes led to transient expressions of guilt. However, to our knowledge no parent actually renounced his religion as a result of this experience. In fact, it was common for a parent to report an eventual "return to religion," and express sympathy for any of the other parents who did not have sufficient religious faith to help them in this time of need.

Hope and Anticipatory Grief

The element of hope as it refers to a favorable alteration of the expected sequence of events, though hard to evaluate, is of general clinical importance (Marmor 1963; Menninger 1959), and was universally emphasized by the parents. Comments would be made such as "Without hope I could never keep going . . . though I know deep down nothing really can be done." Unlike massive denial, hope did not appear to interfere with effective behavior and was entirely compatible with an intellectual acceptance of reality. That the persistence of hope for a more favorable outcome does not require the need to intellectually deny the child's prognosis is of clinical significance, as it differentiates hope from defense patterns that potentially may greatly distort reality. Hope actually helped the parents accept "bad news" in that the ward physician would often couple discouraging news with some hopeful comment.

As the disease progressed in the children, there was usually a corresponding curtailment of hope in the parents. Whereas at first they might hope for the development of a curative drug, as the child became increasingly ill, the hope might be only for one further remission. Parents would note that they no longer were making any long-range plans and that they were living on a day-to-day basis. The hopes regarding their children would tend to be so short-term and limited that parents would find themselves preoccupied with a question such as whether their child would be well enough that evening to attend a movie, rather than think about his ultimate fate. This gradual dissipation and narrowing of hope appeared inversely related to the increasing presence of what has been called anticipatory grief (Lindemann 1944).

The amount of grieving in anticipation of the forthcoming loss varied greatly in the individual parents, and in a few, never was obvious at any time during the child's clinical course. However, in most, as noted by others (Natterson and Knudson 1960), the grief process was usually quite apparent by the fourth month of the child's illness, frequently being precipitated by the first acute critical episode in the child's disease. Grieving then gradually evolved as the disease progressed and any death on the ward often had a potentiating effect.

The signs and symptoms of this anticipatory mourning process were not as well defined as in an acute grief reaction. However, it was common for parents to complain of somatic symptoms, apathy, weakness, and preoccupation with thoughts of the ill child. Sighing was frequently observed, and many parents would occasionally cry at night and appear depressed. At other times there seemed to be an increase in motor activity and a tendency to talk for hours about the ill child, an observation consistent with the findings of Lindemann (1944).

The process of resigning oneself to the inevitable outcome was frequently accompanied by statements of wishing "it was all over with." The narrowing of hope and the completion of much of the grief work was described by one mother who stated: "I still love my boy, want to take care of him and be with him as much as possible . . . but still feel sort of detached from him." In spite of feeling "detached" from her child, this mother continued to be most effective in caring for and comforting her child, with no evidence of physical abandonment. Richmond and Waisman (1955) have commented on the usefulness of this anticipatory mourning in stepwise preparing the parent for the eventual loss, and the few parents in our study who did not display such behavior experienced a more prolonged and distressing reaction after the child actually died.

TERMINAL PHASE

Terminal Episode and Death

The parents realized that the clinical condition was much more serious when all of the established chemotherapeutic agents had been exhausted, this event marking what might be considered the beginning of the terminal phase of the illness. Characteristically at this time, there was an acceleration of the grief-work or the actual precipitation of mourning in those few individuals who previously had denied the prognosis, and to the staff, the parents often appeared resigned to the fact that their child would die. Often, as previously described (Richmond and Waisman 1955), parents would become increasingly involved in the care of other children on the ward, and occasionally a parent would openly express the desire to resume a more normal life and return to the other children at home. Though these feelings prevailed, there still were residuals of hope, if only that the child might "just smile once more" or "have one more good day." During this terminal period, the knowledge that the doctor "who knows the case best" would be in daily seemed of particular importance. However, in spite of this appreciative attitude, the parents were also less understanding and easily became annoyed when even minor things did not go exactly according to plan. There were apt to be frequent, though brief, expressions of irritation or anger, often followed by spontaneous denial of such feelings. These transient manifestations of hostility might have been related to the direct challenging of an underlying, unrecognized belief in the omnipotent nature of the doctors and the

hospital, or in some cases, a displacement of unconscious resentment and ambivalence from the ill child to the medical staff.

In this setting, the child's death was generally taken calmly, but
with the appropriate expression of affect. Outbursts of uncontrollable grief or open
expressions of self-blame were the exception, and usually there was some indication
of relief that the child was no longer suffering. There were arrangements, telephone
calls, and decisions to be made, and characteristically the father again assumed
the more dominant and supportive role, just as he had shortly after the diagnosis
had first been made.

The death of the child therefore did not appear to be a severe superimposed stressful situation, but rather an anticipated loss at the end of a long
sequence of events. This was also reflected in the 17-hydroxycorticosteroid exertion
rates (Friedman, Mason, and Hamburg 1963), in that there was not one parent
who showed a marked rise during the last day of urine collection, which frequently
included the time the child had actually died, nor were plasma corticosteroid
elevations observed several hours after the child's death (Friedman, Mason, and
Hamburg unpublished data). These findings might in part be due to the parents
not yet experiencing the emotion, as many of them remarked that they "just
cannot believe that it's all over . . . it just hasn't hit yet."

Follow-up Observations

The parents of the children who died relatively early in our study
were invited to return to NIH for a three-day period. Twenty-three parents were
thus approached; 18, including 8 couples, accepted and were seen three to eight
months after the end of their children's illness. In addition, three parents who
lived in the immediate vicinity of NIH were also available for study during a
comparable period.

The grief reactions following the actual loss of the children, as related
by these parents, were very similar to, though in some cases not as intense as,
those following a sudden loss (Lindemann 1944), and the mourning usually became much less pronounced after three to six weeks. There was a tendency for
feelings of guilt and self-blame to be verbalized, often for the first time, and as
others (Solnit and Green 1959) have noted, repeated reassurance from the doctor
was frequently quite comforting during this period. One might speculate that in
some cases an unconscious or barely conscious wish for relief of tension through
the child's death during the terminal phase provided the motivation for such
expressions of guilt during the mourning period.

Of the 18 parents who returned to NIH after the child's death, 16
felt that the return had been a helpful experience. Some of these parents believed
that they "would have been drawn back," even if they had not been invited to
again participate in the study. This feeling existed in the face of a "dread about

returning," sometimes accompanied by a tendency to think of their child as still a patient at the hospital. In these parents, there was a feeling of relief soon after arrival at NIH, expressed as "It wasn't anywhere near as hard as I thought it would be," followed by statements to the effect that returning to NIH "has put a period on the whole affair . . . it now seems more real that Jimmy is not with us." In our opinion, this suggests that an unconscious remnant of denial persisted in many parents, reflecting a previous denial process that was not always readily apparent when the child was still alive. This apparent acceleration in the termination of the grief process was not reported by two parents who did not appear to have accepted their loss to any significant degree, though approximately six months had elapsed since the death of their children.

Though our follow-up observations are still limited and confined to 24 couples, it is known that five mothers became pregnant either during or immediately following their child's illness. There is not sufficient data in three cases to judge whether the pregnancy was planned, but in the other two there was a deliberate effort to conceive. One additional couple attempted to adopt a child approximately four months after their own child had died, and in one other family, the mother is attempting to become pregnant some six months after their youngest child died.

None of the parents who have thus far participated in our follow-up study have reported an increased incidence of somatic complaints or minor illnesses, nor have any of the parents developed any acute medical problems requiring hospitalization subsequent to the actual loss of their child. However, it is recognized that the follow-up period has been of inadequate length to make any statements regarding the possible relationship of unresolvable object loss and the grief reaction to the development of disease, as has been suggested by Schmale (1958) and Engel (1961).

IMPLICATION FOR PHYSICIANS AND CONCLUSIONS

Each parent of a child with a fatal disease reacts to the tragedy in a unique manner, consistent with his particular personality structure, past experiences, and the individualized meaning and specific circumstances associated with the threatened loss. In general, optimal medical management depends on the physician's awareness and evaluation of certain aspects of this specific background information. However, the parents of children with leukemia do share many similar problems that are inherent in the situation, and certain modes of adjustment commonly occur in a characteristic sequence. The parental behavior, though not stereotyped, is therefore predictable to some degree.

Characteristically, most parents are unable to incorporate detailed information regarding the disease and its clinical course during the first days after learning the diagnosis. The physician should therefore concentrate on explaining the child's acute condition and keep his guidance relevant to the immediate problem, helping the parents with whatever decisions must be made. Sufficient time and privacy should be available to allow the parents to ask their questions, repetitiously at times, since this is one of the processes by which they come to accept the tragic diagnosis. If referral to a larger medical center is contemplated, the parents should be led to have realistic expectations, neither anticipating a "cure" nor frightened by statements that "nothing can be done."

After the child's medical management has been decided and the immediate problems subside, the parents should be furnished with sufficient information about leukemia[2] to allow them to realistically help in the care and handling of their child. Such information also aids them in resolving any feelings of guilt or sense of responsibility for their child's illness. However, requests for detailed medical information, such as the daily laboratory findings, should be discouraged and evaluated in terms of what underlying needs the parents are attempting to fulfill. The physician should appreciate the frequent attempts of parents to find some "meaning" or "cause" for their child's illness, and unrealistic etiologic explanations should only gradually be questioned. In order to avoid unnecessary confusion and anxiety, all medical information should, whenever possible, be communciated to the parents by the same physician.

The physician should be alert to the problems of the hospitalized child, and parents should be informed, when indicated, that overt manifestations of apathy, depression and hostility are often the natural consequence of prolonged illness and hospitalization in children. Apparent by-passing of parental authority, or even open rejection of the parents by the child, may precipitate episodes of anxiety and guilt in the parents, and every attempt should be made not to further undermine the parental role. During the child's hospitalization, nurses can be particularly helpful in guiding parents, especially fathers, in effective participation in their child's care. At the time of discharge, parents should be instructed about the physical and emotional care of their child, reassured regarding their adequacy to meet the demands of the situation, and advised of the availability of prompt medical help during this period. Special emphasis should be paid to discussing what activities are reasonable for the child, with the aim of preventing undue restrictions and over-protection.

Coping mechanisms observed in parents should be viewed in terms of how such behavior contributes, or interferes, with meeting the needs of the ill child and other family members, yet not neglecting to appreciate the protective function such behavior has in keeping anxiety and depression within tolerable limits for the individual parent. There are many appropriate ways for parents to master the situation and advice should be consistent with the individual's particular coping pattern, with attention paid to the expectations and demands that may be made by friends and relatives. An acceptance and understanding of anticipatory grief can further enable the physician to help parents adjust to their inevitable and painful loss, though the child's physician should not modify his course of treatment because of this anticipatory mourning experienced by the parents. Expressions of guilt or hostility should not be considered abnormal unless they are extreme and persistent; in these cases further evaluation, and perhaps psychiatric consultation, is indicated.

The physician should not underestimate the importance of his mere presence, to both the child and the parents. Parents particularly need his support when their child first becomes seriously ill, even though in reality a remission is likely to follow. Though the physician must keep somewhat "emotionally distant" from the family he is treating in order to maintain his own effectiveness and objectivity, his empathy and understanding are vitally important in caring for the child with a fatal disease and the child's family.

NOTES

1. The ward physicians at the National Cancer Institute have the title of Clinical Associate, having completed internship and at least one year of residency prior to their NIH experience. During each year of this study, there were three ward physicians assigned to the children's floor, each spending nine months on this and an adult service.

2. A publication entitled "Childhood Leukemia: A Pamphlet for Parents" is available to physicians for distribution to parents from the Information and Publications Office, National Cancer Institute, Bethesda, Maryland.

19

The College Student and Death

EDWIN S. SHNEIDMAN

The college student is—by virtue of his or her time of life (typically about twenty years of age) and his or her place in the world (in a setting of ideas and stimulation, books and learning)—in a highly dramatic, life-expanding situation. College life, for most, is exciting. Thus the threat of death, which does nothing but diminish and annihilate, is, especially for a college student, a dramatically devastating trauma. It is the essence of the wrong event at the wrong time, the worst of winter's blasts in the summer of life, terribly premature, horribly out of season with life's flow, the most dire occurrence at the most inauspicious moment.

Independent of our democratic pretensions, we tend not to be egalitarian about death, and perhaps rightly so. We mourn the death of a young gifted person, a beautiful person, more than that of an old person, a wicked person, or even an ordinary person. And, in general, we mourn the death of a college student—at the threshold of full adult life, trained, bright promise unfulfilled—more than any other.

The raw facts are illuminating but not reassuring. United States statistics about college-age death (U.S. Department of Health, Education and Welfare 1970) inform us that in 1969 the percentage of the total population between 15 and 19 years of age was 9.1, between 20 and 24 years, 7.8; in 1968 the reported number of all deaths in the United States was almost 2 million (1,930,082); the percentage of deaths for the 15- to 19-year-old and the 20- to 24-year-old group was each around 1. The mortality rates (per 1000 in that age group) were 1.1 and 1.4, respectively. Those years are obviously a time of life—except for death in war—when death is an event of relatively infrequent occurrence. As to the reasons for death, the four leading causes of death in the United States for ages 15 to 24 for both sexes are accident, homicide, malignant neoplasms, and suicide. The school years are obviously a time of life when the threats to life itself are not so much from internal disorders of the soma, but rather from threats by others in the environment and from imprudencies from within the self.

In every life, the decade of the twenties, from the late teens to age 29, is the time of life which, for many, is a make-or-break era (Shneidman 1971b). That is a time when one has to stand on one's own two feet and face the world. In another setting (Shneidman 1967) I have discussed three types of crises as they relate to time of life; one, called an *intratemporal crisis,* which occurs within a time of life such as adolescence or middle age; a second, called an *intertemporal crisis,* which occurs as one turns the corner from one stage of life to another, e.g., the crisis of moving from being a child to becoming an adolescent, or from being an adolescent to becoming an adult, involving the trauma of moving through life; and a third, called an *extratemporal crisis,* which relates to those crises which are out of phase with one's time of life. The latter describes the individual who is, so to speak, developmentally precocious, way ahead of his or her own years, too mature, an old person in his or her teens; or, conversely, those crises which happen to persons who are "retarded" in the sense of being immature, almost childish, infantile, too young for their years. Obviously, optimal movement through life implies that one develops as one is pushed along by inexorable time. In *Pierre,* Melville says, "Oh what quenchless feud is this, that Time hath with the sons of men." And so it is that we are pushed willy-nilly, screaming, kicking, sometimes willing the obligatory, not only from day to day but from birthday to birthday and from decade to decade. College students can have all of these three types of personal crises.

College time is a fulcrum point; college commencement is both an ending and a beginning. The college student's view of his or her relationship to death is essentially that of a person far removed from death, and yet at that time when life and love and death are all highly romanticized. The romaticization of death—death as lover, death as special, death as arcane, death as heroic—is a separate and fascinating topic (Shneidman 1973). The very topic "death and the college student" implies that there are stages in the human life cycle; infancy, childhood, young adolescence, a time for college, adulthood, etc. And further, it implies that one's basic orientations and attitudes to the topic of death and to one's own death change and develop (and sometimes even mature) as one moves through life's time. The most widely recited statement of this apparently ubiquitous fact about the stages of life is Jacques's speech on the seven ages of man in Act II, Scene vii of *As You Like It.* ("All the world's a stage, and all the men and women merely players.")

In our own century, a number of psychologically oriented authors have elaborated on or explicated this archetypal theme. On first appearance the most simple (but perhaps, on reflection, the most profound) opinion is that of C. G. Jung (1933). He propounds a two-phase view: That life is made up of an upward movement toward that moment when one perceives his or her mortality (somewhere usually in middle age) followed by a second stage of life, in which the primary task is to prepare for one's own death. This turning point in life can be called the "noon-day" of life. It is essentially a "watershed" view of life. Charlotte Buhler (1961) discusses the various stages in the course of the human life cycle; Gerald Heard (1963) writes of the five ages of man; Ernest Schachtel (1959) speaks of the important periods in what he calls the "human metamorphosis," Harry Stack Sullivan (1953) talks about the developmental epochs in the human life cycle; and there are others.

Perhaps the best known twentieth-century explication of the stages of life is Erik Erikson's (1963) conceptualization of the development of human personality in eight hierarchical psychosocial or psychosexual stages, a scheme which implies that one needs successfully to resolve one stage before going on meaningfully to the next stage. In puberty and adolescence, the fifth stage, the core issues revolve around identity versus role confusion; in young adulthood the issues are intimacy versus isolation.

In relation to intimacy versus isolation, one is reminded of Francis Bacon's thought that to love is to give hostages to fortune. The alternative however is isolation, not risking, not daring, not investing, not loving—hoping not to be vulnerable. For most of us the risk of being vulnerable and suffering loss seems more desirable than to be lonely, loveless, and to live a life that is essentially barren and arid. Hiram Haydn (1974), in talking about his great friend Henry A. Murray, said: "Never to have been in love is never to have lived fully; never to have had a friend about whom one feels the way I have described constitutes an equal deprivation of life." Death is the irreversible stopping of the living interaction with all those loves and relationships. It is what Melville's anguished Captain Ahab cries at the death of the Parsee in the penultimate chapter of *Moby Dick*: "Gone?—gone? What means that little word? What death-knell rings in it, that old Ahab shakes as if he were the belfry."

ATTITUDES TOWARD DEATH

Recently I wrote an article on death for a popular psychology journal, *Psychology Today* (1970), which included a 75-item questionnaire on death and then, several months later, published the results of the questionnaire findings. The single biggest surprise in the results was the sheer volume of responses. Within a month of the original article more than 30,000 readers returned the death questionnaire (and more than 2000 of them sent substantial letters with their replies), breaking the record set by previous questionnaires in that journal on the topics of sex, violence, and drugs. For the 1971 report I chose a random sample of 500 responses—a sampling of about 1 in 60. This present section is a first report on the 90 college students included in that sample of 500—18 percent of the initial sample, and representing around 5400 college students among the 30,000 respondents.

America's current attitude toward death is deeply ambivalent: awe of death and an attraction to death; risking death and loving life; wanting happiness and behaving in self-destructive ways; regarding death as taboo and insisting on a new permissiveness to talk about it; an obsession with The Bomb and a deep concern with spiritual rebirth. We live in a death-conscious time, in which people, the center of their own world, boldly assert that they are not psychologically degradable.

Views of death have undergone radical changes in the last few generations—perhaps the first major radical changes since the seventeenth century of Descartes. The Cartesian view of death is tied to a view of the individual as essentially a biological vessel, subject to the whims of fate or fortune. Death is one such whim. The Cartesian philosophic spirit necessarily implies a fatalistic view of life.

The results of the death questionnaire unequivocably demonstrate the demise of fatalism. Contemporary college students—and perhaps most twentieth-century people—have made themselves the center of their own universe, and have put themselves back into their own death. They recognize death and dying as aspects of living. Thanks primarily to Freud, college students see the individual as playing conscious and unconscious roles in his or her own fate. Most students believe in the possible influence of psychological factors on death; 96 percent either "firmly believe" or "tend to believe" that psychological factors can influence or even cause death, and half believe that most persons participate consciously or unconsciously in their own deaths.

Many elements go into shaping people's views of life and death and the part they play in either by their own volition. The usual experiences with death in America have changed dramatically over the last two generations. It used to be that almost everyone, by the time of adolescence, had personally witnessed a death, usually at home, of some loved one—a baby brother or sister, a mother or father. Today most dying is done in hospitals, largely out of sight, and always under formal institutional regimen.

The interface between religion and death is especially fascinating. Numerous studies have shown that nominal religious affiliation is not enough to understand religious conviction. But we asked for "religious background," which allowed us to see that people's religious environment, whether they accept or reject the tenets of their faith, whether they stay with the church of their parents or leave it, certainly affects many of their attitudes toward death. Important in most current attitudes toward death is one's own estimate of his or her religiosity. Among college students the "antireligious" are twice as numerous as the "very religious"—a sharp difference from the total *Psychology Today* sample.

While most of the antireligious college students say that religion plays no role in their own attitudes, a substantial number report that religion has significant impact on them, apparently pushing them away from the traditional religious outlooks on death. Students who consider themselves not hostile to organized religion are less likely than the antireligious to attribute a very significant role to religion.

If religion does not play a significant role in forming attitudes toward death in this secular age, what does? Introspection and meditation, say over one-third of the students. Given another choice and asked to apply the influences to their own deaths, about one-third reinforce their first choice by selecting existential philosophy as the most important influence. They mention Camus and Hesse often.

If we put together attitudes at various ages in reference to beliefs, we find—with no great surprise—that attitudes toward death change as one matures. Typically, religious beliefs become more secular or scientized. One then sees death simply as the end of life. The typical childhood conception of death is in terms of an afterlife, which for most involves ideas of heaven or hell (57 percent), but by young adulthood, the percentage of individuals who believe in an afterlife as their primary view of death has been cut almost in half to 30 percent. From late adolescence on, the largest single percentage see death simply as the final process of life. Consistent with this view, the most distasteful aspect of death for college students is that "one can no longer have any experiences."

The findings of the questionnaire point to the fact that over the past generation or two there has been a tremendous secularization of death. Nowadays people die ascetically in antiseptic hospitals rather than aesthetically in their homes. The physician has replaced the priest; the doctor is today's magician who has the power to extend life, our new escort from this vale of tears. The funeral industry directs the forms of mourning, ushering us from burial to bereavement.

Historian Arnold Toynbee (1969) has written that death is essentially a two-person affair, involving both the survivor and the decedent. He further asserts that if a married person truly loves the spouse, that person will wish the spouse to die *first*, so the spouse will be spared the anguish of bereavement. Student respondents to the death questionnaire divide on this issue: 17 percent say yes and 23 percent say no; most (60 percent) are undecided. The reasons they give for yes and no responses are about equally divided between selfish and selfless reasons. One is reminded of what Lord Nelson is reported to have said as he lay dying aboard the *Victory*: "The pain is so great that one might wish oneself dead, but one would like to live a little longer, too." As ambivalence is the keystone of life, so is it a characteristic of death.

One twenty-year-old college student wrote about the death questionnaire: "If I pass this test do I get immortal life as a prize? Think what a bummer that would be. Fear of death puts a little excitement into life. R.I.P."

CONCEPTUALIZATIONS OF DEATH

It is as true nowadays as when Professor Henry Murray wrote, one short generation ago (specifically in 1949), "that the American of today has no compelling religious belief, no certainty of a moral order, no articulate philosophy, no heart's vision that demands aesthetic utterance." Are contemporary college students a generation adrift? We have seen that they do not think about death more often than most people, and we are not surprised, as we reflect upon it, that when they are asked to write about death, they are able to do so in a rather sensitive and articulate way. In the *Psychology Today* study, most college students viewed death (as did most of the respondents) as "The end; the final process of life" (26 percent) and were most distressed (36 percent) by the notion that death meant that they could no longer have any experiences, that it was a stopping of the mind's introspective flow—a rather twentieth-century psychological and phenomenological view of "cessation."

A group of college students (enrolled in a course on death and suicide) were asked: "What does death mean to you? How do you conceptualize your own death?" The following quoted paragraphs are a sampling from among hundreds of responses. Here are a few:

Death means the end of consciousness. Like dreamless sleep, like before birth—no memories. Nothing. The body decays, its elements become part of the earth so when one dies he gives back to the earth.

Life is accidental, but I cannot understand the concept of myself. What makes the peculiar accident of my mother and father called *me,* feel like *me* and not like my brother? Because of this, I'm not sure that I don't believe in reincarnation if not of the soul. Then the possibility that a random collision of atoms will create another me who thinks and feels.

The part of *me* which conceptualizes cannot conceptualize "not conceptualizing," therefore it is impossible for me to think of my own death without removing myself to a pin point of time and observing, not-me—and in this act my conceptualization faculty is still present. (Male—age 21)

Another:

Death signifies the termination of all meaning your life has begun to assume through careful working through of your ideas. It comes, and it drops one into a void from which he can never return. It destroys all which one held of any worth, of any value whatsoever. It robs one of his life. But it also provides a cease-fire, an escape from the almost unendurable suffering to which one has submitted, an oblivion, an out at last. Death is a long, long sleepless sleep. One returns to nothingness, and then it is as if one had never existed. It makes all of one's efforts to confront himself, to confront the world, to confront the passage of time—so stupid, in retrospect (not that the dead person is able to indulge in retrospection), so futile, so worthless, so absurd. Death is the crowning absurdity to a pathetically meaningless life anyway. (Female—age 21)

Another:

I'm not really certain that I've formed an absolute idea of death. I see death as something very *final* and permanent. It is the end of what I know now as existence. I cannot conceive of non-existence. When I try to picture my death, even though I no longer have a body, *I* am still conscious and I am still myself. Yet, when I try to think of it rationally, it only seems reasonable that when I die, that is the end. It's just a part of the natural cycle of the whole life-decay process. Man is a product of natural selection and the fact that he is able to worry about death and must create for himself consolations of afterlife is his way of accepting what is for every other creature a part of living.

Another way of explaining it is that in nature, a flower, for example, blooms and then eventually dies and all its material remains decay and it's gone. Then the next spring another flower blooms from the same bud and so life and flowers continue. But the flower that followed the first flower was a different flower; the first flower is gone and while every year there will be a flower, that first flower will never *be* again. (Female—age 18)

A sizable number of student reflections touch on what is, in its potential magnitude for human destruction, the most impactful manner of death in history: megadeath—the possibility of killing millions in the flash of a moment.[1] I have been led by my students to believe that the haunting omnipresence of The Bomb underlies, in some sinister but discernible way, much of the malaise, disenchantment, and incivility of youth in our time, reflecting a breakdown of national and international morality which has been "the story of their lives." As one student said: "The Bomb lives!" by which he meant that, at some surface or deep level of consciousness, the specter of nuclear destruction hangs on the air like an unmovable cloud.

THE STUDENT AS DIRECT VICTIM

The majority of college-age deaths—55 to 60 percent—are related to accidents. They are sudden, ugly in their emotional impact, traumatic for the survivors, shocking. But youth is a time for risk taking and "accidents can happen." It is difficult (and perhaps unseemly) to compare the abrasiveness of one kind of death with another, but death from cancer seems to be an especially burdensome death for the survivor—and, of course, for the benighted victim. To die of cancer in one's teens or twenties, in college, seems a particularly "unfair" and tragic thing.

One then dies over a period of time, sees oneself growing sicker and weaker, slipping toward death, experiences the anxious concern of loved ones, and is usually the living (but failing) object of frantic medical efforts.

The following case involves a college student who was feeling rather poorly, couldn't quite diagnose his own symptoms, went to his physician, and was sent by his physician to a hematologist who diagnosed him as having acute myelogenous leukemia. This young man, a student in a local university, was, when first seen by me, a patient in the university hospital. His doctor requested that I see him because of his cantankerous behavior on the ward, his shouting at nurses, his swearing, and what the doctor described as his "bitchy behavior." When I first saw him, he was sitting up in bed, behaving in a rather feisty and imperious way to the others in the room. I greeted him at the outset by saying that I had heard that he had been misbehaving. He seemed to like that approach, and we hit it off quite well from the beginning. In my own heart I decided to see him because I felt that he was in for a rough time, and with his own defenses and alienating behavior, he might turn people away from him and have an unnecessarily psychologically painful death. I began to see him almost every day, alone, just he and I. It developed that he was an only child, his father was dead, and his relationship with his mother for the past several years could be characterized as a running verbal hostile fight. The content of our sessions grew more serious as he became increasingly ill. He sobered and matured enormously within a matter of weeks, and without any leading on my part, chose to talk openly about his impending death.

The session reproduced below (with some minor editing) is one recorded with his knowledge and reproduced here with the permission which he willingly gave before he died. It is several weeks after the first meeting. At this time he was quite ill, extremely weak, physically wrung out, and painfully aware of his downhill course. He died about a week after this session.

> ES: The nurse told me that you had a bad night.
> ST: Yes, it has been pretty bad lately. I am giving up. I want it to be over. I don't expect any miracles anymore. It is going to be a slow process. Maybe not so much a painful process but a slow process. I would like to get out and then I would also like to get to sleep and die. I don't know what to say. I am just tired. I woke up this morning and I was really frightened, just saying "Dear God, dear God, what am I going to do?" But dear God, dear God doesn't answer.
> ES: Were you really frightened?
> ST: Yes. Really frightened.
> ES: What was it fear of?
> ST: Of the unknown and of another day. Dr. Shneidman, if there was a way that I could end it now, I would do that. It is taking so long. I don't have much patience I guess.

ES: I am sure this is a trial for you in many deep ways, including that one.

ST: How do you do it?

ES: There is no easy way. You endure it, and then if you are lucky, you can look back on it. I wish I could give you some nice moral, common sense statement.

ST: I'm scared. You said you would say what death was. You said it was something I wouldn't know anything about. If I can only be sure that it would be peaceful. Will it be peaceful?

ES: I can practically guarantee it.

ST: This is so important. It is almost more important than anything else that it be peaceful.

ES: I am convinced of that.

ST: My mother still wants to believe that maybe something can happen. I suppose I do also.

ES: So do I.

ST: My mother has become so important.

ES: In what ways have your relationships with your mother changed in the past few weeks? They have obviously changed.

ST: I have loved her. I have let myself love her without feeling that she was going to emasculate me. I have let her love me. I have let her be a mother. She has been so beautiful. I get more comfort from her than from anybody else.

ES: Do you think it took your illness for that to happen?

ST: I don't know. I know for me it has, because now there is no reason to be wary of her castrating tendencies because she really means well for me. She brings me such comfort. She is so selfless. Crying is not supposed to help, yet it hurts when you get a fever, and you sweat a lot which is what I do. Life is so. . . . I don't know.

ES: In what other ways have you changed?

ST: It is a hard question. I don't know if I could be honest because I could say one thing now, but if it happened, I might do something else. For one thing, I would be very wary about all health things. I think I would know myself a little better, a lot better. I would look upon myself as a much better person. I think I would be less concerned about my physical appearance, although I don't think I would ignore it. I think I would be less selfish, more concerned with trying to get the most out of every day. If there was a God, if there was somebody that knew, that I could pray to to perform this miracle, I would be most thankful, and I would show it in every way I could. The idea of recovery is so farfetched, so unreal. I don't have a chance. I want to live so much, I do. I don't want to die now. Right now, all they think about is getting me out of the hospital for a few days and then taking me back in, doing as good a job as possible of keeping me alive as long as possible, which is something I really don't want to do, because if it's over, isn't it over? Isn't that the natural way? My mother keeps saying to take each day as it comes, but it is extremely difficult. I had a lot of trouble doing that before. I am having even more trouble doing it now. I went to bed last night after listening to you talking about it, I went to bed feeling good. It was very comforting, but then I woke up this morning, and I was in this terror, just like I need constant reassurance that I have been a good person and that there is someone there to love me. They told me I had a really good chance. They have tried everything. Now a perfectly good person with an awful lot to give is going to die. A young person is going to die. His death is going to be senseless. Do you fear death?

ES: Of course.

ST: I was just wondering about somebody who is more or less a specialist in the area of death, how he felt about it.

ES: I am as human as anybody. There are different levels of me just as there are different levels of you. I think I am very close to you. Like you, I don't like illness, pain, inactivity, uncertainty, death.

ST: I feel peaceful now.

ES: I will come to see you tomorrow.

ST: I hope I will still be here.

What is to be noted in the above exchange is not so much the focus on any single affective state, but rather the wide panoply of human emotions which is displayed in this relatively brief session. To list some of them, we can note his anguish, his puzzlement, the thread of hope and yearning beyond realistic probability. Also, his diffuse anger at "dear God" who doesn't answer his pleas and prayers, his resignation, his despair, his fantasied escape. And more than this, "irrational," simultaneous presence of seemingly contradictory emotions. That is the way the death scene is played. It is not a series of discrete feeling states, displayed cleanly, seriatim; rather it is a confluence and a booming flux of cries and whispers of simultaneous hope and hopelessness, of yearnings for help and declarations of helplessness. All these zigs and zags occur on an essentially down-hill curve of which the person himself or herself often has some deep presentiment. The task of the clinical thanatologist is made both more painful and more tolerable by the fact that in practically every case "all" that he or she needs to do is to be with the dying person, close by, even touching hands, and responding to the needs of the person to talk about any topic as that person moves into death.

One more vignette: At the beginning of one of my courses on death and suicide I was approached by a lovely young woman who, although she was animated and obviously bright (and was, as I learned after her death, a member of Phi Beta Kappa), seemed to be somewhat ill. For one thing she wore bandaids on each of her fingers. During our first conversation I asked her what was wrong, to which question she responded by telling me that she had scleroderma—a disease with an often-fatal outcome. I puzzled aloud as to whether or not she ought to take the course, but when she said that she would really like to try and if it became too onerous in content she would drop it, I consented to let her enroll. I came to know her rather well. She completed the course, but within a few weeks entered the hospital fighting for breath and died of her disease within a matter of days. In her hospital room she said to me: "I badly don't want to die, but most of all I don't want to die badly." She was a remarkable and fine person. Her husband has given me portions of her diary and his permission to reprint these excerpts written a few weeks before she died.

I've just experienced several days of deep depression, full of morbid thoughts of death and illness. The thing that disturbs me about such depressions is my uncertainty as to their generation and cause. If they are psychochemical or endocrinological in origin then I can dismiss them much more easily than if I believe they are the upwelling of some great hidden angst. Are they the maudlin, morbid reflections of a chemically unbalanced brain? This is somewhat of an alienating idea, those thoughts aren't *me*, they're just my body acting up. Having read more deeply into existentialist ideas lately it's intellectually somewhat emotionally repugnant to me to alienate my "inner self." But with such thoughts of death, decay, the aging in my own body and mind, my love for Bob and my pain at eventually leaving him—all inevitably *true*—(I can't dismiss them as fantasies). I can't live happily. Solomon says life isn't meant to be happy, but I'm thinking that I prefer the delusion if such feelings as I have are the alternative.

I'm sitting outside in the patio. The sun warm and a tiny bit burning on my back, the sky blue and clear, the air fresh and just tinged with the smell of perspiration that always accompanies sunbathing, the birds twittering music from somewhere, distant car horns. It's hard to concentrate on being anguished! So I'll stop and enjoy being, now.

Barring the accidents that we all are subject to, a woman my age would see herself comfortably in young adulthood, with a long future. Conversely someone with "6 months to live" would know that . . . but I am constantly aware—afraid that each day may bring the accident, or asphyxiation or choking, or pneumonia that could be quickly fatal. Will this reaction be uneventful, save for discomfort on my part due to my illness? Or will it end in disaster?

Too, I don't know whether I am a "normal" appearing person or not. I thought I was with perhaps a few unusual signs—short fingers, mouth open. Now I feel that (someone made some comment on this last night) I don't appear normal to others and a great ego defense is down. Am I sick? Am I well? What am I capable of doing? What *should* I do? What do others think I should do? When will I have to admit I can no longer make it to school for a few hours each day, three or so days a week? What can I do then? When will it happen? I (like probably everyone else with a problem) feel that it's especially cruel for me—to appear to be healthy and to be so weak as to not be able to walk a block or so without panting and stopping. Death is so close and yet, possibly so far away.

THE STUDENT AS SURVIVOR

As often as a college student is direct victim, another college student (lover or spouse) is the targeted survivor-victim of the death. Grief and mourning in one's teens and twenties for a contemporary is a heavy burden that comes out of season. To be a widow or widower in college is an especially cruel life blow. Melville's Redburn says: "Talk not of the bitterness of middle-age and after life: a boy can feel all that, and much more, when upon his young soul the mildew has fallen. . . . Cold, bitter, cold as December, and bleak as its blasts, seemed the world then to me; there is no misanthrope like a boy disappointed, and such was I, with the warm soul of me flogged out by adversity." These lines begin to approach what the death of a college spouse can do.

There are some especially good recent publications on bereavement, chief among them Parkes's *Bereavement* (1972) and Glick, Weiss, and Parkes's *The First Year of Bereavement* (1974). One of the main findings of these studies seems to be that widows and widowers of any age (twenty through eighty), compared with matched nonwidowed individuals of that same age, suffer a higher rate of morbidity (serious illnesses, hospitalizations, accidents, physical complaints, and psychological distress) and a higher rate of mortality. Bereavement is a serious state, amounting almost to a life-threatening illness. Being a survivor-victim is being a person at risk.

The following is part of a recorded interchange between me and the college student widower of the young woman whose words I have just quoted. The portions of verbatim text fill in the details and tell us many things about the burden and the course of grief in a college student survivor.

> ES: Now to start with, your relationship with Edith was unusual in that you knew she was ill from the beginning.
>
> R: That's correct, I first met her ten years ago, she was eighteen. I was talking with this friend saying I'd really like to meet a girl who was intelligent and particularly knew something about music, particularly Bach. And she said she knew a girl and gave me her name and phone number; so I called her up, it was a blind date and that was that. It was just after her illness had been diagnosed

and her parents, if I remember correctly, told me about it . . . when they saw that we were becoming serious, after we had been courting for some time. And I really didn't know exactly what the disease was, I mean as far as life span was concerned.

ES: Did they tell you the name of the disease?

R: Yes.

ES: Did you look it up?

R: No. As I think of it now, I wonder why I didn't try to find out more. Maybe I was afraid. I don't know. I knew her life would be shortened, but I don't think I really allowed myself to think about it or to find out exactly what it was. It was terminal about eight years after. I have thought about it, because it seems to me strange of my not pursuing it. She was the first girl I guess I really had a good meaningful relationship with, and I think I might have been very frightened to find out the truth. But I didn't want to know. . . . We went to Europe in the summer two years before she died, and when she came back, she had some sort of bronchial thing that never cleared up. And when we saw that we realized it was kind of a significant thing. She would draw the same sort of conclusion and talk about it. The fact that she was not getting better, that the disease was progressing along its course. I'd see things and realize that it was true, but then I'd sort of block it out, trying to deal with the right now. . . . The more I think of it, the more I really realize I think I blocked a tremendous amount out.

ES: Her death was not totally unexpected to you. When she came into the hospital, she was struggling and failing. You knew she was in serious physical trouble. This is a delicate question. Please tell me how you were told that she had died, and then what happened?

R: The doctor that had been attending her told me when I came in that morning to see her, and he brought me aside. He took me somewhere. I think he gave me a tranquilizer. He was a resident. I was extremely impressed with him. I was probably in shock, but I remember the clear thing I did feel was some sense of relief that I don't have to wait any longer. That incredible waiting that I realized I had been going through was suddenly over. But then there was this, I don't know. . . . I went home alone from the hospital, alone, really alone. I really don't recall what happened the rest of the day. I think that a good friend of ours stayed with me that night. I was feeling very freaked out. I must have gone around for maybe a week or so before I really began to feel the loneliness and her loss. I finally stopped running around taking care of everybody, and really felt the mourning, really felt her loss.

ES: What did that mourning feel like?

R: I wouldn't know how to describe it. It's a feeling inside of having an incredible emptiness. I felt sort of at a loss, kind of wondering how my life was going to continue. How it possibly could go on. Everything sort of like disintegrated. Sort of like a piece of me just was kind of lost.

ES: Did you have certain patterns or habits of expectations, of wanting to talk to her or expecting to see her?

R: Yes, that happened a few times. I'd look at a doorway, maybe to the bedroom from the living room, and expect her to come walking through.

ES: What helped the most?

R: I don't know that there's any one thing that helped me the most. Perhaps Susan, probably has helped a lot. Even though it was after a year, she forced me to the issue of dealing with Edith, really moving her out of the apartment, and started showing me things. About six months after Edith died, I went around and grabbed everything that had anything to do with her and put them in boxes and shoved them in the closets; but still Edith was in the closet. She was still there. We moved things round the apartment to make it different. I started doing some of those things, but she just kept saying that she really felt it wasn't her place, that it was still Edith's. She wanted it to be hers. So she did force me a great deal.

ES: Did you get rid of all her things?

R: Oh no. As a matter of fact we have some pottery that Edith had made that we use, that I had never thought of using before.

ES: Do you sleep in the same bed that you had before?

R: Yes, but I've moved the bed in the room and I sleep on the other side of the bed.

ES: Advertently?

R: Yes. I did that purposely.

ES: Does Susan know that you made these changes?

R: I've told Susan that the bed used to be in a different location, and I never made anything of it. I did this about six months after Edith died, before I met Susan. I did a few things, painted one of the walls, and a few things like this, rearranged the furniture. But there was still the other thing. It was very hard for me to commit myself to Susan. This was a big problem. This is over two years now. We've been married for several months and had been going together for two years. I took all that time to make a commitment.

ES: Why was that?

R: I don't know. I searched in myself a lot for what it was. And I wasn't really able to grab it. I'm sure that part was really there. A part of it was the holding on. I'm sure that was also a large part of it. I don't think it was until Susan and I were married that we went through all the boxes in the closets, took all the stuff, and decided either to throw it away or use it, to get it out of the closet, literally and figuratively.

ES: Did you make any inquiries as to Susan's state of health? Did you ask her, for example?

R: Susan is very healthy. I don't recall. I might have asked her, but I'm conscious of the fact that I certainly noticed her health. She's also younger than I am by a few years, and I thought of that. You know what that means. I think part of that means that I don't want to live longer. I don't. I don't want her to die before I do. I'm sure that's there. I'd be surprised if it weren't. . . .

ES: I knew Edith and then I knew you. How did that work out?

R: Well, I think I came to you. I'm not sure if it was because you knew her. I think that was part of it, because you did know her and you knew me through her. But I think it was because of you yourself. I felt you were the type of person who could help me.

ES: In what way?

R: I can't recall, whatever, but I think that some of the things that you said at the time helped me, helped to alleviate my desperation that I felt. A few times I did come in I was feeling pretty desperate. Completely kind of lost and floundering. But that worked out.

THE STUDENT AS THANATOLOGIST

Admittedly, a college course on death is still a somewhat unusual curriculum offering. Yet in the last few years there has been a pleasant proliferation of courses on this topic at universities throughout the country. These courses are typically well subscribed and typically described by the students as an exceptionally rich college course experience (Shneidman 1972, 1976).

What is most rewarding in teaching undergraduate courses on death is the growth that one sees in students in the brief interval of a semester. One hears often from them that the course—the reading, the video and audio tapes of dying persons, the plays (i.e., *Quiet Cries*), the guest speakers, the lectures, the afterlecture rap periods—has helped them personally in their wrestlings with the notion of death (and in other aspects of their lives also), and more than occasionally one hears that the course has pointed them toward a decision to enter the helping professions, specifically, to work with dying persons.

In relation to death, the college student can also be a helper, giving succor to dying persons and to their loved ones. Rather than attempting to describe a college student in this role, I asked a young man (who attends one of my training seminars on thanatology at the UCLA Neuropsychiatric Institute) to write of his own feelings and experiences related to thanatological work.[2] Here is his brief report:

I am a graduate student in Clinical Psychology, in my 20's, currently (1975) doing my internship year at the UCLA Neuro-Psychiatric Institute. A large portion of my program is taken up through my work on the Psycho-Somatic-Liaison Consultation Service where I am assigned to the Medical and Surgical/Oncology Service. I requested this particular service specifically because of special circumstances in my own life and because of a large and significant gap in my training as a clinical psychologist. These two factors above all others, I believe, have led me to seek out intensive training in the area of Clinical Thanatology, i.e., psychotherapeutic intervention into the lives of those with life-threatening illnesses.

The personal life stress event which started me on this unusual training path was the unexpected terminal cancer diagnosis of my mother. Ten years previous to my mother's illness my aunt (her sister) had died a physically and psychologically agonizing death from cancer with my entire extended family, including my mother, determined to keep the reality of her illness from her, and from themselves as much as possible. I was determined from the moment of learning my mother's diagnosis that she would die what I later was to hear labeled as "an appropriate death." At the time I had no label, no understanding of how to deal with it, but I vowed to myself that I would learn at the earliest opportunity.

It is now a year since my mother died and I am partially on the way to learning how to cope with death from a professional and even hopefully a personal standpoint. I have been involved in a training program heavily weighted toward intensive clinical involvement which has included intensive supervision as well as a didactic and case oriented seminar on psychotherapy with the dying.

My primary interests are in the areas of the functioning of social systems and especially in the dynamics of the family unit. These, I have found, fit well into my thanatological work. I am primarily concerned with the impact of a terminal illness on the nuclear and extended family system. I participate in family therapy on the unit and have started a multiple conjoint family therapy group where several family units meet together (without the ill members of their families) to cope with their problems collectively. All of this is not to minimize my concerns for the individual who is bedridden with a life-threatening illness, but to assure psychological support reaching the "survivor-victims" who are also caught up in the wake of the illness.

I work a large number of hours with the nursing and medical staffs. This is largely done in group contexts on a formal basis. I meet with each shift of nurses in a separate group, because each shift is a dynamically different interpersonal working system with its own strengths, deficits and problems. I also meet with the medical staff weekly in "psychosocial rounds." This is a time, on an overt level, when each patient's psychological and social realm is considered, but covertly, on a process level, it is a time when medical staff can ventilate feelings about their patients which depart from the usual medical protocol. The most meaningful interchanges for me with medical and nursing staff are the hallway conferences which are spontaneous in nature and are times when real feelings and creative thoughts are generated toward the "person" part of the patients and their families.

I never before have needed as extensive a personal support system for myself as I do now in relation to my work in thanatology. I rely heavily on my two hours per week of individual supervision as well as a group seminar which often becomes a supportive milieu. Lastly, I rely on the support of my wife who is a continual source of solace in this taxing work which I do sometimes bring home and carry with me more than occasionally.

What is of keen interest to me is how this "job description" is necessarily infused with personal feelings and personal reactions. We are given more than subtle clues to the "psychodynamics of occupational choice," and we see the importance—the vital necessity—of meaningful "support systems" for a person involved in the psychological abrasive reactions that thanatological work invariably engenders.

.   .   .   .

NOTES

1. No serious student of mass murder by the state in our time can afford to miss reading Gil Elliot's searing book *The Twentieth-Century Book of the Dead* (New York: Ballantine Books, 1972), a volume which lists the 110 million people killed by government action since 1900. Further, better to understand the *secularization* of death in this century, it is useful to compare current attitudes with the religious aura that surrounded death in another "death-laden" time, specifically during the great plagues of the mid-fourteenth century, as fascinatingly described in Philip Ziegler's *The Black Plague* (Middlesex, England: Penguin Books, 1969).

2. I wish to thank David Wellisch for writing this report at my request and for permitting me to use it in this chapter.

20

The Effects of Bereavement on Mortality: A Social Psychological Analysis

WOLFGANG STROEBE, MARGARET S. STROEBE, KENNETH J. GERGEN, and MARY GERGEN

All married persons face the possibility of their mate's death. For half the married population widowhood will become a reality. Bereavement in most cultures can be a period of intense grief, uncertainty, stress, doubt, and self-criticism. Within recent years investigators have also begun to ask whether bereavement may not have more severe effects. Specifically, can loss of a mate affect the longevity of the survivor? If so, what is the magnitude and generality of such a *"loss effect"*? Who is at greatest risk of mortality following the death of the spouse? What factors differentiate those for whom loss has a major impact from those who remain more resilient? From what physical causes are the bereaved most likely to die? What is the duration of the risk period following bereavement? Can we identify physiological and/or psychological mechanisms to account for these potentially fatal effects of partner loss? In the present essay, we shall first examine evidence relevant to various aspects of the loss effect, its magnitude, generality, and specific forms. We shall then discuss the cognitive and social psychological processes which are likely to contribute to the loss effect.

THE LOSS OF A SPOUSE AND MORTALITY

Cross-Sectional Studies

In everyday life, intimations of the higher risks of the widowed are pervasive. The "broken heart" notion is a recurrent theme and inexhaustible source

Parts of this essay are an extension of ideas formulated by the authors in a German publication (Stroebe et al. 1980).

of inspiration in literature and the arts. It would appear that there is very good empirical support for these popular beliefs. Analysis of national mortality statistics, giving death rates by marital status, reveals a consistent relationship between bereavement and death. A simple analysis of census information published by the Office of Population Censuses and Surveys for England and Wales (OPCS) for the year 1974 illustrates this relationship. Included in table 20.1 are the ratios of the death rates of the widowed to those of the married. These ratios indicate the magnitude of the excesses in widowed mortality over the married. The table shows that widowed mortality is excessive for every age-group, and for both sexes. The excesses for widowers compared with married men are consistently larger than the excesses for widows compared with married women. For example, widowed males in the 20–24 age category are 17 times more likely to die than their married counterparts, while widowed females in this same age category are 10 times more likely to die than married females. This high rate slowly declines until the later years when the ratio becomes less than 2 to 1.

However, it is also important to note that not only the widowed but also other single statuses—the never married and the divorced—have excessive rates compared with the married. The ratios also show similar patterns for these other unmarried statuses: more excessive rates are found for the younger, and for males, although these differences are generally not as marked as for the widowed. It seems, then, that the high risk of mortality is not unique to those who have lost their spouses to death. Other unmarried groups are similarly susceptible.

Table 20.1. Mortality in England and Wales, All Causes, 1974

Unmarried category (ratio)	Age-group											
	20–24	25–29	30–34	35–39	40–44	45–49	50–54	55–59	60–64	65–69	70–74	75+
Single												
Male	1.92	2.44	2.64	2.39	2.11	1.80	1.67	1.54	1.34	1.22	1.13	1.13
Female	1.63	2.74	2.78	2.13	1.92	1.29	1.44	1.32	1.27	1.15	1.12	1.46
Widowed												
Male	17.25	6.27	3.66	2.86	2.22	2.12	1.66	1.57	1.53	1.44	1.34	1.50
Female	10.01	4.25	4.20	1.24	1.94	1.47	1.44	1.30	1.29	1.19	1.18	1.59
Divorced												
Male	2.94	2.10	2.45	2.25	1.87	1.81	1.84	1.57	1.61	1.38	1.36	1.40
Female	3.59	1.60	1.67	1.77	1.61	1.43	1.43	1.30	1.28	1.15	1.06	1.53

Note: Population and mortality figures are taken from publications from the Office of Population Censuses and Surveys, DH1 No. 1, FM2 No. 2 (1977a,b).

Ratios are derived from the crude age- and sex-specific death rates (using total deaths registered in England and Wales, and total mid-year population estimates) for various marital status groups. These ratios are calculated by dividing the mortality rate of the unmarried status (for the specific age and sex group) by the comparable death rate for the married. Thus, a coefficient of 2.00 means that the mortality rate of the widowed is twice as high as that for the married.

Clearly, more extensive data are necessary to determine the existence of a loss effect.

What is the generality of these findings? Support for the basic pattern of excess mortality derives from a variety of sources. Over a century ago Farr (1859) noted the low mortality of the married compared to the widowed as evidenced in French national statistics. More recently, Kraus and Lilienfeld's (1959) epidemiological analysis of U.S. death rates for 1949–51 indicated a pronounced tendency for the widowed to die prematurely, as compared to the married. There are many other studies of a cross-sectional nature generally confirming the loss effect, and the subsidiary findings that, compared with married counterparts, widowers have relatively more excessive rates than widows, and that younger widowed have more excessive rates than do older (for a review, see Stroebe et al. 1981).

Although cross-sectional analyses are an asset because they give a general indication of the magnitude and range of potential loss effect, tracing of cause and effect sequences in such epidemiological or demographic surveys is not typically permissible. Further, if we do regard these cross-sectional results as indicative of a bereavement–mortality relationship, we are faced with a number of issues which are difficult to clarify. For instance, why should widowers be at higher risk than widows? One might easily generate the opposite hypothesis, that widows are faced with more overwhelming problems on the death of their husbands than vice-versa. And why should the young be more prone to a deleterious loss effect than the old? The old are more likely to be in poor health before bereavement than the young, so that this additional stressful event would be expected to have more extreme consequences. Let us then consider results from longitudinal research.

Longitudinal Investigations

One of the major advantages of longitudinal investigations is that, in contrast to cross-sectional studies, they provide information on the length of time that the widowed survive their spouses. If we postulate a loss effect, we would predict a *rise* in death rates in the period closely following the death of the spouse, when grief is most acute. In longitudinal studies one can compare the mortality experience of the recently bereaved with those of longer duration. Theoretically, there is also the possibility of more closely examining age and sex differences and causes of death in widowed mortality by relating these variables to duration of bereavement.

Unfortunately, longitudinal studies of the loss effect are rare, and those that exist are often marred by methodological problems. Such problems are due in large measure to the complexities of conducting such research. Sample size is, for example, a critical problem in tracing the loss effect on a longitudinal basis. To illustrate, the rate of mortality (per 100,000) for widowers age 70–74 shown in the 1974 census of England and Wales (OPCS 1977a,b) is 8180.73. That is, 8 of these widowers per 100 would be expected to die in any given year. Among comparable married men, the mortality rate is 6114.32. That is, 6 per 100 would be expected to die in a similar period. Additionally, while the mortality ratios of the recently widowed to married would be expected to show a greater difference, the differences in actual numbers per 100 cases would still be unlikely to be large enough to be statistically reliable in a small sample. It is evident from these figures that longitudinal studies would need large samples for any statistically reliable difference to be observed.

Several longitudinal studies that have tried to assess the effects of widowhood on death rates do prove useful. Taking data from death certificates, Young, Benjamin, and Wallis (1963) investigated the "duration effect," that is, the time lapse between the deaths of a couple, among 4,486 widowers whose wives had died in 1957. Unfortunately, widows could not be included in this study as death certificates of men do not identify their spouses in a way that enables them to be followed up, whereas widowers do feature on the death certificates of their wives. Mortality rates for the widowers for the first six months and for each year following bereavement for a period of five years were compared with those for married men. Young, Benjamin, and Wallis reported that the only ratios which were consistently greater than unity (i.e., demonstrated a loss effect) were for those dying within six months of becoming widowed. After this period the rates fell back rapidly to the level for married men. The increment in the first six months was approximately 40 percent (i.e., a widowed to married ratio of 1.4).

A follow-up of this investigation was conducted by Parkes, Benjamin, and Fitzgerald (1969), who examined mortality rates of this sample for four additional years. They found that from the fifth year onwards the mortality rates of the widowers were slightly below those for the married men. Thus, the increase in mortality risk among older widowers does appear to be confined to the first six months of bereavement.

Additional support for these findings comes from a Swedish study (Ekblom 1963) that included both widowers ($n = 351$) and widows ($n = 283$). All were aged 75 at the time of partner loss. Ekblom compared the frequency of mortality among this group with age- and sex-specific mortality rates for the married, as obtained from official Swedish statistics. In the first six months 26 of the widowed (14 males and 12 females) died, compared with an expected figure of 19 (a widowed to married ratio of 1.36). This increase thus supports the Young, Benjamin, and Wallis (1963) finding that the loss effect for widowers occurs in the six months immediately following the death of a spouse. As in the Young, Benjamin, and Wallis study, a decline in excess risk was noted during the following one and a half years (the expected number of deaths in fact exceeded the actual for this period). However, in contrast to Young, Benjamin, and Wallis, Ekblom found that in the third year of bereavement there was again an excess for the widowed. It is interesting to note that this was due entirely to death of widows and not widowers. Unfortunately, as the Young, Benjamim, and Wallis study was confined to widowers, we cannot compare the Swedish and British studies for a sex difference in the duration of risk period. The basic patterns of results do seem very similar to the results of the British studies reported above, but it should be noted that the differences observed in the Swedish study were only tendencies, as Ekblom could not obtain large enough samples to furnish statistically significant results.

A further British study by Cox and Ford (1964) fulfills the requirement regarding sample size. The mortality among 60,000 widows under 70 years of age was examined for a period of five years following the deaths of their husbands. These investigators reported a rise in mortality over expected rates (derived by calculating the mortality rates for the entire period) in the second but not the first year of bereavement. After this peak in the second year the rates became comparable to the expected rates. As the study was based on widows who had applied for widows' pensions, it could have excluded those from the sample who died in the first year and thus had no time to apply for a pension. This might account for the similarity between observed and expected rates for the first year. It is also difficult to compare the Cox and Ford (1964) results with other studies, due to procedural differences and the time period under investigation (i.e., 1927).

However, McNeill (1973) designed a longitudinal study that promised to provide much needed information on sex and age differences in the loss effect. The investigation was planned on a large scale and included mortality data on 9,247 widowed (6,310 widows and 2,937 widowers) in Connecticut. This widowed mortality rate was compared with expected rates. In this investigation the latter were not the married rates but those of the general population of the state. The cohort was followed for three and a half years, with the aim of determining for which of the sexes, at what age, and at what time interval after bereavement the risk of death was most excessive for the survivor.

The bereaved included in the study ranged in age from 20 to 74. Those over 44 were stratified into quinary age-groups; those under 45 were combined into one group so that it would be comparable in size to the older age categories. McNeill reported that the risk of death for the widowed compared with expected rates *declined* with age. Only under 60 years of age were observed deaths significantly excessive compared to expected rates. This decline is in line with the pattern found in cross-sectional surveys (cf. table 20.1), and also the longitudinal study by Young, Benjamin, and Wallis (1963), although these latter sources show *some* excess over expected rates even among the elderly. A sex difference in time-period of highest risk was also found by McNeill: for widowers under 60 years the peak in deaths was during the first six months, whereas for widows the greatest risk was during the second year of bereavement. As in other studies, observed rates after the first two years returned to a level that was generally comparable with expected rates.

In view of its scope (large sample, analyses by age, sex, and cause of death), the McNeill study promised more enlightenment on the bereavement–mortality relationship than any other longitudinal investigation. Interpretation of the above results is, however, severely hampered by the fact that the expected rates very often exceeded the observed (widowed) rates. In fact, taking the entire three-and-a-half-year period, the overall excess of the expected to the observed rates for widowers was significant at the 1 percent level. Thus, one can hardly interpret this study as generally supportive of the bereavement–mortality relationship.

In a longitudinal study by Rees and Lutkins (1967), a significant loss effect has been found in a comparatively small sample. This ingenious study, conducted in a small town in South Wales, differed in several respects from the other longitudinal studies. First, it was carried out prospectively, for a period of six years, from 1960 onwards. Furthermore, Rees and Lutkins isolated 370 cases in which a death had occurred and extended the investigation of the impact of bereavement on mortality to include its effect on parents, siblings, and children. The total number of relatives included in this survey group was 903. The control group ($n = 878$) was composed of the relatives of a further group of 371 local residents ('hypothetical death group'), the latter being matched for age, sex, and marital status with the deceased individuals. This study found highly significant differences in mortality between the relatives in the bereaved and the relatives in the control group. During the first year, 43 (4.76 percent) of the bereaved group and 6 (0.68 percent) of the control group died, a difference that was highly significant. During the second year the excess was no longer significant, and in subsequent years it declined further, to the level of the control group.

Rees and Lutkins analyzed the mortality for the various relatives separately. For the widowed (51 widowers, 105 widows) the mortality rate was higher in the first year: 12.2 percent died compared with 1.2 percent of the controls. The mortality rate for widowers was reported to be significantly higher than for widows. In the first year 19.6 percent of the widowers and 8.5 percent of the widows died; but as males have a higher mortality rate than females, the sex difference may be more clearly expressed in terms of excesses over controls. If we do this, we find that widows to female controls have a higher excess (no control females died in the first year of "bereavement") than widowers to male controls. This result is contrary to all our other findings. However, the Rees and Lutkins results confirmed the finding of Young, Benjamin, and Wallis (1963) that the highest risk period for widowers was the first six months after the spouse's death.

Among the other close relatives, the risk of mortality was excessive during the first year, and this reached significance when the other relatives were combined, and for the children and siblings. The loss effect seems not to be confined to marital partners, though detailed stratification of the relative susceptibility of other close relatives is difficult to make from this study, as the sample sizes are not large enough, and as information on age distribution of the relatives was not given. Nor do we have details of causes of death for either spouse. It would be useful to replicate and to extend this study, particularly in view of a criticism by Parkes, Benjamin, and Fitzgerald (1969) that the differences in mortality rates between widowed and controls may be due in part to the surprisingly low rate of mortality for the controls—the latter is much lower than the mean for married persons of the same age from national statistics.

A few studies have reported no increase in death risk for the recently bereaved; but on close examination none of these investigations convincingly discredits the loss effect. In some (e.g., Clayton 1974; Shepherd and Barraclough 1974) small sample sizes and other methodological shortcomings are probably responsible for the discrepancy. In others (e.g., Ward 1976) the loss effect may be reduced because bereavement followed an extended illness, and death of the spouse was expected. Such expected deaths typically lead to better bereavement outcomes than is the case for unexpected deaths (see, e.g., Parkes 1972).

Conclusions. Most longitudinal studies do seem to point to a period of heightened risk in the first six months of bereavement. This relationship seems to be more pronounced for the widowers than for widows. Some studies have concluded that widows are most susceptible after a longer time-lapse. However, this conclusion must await more detailed study. Further investigations are also needed to compare the mortality risk according to duration of bereavement in widowed of different ages.

CAUSES OF DEATH IN THE WIDOWED

Further support for the loss effect would be provided if the excess mortality rates of the widowed could be attributed to physical causes for which there is a strong psychological underpinning. Unfortunately, only limited information is available on the causes of death among the widows and widowers, and across age-groups. Governmental statisticians no longer list "Griefe" as a cause of death, as was done, for example, in the mortality tables of the City of London in 1657 (McNeill 1973). These deaths among the widowed were "characterized by rupture of auricles and ventricles," and were attributed to a "broken heart." Limitations in possible inferences from present-day diagnoses still persist, in part because people seemingly die from only one disease, namely, the one considered by the attendant physician to be the most important in bringing about the demise of the patient. That such diagnoses are problematic is indicated in studies comparing cause of death as given on death certificates with postmortem examination. Parkes, Benjamin, and Fitzgerald (1969) reported a lack of concurrence to the extent of 28 percent from a national survey. One must hope, then, that the inaccuracies are spread evenly across the marital status groups. One further limitation in available data is that causes of death in marital partners are rarely listed together; therefore it is difficult to assess the contribution to the mortality rates of a number of alternatives to the loss effect (which we discuss in the next section) such as mutual infection, joint accident, or shared unfavorable environments.

One of the most detailed accounts of causes of death across marital status groups was published by the National Center for Health Statistics (NCHS) in 1970. Data for the total United States population for the 1959/61 period were included in this analysis. The report gives information not only on the leading causes of death among the widowed, but also specifies those causes for which risk of death shows an increase in comparison with the still-married. The discussion here will be confined to the data for white citizens, as mortality patterns for black citizens are remarkably different, and consideration of them is beyond our scope.

Interestingly, calculations made from the data show that the three *leading* causes of death for all widowed (white citizens) are identical to those for all married: arteriosclerotic heart and coronary disease is the major killer, followed by strokes, and then cancer of the digestive organs and peritoneum. However, those causes of death that show *excesses* for the widowed with the corresponding married rates are of interest. Table 20.2, compiled from the NCHS (1970) publication, shows widowed to married mortality ratios for specific causes of death, ranked according to magnitude of excess for the widowed. One characteristic of these results is that the two leading causes of death (arteriosclerotic heart disease, including coronary heart disease, and vascular lesions of the central nervous system) do *not* have the largest excesses. In fact, for widows they rank third and fourth in excess over married women's rates, while for widowers, these rank only seventh and eighth in excess. However, the ratios do indicate that in equal-sized groups, for every two married people who die from heart attacks and strokes, three widowed people die. The most dramatic increases in risk come from suicide, accidents, liver cirrhosis, and tuberculosis. While the risk of dying of a "broken heart" is high among the widowed, the risk of an unsavory death rises even more.

Carter and Glick (1976) presented comparable information for 15–64-year-olds. Low excesses (compared to the married) were found for coronary and other myocardial disease, but also notably for many of the cancers. Excesses among widowers ranging from four to seven times as high as married men's were found for accidental fire and explosion, suicide, and tuberculosis. For widows the most extreme excesses were for motor vehicle accidents, homicide, and accidental fire and explosion. Overall, the widowed do seem to die from those causes in which

Table 20.2. Mortality Ratios of Widowed to Married. Standardized marital status–mortality ratios for white persons for selected causes of death, in order of relative excess ratios of widowed to married, U.S., 1959–1961.

Widowers		Widows	
1. Homicide	2.69	1. Accidents (other than motor vehicle)	1.84
2. Liver cirrhosis	2.42	2. Suicide	1.66
3. Suicide	2.39	3. Arteriosclerotic heart, including coronary, disease	1.48
4. Accidents (other than motor vehicle)	2.27	4. Lesions of CNS	1.47
5. Tuberculosis	2.17	5. Tuberculosis	1.43
6. Motor accidents	1.99	6. Liver cirrhosis	1.31
7. Vascular lesions of central nervous system (CNS)	1.50	7. Homicide	1.28
8. Arteriosclerotic heart, including coronary, disease	1.46	8. Cancer of digestive organs and peritoneum	1.23
9. Diabetes	1.41	9. Cancer of cervix	1.18
10. Cancer of digestive organs and peritoneum	1.26	10. Cancer of respiratory system	1.18
11. Cancer of respiratory system	1.26		

Source: NCHS, 1970 (Series 20, No. 8A, compiled from tables 2, 10, 37, and 47).

Note: The "selected causes" are composed, for the most part, of categories which contribute to the four leading causes of death (ICD Nos. 400–402, 410–443, 140–205, 330–334, E800–E962). Also included are liver cirrhosis, diabetes, suicide, homicide and tuberculosis. For further details see NCHS (1970), p. 2.

psychological factors can be presumed to play a crucial role. This argument has been elaborated by Gove. He concluded that the evidence on specific types of mortality suggests that the excesses among the unmarried:

can be largely attributed to characteristics associated with one's psychological state (1973:61).

More precisely, he argued that:

the variations in the mortality rates are particularly large where one's psychological state (1) appears to play a direct role in death, as with suicide, homicide, and accidents, (2) is directly related to acts such as alcoholism that frequently lead to death, and (3) would appear to affect one's willingness and ability to undergo the drawn-out and careful treatment required for diseases such as tuberculosis. In contrast, there is little difference between the marital status in the mortality rates for diseases such as leukemia and aleukemia, where one's psychological state has little or no effect on either the etiology of the disease or treatment (1973:61).

Gove's comments did not elaborate on the meaning of "psychological state," and even more critically, omitted any reference to, or analysis of, the major causes of death: heart disease and strokes. Yet arteriosclerotic heart disease and vascular lesions of the central nervous system together account for approximately 50 percent of the total deaths in each group (i.e., for all marital statuses, males and females, white citizens over fifteen years, 1959–61). The excess rate among the widowed (3 to 2) is sizable, and may reflect the added psychological stress of bereavement on the widowed. While not as dramatic in excess as the relatively rare instances of homicide and suicide, the excess rate is quite substantial, particularly if one takes into account the vast numbers of people affected by these ailments, and the statistical problem of showing great excesses for such overwhelming causes of death.

Just as longitudinal investigations supplement the cross-sectional with regard to the incidence and the prevalence of mortality among the bereaved, so are they also desirable for obtaining information on causes of death in the recently bereaved. Comprehensive as the above cross-sectional data on causes of death are, it is important to remember that the "widowed" in these statistics exclude all those who have remarried, and remarriage rates, particularly for males, are high. Carter and Glick provided some indication of the general magnitude of this "reselection factor": "Of the 15.3 million persons . . . whose first or last marriage had ended in widowhood, 11.7 million, or three-fourths, were still widowed at the time of the census" (1976:438). According to this information, then, we have to expect that a quarter of the widowed are no longer categorized in this marital status group, and that data concerning these individuals are not available for inclusion in the widowed sample.

Evidently, information is needed on causes of death in the recently bereaved (among whom remarriage is rare), but very little research is available that goes into sufficient detail for our purposes. Suicides and accidents appear to be very excessive among recently bereaved males (McNeill 1973; MacMahon and Pugh 1965). In contrast with the comparatively low *excesses* from diseases of the heart found in cross-sectional studies, death from these causes also accounts for a high proportion of the excess rates among recently bereaved widowers (McNeill 1973; Parkes, Benjamin, and Fitzgerald 1969). McNeill (1973) further reported that cancer accounted for a significant proportion of the excess mortality among widows in the second half-year of bereavement and that, similar to the cross-sectional data, there were significant excesses in death rates from liver cirrhosis and alcoholism for both males and females in the second and third years of bereavement.

Conclusions. Perhaps of particular significance is the finding that the widowed in general (that is, disregarding the duration of bereavement) have fairly low excess levels for deaths from heart diseases compared with the married, whereas among the recently bereaved, heart diseases feature not only as the main cause of death, but also as the disease which accounts for most of the excess in death rates. This seems highly consistent with research which has linked diseases of the heart with stress (e.g., Glass 1977), for loss of a partner places great stress on the remaining spouse, especially in the first few months (cf. Lynch 1977). Furthermore, in numerous studies of the recently widowed (e.g., Maddison and Viola 1968; Maddison and Walker 1967; Parkes and Brown 1972) signs of depression and general emotional disturbances (restlessness, sleeplessness, inability to make decisions, etc.) and increased presence of physical disability have been demonstrated. The widowed are also found to drink more alcohol, smoke more, and generally to neglect their health more than the non-bereaved. And as we have seen, the widowed (as far as the evidence goes) frequently die from causes that are related to these symptoms.

Despite the lack of reliable or detailed research on causes of death among the widowed, taken together the analyses reported above seem to point towards an interpretation of the bereavement–mortality relationship which emphasizes the role of psychological factors. The widowed in general, but particularly the recently widowed, appear to be vulnerable to those specific types of mortality which are affected by psychological variables. Support comes not only from the pattern of highly excessive death rates from heart diseases in the recently bereaved, but also from such diseases as liver cirrhosis, cancer, and from suicide, in which (either directly or indirectly) psychological factors can affect the etiology to a far greater extent than is possible, for example, in the case of leukemia and aleukemia (cf. Gove 1973). Precisely how psychological variables operate to affect the bereaved's life chances is our concern in the remainder of this chapter, after alternative explanations for the observed relationship between widowhood and mortality have been discussed.

.   .   .   .

THE CAUSES OF HOPELESSNESS: A SOCIAL PSYCHOLOGICAL APPROACH

A marital couple can be considered a small social group in which members, as in any social group, fulfill certain functions for each other and in which each has certain tasks to perform. The loss of a partner should lead to deficits in a number of areas which can broadly be characterized as *social validation, social support, task performance,* and *social protection.* The surviving partner should experience problems in socially validating a wide range of his or her judgments, he or she should suffer a marked deficit in social and emotional support and, furthermore, will have to take over those parts of the group task which had formerly been performed by the partner. Finally, he or she may find deprivation of the social protection of the marital group anxiety-arousing.

Loss of Social Validation of Personal Judgments

Effective behavior, and the accompanying feeling of having control over one's own outcomes, requires an assessment of reality that may take place under highly ambiguous circumstances. So, too, one's assessment of self-worth is not always an easy one to accomplish with confidence. Such decisions may thus be maximally dependent on social comparison processes (Festinger 1954). Loss of a partner, that is, of someone who fulfilled a central role in comparison processes, may lead to drastic instability of such judgments. In order to evaluate whether one has sufficient ability to solve a specific problem, one needs to have not only a realistic and stable assessment of one's own competence, but also an accurate judgment of the complexity of the task in question. According to Kelley (1967), consensus information (that is, information regarding others' reactions) is as important for the correct attribution of stable characteristics to the environment as it is for characteristics of the person himself. Due to the closeness of the relationship between marital partners, one's spouse is likely to be one of the main sources of consensus information. With the death of the partner, this important source of information is lost, and consequently, confident assessment of one's achievements and capabilities are far more difficult.

Social comparison processes may also play an important part in judging the appropriateness of one's own emotional responses (Schachter 1959). When a spouse is lost, one may face a myriad of questions about what one should be feeling emotionally, what plans are appropriate, how one is to live a life alone, what level of spending is appropriate for a person of single status, and so on. Not the least of such questions may concern one's own sanity. As Glick, Weiss, and Parkes (1974) have shown, almost 40 percent of those bereaved are fearful at one time or another that they may be "going crazy." Matters of sanity are typically very ambiguous, and without a close relation to assure one that his or her actions, emotions, or thoughts are "merely the result of temporary stress," as opposed, let us say, to "deep emotional trauma," the fear that one is a borderline psychotic may continue unabated. In sum, to the extent that the survivor is unable to locate sources enabling a successful definition of reality, the negative effects on health and death rate may be increased.

Loss of Social and Emotional Support

Broad agreement exists within the helping professions concerning the central, if not critical, role played by self-esteem in the emotional well-being of the individual. The neo-Freudian analysts furnished perhaps the initial insights into the significance of self-regarding attitudes in the life of the individual. Horney's method of treatment was chiefly centered around the problem of reducing the patient's feelings of "basic inferiority," which feelings were believed to be at the root of various neurotic patterns. Adler's concept of the "inferiority complex" and Erikson's (1963) elaboration of the crisis between competence versus inferiority, underscores many of the same concerns. More recently, Carl Rogers (1959, 1968) has constructed a theory of therapy and personal growth based on the assumption that the major problems motivating the individual to seek therapeutic consultation most frequently stem from depleted feelings of self-regard. Much of the data generated by Rogers and his colleagues lends support to this assumption. Additional support emerges from other realms of the socio-behavioral sciences where theorists consistently point to the fulfillment of esteem-needs necessary to optimal human functioning (cf. Adler 1930; Becker 1967; Horney 1950; Maslow 1962). In general, then, it would appear that people are frequently concerned with their worth or value, and that feelings of personal worth are furnished primarily through social sources. Expression of regard or love, indications of trust, communications of praise, and even the other's provision of material resources may all serve to bolster one's feelings of self-worth or esteem.

This line of argument enhances our understanding of the loss effect. With the death of a close relation one often loses a major source of personal esteem. With their love and unconditional positive regard, partners in a happy marriage can repair many of the damages that the other's self-esteem may have suffered in the course of a day. Thus, with the loss of his or her partner, the individual may face a significant lowering of self-regard. This decrement may be accompanied by a lowered motivation to engage in health-sustaining activities, and an increased reliance on drugs (including alcohol and tobacco) for reducing suffering and furnishing a transient sense of security. All such outcomes should lend themselves to a decline in health. In effect, to the extent that the loss of a close relation is accompanied by a decrease in expressions of positive regard for the survivor, the survivor may experience a loss of self-worth and a decrement in personal health and increased vulnerability to death.

Loss of Material and Task Supports

Although little discussed in the traditional literature on bereavement, there is good reason to believe that a surviving spouse frequently confronts a substantial loss of material and task supports. Primary among the former, of course, may be the loss of a reliable income. However, additional material losses may frequently include one's living quarters, health insurance, the caretaking of one's home, and the provision of meals. In the traditional family, where role differentiation occurs, a spouse also has a number of tasks to fulfill, such as bringing up children, preparing food, cleaning the house, clearing snow, etc. The higher the specialization of these roles in a marriage, the more drastic are the effects of loss of one of the partners. For example, if a husband has never been concerned with running the household, the death of his wife may present a number of difficult problems. If a wife has never carried out heavy manual labor or been responsible for financial accounting, she may also come under great strain. Although these difficulties may be minimized with the help of an extensive "social support network" (Kobrin and Hendershot 1977; Lopata 1973; Walker, MacBride, and Vachon 1977), such tasks may be highly stressful and thus lead to an increase in physical vulnerability.

Loss of Social Protection

In a scholarly analysis of functions of grief, Averill argued that "it is the biological function of grief to ensure group cohesiveness in species where a social form of existence is necessary for survival" (1968, 1979:347). This suggestion rests on the assumption that since such animals have a greater chance of survival in the group, where they are better protected against predators, there is evolutionary pressure to establish instinctual mechanisms which would make leaving the group painful for the individual animal. A similar suggestion has been made by Bowlby (1969) who postulated that children are born with an innate propensity to be near an attachment figure, a role usually taken over by their mothers. Separation anxiety, or—in the case of permanent loss—severe grief reactions, are thus assumed to have a biological function, ensuring cohesiveness, even if they lead to distress or physical detriment for the bereaved. This view, which is also shared by Parkes (1972), is in clear opposition to Freud's (1917) claim, that it is the function of grief to foster the detachment of the bereaved from the lost love object.

If it were the biological function of attachment to keep the individual protected against dangers, the question should be raised whether at a psychological level (a) there is an increase in need for affiliation in situations of threat, and (b) whether the presence of others actually reduces stress and anxiety.

With regard to the first point, research by Schachter (1959) clearly demonstrated that fear elicits affiliation. Subjects who expected to receive severe electric shocks showed a greater preference to wait with others than subjects who anticipated only mild shock treatment. While there is also evidence for the anxiety-reducing property of the presence of others in fear-arousing situations, the mechanisms which mediated fear-reduction have not yet been clearly identified (Cottrell and Epley 1977; Epley 1974). Nevertheless, the fact that the presence of a companion has been demonstrated to lessen the emotional reaction to fear-arousing situations suggests that the loss of a loved companion should make life more stressful for the surviving partner. Since, in this case, the noxious effects are not due to the loss experience itself, but to the absence of a partner, lack of socially mediated stress-reduction might be one of the factors contributing to the greater mortality of the never-married and divorced as compared with married persons.

A second process which may be important in this context is that of "diffusion of responsibility." Sharing decisions lessens the load of responsibility for the decision-makers. Although the evidence is less than clearcut (Lamm and Myers 1978), the fact that under certain conditions groups make more extreme decisions than individuals may be partly attributed to a diffusion of responsibility among group members. Applied to a marital couple, this would mean that decision-making is likely to be experienced as more stressful if one of the partners should suddenly be faced with the necessity of arriving at decisions (or facing responsibilities) without being able to consult the other. In this way, the loss of a partner would add considerable strain to the life of the other.

The implications of this research for differential prediction of the loss effect are somewhat complex. With regard to the anxiety-reducing property of the presence of others, predictions would depend on the precise mechanisms mediating this effect. If the *mere* presence of others lessens anxiety, then partner loss should always have a deleterious effect. If, on the other hand, the anxiety-reducing effect is achieved by the other person serving as a calm model, consequences of partner loss are difficult to predict. With regard to decision-making, predictions can be arrived at more easily. Loss of a partner should be the more stressful, the more the couple has been used to arriving at decisions only after joint deliberation.

Conclusions. According to the analysis presented above the consequences of losing a marital partner should be the more severe, the closer the relationship between the partners, the greater the role differentiation within the marital group, and the fewer alternative persons are available who could serve part of the functions formerly fulfilled by the partner. While the absence of strong positive affective bonds between the partners may imply that they will no longer serve each other as sources of social and emotional support, it should leave their willingness and ability to fulfill social-validational, task-related and social protection functions for each other unimpaired. Even if the marriage is no longer completely harmonious, the partners might still value the other's judgments and they will certainly still have to depend on each other for performing the tasks necessary to keep the family going.

Thus, it would follow from a social psychological model that the loss of a partner should lead to some of the same problems whether caused by death or divorce. This prediction is consistent with findings by Weiss (1976) that partners who had voluntarily separated reported frequent experiences of separation anxiety, uncertainty, disorientation and other reactions which are quite familiar from psychiatric studies of the widowed (Parkes 1972). It also is consistent with the higher mortality rates of the divorced compared with the married.

.   .   .   .   .

CONCLUSIONS

Interest in the psychology of death and bereavement has grown at a rapid rate over the past decade. Both the *Annual Review of Psychology* and the *Psychological Bulletin* published reviews in these domains in 1977 (Kastenbaum and Costa 1977; Rowland 1977). Two additional volumes (Kastenbaum and Aisenberg 1972; Schulz 1978) have summarized and integrated the psychological literature in the field, and an international journal for the study of "dying, death, bereavement, suicide, and other lethal behaviors," namely, *Omega—The Journal of Death and Dying,* has been established. Yet, to our knowledge, there has been no systematic psychological investigation of the factors underlying the apparent risk of death among the widowed. As we have seen, many investigations have attempted to document the loss effect, but the reasons for its existence remained obscure. Since Freud's pioneering work, psychological research has primarily concentrated on problems of adjustment to death by the terminally ill, and on general attitudes towards death. Psychological investigations on loss and grief following the death of a loved one (e.g., see Lindemann 1944; Schoenberg et al. 1975) have been chiefly concerned with the dynamics and sequential character of the grieving process. The most detailed description and theoretical analysis of responses to loss through death—that by Bowlby (see 1969, 1973, 1980)—has focused on children (particularly on their responses to the loss of a parent). Adult responses to loss of a spouse were discussed mainly for the purposes of comparison with childhood grief and mourning. It was our aim, therefore, at this juncture to raise the question more specifically as to the underlying mechanisms of the loss effect among spouses, for only following an analysis of these cognitive and social psychological factors can effective ameliorative programs be planned and implemented.

We have seen that the mortality rates of the widowed are excessive compared with married controls of comparable age and sex; but it is most important for the planning of intervention measures among the bereaved to remember that only a small proportion of the bereaved population actually suffers psychological and physical reactions which eventuate in early death. The majority of the widowed recover from the grief process and return to normal life. Thus, there are clearly individual differences in reactions to bereavement, and, in our opinion, psychological investigations of these differences are now necessary in order to identify this high-risk group. In addition to the identification of the risk group, prevention requires the opportunity to administer therapy. Such a therapy program must, however, be constructed on the basis of a theoretical and empirical account of the processes responsible for the potentially fatal effects of widowhood.

Each of the factors discussed above probably contributes a small part to the development of pathological reactions in bereavement. Although epidemiological studies provide a preliminary foundation for development and examination of the effects of bereavement, such a theory will ultimately have to be buttressed by more thorough psychological investigation.

Part VI

Stress Management

Psychologists, physicians, and others have offered scores of suggestions and techniques for managing stress more efficiently. While empirical validation of effectiveness is lacking in many instances, the popularity of stress management strategies continues to soar. Selections in Part VI are offered as some examples of currently popular stress management guidelines, as well as of contemporary criticism and controversy in this area. (A more complete accounting of stress management procedures may be found in Davis, Eshelman, and McKay 1982; Girdano and Everly 1979; and Greenberg 1983.)

Benson's best-selling book, *The Relaxation Response* (1975), brought to national attention a relatively simple meditative procedure that was heralded as being not only easy to use but also potentially effective as an adjunct in the treatment of stress-related diseases such as hypertension. Benson argues that eliciting the Relaxation Response (e.g., lowered heart rate, decreased oxygen consumption and rate of metabolism, increased skin resistance, alpha brain-wave emissions, etc.) on a regular basis will greatly help one in coping with the stresses of everyday life. Benson's technique is a meditative one and shares many characteristics in common with the more popular forms of meditation such as Transcendental Meditation, Zen Buddhism, and Yoga. The four basic components for eliciting the Relaxation Response are: a quiet environment, a mental device (known as a "mantra" in most forms of meditation), a passive attitude, and a comfortable position.

Benson addresses several important issues in his selection. First, he clearly points out that individuals with medical problems should only practice his procedure under the strict supervision of a physician. Second, Benson notes that his technique is not the only way to elicit the Relaxation Response—prayer and traditional forms of meditation, for example, also bring about this state. And, third, the Relaxation Response is quite different from physiological reactions during sleep. For example, during meditation slow brain waves (alpha waves) increase in intensity and frequency—this does not typically occur during sleep. In other words, sleep is no substitute for meditation.

One of the more recent links between styles of living, coping, and somatic illness has been suggested by Friedman and Rosenman (1974), who argue that a primary cause of coronary heart disease is a distinctive pattern of behavior they call Type A. This behavior pattern involves constant pressured interactions with the environment and a compelling sense of time urgency, aggressiveness, competitiveness, and generalized hostility. In a sense, this pattern is the Type A's mode of coping with internalized societal values of achievement and the work ethic. A number of investigators (e.g., Rahe, Ward, and Hayes 1979; Roskies 1980; Roskies et al. 1978; Suinn 1979) have attempted to modify Type A behaviors with a variety of techniques. Our second selection in this section is by Chesney and Rosenman (1980). This paper clearly summarizes some of the issues and strategies relevant to Type A behavior and its modification.

Several points are worth mentioning about the Chesney and Rosenman article. First, *modification* of Type A behavior does *not* mean changing a Type A person into a Type B (a more relaxed, unhurried individual). The goal of modification is to *temper* or reduce excessive Type A behaviors in order to reduce the risk of coronary heart disease. Second, research on modifying Type A behavior is relatively new and sparse—long-term adverse effects (if any) of such alterations remain largely unknown at this time. But, at any rate, short-term benefits such as increased life satisfaction, often improved productivity, and gains in health represent significant and worthwhile outcomes. Third, though this article was written for professionals, it has no references. Note 1 contains an address to contact should you wish a list of references for the studies and strategies mentioned in the article.

In the next selection, Janis (1983) discusses "stress inoculation" from the standpoint of stress prevention and management, particularly in the context of health care. Janis has been a pioneer in the stress field, and the first part of his paper traces historically many of his important studies—ranging in emphasis from how people cope with the stresses of combat to those of surgery and post-decisional crises. One of the major conclusions drawn from his studies is that people can tolerate stress better when they are given realistic warnings and relevant reassurances in advance about what is to happen to them. This preparation, which Janis previously called "emotional inoculation," is believed by Janis to stimulate the "work of worrying"—a process of mentally rehearsing the impending danger and its possible costs and preparing for them. In later parts of his paper, Janis discusses some clinical applications derived in part from his theoretical and empirical work. Using the more contemporary term, "stress inoculation" (after Meichenbaum 1977), Janis reviews the procedures typically involved in stress inoculation and how they have been used to alleviate or cure stress-related emotional and physical disorders. The final part of Janis' paper is devoted to instances where preparatory information has proven ineffective or detrimental to individuals and, to discussions of possible crucial ingredients of successful stress inoculation (such as encouraging contingency plans and fostering a sense of self-confidence, hope, perceived control, and personal commitment). (For further information on stress inoculation, see Meichenbaum and Jaremko 1983.)

Our next selection, by Bramson, deals with an all-too-common problem, how to deal with difficult people. Coping effectively with difficult people means being able to take actions "to right the power balance, to minimize the impact of others' difficult behavior in the immediate situation in which you find yourself" (1981:5). There are many patterns of difficult behavior and in his book (*Coping With Difficult People*), Bramson identifies seven of the most disruptive or frustrating: hostile-aggressives, complainers, silent and unresponsives, super-agreeables, negativists, know-it-all experts, and indecisives. In Bramson's selection, he offers numerous suggestions for coping with any of the above-mentioned difficult behavior patterns.

While we find Bramson's work interesting and relevant to the lives of most people, we also find ourselves wondering about the validity of his classification scheme and suggestions. As stated in his book, Bramson has developed his views based on years of observation (watching and interviewing) hundreds of workers in numerous settings and organizations. But, the method of data collection is never made explicit; nor are we told of the empirical procedures used in deriving his seven categories of difficult behavior patterns. Regarding his suggestions for coping effectively with difficult patterns of behavior, Bramson notes that they have been "tried out and tested by many people" (1981:3). Overlooking the obvious vagueness of such a statement, one could ask whether Bramson's suggestions are appropriate for use by all people in all circumstances involving difficult people (of all types) or whether more specificity is in order. These, and other, points of concern need not detract from the potential usefulness of Bramson's work but, they do suggest some of its possible limitations.

Roskies' (1983) selection is actually a journal review of four stress management guides. It is written with great charm and humor, and makes some rather cogent points regarding the self-help literature. While it might be misleading to view the four books discussed by Roskies as representative of the entire stress management field, they nevertheless do represent fairly typical contemporary offerings for the general public. We include Roskies' review here not because of what it offers regarding the four specifically-mentioned books, but because of what it has to offer in the way of guidelines for evaluating self-help manuals in the stress and coping field.

Drug and alcohol abuse, smoking, compulsive overeating, and other habits are sometimes adopted as ways of coping with stress. Because such habits are often dangerous to health, illegal, and so on, people will at times decide to "kick the habit." When done with the help of professionals, the statistics regarding quitting are not particularly encouraging—leading some to conclude that addictions are almost impossible to overcome. In our next selection, Peele (1983) provides an optimistic picture of the effectiveness of *self-help* in many cases of addiction. He argues that reliance on professionals is detrimental to success because it fosters dependency on another (namely, on the therapist) and a sense of not being responsible for one's own behavior. Peele also takes issue with the usual explanation of addictions—that they are entirely biologically based. He believes addictions are caused partly at least by the individual's social situation, attitudes, and expectations. The stages of self-cure, according to Peele, include: accumulated unhappiness about the addiction, a moment of truth, changing patterns and identity, and dealing with relapses.

Peele's article was written for a popular magazine and thus while it makes reference to research studies, details are sketchy. Moreover, his views are certain to alienate those professionals who see addictions as "disease." As but one example of the controversy generated by Peele's position, consider the traditional warning given to recovered alcoholics by groups such as Alcoholics Anonymous. The warning is that a recovered alcoholic must never have another drink, lest he or she will once again become hooked by uncontrollable drinking. But, as Peele suggests, the addict who successfully modifies his or her life can control occasional lapses. Regarding the alcoholic in particular, preliminary studies do suggest that controlled drinking is a possibility—at least for some recovered alcoholics (e.g., Marlatt, Demming, and Reid 1973; Sobell and Sobell 1976). Though these and related studies are controversial (e.g., see Marlatt 1983), they nevertheless do highlight Peele's stance and provide some support for it. All in all, Peele's article raises some extremely important issues and concerns regarding the management of self-destructive coping behaviors.

Apropos of many of the points made by the selections included in this section is a story recounted by Selye regarding the two sons of an alcoholic—one also an alcoholic and the other, a teetotaler. When they were asked to explain their very different drinking behaviors, they both replied, "With a father like that, what do you expect?" Selye believed this anecdote illustrates an important lesson to be drawn from stress research:

that it is not what we face but how we face it that matters. Though internal and external factors influence or even determine some responses, we do have limited control over ourselves. It is the exercise of this control, or the lack of it, that can decide whether we are made or broken by the stress of life. (1980b:143)

21

The Relaxation Response

HERBERT BENSON

The case for the use of the Relaxation Response by healthy but harassed individuals is straightforward. It can act as a built-in method of counteracting the stresses of everyday living which bring forth the fight-or-flight response. We have also shown how the Relaxation Response may be used as a new approach to aid in the treatment and perhaps prevention of diseases such as hypertension. In this chapter, we will review the components necessary to evoke the Relaxation Response and present a specific technique that we have developed at Harvard's Thorndike Memorial Laboratory and Boston's Beth Israel Hospital. We again emphasize that, for those who may suffer from any disease state, the potential therapeutic use of the Relaxation Response should be practiced only under the care and supervision of a physician.

HOW TO BRING FORTH THE RELAXATION RESPONSE

[Earlier] we reviewed the Eastern and Western religious, cultic, and lay practices that led to the Relaxation Response. From those age-old techniques we have extracted four basic components necessary to bring forth that response:

(1) *A Quiet Environment*
Ideally, you should choose a quiet, calm environment with as few distractions as possible. A quiet room is suitable, as is a place of worship. The quiet environment contributes to the effectiveness of the repeated word or phrase by making it easier to eliminate distracting thoughts.

(2) *A Mental Device*
To shift the mind from logical, externally oriented thought, there should be a constant stimulus: a sound, word, or phrase repeated silently or aloud; or fixed

gazing at an object. Since one of the major difficulties in the elicitation of the Relaxation Response is "mind wandering," the repetition of the word or phrase is a way to help break the train of distracting thoughts. Your eyes are usually closed if you are using a repeated sound or word; of course, your eyes are open if you are gazing. Attention to the normal rhythm of breathing is also useful and enhances the repetition of the sound or the word.

(3) *A Passive Attitude*

When distracting thoughts occur, they are to be disregarded and attention redirected to the repetition or gazing; *you should not worry about how well you are performing the technique,* because this may well prevent the Relaxation Response from occurring. Adopt a "let it happen" attitude. *The passive attitude is perhaps the most important element in eliciting the Relaxation Response. Distracting thoughts will occur. Do not worry about them. When these thoughts do present themselves and you become aware of them, simply return to the repetition of the mental device. These other thoughts do not mean you are performing the technique incorrectly. They are to be expected.*

(4) *A Comfortable Position*

A comfortable posture is important so that there is no undue muscular tension. Some methods call for a sitting position. A few practitioners use the cross-legged "lotus" position of the Yogi. If you are lying down, there is a tendency to fall asleep. As we have noted previously, the various postures of kneeling, swaying, or sitting in a cross-legged position are believed to have evolved to prevent falling asleep. You should be comfortable and relaxed.

It is important to remember that there is not a single method that is unique in eliciting the Relaxation Response. For example, Transcendental Meditation is one of the many techniques that incorporate these components. However, we believe it is not necessary to use the specific method and specific *secret,* personal sound taught by Transcendental Meditation. *Tests at the Thorndike Memorial Laboratory of Harvard have shown that a similar technique used with any sound or phrase or prayer or mantra brings forth the same physiologic changes noted during Transcendental Meditation:* decreased oxygen consumption; decreased carbon-dioxide elimination; decreased rate of breathing. In other words using the basic necessary components, any one of the age-old or the newly derived techniques produces the same physiologic results regardless of the mental device used. The following set of instructions, used to elicit the Relaxation Response, was developed by our group at Harvard's Thorndike Memorial Laboratory and was found to produce the same physiologic changes we had observed during the practice of Transcendental Meditation. This technique is now being used to lower blood pressure in certain patients. A noncultic technique, it is drawn with little embellishment from the four basic components found in the myriad of historical methods. We claim no innovation but simply a scientific validation of age-old wisdom. The technique is our current method of eliciting the Relaxation Response in our continuing studies at the Beth Israel Hospital of Boston.

1. Sit quietly in a comfortable position.
2. Close your eyes.
3. Deeply relax all your muscles, beginning at your feet and progressing up to your face. Keep them relaxed.
4. Breathe through your nose. Become aware of your breathing. As you breathe out, say the word, "ONE," silently to yourself. For example, breathe IN . . . OUT, "ONE"; IN . . . OUT, "ONE"; etc. Breathe easily and naturally.
5. Continue for 10 to 20 minutes. You may open your eyes to check the time, but do not use an alarm. When you finish, sit quietly for several minutes, at first with your eyes closed and later with your eyes opened. Do not stand up for a few minutes.
6. Do not worry about whether you are successful in achieving a deep level of relaxation. Maintain a passive attitude and permit relaxation to occur at its own pace. When distracting thoughts occur, try to ignore them by not dwelling upon them and return to repeating "ONE." With practice, the response should come with little effort. Practice the technique once or twice daily, but not within two hours after any meal, since the digestive processes seem to interfere with the elicitation of the Relaxation Response.

The subjective feelings that accompany the elicitation of the Relaxation Response vary among individuals. The majority of people feel a sense of calm and feel very relaxed. A small percentage of people immediately experience ecstatic feelings. Other descriptions that have been related to us involve feelings of pleasure, refreshment, and well-being. Still others have noted relatively little change on a subjective level. Regardless of the subjective feelings described by our subjects, we have found that the physiologic changes such as decreased oxygen consumption are taking place.

There is no educational requirement or aptitude necessary to experience the Relaxation Response. Just as each of us experiences anger, contentment, and excitement, each has the capacity to experience the Relaxation Response. It is an innate response within us. Again, there are many ways in which people bring forth the Relaxation Response, and your own individual considerations may be applied to the four components involved. You may wish to use the technique we have presented but with a different mental device. You may use a syllable or phrase that may be easily repeated and sounds natural to you.

Another technique you may wish to use is a prayer from your religious tradition. Choose a prayer that incorporates the four elements necessary to bring forth the Relaxation Response. We believe every religion has such prayers. We would emphasize that we do not view religion in a mechanistic fashion simply because a religious prayer brings forth this desired physiologic response. Rather, we believe, as did William James, that these age-old prayers are one way to remedy an inner incompleteness and to reduce inner discord. Obviously, there are many other aspects to religious beliefs and practices which have little to do with the Relaxation Response. However, there is little reason not to make use of an appropriate prayer within the framework of your own beliefs if you are most comfortable with it.

Your individual considerations of a particular technique may place different emphasis upon the components necessary to elicit the Relaxation Response and also may incorporate various practices into the use of the technique. For example, for some a quiet environment with little distraction is crucial. However, others prefer to practice the Relaxation Response in subways or trains. Some people choose always to practice the Relaxation Response in the same place and at a regular time.

Since the daily use of the Relaxation Response necessitates a slight change in life-style, some find it difficult at first to keep track of the regularity with which they evoke the Response. In our investigations of the Relaxation Response, patients use the calendar reprinted for your convenience (see Benson 1975:180–81). Each time they practice the Relaxation Response, they make a check in the appropriate box.

It may be said, as an aside, that many people have told us that they use our technique for evoking the Relaxation Response while lying in bed to help them fall asleep. Some have even given up sleeping pills as a result. It should be noted, however, that when you fall asleep using the technique, you are not experiencing the Relaxation Response, you are asleep. As we have shown, the Relaxation Response is different from sleep.

PERSONAL EXPERIENCES
WITH THE RELAXATION RESPONSE

Several illustrations of how people include the practice of the Relaxation Response in their daily lives should answer the question that you may now be posing: "How do I find the time?" One businessman evokes the Relaxation Response late in the morning for ten or fifteen minutes in his office. He tells his secretary that he's "in conference" and not to let in any calls. Traveling quite a bit, he often uses the Relaxation Response while on the airplane. A housewife practices the Relaxation Response after her husband and children have left for the day. In the late afternoon, before her husband comes home, she again evokes the response, telling her children not to disturb her for twenty minutes. Another woman, a researcher, usually awakens ten or twenty minutes earlier in the morning in order to elicit the Relaxation Response before breakfast. If she wakes up too late, she tries to take a "relaxation break" rather than a coffee break at work. She finds a quiet spot and a comfortable chair while her co-workers are out getting coffee. On the subway, a factory worker practices the Relaxation Response while commuting to and from work. He claims he has not yet missed his stop. A student uses the Relaxation Response between classes. Arriving fifteen minutes early, he uses the empty classroom and says he is not bothered by other students entering the room. If the classroom is in use, he simply practices the response sitting in the corridor.

The regular use of the Relaxation Response has helped these people to be more effective in their day-to-day living. The businessman feels he is "clearing the cobwebs" that have accumulated during the morning. He also states he often gets new perspectives on perplexing business problems. The housewife, before regularly eliciting the Relaxation Response, found it very difficult to face the prospects of preparing dinner and getting the family organized for another day. She now feels more energetic and enjoys her family more. The researcher no longer requires two cups of coffee in the morning to get started at work, and the factory worker notes he "unwinds" going home. The student says he is more attentive and hardly ever falls asleep during lectures. He even attributes better grades to his regular elicitation of the Relaxation Response.

The examples of when people practice the Relaxation Response are numerous. You must consider not only what times are practical but also when you feel the use of the Relaxation Response is most effective. We believe the regular use of the Relaxation Response will help you better deal with the distressing aspects of modern life by lessening the effects of too much sympathetic nervous system activation. By this increased control of your bodily reactions, you should become more able to cope with your uncertainties and frustrations.

The following two descriptions of people who have regularly used the Relaxation Response for specific problems show how they feel the Relaxation Response has been of help to them. A young man, who suffered from severe anxiety attacks, reports that he often felt fearful, nervous and shaky, tense and worried. After practicing the Relaxation Response for two months, he rarely suffered from attacks of anxiety. He felt considerably more calm and relaxed. Usually, he practiced the technique regularly twice a day, but he would also practice it when he began to feel anxious. By applying the technique in such a manner he found he could alleviate these oncoming feelings. In short, he felt that the practice of Relaxation Response had significantly improved his life.

Our second illustration is from a woman with moderate hypertension. She has a strong family history of high blood pressure, and the regular practice of the Relaxation Response has lowered her blood pressure. She has been practicing the technique using the word "ONE" for over fourteen months. Her own words best convey what the response has meant for her.

"The Relaxation Response has contributed to many changes in my life. Not only has it made me more relaxed physically and mentally, but also it has contributed to changes in my personality and way of life. I seem to have become calmer, more open and receptive especially to ideas which either have been unknown to me or very different from my past way of life. I like the way

I am becoming; more patient, overcoming some fears especially around my physical health and stamina. I feel stronger physically and mentally. I take better care of myself. I am more committed to my daily exercise and see it as an integral part of my life. I really enjoy it, too! I drink less alcohol, take less medicine. The positive feedback which I experience as a result of the Relaxation Response and the lowered blood pressure readings make me feel I am attempting to transcend a family history replete with hypertensive heart disease.

"I feel happier, content, and generally well when I use the Relaxation Response. There is a noticeable difference in attitude and energy during those occasional days in which I have had to miss the Relaxation Response.

"Intellectually and spiritually, good things happen to me during the Relaxation Response. Sometimes I get insights into situations or problems which have been with me for a long time and about which I am not consciously thinking. Creative ideas come to me either during or as a direct result of the Relaxation Response. I look forward to the Relaxation Response twice and sometimes three times a day. I am hooked on it and love my addiction."

We should also comment about the side effects of the Relaxation Response. Any technique used to evoke the Relaxation Response trains you to let go of meaningful thoughts when they present themselves and to return to the repetition of the sound, the prayer, the word "ONE," or the mantra. Traditional psychoanalytic practice, on the other hand, trains you to hold on to free-association thoughts as working tools to open up your subconscious. Thus, there is a conflict between the methods of the Relaxation Response and those used in psychoanalysis. Persons undergoing psychoanalysis may have difficulty in disregarding distracting thoughts and assuming a passive attitude, and it may therefore be more difficult for them to elicit the Relaxation Response.

A basic teaching of many meditational organizations is that if a little meditation is good, a lot would be even better. This argument encourages followers to meditate for prolonged periods of time. From our personal observations, many people who meditate for several hours every day for weeks at a time tend to hallucinate. It is difficult, however, to draw a direct association between the Relaxation Response and this undesirable side effect because we do not know whether the people experiencing these side effects were predisposed to such problems to start with. For example, proponents of some meditative techniques evangelistically promise relief from all mental and physical suffering and tend to attract people who have emotional problems. There may be a preselection of people who come to learn these techniques because they already have emotional disturbances. Furthermore, the excessive daily elicitation of the Relaxation Response for many weeks may lead to hallucinations as a result of sensory deprivation. *We have not noted any of the above side effects in people who bring forth the Relaxation Response once or twice daily for ten to twenty minutes a day.*

One should not use the Relaxation Response in an effort to shield oneself or to withdraw from the pressures of the outside world which are necessary for everyday functioning. *The fight-or-flight response is often appropriate and should not be thought of as always harmful. It is a necessary part of our physiologic and psychological makeup, a useful reaction to many situations in our current world.* Modern society has forced us to evoke the fight-or-flight response repeatedly. We are not using it as we believe our ancestors used it. That is, we do not always run, nor do we fight when it is elicited. However, our body is being prepared for running or for fighting, and since this preparation is not always utilized, we believe anxieties, hypertension and its related diseases ensue. The Relaxation Response offers a natural balance to counteract the undesirable manifestations of the fight-or-flight response. We do not believe that you will become a passive and withdrawn person and less able to function and compete in our world because you regularly elicit the Relaxation Response. Rather, it has been our experience that people who regularly evoke the Relaxation Response claim they are more effective in dealing with situations that probably bring forth the fight-or-flight response. We believe you will be able to cope better with difficult situations by regularly allowing your body to achieve a more balanced state through the physiologic effects of the Relaxation Response. You can expect this balanced state to last as long as you regularly bring forth the response. Within several days after stopping its regular use, we believe, you will cease to benefit from its effects, *regardless* of the technique employed, be it prayer, Transcendental Meditation or the method proposed in this book.

22

Strategies for Modifying Type A Behavior

MARGARET A. CHESNEY and
RAY H. ROSENMAN

The marked increase in coronary heart disease (CHD) in most industrialized societies since World War I amounts to a twentieth-century epidemic that cannot be attributed simply to a larger population of older persons or to improved methods of diagnosis. There is now a large body of evidence pointing to multiple causes. Among these, blood pressure, serum cholesterol and certain lipoprotein levels, cigarette smoking, diet, and degree of physical activity are generally believed to be the most strongly associated with CHD risk. Still, these factors are unable to explain more than a fraction of the "epidemic," and they do not predict the occurrence of CHD in specific individuals.

The continuing search for additional causes has led to recognition of certain psychosocial factors that appear characteristic of the twentieth century. Several investigators have found such individual traits as hostility, competitiveness, ambitiousness, work orientation, and compulsive activity characteristic of some CHD patients. These personality traits apparently interact with the Western industrialized environment and result in a specific pattern of behavior, labeled Type A, that has been reported to be causally associated with the increased incidence of CHD in such societies.

The possibility of modifying Type A behavior to decrease CHD risk is now being studied. How this can be done and the results that might be achieved are discussed in this article.[1]

Behavior as a Risk Factor

Individuals classified as having the Type A behavior pattern are striving to achieve in a constant struggle against other persons, things, and time. In this struggle, the Type A person is alert, work-oriented, impatient, and chronically hurried. He or she shows enhanced aggressiveness, competitiveness, ambitiousness, and adrenergic arousal.

Persons without these characteristics are labeled Type B. They too may be concerned about their work, but they do not show the aggressiveness, competitiveness, hostility, or impatience that is characteristic of persons with Type A behavior.

After more than two decades of research, in 1978 the Type A Behavior Pattern (TABP) was recognized as a new CHD risk factor by a panel of experts convened by the National Heart, Lung and Blood Institute. This panel concluded that:

This increased risk is over and above that imposed by age, systolic blood pressure, serum cholesterol, and smoking, and appears to be of the same order of magnitude as the relative risk associated with any of these factors.

Recognition of Type A behavior as a CHD risk factor was based primarily on the Western Collaborative Group Study (WCGS), a longitudinal study of 3,524 men in the San Francisco Bay Area. The eight-and-a-half-year investigation found that men initially assessed as Type A had twice the rate of primary CHD and an even greater rate of recurring coronary events as the Type B subjects. These differential ratios prevailed after statistical adjustment for all other risk factors. The Framingham Study and others have now confirmed TABP as a major risk factor.

Is Changing Behavior Beneficial?

There is little incontrovertible evidence so far that programs to alter diet, physical activity, or serum cholesterol have reduced CHD risk significantly. It may be that improved results from such methods will require that they be started during childhood rather than in adults with already established disease. In Type A adults, improved results will probably also require modification of TABP, especially for secondary prevention.

Research is currently under way to evaluate methods for modifying TABP. For example, studies with CHD patients as well as with healthy subjects at Colorado State University and the University of Montreal have demonstrated significant reductions in serum cholesterol and blood pressure following TABP modification.

Another study evaluated a group modification program instituted as part of post-myocardial infarction rehabilitation at the U.S. Naval Hospital in San Diego. Participants in this behavioral intervention program showed significantly less coronary morbidity and mortality than post-MI patients who received only standard rehabilitation measures.

Although these promising studies dealt with small numbers of subjects and with inadequate measures for assessing effectiveness, they do indicate the possible benefits of Type A modification for preventing primary CHD and recurring morbidity.

What Measures Are Needed?

If Type A behavior is to be modified, at least one of its three interacting causal factors has to be addressed: (1) the demands of the environment; (2) the individual's interpretation of these demands as challenges; and (3) the individual's challenge-elicited responses. Detailed discussions of TABP modification can be found elsewhere. Here, we present only a brief overview of recommendations for dealing with each of these three factors.

Environmental demands. In the environment of Western industrialized societies, such Type A behaviors as winning and rising to the top quickly are viewed as signs of success and are rewarded. Additionally, today's urban environment places increasing demands on the individual, and too often the environment cannot be altered to reduce the stress it imposes.

As clinicians, you are not often given the opportunity to advise sweeping environmental changes. But you can recognize those environmental stressors over which patients have some control, and you can make recommendations to your patients. For example, patients may be in a position to change their work schedules and give themselves work places that cause less stress by reducing noise, clutter, and interruptions.

Perceptions and reactions to stress. It is more often possible to modify an individual's perception of environmental stressors, with resulting reduction in adrenergic arousal, than to effect environmental change. However, altering perceptions and interpretations of environmental stressors often requires the person to develop new philosophic guidelines.

These guidelines must temper the Type A person's beliefs that competitive drive, time urgency, speed, and hyperarousal have been primarily responsible for his major accomplishments and that reducing competitive drive and habitual acceleration of actions will lead to diminished power, prestige, and income. If these beliefs are not modified, Type A individuals cannot often be motivated to alter their behavior.

The clinician's job is to convince such individuals that severe TABP is not responsible for their major accomplishments, that their true goals are not reached any faster by speeding up daily activities, and that following up each achievement with yet another ill-defined goal often prevents them from experiencing the satisfactions they seek but rarely attain by chronically rushing through life.

Conversely, these persons have to be convinced that alternative behaviors are not a threat to their socioeconomic well-being or control of their environment. They need to be shown that pacing themselves and working at one task at a time can be more efficient, even more productive, and that this way of working does not have the physiologic risk of their Type A behavior pattern.

Effecting Behavior Change

To convince the Type A individual to embark on a modification program, the goal of intervention has to be made clear. TABP modifications do not attempt to change a Type A individual into a Type B. Instead, intervention aims to temper TABP so as to reduce the CHD risk it carries. Clinical evidence suggests that in attaining this goal individuals gain in efficiency and productivity. This outcome should be emphasized because it is particularly valued by Type A persons.

It is important also to point out the gains in health, life satisfactions, and the sense of well-being that can accompany behavior modification. That these gains can result from modifying TABP was shown in the previously mentioned Montreal study. Program participants continued to work the same number of hours and carry the same responsibility but reported enjoying life more.

As clinicians know too well, it is one thing to recommend to patients that they make life-style changes, another and more difficult job to get their adherence. The following are strategies you can use to help patients succeed in TABP modification. The short-term results have shown them effective for changing behavior, but there are not yet enough data to assess their long-term efficacy.

STRATEGIES

Self-Observation

Because Type A individuals are often unaware of their behavior, self-observation is a critical first step. It teaches the person to witness such daily experiences as the struggle in commuting to work, the schedule bulging with activities without adequate breaks, the battle with the clock, and the impatience and irritation with others that too often are manifested in facial tension and vocal outbursts.

For self-observation, a patient should be instructed to keep a log of incidents that arouse such Type A behaviors as anger, anxiety, frustration, or time-urgency. This record serves as an incentive to change, a source of target behaviors for modification, and a benchmark against which progress can be measured.

Self-Contracting

Awareness of problem behaviors is necessary but is often insufficient by itself to bring about change. For lifelong habits to be modified, specific behaviors in specific situations need to be isolated and changed. One particularly effective procedure for promoting this is self-contracting, in which a patient puts in writing—the contract—a commitment to change a certain adverse daily pattern of behavior. For example, patients may contract to:

> Avoid rushing by walking at a more relaxed pace at work
> Often eat lunch alone, without reading or working, and avoid the regular "business" meal
> Drive more slowly in the city and not exceed 55 mph on the highway
> Listen to relaxing music rather than dictate while driving or feel frustrated at other drivers
> Start work earlier or stay at work a little longer to avoid the habitual need to bring work home
> Spend 15 minutes once or twice a day practicing deep relaxation or take a brisk walk to replace a coffee break
> Exercise 30 minutes three times a week. (Programs of regular appropriate exercise reduce adrenergic arousal and may enhance an individual's ability to cope with day-to-day stressors.)

To be effective, such procedures must avoid certain pitfalls. For example, in self-contracting, the behaviors should be clearly defined rather than presented as an abstract concept. Thus, the person contracts to "avoid rushing by walking at a relaxed pace at work" rather than, vaguely, to "slow down at work."

In addition, it is important to propose only a few changes in each contract. If too many are simultaneously outlined, the probability increases of a patient's giving up. Instead, he or she should follow each successfully completed contract with a new one.

New habits can be established only if they are practiced. To be most effective, each contract should specify the number of times a day that the patient will perform drills of each new behavior. For example, patients might contract that between 10 and 11 A.M. each work day, they will focus on decelerating all speech and motor movements.

Modeling

The most effective way to learn a complicated new set of behaviors is to watch someone else, a successful "model," carry out the desired behavior.

In Type A modification efforts, you can serve as a model for patients by engaging in desirable behaviors: exhibiting humor rather than anger, having realistic and flexible schedules rather than overscheduling, and using decelerated rather than frenetic movements.

Research has shown that individuals who are still involved in the process of learning to alter their behavior patterns are more effective as models than individuals who are masters of the desired behaviors. Therefore, Type A clinicians who are coping with stressors and clearly attempting to modify their own TABP can be models as influential as Type Bs who do not experience stress—perhaps even more so.

You can also encourage patients to select as models other successful individuals with whom they are acquainted. It is not necessary for these lay-models to be aware of their role. Patients can simply study their models' reactions to daily stressors and their activities and imitate them. For example, one patient, explaining how he managed to respond calmly to an irate employee, stated: "I just told myself to handle this fellow like Dick would."

Muscular Relaxation

Lowering excessive adrenergic arousal is an important goal in TABP modification, and relaxation strategies can help. Training in progressive relaxation, both by itself and when facilitated by biofeedback, has been shown to have psychologic and physiologic benefits, including lowered adrenergic arousal.

The effectiveness of specific relaxation techniques for TABP has not been investigated, but relaxation procedures have been an integral part of TABP intervention programs to date. Once individuals are thoroughly trained to obtain deep muscle relaxation, they are able to relax in less than a minute. They can then be trained to recognize signs of tension or arousal and to use these early signs as cues for relaxation.[2]

Dealing with Hostility

A critical and particularly difficult problem you may have to deal with when trying to modify a Type A person's behavior is the hostility that often grows out of excessive impatience and competitiveness. In the course of development of TABP, hostile aggressiveness is fostered. Perhaps because Type A individuals place winning and achievement as the ultimate goals, they perceive most other individuals as competitors and threats. The Type A person's brand of hostility may be described as "free floating," reflecting its capacity to be touched off by even the slightest provocation.

There is no known strategy for changing hostility, as there is for reducing adrenergic arousal. However, as is the case with other facets of TABP,

Type A patients should be instructed to observe and monitor their frustration, anger, and hostility in the self-observation log. By doing so, certain situations will emerge that provoke these negative emotions. Then, similar to and in conjunction with the other target behaviors, the Type A person can contract to plan events that will encourage humor, affection, and friendship.

For example, the Type A person who becomes hostile while driving might use mass transit or join a carpool. Another individual who becomes hostile when waiting in lines might perform a drill of selecting the longest line and spending the time smiling at passers-by and chatting with others in line. Yet another individual who feels rushed and alone might contract to lose some acquaintances and plan more time for friends.

Group-Oriented Modification

Modifying hostility as well as other Type A behaviors may be more effective when it is done in a structured group therapy format. The group therapy approach has several advantages that are not found in one-to-one treatment.

First, the group provides an opportunity for working with others on a common problem. Thus the group addresses the Type A individual's characteristic preference for working alone. Second, other persons in a group serve as models for one another and can share problems and potential solutions. Third, the group allows subjects to role-play, drill, and practice their new behaviors in an environment that provides candid feedback while being supportive. Finally, the group is more economical for a therapist pressed for time.

Will It Work?

We do not yet know the long-term potential of Type A behavior modification for primary CHD prevention or even the shorter term potential for secondary prevention. However, the need for prevention of recurring coronary morbidity and sudden death is particularly great.

If modification of Type A behavior had negative side-effects, we would be unwise to advocate it, but no such effects have been observed to date. Tipping the balance in favor of appropriate modification is the evidence (admittedly small to date) of significant benefits—reduced CHD risk and increased life satisfactions. There is also the possibility that through attempts to modify Type A behavior, we will learn more about psychologic factors relating to CHD risk that we can apply with increasing benefit in the future.

NOTES

1. A list of references for the studies and strategies mentioned in this article may be obtained by writing to: CONSULTANT, Box A, 500 W. Putnam Ave., Greenwich, CT 06830.

2. For training in relaxation and stress management, patients can be referred to psychiatrists or licensed psychologists specializing in behavior modification approaches.

23

Stress Inoculation in Health Care: Theory and Research

IRVING L. JANIS

S tress inoculation involves giving people realistic warnings, recommendations, and reassurances to prepare them to cope with impending dangers or losses. At present, stress inoculation procedures range in intensiveness from a single ten-minute preparatory communication to an elaborate training program with graded exposure to danger stimuli accompanied by guided practice in coping skills, which might require fifteen hours or more of training. Any preparatory communication is said to function as stress inoculation if it enables a person to increase his or her tolerance for subsequent threatening events, as manifested by behavior that is relatively efficient and stable rather than disorganized by anxiety or inappropriate as a result of denial of real dangers. Preparatory communications and related training procedures can be administered before or shortly after a person makes a commitment to carry out a stressful decision, such as undergoing surgery or a painful series of medical treatments. When successful, the process is called stress inoculation because it may be analogous to what happens when people are inoculated to produce antibodies that will prevent a disease.

OBSERVATIONS DURING WORLD WAR II

The notion that people could be prepared for stress was very much in the air

Preparation of this chapter was supported in part by Grant No. 1R01 MH32995-01 from the National Institute of Mental Health. I wish to express my thanks to Marjorie Janis, Leah Lapidus, Donald Meichenbaum, and Dennis Turk for valuable criticisms and suggestions on revising earlier drafts.

during World War II. I was rather forcibly introduced to that notion shortly after I was drafted into the Army in the fall of 1943. Like millions of other American soldiers who received basic military training at that time, I was put through what was called a "battle inoculation" course. It included not only films, pamphlets, and illustrated lectures about the realities of combat dangers but also gradual exposure to actual battle stimuli under reasonably safe conditions. The most impressive feature of the battle inoculation course was that each of us had to crawl about eighty yards under live machine-gun fire in a simulated combat setting that was all too realistic.

Later on, as a member of an Army research team of social psychologists under the leadership of Samuel Stouffer and Carl Hovland, I had the opportunity to collect and analyze pertinent morale survey data and clinical observations bearing on stress tolerance. In a chapter on fear in combat in *The American Soldier: Combat and Its Aftermath* (1949), I discussed the battle inoculation course. Although its effectiveness had not been systematically investigated during the war, I noted that correlational data from morale surveys indirectly supported the conclusion that "having the experience of escaping from danger by taking successful protective action and having practice in discriminating among [battle] sound cues can be critical factors in the reduction of fears of enemy weapons in combat" (p. 241). In a more speculative vein, I also suggested other ways in which exposure to stress stimuli during basic military training might facilitate coping with the stresses of combat: Battle inoculation training could "increase motivation [of the soldier] to acquire combat skills" and to "develop some personal techniques for coping with his emotional reactions—such as focusing his attention upon the details of his own combat mission as a form of distraction, frequently asserting to himself that he can take it, or some other . . . verbalization which reduces anxiety" (p. 224).

Battle inoculation training was given only after trainees had received ample training opportunities to build up a repertoire of combat skills. I pointed out that this type of preparation for combat could help to reduce the disruptive effects of fear in two ways:

(1) the general level of anxiety in combat would tend to be reduced in so far as the men derived from their training a high degree of self-confidence about their ability to take care of themselves and to handle almost any contingency that might threaten them with sudden danger; and (2) the intensity of fear reactions in specific danger situations would tend to be reduced once the man began to carry out a plan of action in a skilled manner (1949:222–23)

In a critical review of the evidence bearing on fear in combat, Rachman concludes that, with minor exceptions, the available correlational data support these propositions, which are consistent with Bandura's (1977) recent emphasis on the positive behavioral changes resulting from an improved sense of self-efficacy:

In sum, troops who expressed a high degree of self-confidence before combat were more likely to perform with relatively little fear during battle; however, a minority who expressed little confidence in themselves also performed well . . . [and] another minority . . . expressed a high degree of self-confidence before combat, but experienced strong fear during it. (Rachman 1978:64)

To some extent, the minor deviant findings may be attributed to the imperfect reliability of the measures of self-confidence and of fear in combat. Further, as Rachman suggests, they may result from the relatively low correlations among subjective fear, physiological disturbances, and avoidance behavior that makes for inadequate performance. Rachman cites evidence that "the physiological aspects of fear are most susceptible to habituation training" and predicts, therefore, "that this component will decline as combat experience increases, provided the soldier succeeds in avoiding traumatic exposures" (1978:64–65). Although at the time we knew very little about how habituation or related stress inoculation processes work, the data from studies of combat soldiers during World War II clearly highlighted the value of preparatory training experiences for improving men's coping responses when they subsequently encounter danger.

A few years after the end of that war, when reviewing the studies bearing on fear reactions of civilians exposed to air war during World War II, I again encountered indications that realistic warnings and gradual exposure to stress stimuli might have positive effects as "psychological preparation for withstanding the emotional impact of increasingly severe air attacks" (Janis 1951:155). I was especially impressed by Matte's (1943) observations of Londoners standing for long periods of time silently and solemnly contemplating the bombing damage. These observations, together with his clinical interviews, led him to infer that the Londoners were "working-through" the current air-raid experience in a way that prepared them psychologically for subsequent ones. He surmised that their gradual realization of the possibility of being injured or killed minimized the potentially traumatic effects of a sudden confrontation with air-raid dangers and at the same time heightened their self-confidence about being able to "take it." Rachman's review of the evidence from wartime research emphasizes the unexpectedly high level of stress tolerance displayed by heavily bombed people in England, Germany, and Japan during World War II. He points out that "some of the strongest evidence pointing to the tendency of fears to habituate with repeated [nontraumatic] exposures to the fear-provoking situation, comes from these [World War II] observations of people exposed to air raids" (1978:39).

The value of psychological preparation was also implied by impressionistic observations of how people reacted to social stresses during World War II.

Romalis (1942), for example, reported clinical observations suggesting that the American women who became most upset when their husbands or sons were drafted into the Army tended to be those who had denied the threat of being separated. These women, according to Romalis, were psychologically unprepared because they had maintained overoptimistic beliefs that their husbands or sons would somehow be exempt from the draft. When the threat of being separated actually materialized, they reacted with much more surprise, resentment, and anxiety than those women who had developed realistic expectations.

RESEARCH ON SURGERY

While studying stress reactions in a series of case studies of surgical patients during the early 1950s, I observed numerous indications that preparatory information could affect stress tolerance. My first series of case studies on the surgical wards led me to surmise that the earlier observations on psychological preparation of people exposed to military combat and air-war disasters might have broad applicability to all sorts of personal disasters, including surgery and painful medical treatments. I was able to check on this idea by obtaining survey data from 77 men who had recently undergone major surgical operations (Janis 1958:352–94). The results indicated that those surgical patients who had received information beforehand about what to expect were less likely than those given little information to overreact to setbacks during the postoperative period. Although no dependable conclusions about the causal sequence could be drawn from these correlational results, they led to subsequent experiments on the effects of giving patients various kinds of preparatory information intended to increase their tolerance for the stresses of surgery.

      Supporting evidence for the effectiveness of anticipatory preparation for stress—information about what to expect combined with various coping suggestions—has come from a variety of controlled field experiments with adult surgical patients (e.g., DeLong 1971; Egbert et al. 1964; Johnson 1966; Johnson et al. 1977; Schmidt 1966; Schmitt and Wooldridge 1973; Vernon and Bigelow 1974). Similarly, positive results on the value of giving psychological preparation have also been reported in studies of childbirth (e.g., Breen 1975; Dick-Read 1959; Lemaze 1958; Levy and McGee 1975) and noxious medical procedures (e.g., Johnson and Leventhal 1974).

      The research with surgical patients indicates that preparatory information can inoculate people to withstand the disruptive emotional and physical impact of the severe stresses of surgery. Like people traumatized by an overwhelming wartime disaster, those who are not inoculated experience acute feelings of helplessness and react with symptoms of acute fright, aggrievement, rage, or depression. In this respect, the natural tendency of ill people to deny impending threats during the preoperative period is likely to be pathogenic.

A number of interrelated cognitive and motivational processes that may mediate the effects of stress inoculation are suggested by case studies of how hospitalized men and women react to severe setbacks after having decided to accept their physician's recommendation to have an operation (Janis 1958:352–94; 1971:95–102). Most of the case studies deal with surgical patients who for one reason or another were not psychologically prepared. These patients were so overwhelmed by the usual pains, discomforts, and deprivations of the postoperative convalescent period that they manifestly regretted their decision and on some occasions actually refused to permit the hospital staff to administer routine postoperative treatments. Before the disturbing setbacks occurred, these patients typically received relatively little preparatory information and retained an unrealistic conception of how nicely everything was going to work out, which functioned as a blanket immunity type of reassurance, enabling them for a time to set their worries aside. They sincerely believed that they would not have bad pains or undergo any other disagreeable experiences. But then, when they unexpectedly experienced incision pains and suffered from all sorts of other unpleasant deprivations that are characteristic of postoperative convalescence, their blanket immunity reassurance was undermined. They thought something had gone horribly wrong. They could neither reassure themselves nor accept truthful reassurance from physicians and nurses.

Taking account of the surgery findings and the earlier research from World War II, I suggested that it should be possible to prevent traumatic reactions and to help people cope more effectively with any type of anticipated stress by giving them beforehand some form of "emotional inoculation," as I then called it (Janis 1951:220–21; 1958:323). (Subsequently, Donald Meichenbaum [1977] called it "stress inoculation," which I now think is a better term.) For people who initially ignore or deny the danger, the inoculation procedure, as I have described it (Janis 1971:196–97), includes three counseling procedures: (1) giving "realistic information in a way that challenges the person's blanket immunity reassurances so as to make him aware of his vulnerability" and to motivate him "to plan preparatory actions for dealing with the subsequent crisis"; (2) counteracting "feelings of helplessness, hopelessness, and demoralization" by calling attention to reassuring facts about personal and social coping resources that enable the person "to feel reasonably confident about surviving and ultimately recovering from the impending ordeal"; and (3) encouraging "the person to work out his own ways of reassuring himself and his own plans for protecting himself." The third procedure is important because in a crisis many people become passive and overly dependent on family, friends, and authority figures, such as physicians; they need to build up cognitive defenses involving some degree of self-reliance instead of relying exclusively on others to protect them from suffering and loss. The first two counseling procedures require careful dosage of both distressing and calming information about what is likely to happen in order to strike "a balance between arousal of anticipatory fear or grief on the one hand and authoritative reassurance on the other" (Janis 1971: 196). For persons whose initial level of fear is high, however, only the second and third procedures would be used.

In my theoretical analysis of the psychological effects of preparatory information, I introduced the concept of "the work of worrying" to refer to the process of mentally rehearsing anticipated losses and developing reassuring cognitions that can at least partially alleviate fear or other intense emotions when a crisis is subsequently encountered (Janis 1958:374–78). The "work of worrying" is assumed to be stimulated by preparatory information concerning any impending threat to one's physical, material, social, or moral well-being. For example, it may play a crucial role among men and women exposed to the physical and social stresses of tornadoes, floods, and other natural disasters. Wolfenstein reports having the impression from her review of disaster studies that the people who seemed to cope best and to recover most quickly were those who received unambiguous warnings beforehand and who decided to take precautionary action on the assumption that they could be affected personally. She suggests that among people who deny that any protective measures are necessary up to the last moment, "the lack of emotional preparation, the sudden shattering of the fantasy of complete immunity, the sense of compunction for failing to respond to warnings contribute to the disruptive effect of an extreme event" (1957:29).

RESEARCH ON OTHER POSTDECISIONAL CRISES

Essentially the same adaptive cognitive and emotional changes that were discerned following stress inoculation in surgical patients have been noted in many case studies and in a few field experiments that focus on people who have encountered setbacks and losses when carrying out other decisions, including typical problems arising after choosing a career, taking legal action to obtain a divorce, and making policy decisions on behalf of an organization (Janis and Mann 1977). Stress inoculation is also pertinent to the problems of backsliding recidivism, which plagues those health-care practitioners who try to help their clients to improve their eating habits, stop smoking, cut down on alcohol consumption, or change their behavior in other ways that will promote physical or mental health (see Janis and Rodin 1979). Similarly, preparatory communications given prior to relocation of elderly patients to a new nursing home or to a hospital have been found to be effective in reducing protests and debilitation (Schulz and Hanusa 1978).

Recently stress inoculation has begun to be used in schools to prevent teenaged children from becoming cigarette smokers. A controlled field experiment with seventh graders showed that significantly fewer teenagers become smokers by the end of the school year if they were exposed to an experimental program of stress inoculation designed to counteract the overt and subtle social pressures, such as dares from friends, that frequently induce smoking (McAlister, Perry, and Maccoby 1979). The stress inoculation procedures, which were given after the students committed themselves to the decision to be nonsmokers, included role-playing skits to represent the various social inducements to smoke, specific suggestions about how to handle difficult situations when confronted with peer-group pressures, and rehearsals of appropriate cognitive responses of commitment to resist the pressures.

All of the various studies just cited on postdecisional crises support the same general conclusion that emerged from the earlier surgery studies, namely, that many people will display higher stress tolerance in response to losses and setbacks when they attempt to carry out a chosen course of action if they have been given realistic warnings in advance about what to expect, together with cogent reassurances that promote confidence about attaining a basically satisfactory outcome despite those losses and setbacks.

CLINICAL USES IN TREATING EMOTIONAL AND PHYSICAL DISORDERS

During the past decade, stress inoculation has been extensively used by clinical practitioners who have developed what they call a "cognitive-behavioral modification" form of therapy (see Goldfried, Decenteco, and Weinberg 1974; Meichenbaum 1977; Meichenbaum and Turk 1976, 1982b). In the earlier work I have just reviewed, stress inoculation was introduced to *prevent* the damaging psychological consequences of subsequent exposures to stress, such as demoralization, phobias, and psychosomatic disorders. In contrast, this new trend in clinical psychology uses stress inoculation to *alleviate* or *cure* the stress-related disorders from which patients are already suffering.

The procedures described by Donald Meichenbaum and his associates for clients suffering from phobic anxiety, such as excessive fear of needles used in injections and blood tests, include three main steps. The first step is to give preparatory information about the stressful situations that evoke the anxiety symptoms. Just as in the surgery cases, the client is told about (a) the negative features of the situations that arouse anxiety, including the possibility of high physiological arousal and feelings of being emotionally overwhelmed, and (b) the positive features that are reassuring and that can lead to the development of more effective ways of managing the situation. A major goal of this initial educational phase, which is usually conducted by means of questions in a type of Socratic dialogue, is to help the clients reconceptualize their anxiety symptoms so that what they say to themselves when confronted with the phobic situation will no longer be self-defeating but will be conducive to effective action. Another somewhat related goal is to enable the client to grasp a more differentiated view of anxiety as comprising both cognitive appraisals of threat and physiological arousal. This differentiation sets the stage for the next phase.

The second phase is intended to help the client develop a new set of coping techniques that modify distressing cognitions and physiological arousal. The client is not only encouraged to make use of coping skills already in his or her repertoire but is also given training in new "direct-action" skills, such as relaxation exercises that can be used to reduce emotional arousal in anxiety-provoking situations. A major goal of this phase is to prepare the client to react in a constructive way to early warning signs, before the full onset of the anxiety symptoms. In addition to direct-action skills, cognitive coping skills are also discussed in collaborative interchanges designed to help the client work out his or her own coping strategies. The counselor gives suggestive examples of positive self-talk that might promote effective coping, such as "I can handle this situation by taking one step at a time." Some of the recommended self-talk is also likely to enhance the client's sense of self-efficacy after each successful trial—for example, "I can do it, it really worked; I can control my fear by controlling my ideas."

The third phase involves applying the new coping skills to a graded series of imaginary and real stress situations. The procedures used in this phase are based on the pioneering work of Seymour Epstein (1967), who emphasized the importance of "self-pacing" and exposure to small doses of threat in the acquisition of coping skills for mastery of stress among men engaging in such dangerous activities as parachuting and combat flying. In the graduated practice phase of stress inoculation, the patient is given role-playing exercises and also a series of homework assignments involving real-life exposures that become increasingly demanding.

Favorable results from using this type of stress inoculation have been reported in clinical studies of clients suffering from a variety of emotional symptoms, including persistent phobias (Meichenbaum 1977); test anxiety (Goldfried, Linehan, and Smith 1978; Meichenbaum 1972); social anxiety and shyness (Glass, Gottman, and Shmurack 1976; Zimbardo 1970); speech anxiety (Fremouw and Zitter 1978; Meichenbaum, Gilmore, and Fedoravicious 1971); depression (Taylor and Marshall 1977); and outbursts of anger (Novaco 1975). Essentially the same procedures have also been used successfully with patients suffering from certain kinds of physical ailments, most notably those involving sporadic or chronic pain (Turk 1977; Turk and Genest 1979). From the clinical research that has been done so far, it appears that a package treatment combining the various kinds of intervention that enter into this type of stress inoculation can sometimes be effective with some patients, but it is not yet known which interventions are essential and which are not (see Meichenbaum and Turk 1982a). Nor do we know very much at present about the conditions under which giving preparatory information or administering any of the other component interventions is likely to succeed or fail.

When Preparatory Information Fails

Here and there in the prior research on stress inoculation one can discern a few rudimentary indications of the conditions under which preparatory information is ineffective or even detrimental. From the very outset of my research on surgery it was apparent that, although preparatory information is advantageous for many patients, it definitely is not for some of them (Janis 1958:370–74). In numerous instances of failure, the main source of difficulty seems to be that the message is too meager to influence the patients. Very brief preparatory messages that take only a few minutes to convey information about impending threats are usually too weak to change a patient's expectations or to stimulate the development of effective self-assurances, and therefore have no effect at all. At the opposite extreme, some patients receive very strong preparatory communications from their physicians and friends, which unintentionally stimulate anxiety and feelings of helplessness that decrease rather than increase stress tolerance. Like an overdose of antigens, an overenthusiastic inoculation attempt can produce the very condition it is intended to prevent.

Other sources of detrimental effects have to do with the nature of the stress to which the person is subsequently exposed. For example, I have observed that at least a small minority of surgical patients have become extremely upset when told in advance that they are going to be given certain intrusive treatments such as enemas, catheterization, or injections (Janis 1958:387). These patients apparently imagine each of these routine treatments as being much worse than it really is. When the time comes to have it, they become so emotionally aroused that they are unresponsive to the physicians' or nurses' reassurances and resist to such an extent that the treatment is either botched or cannot be carried out at all. Some practitioners report that they obtain better cooperation if they give no preparatory information about a disturbing procedure of short duration, such as an enema, until they administer it, at which time they give the patient reassurances along with instructions about what to do (see Janis 1958:394).

In the instances I have just been discussing, the stress episode itself is relatively mild because the patients do not undergo acute pain or prolonged discomfort and an authority figure is present to reassure them that they are doing fine. Perhaps stress inoculation is most applicable for those episodes of stress that are painful or of long duration and that are likely to occur at times when no one will be around to give reassurances.

More recent research with surgical patients has shown that, as expected, preparatory information is not uniformly effective. (For a review of inconsistent effects of preparatory information given to surgical patients, see Cohen and Lazarus 1979). In a number of studies that found no significant effects on psychological or physical recovery, only brief messages were given to the patients, describing what the stressful experiences would be like in the operating room and during convalescence. For example, a field experiment by Langer, Janis, and Wolfer (1975) found that a brief message containing standard preparatory information was ineffective, whereas a special form of psychological preparation that presented detailed instructions about a cognitive coping device (which I shall describe later) proved to be highly effective in helping patients to tolerate postoperative stress.

Johnson et al. (1977) found that preparatory information about what to expect was ineffective for patients having one type of operation (herniorrhaphy) but was highly effective for those having another type (cholecystectomy). These findings may be in line with the earlier observations suggesting that the success of inoculation attempts will vary depending upon the nature of the stress.

Psychological preparation for childbirth, which for several decades has been extensively applied to hundreds of thousands of women, has often been investigated (e.g., Chertok 1959; Doering and Entwhistle 1975; Huttel et al. 1972; Tanzer 1968). In general, most of the studies of pregnant women, like those of surgical patients, document the value of giving preparatory information and coping suggestions. But occasional failures have also been reported (e.g., Davenport-Slack and Boylan 1974; Javert and Hardy 1951). Some women experience severe pains during childbirth despite being given one or another form of psychological preparation. Essentially the same can be said about psychological preparation for other types of pain. Turk and Genest (1979) have reviewed over two dozen systematic evaluation studies of psychological treatments designed to help people suffering from persistent backaches, recurrent headaches, or other chronic pains. Most of the treatments include giving preparatory information about recurrent distressing events that might precipitate or exacerbate the patient's pains, together with suggestions about how to cope more effectively with the stresses. A major conclusion that emerges from all these studies, according to Turk and Genest, is that when the psychological treatments include preparatory information about expected stresses and suggestions about how to cope with the stresses, they are generally effective in helping to alleviate chronic pains, but not with all patients in all situations.

Turk and Genest suggest a number of important factors that may influence the outcome of stress inoculation for patients suffering from chronic pain—the degree of threat perceived by the patient, the perceived effectiveness of the information, the mode or channel used to present the preparatory message, and individual differences in coping style and self-confidence. They point out, however, that these factors await systematic investigation, as do the various ingredients of the treatments that have been found to be effective.

In summary, many findings, both old and new, from studies of psychological preparation for surgery, childbirth, and the stresses associated with chronic pain show that stress inoculation often works but sometimes does not. Obviously, the time has come to move on to a more sophisticated phase of research, to investigate systematically the conditions under which stress inoculation is effective. In this new phase of research, which has just recently begun, the investigators' primary purpose is no longer merely to evaluate the overall effectiveness of stress inoculation procedures, to find out if one or another compound treatment program is successful in building up tolerance for one or another type of stress. Rather, the purpose is to find out which are the *effective components* of the stress inoculation treatments that have already been found to be at least partially successful in past research and to determine the conditions under which each component has a positive effect on stress tolerance. This new phase of analytic research on components includes investigating several factors simultaneously in an analysis of variance design so that interaction effects can be determined, which help to specify in what circumstances and for which types of persons certain of the components of stress inoculation are effective. In my opinion, this is where stress inoculation research should have started to go a long time ago; fortunately, this is the direction it is now actually taking.

From prior studies, we have already obtained important clues about what could prove to be the crucial components. The variables that appear to be leading candidates are discussed in the sections that follow.

PREDICTABILITY

According to a number of laboratory investigations, a person's degree of behavioral control is increased by reducing uncertainty about the nature and timing of threatening events (Averill 1973; Ball and Vogler 1971; Pervin 1963; Seligman 1975; Weiss 1970). Several experiments indicate that people are less likely to display strong emotional reactions or extreme changes in attitude when confronted with an unpleasant event if they were previously exposed to a preparatory communication that accurately predicted the disagreeable experience (Epstein and Clark 1970; Janis, Lumsdaine, and Gladstone 1951; Lazarus and Alfert 1964; Staub and Kellett 1972). These experiments show that advance warnings and accurate predictions can have an emotional dampening effect on the impact of subsequent confrontations with the predicted adverse events. Predictability may therefore be a crucial component in increasing stress tolerance. This hypothesis implies that when a person is given realistic preparatory information about the unpleasant consequences of a decision, he or she will be more likely to adhere to the chosen course of action despite setbacks and losses.

Although the hypothesis has not been systematically investigated with relation to postdecisional behavior, it appears to be plausible in light of a field experiment by Johnson, Morrisey, and Leventhal (1973) on psychological preparation of patients who had agreed to undergo a distressful gastrointestinal endoscopic examination that requires swallowing a stomach tube. In this study one of the preparatory communications was devoted mainly to predicting the perceptual aspects of the unpleasant procedures—what the patient could expect to feel, see, hear, and taste. Photographs of the examining room and the apparatus were also presented. Effectiveness was assessed by measuring the amount of medication required to sedate the patients when the distressing endoscopic procedure was given, which is an indicator of stress tolerance. The preparatory communication that predicted the unpleasant perceptual experiences proved to be highly effective, significantly more so than a control communication that described the procedures without giving any perceptual information. The effectiveness of the preparatory communication with the perceptual information cannot, however, be ascribed unequivocally to the increased predictability of the unpleasant events, because here and there is also contained reassuring information about the skill of the health-care practitioners and various explanations, which may have involved another variable (discussed in the next section below).

If future research verifies the hypothesis that predictability is a variable crucial to increasing stress tolerance, a subsidiary variable to be considered will be the *vividness* of the perceptual information that is presented, which might make images of expected stressful events more *available,* in the sense that Tversky and Kahneman (1973, 1974) use that term. Psychodramatic role playing, films, and other vividness-enhancing techniques might increase the effectiveness of stress inoculation procedures by increasing the availability of realistic images of the predicted stressful events.

ENHANCING COPING SKILLS
BY ENCOURAGING CONTINGENCY PLANS

Another component of standard stress inoculation procedures consists of information about means for dealing with the anticipated stressful event, providing people with more adequate coping skills. If this component is essential, we would expect to find that people will show more adherence to an adaptive course of action, such as following well-established health rules, if they are given preparatory communications containing specific recommendations for coping with whatever adverse consequences of the decision are most likely to occur. In most of the examples of stress inoculation used in the prior research that has already been cited, two different types of coping recommendations are included. One type pertains to *plans for action* that will prevent or reduce objective damage that might ensue if the anticipated stressful events occur. The second type involves *cognitive coping devices,* including attention-diversion tactics, mentally relaxing imagery, and the replacement of self-defeating thoughts with reassuring and optimistic self-talk, all of which can prevent or reduce excessive anxiety reactions.

A good example of the first type is to be found in the highly successful stress inoculation procedure for surgical patients used by Egbert et al. (1964), which included giving instruction regarding physical relaxation, positions of the body, and deep-breathing exercises that can help to keep postoperative pains to a minimum. Such instruction can be conceptualized as providing a set of contingency plans for dealing with setbacks, suffering, and other sources of postdecisional regret for a course of action that entails short-term losses in order to obtain long-term gains. For example, surgical patients in the study by Egbert and his associates were encouraged to develop the following contingency plan: "If I start to feel severe incision pains, I will use the relaxation and breathing exercise to cut down on the amount of suffering."

Other investigators also report evidence of the effectiveness of stress inoculation procedures that include instruction about behavioral coping techniques for medical or surgical patients (Fuller, Endress, and Johnson 1977; Johnson 1977; Lindeman 1972; Lindeman and Van Aernam 1971; Schmitt and Wooldridge 1973; Wolfer and Visintainer 1975). In all of these studies, the recommendations about coping actions were presented in compound communications, accompanied by other types of information, such as predictions about what stressful events are likely to be experienced. There is no way of knowing, therefore, whether the coping action recommendations were wholly, partially, or not at all responsible for the successful outcome of the stress inoculation. One major study, however, has attempted to tease out the relative effectiveness of the coping recommendations. In their second study of patients who were about to undergo a distressing endoscopic examination, Johnson and Leventhal (1974) compared a preparatory communication about the discomforts and other sensations most likely to be experienced with one that gave specific behavioral coping instructions about how to use rapid breathing to reduce gagging during throat swabbing and what to do to avoid discomforts while the stomach tube was being inserted into the esophagus. These investigators found that each of these preparatory communications was more effective than a standard (control) communication limited to describing the endoscopic examination procedures (given to all subjects in the experiment), but the combined effect was significantly greater than either alone. Thus, the combination of predicting the adverse events that would be experienced with recommending coping actions proved to be the maximally effective form of stress inoculation. If this outcome is replicated in subsequent analytic research on the effectiveness of different components of stress inoculation, a major controversial issue might be settled. We should be able to find out whether information about coping strategies is essential and which combinations with other components are most effective for various types of individuals.

ENHANCING COGNITIVE COPING CAPABILITIES

We turn next to research on the second type of coping recommendations—those pertaining to positive self-talk and other cognitive changes that might increase stress tolerance without necessarily involving any overt coping actions. A few studies provide evidence that people can be helped by preparatory communications that induce them to reconceptualize in an optimistic way the stresses they will undergo. A coping device developed by Langer, Janis, and Wolfer (1975), which involves encouraging an optimistic reappraisal of anxiety-provoking events, was tested in a field experiment with surgical patients by inserting it in a brief preoperative interview conducted by a psychologist. Each patient was given several examples of the positive consequences of his or her decision to undergo surgery (for example, improvement in health, extra care and attention in the hospital, temporary vacation from outside pressure). Then the patient was invited to think up additional positive examples that pertained to his or her individual case. Finally the patient was given the recommendation to rehearse these compensatory favorable consequences whenever he or she started to feel upset about the unpleasant aspects of the surgical experience. Patients were urged to be as realistic as possible about the compensatory features, so as to emphasize that what was being recommended was not equivalent to trying to deceive oneself. The instructions were designed to promote warranted optimism and awareness of the anticipated gains that outweighed the losses to be expected from the chosen course of action. The findings from the controlled experiment conducted by Langer, Janis, and Wolfer (1975) supported the prediction that cognitive reappraisal would reduce stress both before and after an operation. Patients given the reappraisal intervention obtained lower scores on nurses' blind ratings of preoperative stress and on unobtrusive postoperative measures of the number of times pain-relieving drugs and sedatives were requested and administered.

Additional evidence of the value of encouraging cognitive coping strategies comes from a study by Kendall et al. (1977) on the effectiveness of stress inoculation for patients who had agreed to undergo cardiac catheterization.

This is a particularly stressful medical procedure that involves working a catheter up into the heart by inserting it into a vein in the groin. One group of patients was given stress inoculation that included discussion of the stresses to be expected together with suggestions for developing their own cognitive coping strategies, which were encouraged by suggesting various reassurances, modeling cognitive coping strategies, and reinforcing whatever personal cognitive coping responses the patient mentioned. Two other equivalent groups of patients were given different preparatory treatments—an educational communication about the catheterization procedure and an attention–placebo intervention. There was also a no-treatment control group. The patients given the stress inoculation procedure that encouraged them to develop their own cognitive coping strategies showed higher stress tolerance during the cardiac catheterization than those in the other three treatment groups, as assessed by self-ratings and by ratings made by observers (physicians and medical technicians).

One cannot expect, of course, that every attempt to encourage positive thinking among patients facing surgery or distressing treatments will succeed in helping their recovery during convalescence. One such attempt with surgical patients by Cohen (1975), using different intervention procedures from those in the preceding studies, failed to have any effect on indicators of psychological and physical recovery.

Although few studies have been done among patients who are not hospitalized, there is some evidence of favorable effects suggesting that encouraging positive self-talk and related cognitive coping strategies might prove to be successful in many different spheres of health care. In a controlled field experiment, a stress inoculation procedure designed to encourage positive self-talk was found to be effective in helping patients reduce the frequency, duration, and intensity of muscle-contraction headaches (Holroyd, Andrasik, and Westbrook 1977).

Cognitive coping procedures may also be effective for increasing adherence to such health-related decisions as dieting. That this is a likely prospect is suggested by the findings from a doctoral dissertation by Riskind (1982), which was carried out in the Weight-Reduction Clinic under my research program. In this field study, all the clients were given counseling and information about dieting but only one experimental group was given additional instructions to adopt a day-by-day coping perspective rather than a long-term perspective. Riskind found that the coping instructions resulted in a greater sense of personal control and more adherence to the diet (as measured by weight loss) over a period of two months among clients with a relatively high initial level of self-esteem. The results are similar to those reported by Bandura and Simon (1977) for obese patients being treated by behavior modification techniques. The patients who were instructed to adopt short-term subgoals on a *daily* basis ate less and lost more weight than the patients who were instructed to adopt a longer-term subgoal in terms of *weekly* accomplishments.

From the few systematic studies just reviewed, it seems reasonable to expect that recommendations about coping strategies may prove to be ingredients essential to successful stress inoculation. The evidence is particularly promising, as we have seen, with regard to increasing the stress tolerance of medical and surgical patients by encouraging them to replace self-defeating thoughts with positive coping cognitions. A similar conclusion is drawn by Girodo (1977) after reviewing the positive and negative outcomes of treating phobic patients with the type of stress inoculation procedures recommended by Meichenbaum (1977). Girodo goes so far as to say that the only successful ingredients of stress inoculation are those that induce the person to reconceptualize the threat in nonthreatening terms and that all other ingredients are of limited value, serving to divert attention only temporarily from threat cues. Any such generalization, however, gives undue weight to a limited set of findings and would be premature until we have well-replicated results from a variety of investigations that carefully test the effectiveness of each component of stress inoculation.

SELF-CONFIDENCE, HOPE, AND PERCEIVED CONTROL

Many innovative clinical psychologists who have developed stress inoculation procedures and use them in their practice or research emphasize that teaching patients new cognitive skills is a necessary but not sufficient condition for helping them to deal effectively with stressful situations. They say that the patients not only need to acquire adequate coping skills but also, in order to use them when needed, must feel some degree of self-confidence about being successful (see Cormier and Cormier 1979; Meichenbaum and Turk 1982b; Turk and Genest 1979). Inducing the patients to believe that a recommended course of action will lead to a desired outcome is only one step in the right direction; they must also be able to maintain a sense of personal efficacy with regard to being able to "take it" and to do whatever is expected of them (see Bandura 1977). Over and beyond the coping recommendations themselves, reassuring social support may be needed to build up the patients' self-confidence and hope about surviving intact despite whatever ordeals are awaiting them (Caplan and Killilea 1976).

For medical and surgical patients, the key messages include two types of statements along the lines that I have just suggested. One type asserts that the medical treatment or surgery they are about to receive will be successful, which makes them feel it is worthwhile to put up with whatever suffering, losses, and coping efforts may be required. The second type asserts that the patient will be able to tolerate the pain and other sources of stress. Among the "coping thoughts" recommended in the stress inoculation procedure used by Meichenbaum and Cameron (1973) for fear-arousing situations and by Turk (1977) for chronic pain are some that are specifically oriented toward building a sense of self-confidence and hope—for example, "You can meet this challenge," "You have lots of different strategies you can call upon," and "You can handle the situation." Even the standard recommendations concerning positive self-talk, such as "Don't worry, just think about what you can do about the pain," tend to create an attitude of self-confidence about dealing effectively with the stresses that are anticipated. Similarly, the positive effects of the cognitive coping techniques used with surgical patients by Langer, Janis, and Wolfer (1975) may be at least partly attributable to attitude changes in the direction of increased self-confidence. The patients are encouraged to feel confident about being able to deal effectively with whatever pains, discomforts, and setbacks are subsequently encountered, which may help them to avoid becoming discouraged and to maintain hope about surviving without sustaining unbearable losses.

The crucial role of statements about the efficacy of recommended means for averting or minimizing threats of bodily damage is repeatedly borne out by social psychological studies of the effects of public health messages that contain fear-arousing warnings (see Chu 1966; Janis 1971; Leventhal 1973; Leventhal, Singer, and Jones 1965; Rogers and Deckner 1975; Rogers and Thistlethwaite 1970). A study by Rogers and Mewborn (1976), for example, found that assertions about the efficacy of recommended protective actions had a significant effect on college students' intentions to adopt the practices recommended in three different public health communications dealing with well-known hazards—lung cancer, automobile accident injuries, and venereal disease. The findings from this study and from the other studies just cited are consistent with the hypothesis that when a stress inoculation procedure presents impressive information about the expected efficacy of a recommended protective action, it instills hope in the recipients about emerging without serious damage from the dangers they may encounter, which increase their willingness to adhere to the recommended action.

Obviously, it is difficult to test this hypothesis independently of the hypothesis that information inserted to increase coping skills is a potent ingredient of successful stress inoculation. Nevertheless, as I have already indicated, there are certain types of messages that can induce attitude changes in the direction of increased self-confidence and hope without necessarily changing coping skills, and these messages could be used in field experiments designed to determine whether the postulated attitude changes mediate successful stress inoculation. For example, a patient's self-confidence about surviving the ordeal of a painful medical treatment might be increased by a persuasive communication containing an impressive example of a similar patient who had a successful outcome, possibly counteracting a defeatist attitude and fostering an optimistic outlook without increasing coping skills.

There are theoretical grounds for assuming that communications fostering self-confidence and hope will prove to be effective components of stress inoculation, particularly for preventing backsliding among patients who decide to comply with a troublesome medical regimen. Janis and Mann (1977) describe several basic patterns of coping with realistic threats derived from an analysis of the research literature on how people react to emergency warnings and public health recommendations. They postulate that under conditions in which people are aware of serious risks for whatever alternative actions are open to them, there are three main coping patterns, each of which is assumed to be associated with a specific set of antecedent conditions and a characteristic level of stress:

1. *Defensive avoidance*: The decision-maker evades the conflict by procrastinating, shifting responsibility to someone else, or constructing wishful rationalizations that bolster the least objectionable alternative by minimizing the expected unfavorable consequences and remaining selectively inattentive to corrective information.
2. *Hypervigilance*: The decision-maker searches frantically for a way out of the dilemma and impulsively seizes on a hastily contrived solution that seems to promise immediate relief, overlooking the full range of consequences of his or her choice because of emotional excitement, repetitive thinking, and cognitive constriction (manifested by reduction in immediate memory span and by simplistic ideas). In its most extreme form, hypervigilance is referred to as "panic."
3. *Vigilance*: The decision-maker searches painstakingly for relevant information, assimilates it in an unbiased manner, and appraises alternatives carefully before making a choice.

Defensive avoidance and hypervigilance may occasionally be adaptive but they generally reduce one's chances of averting serious losses. Consequently, they are regarded as defective patterns of decision-making. The third pattern, vigilance, generally leads to careful search and appraisal, effective contingency planning, and the most adequate psychological preparation for coping with unfavorable consequences that might otherwise induce postdecisional regret and backsliding.

According to Janis and Mann's (1977) analysis, the vigilance pattern occurs only when three conditions are met: The person must (1) be aware of serious risks for whichever alternative is chosen; (2) hope to find a satisfactory alternative; and (3) believe that there is adequate time to search and deliberate before a decision is required. If the second condition is not met, the defensive avoidance pattern occurs; if the third condition is not met, the hypervigilance pattern occurs.

Observations from prior studies by my colleagues and me in weight-reduction and antismoking clinics indicate that clients often start carrying out a health-oriented course of action without having engaged in vigilant search and appraisal of the alternatives open to them (Janis 1982). The dominant coping pattern in many cases appears to be defensive avoidance—deciding without deliberation to adopt the recommended course of action, which appears at the moment to be the least objectionable alternative, and bolstering it with rationalizations that minimize the difficulties to be expected when carrying it out. Defensive avoidance also appears to be a frequent coping pattern among hospitalized surgical and medical patients (see Janis 1958; Janis and Rodin 1979).

In order to prevent defensive avoidance, according to Janis and Mann (1977), preparatory communications are needed to meet the second of the three essential conditions for promoting a vigilant coping pattern: Assuming that the clients are already aware of the problems to be expected, interventions are needed that foster hope of solving these problems. Such interventions may also be essential for maintaining a vigilant problem-solving approach to whatever frustrations, temptations, or setbacks subsequently occur when the decision is being implemented.

On the basis of prior studies in clinics for heavy smokers and overweight people, it appears plausible to assume that backsliding occurs when one or more major setbacks make the clients lose hope about finding an adequate solution (Janis 1982). If this assumption is correct, we would expect stress inoculation to be most effective in preventing patients from reversing their decisions to follow a medical regimen if the preparatory communications contain information or persuasive messages that foster hope of solving whatever problems may arise from that regimen.

Closely related to patients' attitudes of self-confidence and hope are their beliefs about being able to *control* a stressful situation. Stress inoculation may change a patient's expectations of being in control of a dangerous situation, both with regard to the external threats of being helpless to prevent physical damage and the internal threats of becoming panic-stricken and losing emotional control. The stress inoculation procedures used with surgical and medical patients typically include statements designed to counteract feelings of helplessness and to promote a sense of active control. For example, in the stress inoculation procedures designed by Turk (1978) for patients suffering from chronic pain, the coping thoughts that are explicitly recommended and modeled include "Relax, you're in control" and "When the pain mounts, you can switch to a different strategy; you're in control."

There is now a sizable body of literature indicating that perceived personal control sometimes plays an important role in coping with stress (Averill 1973; Ball and Vogler 1971; Bowers 1968; Houston 1972; Janis and Rodin 1979; Kanfer and Seiderk 1973; Lapidus 1969; Pervin 1963; Pranulis, Dabbs, and Johnson 1975; Seligman 1975; Staub, Tursky, and Schwartz 1971; Weiss 1970).

Some preparatory interventions may make patients feel less helpless by making them more active participants, increasing their personal involvement in the treatment. Pranulis, Dabbs, and Johnson (1975), for example, redirect hospitalized patients' attention away from their own emotional reactions as passive recipients of medical treatments toward information that makes them feel more in control as active collaborators with the staff. Perhaps many of the preparatory communications used for purposes of stress inoculation have essentially the same effect on the patients' perceived control over distressing environmental events, which could increase their self-confidence and hope.

INDUCING COMMITMENT
AND PERSONAL RESPONSIBILITY

Another psychological component that may contribute to the positive effects of stress inoculation is the heightening of commitment. As part of the stress inoculation procedure for a new course of action, such as accepting medical recommendations to undergo surgery, painful treatments, or unpleasant regimens, patients are induced to acknowledge that they are going to have to deal with anticipated losses, which is tantamount to making more elaborated commitment statements to the health-care practitioners. Prior psychological research on commitment indicates that each time a person is induced to announce his or her intentions to an esteemed other, such as a professional counselor, the person is anchored to the decision not just by anticipated social disapproval but also by anticipated self-disapproval (Janis and Mann 1977; Kiesler 1971; McFall and Hammen 1971). The stabilizing effect of commitment, according to Kiesler's (1971) research, is enhanced by exposure to a mildly challenging attack, such as counterpropaganda that is easy to refute. A stress inoculation procedure for medical treatments or surgery might serve this function by first calling attention to the obstacles and drawbacks to be expected (which is a challenging attack) and then providing impressive suggestions about how those obstacles and drawbacks can be overcome (which may dampen the challenging attack sufficiently to make it mild).

Along with inducing increased commitment, stress inoculation tends to build up a sense of personal responsibility on the part of the patient. After hearing about the unpleasant consequences to be expected from undergoing a prescribed treatment and about ways of coping with the anticipated stresses, patients realize all the more keenly that they are personally responsible for the decision to undergo the recommended treatment and for doing their share to help carry it out as effectively as possible, rather than simply being passive recipients of whatever it is that the physician decides to do.

Predictions about each source of stress to be expected and accompanying suggestions convey to the patient the theme "This is yet another problem you must solve yourself; no one else can do it for you." My recent research in weight-reduction and antismoking clinics suggests that such messages may foster long-term adherence to difficult regimens because sticking to it requires that the patients develop attributions of personal responsibility, with a corresponding decline in dependency on the counselor (Janis 1982). My observations are in agreement with those of Davison and Valins (1969), who conclude from their research in a completely different setting that behavior change is more likely to be maintained when people attribute the cause of the change to themselves rather than to an outside agent. A direct implication of this conclusion is that people who seek help in self-regulation will be more likely to adhere in the long run to a new course of action, such as dieting or stopping smoking, if the counselor stresses the client's own role in whatever behavior change occurs (see Brehm 1976: 168; Rodin 1978).

A theoretical analysis by Janis (1982: ch. 2) of supportive helping relationships postulates that when people have the intention of changing to a new course of action that requires undergoing short-term deprivation in order to attain long-term objectives, the incentive value of gaining the approval of a professional advisor or counselor can help to get them started. A supportive norm-setting practitioner can build up and use potential motivating power, according to this analysis, if he or she builds up an image of the helper as a quasidependable source of self-esteem enhancement: The persons who seek help come to realize that they will receive spontaneous acceptance, including times when they reveal weaknesses and shortcomings, *except* when they fail to make a sincere effort to live up to a limited set of norms (see Janis 1982). This expectation of partly contingent acceptance from the helper allows the client to look forward to receiving genuine acceptance and approval much of the time—and perhaps practically all of the time—provided that he or she makes a sincere effort to follow just a few rules recommended by the helper pertaining to only a limited sphere of personal behavior.

A crisis arises, however, when direct contact between the helper and the client is terminated, as is bound to happen when a counselor arranges for a fixed number of sessions to help a client get started on a stressful course of action such as dieting. When the sessions come to an end, even if prearranged by a formal contract, the client will want to continue the relationship, insofar as he or she has become dependent on the counselor for social rewards that bolster self-esteem. The client is likely to regard the counselor's refusal to comply with his or her demand to maintain contact as a sign of rejection or indifference. If this occurs, the client will no longer be motivated to live up to the helper's norms and will show little or no tendency to internalize the norms during the postcontact period.

In order to prevent backsliding and other adverse effects when contact with the helper is terminated, the person must internalize the norms sponsored by the helper by somehow converting *other-directed* approval motivation into *self-directed* approval motivation. Little is known as yet about the determinants of this process, but it seems plausible to expect that internalization might be facilitated by communications themes in stress inoculation procedures that enhance commitment by building up a sense of personal responsibility.

COPING PREDISPOSITIONS

For certain types of persons, as I mentioned earlier, stress inoculation has been found to have no effect and occasionally even adverse effects. The Janis and Mann (1977) theoretical model of coping patterns has some implications for personality differences in responsiveness to stress inoculation. Certain people can be expected to be highly resistant to communications that attempt to induce the conditions that are essential for a coping pattern of vigilant search and appraisal. The difficulty may be that they generally are unresponsive to authentic information that promotes one or another of the three crucial beliefs (that there are serious risks for whichever alternative course of action is chosen, that it is realistic to be optimistically hopeful about finding a satisfactory solution, and that there is adequate time in which to search and deliberate before a decision is required). Such persons would be expected to show consistently defective coping patterns that often would lead to inadequate planning and overreactions to setbacks. In response to acute postdecisional stress, they would be the ones most likely to reverse their decisions about undergoing painful medical treatments.

Elsewhere (Janis 1982: ch. 20), I have more fully elaborated these theoretical assumptions and reviewed the research findings on specific personality variables related to responsiveness to stress inoculation. In the discussion that follows I shall highlight the main findings and conclusions.

A number of studies employing Byrne's (1964) repression–sensitization scale and Goldstein's (1959) closely related coper-versus-avoider test suggest that persons diagnosed as chronic repressors or avoiders tend to minimize, deny, or ignore any warning that presents disturbing information about impending threats. Such persons appear to be predisposed to display the characteristic features of defensive avoidance. Unlike persons who are predisposed to be vigilant, these avoiders would not be expected to respond adaptively to preparatory information that provides realistic forecasts about anticipated stressful experiences along with reassurances. Relevant evidence is to be found in the reports on two field experiments conducted on surgery wards by Andrew (1970) and DeLong (1971). In both studies, patients awaiting surgery were given Goldstein's test in order to assess their preferred mode of coping with stress and then were given preparatory information. The reactions of the following three groups were compared: (1) copers, who tended to display vigilance or sensitizing defenses; (2) avoiders, who displayed avoidant or denial defenses; and (3) nonspecific defenders, who showed no clear preference. In Andrew's (1970) study, preparatory information describing what the experience of the operation and the postoperative convalescence would be like had an unfavorable effect on the rate of physical recovery of avoiders but a positive effect on nonspecific defenders. Copers recovered well whether or not they were given the preoperative information. In DeLong's (1971) study, avoiders were found to have the poorest recovery whether or not they were given preparatory information, and copers showed the greatest benefit from the preparatory information. The findings from the two studies show some inconsistencies but they agree in indicating that persons who display defensive avoidance tendencies do not respond well to preparatory information.

Correlational evidence from studies of surgical patients by Cohen and Lazarus (1973) and Cohen (1975) appears to contradict the implications of the studies just discussed bearing on vigilance versus defensive avoidance. These investigators report that patients who were rated as "vigilant" before the operation showed poorer recovery from surgery than those rated as "avoidant." This finding seems not only to contradict the earlier surgery findings but also to go against the expectation from the conflict-theory model that people who are vigilant will cope better with unfavorable consequences of their decisions than will those whose dominant coping pattern is defensive avoidance. But there are two important considerations to take into account. One is that Sime (1976) attempted to replicate Cohen and Lazarus' (1973) finding using the same categories but was unable to do so. When there are disagreements like this, one suspects that either there are unrecognized differences in the way in which the variables were assessed or that the relationship between the two variables is determined by an uninvestigated third variable, such as severity of the patient's illness. A second consideration has to do with the way Cohen and Lazarus define "vigilance." A careful examination of their procedures reveals that they did not differentiate between hypervigilance and vigilance. The investigators state that they classified as vigilant any patient who sought out information about the operation (which hypervigilant people do even more than vigilant ones) or who were sensitized in terms of remembering the information and displaying readiness to discuss their thoughts about the operation. (Again, the hypervigilant people tend to be much more preoccupied with information about threatening consequences than those who are vigilant.) The one example Cohen and Lazarus give of a so-called vigilant reaction would be classified as "hypervigilant" according to the criteria given in Janis and Mann

(1977:74, 205–06): "I have all the facts, my will is all prepared [in the event of death] . . . you're put out, you could be put out too deep, your heart could quit, you can have shock . . . I go not in lightly." Consequently, the correlation observed by these investigators might be attributable to the relationship between preoperative *hypervigilance* and low tolerance for postoperative stress, which has been observed by other investigators (Auerbach 1973; Janis 1958; Leventhal 1963). Auerbach (1973), for example, found that surgical patients who showed a high state of preoperative anxiety relative to their normal or average level (as assessed by the State–Trait Anxiety Inventory developed by Spielberger, Gorsuch, and Lushene 1970) obtained poorer scores on a measure of postoperative adjustment than did those who showed a relatively moderate level of preoperative anxiety.

In Auerbach's study, the postoperative adjustment of the patients who showed moderate preoperative anxiety was found to be superior to that of the patients who showed relatively low anxiety as well as those who showed relatively high anxiety before the operation. In disagreement with contradictory findings reported by Cohen and Lazarus (1973) and by several other investigators, Auerbach's data tend to confirm Janis' (1958) earlier finding of a curvilinear relationship between the level of preoperative anxiety and postoperative adjustment. Such data are consistent with the "work of worrying" concept, which assumes that inducing vigilance in surgical patients (manifested by a moderate level of preoperative fear or anxiety) is beneficial for postoperative adjustment (Janis 1958; Janis and Mann 1977). But it is essential to take note of the disagreements in the correlational results obtained from many nonintervention studies in the research literature on the relationship between level of preoperative fear or anxiety and postoperative adjustment, which can be affected by a number of extraneous variables that are difficult to control even when they can be recognized (see Cohen and Lazarus 1979). It would not be worthwhile, it seems to me, for investigators to carry out more such correlational studies because even a dozen or two of them cannot be expected to settle the issue. I think it is realistic, however, to hope for dependable conclusions about the postoperative effects of arousal of vigilance before surgery—and also about the interacting effects of such arousal with personality characteristics—if a few more well-controlled *intervention* studies are carried out in which preparatory information designed to induce vigilance is used as an independent variable and is not confounded with social support or with any other potentially potent variable.

Complicated findings on another predispositional attribute were obtained by Auerbach et al. (1976) in a study of stress inoculation for dental surgery. Using Rotter's (1966) personality measure of locus of control, these investigators found that "internals" (patients who perceive themselves as having control over the outcome of events) responded positively to specific preparatory information about the surgical experiences to be expected, obtaining higher ratings on behavioral adjustment during surgery than those who were not given the preparatory information. In contrast, "externals" (patients who perceive themselves as primarily under the control of external circumstances) obtained lower adjustment ratings when provided with the specific preparatory information. But subsidiary findings show the reverse outcome when the patients were given general preparatory information that was not directly relevant to their surgical experience.

As is so often the case with the correlational data obtained in personality research, the findings can be interpreted in a number of different ways and it is difficult to determine which interpretation is best. For example, since prior research shows that "externals" tend to be more defensive than "internals," the main finding could be viewed as consistent with the hypothesis that persons who are predisposed to adopt a defensive avoidance coping pattern fail to show increased stress tolerance when given preparatory information about the specific stress experiences that are to be expected. An alternative interpretation would be in terms of the importance of perceived control: maybe only those patients who are capable of perceiving themselves as influencing what happens develop adequate coping responses when given preparatory information about anticipated stressors. In any case, the complex findings from the many studies of personality variables suggest that, in order to increase the percentage of patients who benefit from stress inoculation, it will be necessary to hand-tailor the preparatory information in a way that takes account of each individual's coping style.

When opportunities for stress inoculation are made available, personality factors may play a role in determining who will choose to take advantage of those opportunities and who will not. A study by Lapidus (1969) of pregnant women indicates that when preparatory information about the stresses of childbirth is offered free of charge, passive-submissive women who are most in need of stress inoculation are unlikely to obtain it if it is left up to them to take the initiative. On various indicators of field dependence–independence, cognitive control, and flexibility, the pregnant women who chose to participate in a program that offered psychological preparation for childbirth differed significantly from those who chose not to participate. The participants were more field-independent and displayed stronger tendencies toward active mastery of stress than the non-participants, many of whom showed signs of strong dependency and denial tendencies.

In order to take account of individual differences in coping style and other personality predispositions, it may be necessary in each clinic or hospital to set up a number of different preparation programs rather than just one standard program. The patients would probably have to be screened in advance for their knowledge about the consequences of the treatment they have agreed to undergo as well as for their capacity to assimilate unpleasant information. At present, health-care professionals have to use their best judgment in selecting what they think will be the most effective ingredients of stress inoculation for each individual facing a particular type of stress. Until more analytic research is carried out on responsiveness to each of the major components of stress inoculation, the hand-tailoring of preparatory information and coping recommendations will remain more of an art than a science.

CONCLUSION

The main point emphasized throughout this article is that sufficient research has already been done on the effectiveness of stress inoculation to warrant moving to a new stage of attempting to identify the factors that are responsible for the positive effects. Analytic experiments are needed that attempt to determine the crucial variables by testing hypotheses based on theoretical concepts about basic processes. These can be carried out as field experiments in clinics and hospitals where large numbers of patients are awaiting distressing medical treatments or surgery. With regard to the problems of internal validity and replicability of the findings, investigators can use standard methodological safeguards, such as random assignment of patients to conditions, that have evolved in experimental social psychology and personality research during the past three decades. The major goal should be to pin down as specifically as possible the key variables (and their interactions) that are responsible for the positive effects of stress inoculation on increasing tolerance for adverse events, including those losses that disrupt adherence to health-promoting regimens.

The key variables that should be given priority, in my opinion, are the ones suggested by theory and prior research, as discussed in the preceding sections—(1) increasing the predictability of stressful events, (2) fostering coping skills and plans for coping actions, (3) stimulating cognitive coping responses such as positive self-talk and reconceptualization of threats into nonthreatening terms, (4) encouraging attitudes of self-confidence and hope about a successful outcome with related expectations that make for perceived control, and (5) building up commitment and a sense of personal responsibility for adhering to an adaptive course of action.

24

Toward Effective Coping: The Basic Steps

ROBERT M. BRAMSON

Underlying the coping process are six fundamental steps that will help you cope successfully, no matter what type of Difficult Person you need to deal with. (1) Assess the situation. (2) Stop wishing the Difficult Person were different. (3) Get some distance between you and the difficult behavior. (4) Formulate a coping plan. (5) Implement your plan. (6) Monitor the effectiveness of your coping strategy, modifying it where appropriate. Let's look at each of these steps in turn.

ASSESS THE SITUATION

At work, as in the rest of life, we encounter many situations in which others seem to cause us difficulty. A co-worker turns grumpy and uncommunicative, the boss blows his stack over a minor mistake, subordinates may seem perpetually ready with new excuses about assignments still unfinished, and clients may act as if they know more about our business than we do. Which of these situations involve Difficult People? How do you recognize a Difficult Person when you see one?

The first preparatory step in the coping process is to determine whether or not you are dealing with a Difficult Person or with a situation that is temporarily bringing out the worst in an ordinarily nondifficult person. A well-documented but often unrecognized human tendency is to become irritated over the foibles of others while excusing our own as "just being human." Whenever we run into a frustrating situation, or a "no" to an idea or wish, it is tempting enough to brand others as "difficult." But seeing Difficult People wherever you turn is likely to earn yourself the label you are placing on others—and it won't help you to cope with the situation.

Sometimes, deciding that you are in truth dealing with a Difficult Person is relatively simple. Your assistant who complains to you constantly about other staffers in a passive way will at once be recognized as a Complainer; the boss whose abrasive, hostile manner causes all of his or her subordinates to groan inwardly and turn grimly silent outwardly is a clear Sherman Tank. These are the individuals about whom office gossip revolves, individuals that most people agree are problem-causers.

Other troublesome encounters, however, are not so clear. When criticized by a boss for getting a report in late again, you may secretly feel that he or she has a right to feel angry. The steady customer who complains about the decline in service may have a legitimate beef. Or you may be confused about why your relationship with a neighbor began to deteriorate about six months ago. If coping is to be effective, we need some realistic measures by which to judge whether someone is truly a Difficult Person or a person caught up in an unfortunate but temporary situation.

. . . The Difficult Person is one who acts chronically in a difficult manner. This is the litmus test of whether we are genuinely faced with a Difficult Person, whether we can look for a simpler solution to our poor relations, or whether we should take a closer look at the possibility that we are just seeking an easy excuse for our own problems. To make this test, use the answers to the following questions as guides:

1. Has the person in question usually acted differently in three similar situations?
2. Am I reacting out of proportion to what the situation warrants?
3. Was there a particular incident that triggered the troublesome behavior?
4. Will direct, open discussion relieve the situation?

If your answer to any one of these four questions is yes, chances are you are not primarily dealing with a Difficult Person, even if that person's behavior is now impossible. If your answers are all in the negative, then you probably are confronted with one. Let me elaborate and give some examples from my consulting experience of individuals who might have appeared on the surface to be Difficult People but who actually weren't.

Question 1: Has the Person in Question Usually Acted Differently in Three Similar Situations?

Carl was a first-line data processing supervisor who appeared to have all the earmarks of a Difficult Person. He was surly and unresponsive to an extreme. A few days before I was asked to try to help out, he had suddenly pushed his desk into a corner of the office and piled books so high on one side that it was almost impossible for anyone to see him. Others in the office were alarmed by his erratic behavior and feared what he would do next.

When I talked with other employees in the office, however, they all agreed that Carl used to act quite reasonably and had been a relatively easy person to get along with. Carl's bizarre behavior, it turned out, was the result of a chain of events which began with his rejection for promotion six months before. When he was passed over for promotion, Carl complained to his area's vice-president. The vice-president concluded that Carl had been unfairly treated, and he ordered the heads of his division to establish a training plan so that Carl would know what he had to do in order to move up in the ranks.

It was not surprising that among the division heads there was some resistance to implementing this plan. They were resentful of Carl for having gone over their heads to complain. And Carl, once his meeting with the vice-president became public knowledge, began to feel that others in the office were waiting for him to fail in order to justify their decision not to promote him. Anxious and angry over what seemed to him a cold and unsupportive atmosphere, Carl began to fall down on the job. He turned in his reports late, made silly mistakes, and reduced his contacts with others on the floor to the bare minimum. Moving his desk into the corner was merely the logical expression of his feelings of increasing isolation from and suspiciousness of others.

When this chain of events was untangled, Carl was able to vent his feelings to his own supervisor, who had been shunted to one side when the trouble with the brass had started. He was then transferred to a different division where his effectiveness on the job soon began to return to normal. Carl's problem behavior was primarily situational. Understanding the source of his upset and providing him with a fresh environment was enough to enable him to work effectively and smoothly with others. The clue that Carl wasn't really one of those Difficult People we have described, but rather one whose problems with others could be rather straightforwardly resolved, was that prior to the promotion dispute he had acted quite differently.

Question 2: Am I Reacting Out of Proportion to What the Situation Warrants?

The second question to ask yourself after a series of uncomfortable exchanges with another is whether or not, upon reflection, your own responses to the person seem excessive. If you find yourself reacting negatively to practically everything a particular individual does, it may be that you are responding to something quite specific about the individual, not a systematic pattern of difficult behavior. Consider the following example.

A regional administrator of a federal agency called on me to advise him on what should be done about his silent and unresponsive bureau chief. It had gotten to the point, the regional administrator told me, where everything his bureau chief did infuriated him. He would yell at and abrade his subordinate, but the bureau chief would just sit there and say nothing. Even over minor issues, the regional administrator would blow up at the man. Once, for instance, the bureau chief asked a simple procedural question, and the regional administrator immediately snarled, "Why don't you read what we send you; don't you ever pay attention to what's going on?"

I soon discovered, however, that there was a specific cause for the administrator's upset. He had recently sent the bureau chief instructions on how to handle an important policy meeting. The bureau chief proceeded to do just the opposite of what his boss had requested, and it wasn't long before the administrator heard about it. He stormed into the bureau chief's office and read him the riot act. The bureau chief just sat there in stony silence, then he got up and walked out of the room without saying a word.

As it turned out, and as the regional administrator himself was later to admit, the bureau chief had had very good reasons for altering his presentation at the conference. But because of his boss's approach, he never explained this to him, becoming increasingly unresponsive instead. The administrator, for his part, grew more and more furious because of his subordinate's lack of response. For the regional administrator, the clue that he might not be dealing with a Difficult Person should have been the degree to which he became upset with his bureau chief over subsequent, admittedly minor, matters.

Question 3: Was There a Particular Incident that Triggered the Troublesome Behavior?

The third question to ask yourself after a series of unpleasant incidents with an individual is whether or not there was a particular incident that triggered the difficult behavior. Frequently, posing this question becomes just another way of asking questions 1 and 2. In the above examples, Carl's lack of promotion was the trigger of his troublesome behavior, and the regional administrator's approach and the bureau chief's response to their meeting over the conduct of the policy conference was the spark of the bureau chief's subsequent behavior pattern. In these instances, and others like them, exposing and discussing openly the triggering incidents led to a reasonably productive resolution of the problem.

Question 4: Will Direct, Open Discussion Relieve the Situation?

After thinking through these assessment questions, you may suspect that you're faced with a relationship gone sour rather than with a Difficult Person. In that case, an attempt to untangle the problem through direct discussion with the other person is a useful next step. It, of course, may not alleviate the situation, but you will have satisfied yourself that, with awareness that you might be a part of the problem, you have done your best to work it through. These steps, modified to fit your own style and the circumstances, offer the best chance of success.

First, initiate a conversation, preferably by making an appointment to demonstrate your serious intent and lessen the chance of interruption. Open the conversation with a statement of your own sense that things have not been going well between you. Wait for a reaction. If none is forthcoming, try again with your best guess about an incident that may have opened the breech in your relationship.

In the case of that regional administrator and his bureau chief, it might sound like this: "Murry, I've been thinking about the way we've been getting on each other's nerves lately—did it start when I jumped on you about that policy meeting last January? Are there problems at home? What's happening?" Notice that your last question was open-ended. That will help you to deal with any uncertainty or reluctance in the other person. . . .

If the response you get typifies any one of the Difficult People we've visited, and you can't shake him or her out of it by restating what you've just said, proceed with coping. If, however, he or she begins to open up to you, bringing up old slights, forgotten arguments, or neglected rewards, take pains to avoid explaining it all away. Do *not* give all of the reasons why you did those things that were seen as threatening or demeaning. You will be tempted to do just that, especially if you are of a matter-of-fact turn of mind. But nothing will kill your attempts at resolving the problem sooner than, "Oh, yes, well, you know that when you brought your promotion up at the annual performance review, we had a salary freeze and I couldn't bring it up later because . . ." Instead, as simply as you can, state what your intention was at that time and what it is now: "Well, I can see that what I did left you feeling that the extra work you did wasn't very important to me. That's certainly not what I wanted then, and it's not what I want now. What do we need to do to make sure that it doesn't happen again?" If it appears that what you've said hasn't registered, that is, it is followed by a restatement of those old grievances, try again. But, first, do as careful a job as you can of acknowledging both what's been said and the feelings behind it. . . .

Once the conversation begins to turn toward preventing future occurrences, continue with it. Be ready, however, to acknowledge and then restate your own intentions if the conversation starts to slip.

STOP WISHING THEY WERE DIFFERENT

Perhaps the most valuable single step that anyone can take in preparation for coping with Difficult People is to *stop wishing they were different.* This is far easier said than done.

Think of someone standing over you, pounding the table, shouting and cursing at you. If you're like most people, you'll sit there muttering to yourself something like: "He shouldn't be that way!" or "Why is she acting that way? That's not the way *anyone* should be!" *Not* to feel abused, not to feel that the aggressor should be different, would seem almost out of the question. The problem is this. To the extent that you are sitting there trying to wish your tormenting frog into a prince (or princess) you will be that much *less* able to do just those things that might minimize that terrible behavior.

Blaming Isn't Changing

In situations like the above, we blame something exclusively internal on the other person. We all tend to believe that others are basically like ourselves, that they have similar values, assumptions, and feelings. Consequently, when they do not act as we expect or would like, it is "logical" to assume that their unexpected and unwanted behavior must be due to hostile intentions, a faulty personality, or just plain personal "difficultness." As a result, we conclude that it is up to *them* to change.

Given this very human attribute, what else is there for us to do but plaintively wish that our Difficult Person were different and then feel frustrated when he or she doesn't change? The confounding fact is that Difficult People at times behave rather well. This lends temporary credence to a belief that finally they've changed, only to have this credence undermined when the disliked behavior shows up again. Feeling virtuous and self-righteous for having "done all I can" is very understandable, but unfortunately it won't keep your interaction with that offensive person from falling into the same rut.

The source of the great strength with which this wish can take hold is that deeply buried sense of witching power that is left over from the childhood of each of us. The attempt is an exercise in futility that only sidetracks you from what you *can* do to alleviate the situation.

Giving Up the Magical Wish

The second step toward successful coping, then, is to give up that magical wish. When you look closely, you are likely to be surprised at how much energy you had used in the wishing. Because it is such a valuable aid to coping, in the next few paragraphs I'll suggest some actions you can take to give up the wish that your own Difficult Person were different. Giving up the wish is a letting-go process. You will likely feel a sense of relief as you release this psychic wrestling hold that required great energy yet failed to make anything change.

To help yourself let go of that attempt at magical spell-casting, try to become aware of the strength of that fantasy-filled wish in your own life. It helps. You may feel it as a hope that "this time it will be different." Or it may turn up as that feeling of disappointment and dismay when Barbara, *again,* brings her order book in a day late. Well, why are you so surprised? Even more to the point, why did you tell your supervisor that you would have all the orders in on the same day you set for Barbara, when you knew she was always late?

What a bitter cycle: an unrealistic hope turns to resentment only to be followed by another unrealistic hope. To see yourself in that cycle playing a part that seems out of touch with the actuality of who Barbara is can help you to choose behaviors that will be more appropriate and more likely to gain for you a better, more productive relationship with her. It is with others as they are that you must learn to cope.

GET SOME DISTANCE BETWEEN YOU AND THE DIFFICULT BEHAVIOR

When confronted with Difficult People, we tend to become so wrapped up in the situation—wishing the individuals were different, feeling angry toward them, and upset at ourselves for being dragged into another unpleasant routine—that we're unable to think through more effective responses. Difficult People are difficult to us because they touch off a series of reactions in ourselves which always seem to become part of their game.

In order to be able to cope with Difficult People, to break the destructive patterns of behavior which you fall into with them, you must learn to gain some perspective on their actions, even while they are talking to you. Only by seeing their patterns of behavior and understanding the source of those patterns will you be able to devise an effective strategy for coping with them.

Your goal is a detached and distanced view of that Difficult Person, while he or she is in the process of being difficult (even shortly thereafter may do). Here are some quotations from those who achieved this perspective with their own problem people: "I am looking at her through the wrong end of a telescope; every detail clear, but very far away." "I can see him as if he were sitting in a cage with a label over him." "It's not just me he does this to—he's that way with everyone." "I suddenly saw that if I wait for her to stop complaining and start taking some action on her own, I'll wait forever."

To have a distanced perspective of someone does not mean being cold, unfeeling, or nonunderstanding. My own experience is that the opposite is often true, particularly with those I care about, or need, the most. A truism that usually holds here, too, is: the more you can see others as truly separate from yourself, the more you are able to see them as they are.

Labeling Can Help

Most people feel an inner resistance to the idea of categorizing people, putting them in boxes labeled, "Difficult People," "Indecisive," "Complainer," or whatever. Human beings are immensely complex and adaptable, and no one can be completely reduced to any category. But that doesn't mean that there aren't some very practical reasons for categorizing people. One of these is that labeling people often helps you feel "distanced" from them, especially if they're people with whom you're very involved.

It allows you to see their behavior as happening outside of yourself and your personal responses. That is, it often enables you to see that the Hostile-Aggressive person or the Complainer isn't being hostile or complaining just with you, but that he or she does this to everyone in similar situations. Identifying the kind of Difficult Person you've encountered can in itself help you to take the disturbing behavior less personally. You become less paralyzed wondering what *you* did to bring it on and become more ready for an active, more effective response.

Another practical reason for categorizing people is that by doing so you may gain an insight into their behavior. Regardless of any other attributes they may have, Indecisives have learned to act the way they do because it gets them through, or out of, some kinds of situations. Thus, just recognizing that they are habitually indecisive tells you something about them.

I'm suggesting, then, that while you are doing your business with people who are driving you up a tree, you actively try to think about them in some category of "Difficult Person." It is important, however, that you see the labels and the behavior patterns they describe as *prototypes* rather than *stereotypes*. Using "Complainer" as a stereotype label would imply that all Complainers are alike, a statement far from the truth. What we mean by that label is rather that all Complainers show certain behaviors in common, but in most other ways they are quite different.

Looking at people as if they were specimens does, I think, cut down on spontaneity. Done to extreme, as a means of avoiding intimacy, for example, it is as harmful as being submerged in a relationship. This article is about coping, however, not being spontaneous; for coping a degree of "outside" perspective does seem to help. The purpose of this attempt to gain distance is not to write off your own responsibility for any situation but to free yourself for a more productive and, in the long run, more caring response.

Understanding Can Help

For achieving a broader perspective on a Difficult Person, it does seem to help to *believe* that you understand what it's like to be one. When you can make some sense out of behavior that has previously seemed nonsensical, you feel less confused and helpless—more able to cope.

The kind of understanding that I am suggesting here is "understanding from the inside," to use psychologist George Kelly's term. Think of that someone who has continued to do those frustrating and awful things in the face of negative reactions, hints, resignations, and even open warfare. The task is to imagine how life looks to that person, and to relate that perspective to comparable experiences of your own life.

Gaining and maintaining this kind of understanding is devilishly hard. Can we ever fully succeed with any other person? I doubt it. But even a snatch of such understanding can provide the necessary vantage point that will release you from those patterns of interaction that bring out the worst in everyone.

FORMULATE A PLAN
FOR INTERRUPTING THE INTERACTION

Once you have managed to gain some distance and some understanding of the Difficult Person's behavior, it is time to devise a strategy for coping more effectively with it. The basic tenet that underlies successful coping is a simple but often overlooked fact: the behavior of human beings is highly interactional. Because this fact is often forgotten, most of us are cut off from a source of leverage in our relationships with Difficult People that is there for the using. To see how and why this leverage works, consider the following two possible scenarios that might unfold when I get up to give a talk before a group.

Two Cycles of Behavior

Suppose, in the first instance, that I am addressing a group of supervisors who, unknown to me, have been ordered by their superior to drop everything and come hear me speak. They're resentful of having to take time out from other chores to listen to me, and, under the circumstances, they're not initially interested in my topic.

After I've been talking only a few minutes, I begin to notice that some of the supervisors are nodding off while others are squirming in their chairs or staring out the window. They may be inwardly fuming at what an S.O.B. their boss is for making them come to this meeting and wondering how they'll still be able to make tomorrow's production deadline, but I don't know that. What I notice is widespread boredom and disinterest, which I interpret as solely a response to my speech, and as a consequence begin to feel defensive and self-conscious about my presentation. My voice tightens up, I start stumbling over words, and my delivery begins to sound more tentative. The supervisors notice this change in my presentation. Most become even more irritated with me, now having even more evidence that their resentment at having been forced to attend was well founded. A few, perhaps, may start to feel sorry for me and ask forced questions in an effort to prop me up. But both the visible irritation of the majority and the over-solicitousness of the minority make me feel even more self-conscious. Chances now are great that both I and my presentation will provoke even more irritation and boredom among my audience. Increasingly more tense and disconcerted, I expend more and more energy trying to gain my audience's approval, less and less on the substance of my speech. Thus, I progress to the lowest level of my competency. Later on, perhaps, while trying to understand this disaster I will salve my feelings with the thought that I was faced with an unruly, unappreciative, and completely difficult group.

The above scenario is an example of what I call a *negative interaction cycle*. An initial negative encounter between myself and the audience spiraled into increasingly negative and unproductive interactions between us. Without doubt, the particular way in which I responded to the seat squirming and evidence of disinterest was determined by who I am—my personality and my repertoire of learned responses—but it was something in the specific character of that situation that elicited that set of increasingly incompetent responses (tightening up, etc.) from me.

Now let's look at a contrasting scenario, one that involves a *positive interaction cycle*. Suppose that a few minutes into my talk one of the supervisors remarks that he doesn't know about the others, but as far as he is concerned, what I am saying makes a lot of sense to him and he's eager to hear more. My initial feelings of discomfort begin to diminish, I start to relax, my voice becomes lively, and my tone sounds more self-confident. Others in the group begin to worry less about their deadlines as they pay more attention, perhaps become intrigued by what I am saying, and I, noticing this, begin to feel more relaxed. I am now able to devote full attention to presenting the substance of my talk in an effective manner.

In this instance, the interaction between myself and my audience cycled in a positive direction. Once again, I responded to the audience in the way that I did because I have my particular personality, developed through my own unique past experiences. This time, however, because of an affirming note early in the speech, the outcome was quite different. The cast of characters in these two scenarios is the same. What makes the difference is the quality of the interaction.

Let me put what I've been saying a little more abstractly. The way people behave is not due solely to an early learned set of personality traits, although personality traits certainly have much to do with anyone's behavior. Nor is behavior purely a response to the particular situations in which people find themselves, although it is certainly true that any person will respond differently in different circumstances. There is always a relationship between an individual's personality and the specific situation the person is in, as that person sees it.

Here's the way it works. Personality is simply the repertoire of strategies and tactics for dealing with life that an individual has learned to prefer. Any specific situation at times pulls out and at times inhibits certain of the strategies in that person's armentarium. When my audience acted bored and disinterested, it pushed a "respond" button in me. The question is why did I tighten up, blame myself, but pretend outwardly that nothing was happening, rather than remain calm, suspect that the members of the audience had other things on their minds, and inquire matter-of-factly, or with humor, what the difficulty was. My ability to consistently do the latter increased markedly when I was helped to see that, early on, I had learned to blame myself when others became irritated with me, had developed a very strong need for group approval, and, even worse, had learned that it was improper to comment on what others seemed to think of me. These insights, however, came later. I would not have survived my earlier years on the "seminar circuit" if I had not frequently encountered the second scenario when, certain of at least one member's approval, more positive and productive responses were elicited from me.

What makes a Difficult Person different from the rest of us is that he or she is more likely to respond in ways that manage to get the worst out of everyone. We can all be negative and unproductive in various situations, but defensive, unproductive behavior in the Difficult Person is more frequent, more easily elicited, and at a lower threshold than for the rest of us. What makes it possible to cope with Difficult People at all is that, like everyone else, they have positive responses in their repertoire. If you can learn to avoid doing and saying those things that elicit the negative behavior from a Difficult Person and structure the interaction so as to encourage his or her positive, more productive responses, then you will be coping more successfully with that individual.

The Leverage Is in the Interaction

The primary leverage you have for coping with the difficult behavior of other people is your ability to change the nature of the interaction you are both caught in. You can do this by changing your own piece of it, your own behavior. To do this properly, as we discussed earlier in the chapter, you must mentally step outside the interaction long enough to see that your own behavior was elicited from you by what the other person has done, or at least by what you thought he or she had done.

You are free to change your part in the interaction precisely because you no longer wait for those difficult others to do the remedying. Let me take as an example those wonderfully nice people . . . who promise you anything but don't deliver. Don't you have a right to expect that those people will be honest with you, that they will say, "I cannot have that report in by Thursday, other things have priority," rather than, "Sure, Thursday will be fine"? Of course you do. Everyone has a right to expect that the people they associate with will be candid. The problem is that those overagreeable people just can't be blunt, unless you give them a lot of help. You could emphatically insist on your right to get honest answers, driving those poor overagreeable persons into a panic. Or you can choose to do the work of changing the situation yourself so as to make it easier for the truth to emerge.

IMPLEMENT YOUR STRATEGY

Once you have determined an appropriate plan of attack, the obvious next step toward successful coping is to implement it. Here are some general guidelines on timing and preparation.

Timing

You should choose the moment to implement your strategy with some discretion. There are two main criteria of proper timing. First, you should select a period when the Difficult Person is not overburdened with other problems. For example, if the individual has just been given a huge assignment or just had a run-in with the boss or just separated from his or her mate, it is best to delay putting your plan into effect. When people are under a lot of stress, they tend to be less resilient in their responses to new developments, and will be less likely to react to your confrontation in a fruitful manner. By disrupting their established patterns of behavior when they are under great stress, you also risk their taking their frustrations over that recent separation or fight with the boss out on you.

The second criterion of appropriate timing is whether or not you have the time yourself, and the energy, to carry through with your coping plan. You don't want to confront the Difficult Person once and then seem to fall back because you no longer are able to devote the necessary effort to the interaction between you. Successful coping depends on your ability to pay careful and systematic attention to what happens between you and the Difficult Person. Your attempts to interrupt the interaction between the two of you may not work on the first or second or even third try. A Difficult Person's patterns of habitual response tend to be deeply ingrained, and it may take them awhile to react to your new behavior and develop a new way of responding to it.

Preparation

While my experience has been that the coping methods explained in this book usually work even if they are not carried out with great skill, if you can, it will pay to practice your strategy before actually confronting that Difficult Person. This is especially true with Sherman Tanks, Snipers, and Bulldozers. Practicing what you intend to say in front of a mirror is an effective form of preparation. Be sure to say the words aloud. Perhaps an even better method is to corral a friend or your spouse to go through a dry run with you, playing the role of the Difficult Person. Ready yourself for an abrasive encounter by imagining that Difficult Person standing in front of you shouting and swearing. Then say the coping words as well as you can. Try to visualize the encounter developing just as you hope it will. If your image of a successful interchange falters, start over.

MONITOR THE PROGRESS OF YOUR COPING AND MODIFY WHEN APPROPRIATE

Once you have begun implementing your coping plan, it is important to monitor its effects carefully and modify it if necessary. You may discover, for instance, that your approach has little or no influence because you have misinterpreted the kind of Difficult Person you are confronted with. You may have mistaken, for example, Super-Agreeable behavior for Indecisive. In such a case, there's nothing for it but to heave a sigh and devise a new strategy.

It's also possible that no matter what you do, your attempts at coping will fail to produce many productive results. This may happen because the threshold at which the difficult behavior is triggered is so low that you would have to become a slave to the moods and idiosyncracies of the Difficult Person in order to avoid triggering that defensive behavior. It also may happen because the person is so engrossed in his or her own inner life that what you do in the present has little effect on his or her behavior. For instance, they may explode because of some thought of their own which is unrelated to anything you have said or done. In such circumstances, further attempts to cope would appear clearly counterproductive. When should you abandon coping attempts, and what should you do then?

When to Abandon the Coping Effort

My advice is first to try to cope with the Difficult Person using the methods proposed in the previous chapters, and any others you can invent. Expect to have to persist, plan, and become as skillful as you can, because you are the one supplying the energy and motivation. But if your attempts at coping don't work, literally get as much distance from the Difficult Person as you can. Don't wait two years to ask for a transfer away from that difficult boss, try to arrange it before the interaction has taken too great a toll on both of you. You may both benefit from the change.

The best kind of distance to get from that troublesome other is the easiest and least costly kind. Here are some examples.

Physical distance. Walk away, leaving the scene of action; get yourself transferred to another office; obtain a divider for the office so that at least you don't have to look at the person (and he or she won't have to look at you).

Organizational distance. Move the Difficult Person to a staff position, with no authority over others; transfer yourself into another unit; ask for a different committee assignment.

When considering whether or not to abandon your coping attempts, it is important to remain flexible and not let your pride determine your decision. Acknowledging that your efforts at coping have failed can be a source of wounded pride. You may be tempted to try again, and again, because you can't bear the thought of not being successful at everything you try or because it has become a point of pride for you not to back down from, for instance, a Hostile-Aggressive type. But consider whether, like Dean Edwards in the example below, the benefit of saving that modicum of pride is worth the torment of having to remain in the vicinity of an impossible person.

Dean Edwards was a young, very able project chief in a large organization. Anathema to him was Lee Jackson, the organization's administrative chief, who habitually ignored him in meetings, "overlooked" decisions made by the head of the organization that were favorable to Dean's project, "ordered" Dean's boss to keep Dean away from him, and publicly questioned the value of Dean's project in a sarcastic manner.

After a year and a half of acute distress, Dean, with his boss's approval, designated one of his staff, an older man, as "Project Administrative Officer" and assigned all contact with Lee to this person. During the following two years the project was able to get its most needed administrative support. Dean recognized that he had, in a sense, given in to Lee at some cost to both his ego and his "strong man" image. However, his freedom from debilitating attacks of tension seemed clearly to outweigh those costs.

Remember, *no one* is under a moral obligation to remain in the vicinity of, to keep working with, or even to keep living with, another person whose behavior is demoralizing, severely upsetting, or stress-producing. I emphasize this point because I keep finding people for whom it is not obvious at all. They confuse a practical question of costs and benefits with a moral imperative.

Without doubt, getting yourself, or that Difficult Person, out of the situation *may* be too costly in terms of unmet needs, thwarted ambitions, or pain to those you care about. You may like your job and have few alternatives anyway; you may need to get along with that boss or that manager in order to move into a better position in the company; you may feel a sense of responsibility for your patients even though you can't stand the director of the clinic. The fact that many times we are, to one degree or another, forced to come to terms with Difficult People is what makes learning how to cope with them useful and necessary.

25

Stress Management:
Averting the Evil Eye

Review by ETHEL ROSKIES

Edward A. Charlesworth and Ronald G. Nathan: *Stress Management: A Comprehensive Guide to Wellness*
F. J. McGuigan: *Calm Down: A Guide to Stress and Tension Control*
Martin Shaffer: *Life After Stress*
Charles F. Stroebel: *QR: The Quieting Reflex*

In recent years our traditional understanding of the causes of disease has been transformed by a powerful new concept: stress. From its humble origins as a laboratory term in the 1950s, stress has now become a shorthand symbol for explaining much of what ails us in the contemporary world, invoked to explain conditions as diverse as nail biting, smoking, homicide, suicide, cancer, and heart disease. From an anthropological perspective, stress serves the the same purpose in modern society as ghosts and evil spirits did in former times, making sense of various misfortunes and illnesses that otherwise might remain simply random games of chance (Hocking 1982). One sign of the success of stress in fulfilling this explanatory function is that it in turn has spawned a whole series of spin-offs: burn out, job stress, executive stress, corporate stress, marital stress, and so on.

It would be un-American to accept a new cause for disease without seeking to cure or control it. Thus, it is not surprising that the ranks of self-help manuals have recently been joined by books devoted to teaching us how to manage stress. Among the array of do-it-yourself guides to increasing sexual pleasure, building the body beautiful, and unlocking hidden mental and emotional capacities is a new crop of manuals devoted to taming the killer stress. The stress management guides under review here have all been published within the past year or so, and although the sales pitch varies from threats of dropping dead to promises of maximum well-being, all are dedicated to the premise that the individual can avert or diminish the potential harm of stress by using new, improved coping strategies.

Unfortunately, these stress management guides share one other important characteristic: Judged by the criteria established by *Contemporary Psychology* to evaluate self-help books (Rosen 1981), all are woefully inadequate. Explanations of why and how stress is harmful are simplistic and often inaccurate. Techniques for self-diagnosis are vague, inappropriate, and in some cases may even be harmful to individuals who should probably seek other types of help. Claims for the efficacy of the proposed "cures" are exaggerated and supported mainly by anecdotes and irrelevant statistics. Finally, even though all these manuals are clearly labeled as do-it-yourself treatment programs, not one has been tested in this format.

RESISTING THE FIRST REACTION

As a stress management researcher, my first reaction to this exhibition of apparent pseudoscience was a rapidly rising blood pressure. The temptation was to reduce my personal stress level by writing a scathing review that would once again demonstrate the superiority of pure science and scientists over popularizers. This outburst of moral indignation, however, could not be sustained for long. For even though it provided facile pleasure to take potshots at the many errors of fact and procedure contained in these manuals (it is misleading to infer that stress is the sole or major cause of coronary heart disease, as McGuigan does; it is inappropriate to use the Holmes and Rahe inventory of life changes as a diagnostic indicator of *individual* stress vulnerability, as Charlesworth and Nathan do; etc.), I was soon confronted by the realization that these self-help guides simply reflected many of the inadequacies characterizing current professional practice in the stress management area.

Treatment of stress problems as such is a relatively new area of therapeutic endeavor and lacks the conceptual sophistication and empirical data base already developed for other life-style problems such as alcoholism, obesity, and smoking. Practitioners for these better established disorders can and do complain of low rates of treatment success and high rates of dropout, but at least they are working within a framework of common diagnostic procedures and accepted criteria for evaluating whether a given treatment is a success or failure. Stress management, in contrast, remains uncharted territory in which each individual practitioner not only can propose his or her favorite treatment but also has the liberty to define the problems being treated under the stress rubric and to decide which evaluation criteria, if any, to use. Moreover, there are so few good treatment studies available that even the best clinician is forced, for want of anything better, to rely mainly on personal clinical experience and personal preferences.

With this background it is possible to reexamine these stress manuals from a less negative perspective. Given the reality of the millions of people who, rightly or wrongly, believe that they suffer from harmful stress effects, and given the fact that these manuals provide relatively low-cost and easily accessible forms of intervention, would it not be fairer to judge them by current standards of professional practice rather than by some not-yet-attained ideal? In an area where even the professionals have only minimal empirical support for their preferences, it is possible that the most that one can ask from a self-help manual is that it be not obviously misleading or harmful and that it hold some promise of doing good, at least to some people. A good manual by these criteria would provide the author's definition of the type of stress problem the manual was designed to handle, as well as procedures to permit the reader to decide whether or not he or she had problems that might be characterized by these terms. As far as the treatment itself is concerned, one would expect the proposed treatment to possess at least face validity and to be feasible in terms of the time, effort, and equipment involved. Finally, such a manual would contain a minimum of untruthful assertions, particularly those relating to the dire consequences likely to befall noncompliers and the miraculous benefits to be expected by true believers.

Even with these new criteria it was not possible to rank these books in terms of merit or even personal preference. There was no book that I could endorse wholeheartedly, yet even the least preferred of the four persisted in having some attractive features. For this reason I have simply divided the books into two general categories: McGuigan's and Stroebel's books focus on stress symptoms and disorders and emphasize the use of a single technique, whereas the books by Shaffer and by Charlesworth and Nathan view stress management mainly as a form of health promotion and suggest a wide variety of remedial techniques. The potential consumer, therefore, should consider—in addition to the specific strengths and weaknesses of a given volume—whether he or she primarily seeks relief from stress symptoms or enhancement of quality of life.

STRESS AND THE SINGLE TECHNIQUE

The most appealing characteristic of McGuigan's book is the obvious sincerity and fervor of its author. A long-time disciple of Edmund Jacobson, McGuigan was trained by this pioneer of progressive relaxation in the use of his procedures. McGuigan, in turn, has used Jacobson's technique to treat his own stress symptoms, has taught it both to his patients and to "healthy people," and is fervently convinced of its efficacy. Unfortunately, it is this same fervor that causes the author to overstate his case and that constitutes the major weakness of the book. The introductory chapter conveys the message in vivid newspaper clippings: Stress kills. Reading rapidly through the book, one is left with the impression that excessive tension produced by stress is the major cause of coronary heart disease, ulcers, high blood pressure, depression, fatigue, neuroses, and much more.

The potential benefits of learning the Jacobsonian form of progressive relaxation (those who would stray from the path of Jacobsonian orthodoxy and experiment with other forms of relaxation do so at their peril) are stated in equally strong terms. Although allusion is made to scientific studies, the evidence, except for one badly presented study, is anecdotal. Jacobson himself is cited as claiming that individuals who learn relaxation can add twenty years to their lives. There is speculation that Nelson Rockefeller might have attained his objective of living to 100 had he not canceled his appointment to learn relaxation in favor of a skiing trip. My favorite anecdote of all, however, concerns a patient whose daughter had just tried to commit suicide.

The precipitating events were that the daughter's husband had just abandoned her, and that the daughter had recently had an accident in which an individual in an oncoming car had been killed. The patient's husband was in the process of dying from a combination of coronary heart disease and diabetes. One of her sons was homosexual . . . while the other was dyslexic. . . . [In spite of these problems], she functions well in life, even carrying on her husband's business. She is well trained in Progressive Relaxation at this point, but what is equally important, she routinely practices her relaxation an hour a day. (pp. 92–93)

In spite of its obvious charm, I have placed McGuigan's book at the least preferred end of the continuum because I consider it potentially harmful. Although he makes passing references to the limits of self-taught relaxation as a treatment, the case for learning to reduce tension is so overstated that the high-risk individual for coronary heart disease, the hypertensive, and the depressive—to cite only three instances—might be misled into neglecting other forms of treatment. Even for individuals who do not present potentially dangerous physical and psychological problems, the treatment program proposed here is unlikely to be of much value because of its complexity and length. To learn Jacobsonian relaxation properly, one must buy an audio-casette tape and practice at least one hour a day for at least seventy days. McGuigan gives us no data on the rate of compliance even when the technique is professionally taught; but when used on a self-help basis, it would indeed be rare to find a person who could or would complete the program.

Stroebel's book shares many of the virtues and drawbacks of the McGuigan volume. Like McGuigan, Stroebel himself has experienced a serious stress symptom and has found the cure he proposes to be an effective personal remedy. Thus, he too speaks with obvious sincerity and fervor. Unfortunately, this book also shares the same reliance on scare tactics to motivate individuals to embark on the path to salvation. The introductory chapters are peppered by statistics on the 10 million Americans taking drugs for stress disorders and the 95 million experiencing stress symptoms. The book jacket goes further in claiming that the relaxation technique "might even save your life." In presenting the contrasting outcome of two cancer patients, one of whom learned the Quieting Response and one of whom did not (pp. 55–56), the inferred message is clear: Good patients live, and bad patients die.

Another objectionable characteristic of this book is the attempt to attain a scientific gloss by the use of unscientific methods. The author's personal theory for explaining stress mechanisms—the compass points of healthy and unhealthy stress—might appear scientific to the lay reader, but it is not backed by any empirical support. Furthermore, as a professor of psychiatry at a reputable medical school, the author should be well aware that the number of people adopting a given treatment procedure does not constitute proof of its efficacy.

It is particularly regrettable that Stroebel chose to weaken his case by overkill, because the volume contains a number of very positive features. For one, the author provides some procedures for self-diagnosis and, even more important, a list of conditions under which self-regulation training should not be used without prior medical consultation (pp. 131–32). For another, the author devotes considerable attention to the problems involved in learning new habits and provides detailed instructions for when and how to practice.

The most attractive feature of this volume is the treatment technique itself. Within the repertoire of stress management techniques, relaxation procedures have the strongest empirical support for their ability to produce positive psychological and physiological effects, and the specific relaxation technique advocated here is plausible, easy to learn, and easy to apply. It is unlikely that learning the Quieting Response will provide a magical cure for all one's stress problems, but it is likely that some people may learn the technique by reading the book and that it will do them good.

STRESS AND THE ROAD TO HEALTH

In moving from the previous two volumes to Shaffer's book, we also move from a world of illness to one of health. Now it is no longer a question of simply surviving stress. Instead, the successful user of this manual will learn to combat stress and fatigue, create a positive atmosphere at work, master relaxation skills, relieve tension in the home, and use stressful situations to *thrive*. Shaffer is listed as a clinical psychologist who consults with corporate executives, and his book reflects his clientele. This is a stress book written specifically for the upwardly mobile business executive who seeks to conquer stress in the same way he or she conquers other challenges.

There are a number of positive characteristics to this volume. First, dire warnings of the harmful effects of stress are kept to a bare minimum. Second, the explanation of what stress is goes beyond Selye's General Adaptation Syndrome and Holmes and Rahe's life events inventory to include a consideration of the individual's thoughts and feelings. Third, there is some attempt to provide methods for the individual to analyze his or her personal stress triggers and reactions. Finally, the author is far from doctrinaire in his proposed treatment program. In addition to listing six types of relaxation exercises and describing two in detail, he presents a smorgasbord of stress management techniques ranging from prescriptions for exercise, sleep, and nutrition to proposals for time management, communication skills, positive thinking, and changing the lighting and noise levels in one's office.

It is unlikely that this book will do anyone much harm, but I seriously doubt whether it will do anyone any good. The techniques for self-analysis are time consuming and difficult to follow. It is hard to imagine a Type A business person learning to relax by rapidly skimming through the relaxation advice. As for the rest, there is so much advice given and so few detailed instructions that even the most eager student might soon be discouraged by the over-abundance of what-to-do and the deficiency of how-to-do it.

The book I have left for last, that by Charlesworth and Nathan, is also the one that I had the most difficulty evaluating. In appearance, it is very different from the bright dust jacket and short, snappy text of the usual self-help manual. Here, in contrast, the reader is confronted by over 500 pages of gray printed matter, and the school text appearance is reinforced by the quizzes and suggestions for further reading at the end of each chapter. Paradoxically, however, this is the book that also contains the greatest number of step-by-step instructions, exercises, charts, and self-rating forms.

The text of this volume mirrors its appearance combining as it does a mélange of positive and negative features. For the first 200 pages or so, I had few quarrels with its contents. The goal of stress management (vs. stress elimination) is reasonable and well stated, and the explanation of stressors and how they work is the best of any of the four books under review. There is also a suitable warning for those for whom the use of a stress self-help manual is contraindicated. In terms of the proposed treatment, I have my doubts whether anyone can really learn a complex relaxation or scanning procedure by following written instructions, but at least those provided here are detailed and clear. With the chapter on life-change management, however, the authors begin to skate on very thin ice. What types of life changes produce what types of effects under what types of conditions constitutes a very controversial topic in stress research, and it is a misstatement of current work simply to assert that positive life changes are as potentially harmful as negative ones. It is even more irresponsible to claim that "if you totaled over 300 points on the Social Readjustment Rating Scale, your chances are over 80 percent of having a serious physical or emotional illness during the next two years" (p. 199).

The rest of this manual covers a broad territory. There are exercises for using desensitization as a stress reduction technique (though the example of a needle phobia seems a bit bizarre in the context of this book), followed by a discussion of Type A behavior and suggestions for its modification. From this, the book proceeds to a consideration of irrational beliefs and the use of self-talk to deal with anxiety and anger. Assertiveness training and time management are other topics treated. Finally, there is the obligatory bow to exercise, good nutrition, and weight control. Much useful information and many practical suggestions are included in this survey, but for this reader, at least, the overall impression was one of stimulus overload. It is a well-intentioned, reasonably well-written book, but not one that could legitimately be promoted as a do-it-yourself guide.

In summary, there is not a single one of these stress management guides that I can honestly recommend to those seeking to learn new coping techniques for the purpose either of reducing stress symptoms or simply of improving quality of life. The two books presenting an array of stress management techniques are too vague or complex to be used on a do-it-yourself basis, and the two single-technique manuals are simplistic. Moreover, all four books contain inaccurate and sometimes misleading statements. Forced to choose one book, I would guess that Stroebel's might do the most good, largely because his is a technique that conceivably could be learned by a reader alone. But even this would be a choice without conviction. If these four books constitute a fair sample of what is available—and, regrettably, I think they do—then a really good stress management guide remains to be written.

26

Out of the Habit Trap

STANTON PEELE

A man who had been drunk every night for many years arrived home late, bombed once again. The next morning his mother, with whom he was living, found him staring at himself in the mirror. He turned to her and announced: "I'm giving up drinking and, while I'm at it, smoking." Then he placed a pack of cigarettes and a bottle of beer on the mantelpiece. "What's that for?" his mother asked. He said: "That's so I'll know where to find a smoke or drink if I want one. Then I can just kill myself instead." He has touched neither cigarettes nor booze for nearly ten years.

A union official, noting that the price of cigarettes had risen yet again, put the extra nickel in the vending machine. A coworker laughed at him: "You'll pay whatever they ask." The smoker thought: "God, he's right; the tobacco company has me where it wants me." Then and there, he quit his three-pack-a-day habit forever.

Talk-show host Merv Griffin watched a comedian imitating him— as a fat man. The comic had stuffed himself with padding and Griffin could not bear the caricature. He put himself on a diet and exercise program, and soon showed off his new, thin self to his audience.

Stories like these seldom make the newspapers; for that matter, people who quit their long-standing habits by themselves often go unrecognized by scientific studies. Instead, we hear dire stories about people who can't seem to quit, and gloomy statistics on relapse rates. Among people in therapy to lose weight, stop smoking, kick a drug or drink addiction, as few as 5 percent actually make it.

But here's the irony and the hope: Self-cure can work, and depending on someone else to cure you usually does not.

This is the case for addictions like cigarette smoking and alcoholism, as well as for some more-complex habits. Obesity, for example, may involve compulsive overeating—an addiction to food that some thin people also struggle with for years. But genetics and a lifetime of inactivity and bad eating habits also play a role. Whatever the cause, though, losing weight takes a major change in life-style—and the people who do it best are those who do it on their own.

Therapists tend to fail their clients by undermining self-reliance; they encourage people to rely upon others for cure, and to give up responsibility for their own behavior. But because therapy works so rarely, many researchers have come to view addictions as almost impossible to beat. And that mistake makes habits harder to break.

Many have begun to think of addiction as an exclusively biological process—one that cannot be overcome by psychological effort or will power. In this view, alcoholics have a "disease," a "genetic susceptibility" to liquor. Obese people have a preordained weight level. Smokers are hooked on nicotine, and their bodies cannot tolerate a depletion of the drug.

All of these theories stem from the grandfather addiction of them all, heroin. Everyone knows the image: the suffering heroin addict, inexorably bound to a physiological dependence. The penalty for withdrawal is intolerable agony, so the addict increases the doses until death. Remember *The Man with the Golden Arm*?

For more than ten years, I have been conducting interviews with all sorts of addicts and reviewing the research on all kinds of addiction. Addiction, I've found, may be affected by biological factors, but they are not enough to explain it. True, addiction is caused partly by the pharmacological action of the drug (if it's a drug addiction), but also by the person's social situation, attitudes and expectations. Even people who are constitutionally sensitive to a substance can control their use of it, if they believe that they can.

There is now good evidence for these heretical assertions. The most compelling statistics come from the success of people who cure themselves without therapy:

> University of Kentucky sociologist John O'Donnell, analyzing a national survey of drug use among men in their twenties, found that only 31 percent of the men who had ever used heroin had touched the drug in the previous year.
> Similarly, when American soldiers who had used heroin in Vietnam returned home after the war, over 90 percent of them gave the drug up without difficulty. Addiction experts predicted an epidemic of heroin abuse by the vets, but it never materialized. Washington University psychologist Lee Robins found that even among men who had truly been addicted in Vietnam, only 14 percent became dependent on narcotics in the U.S.
> Harvard psychiatrist George Vaillant found that more than half of the one-time alcohol abusers in a group of several hundred men

had ceased problem drinking (the men had been interviewed over a period of 40 years).

Social psychologist Stanley Schachter at Columbia University, interviewing members of two different communities, discovered that about half of those who had once been obese or hooked on cigarettes had lost weight or quit smoking. The formerly overweight people said they had lost an average of 35 pounds and kept it off for an average of 11 years.

Some of these statistics, admittedly, are open to question. When you're asking people to talk about how they've changed over the past several years, they may paint an excessively rosy picture of their ability to improve themselves. But even if the percentages are inflated, the evidence is still good that people can change for the better, far more than they have been given credit for.

Often, people simply outgrow their bad habits. Sociologist Charles Winick of City College of New York has examined the lives of drug addicts. Many, in Winick's words, "mature out" as they get older. Long-term studies of alcoholics and smokers show the same pattern. Some people even outgrow their teenage cravings for Twinkies and sugar "fixes."

WHY BIOLOGY IS NOT DESTINY

There's other intriguing evidence that hammers away at the theory of the "biological trap" of addiction. For example, most addicts, of all kinds, regularly overcome withdrawal pangs. As Harvard psychiatrist Norman Zinberg and his associates discovered, heroin addicts often cut down or quit their heroin use on their own. Alcoholics often don't need to "dry out" in a hospital, but frequently just go on the wagon with no particular anguish. Practically every cigarette smoker stops at some point—for anywhere from a few days to years. (Orthodox Jews quit weekly for the Sabbath.)

It is actually long *after* the phase of "withdrawal pangs" that most addicts slide back into their habits. When they do backslide, it is not because of a physiological craving as much as it's stress at work or home, or social pressures ("Come on Mort, join us . . . one for the road. . .").

It's also a myth that a single experience of a drug can catch you chemically (hence the "first fix is free" strategy of drug dealers). Most people have to learn to become addicted. As Zinberg found, hospital patients given strong doses of narcotics every day for ten days or more—doses higher than those street addicts take—virtually always leave the hospital without even a twinge of craving for the drug.

For an addiction to develop, the pharmacological effects of a drug have to produce an experience that a person with certain needs, in a certain situation, will welcome. When the need is great enough, people can become "addicted" to almost anything. Addicts may switch not only from one chemical substance to another, but from a chemical to a social "high." Vaillant reports that former alcoholics often shift to new dependencies—candy, prayer, compulsive work, hobbies, gambling.

Addiction also depends largely on people's beliefs about what a substance will do to them. Psychologist Alan Marlatt at the University of Washington found that alcoholics will behave drunkenly when they only *think* they are drinking liquor—but when they're actually drinking tonic and lime juice. He also found the reverse: when alcoholics drink alcohol, but believe it's tonic and lime juice, they don't behave drunkenly.

Despite such evidence, the search has continued, unsuccessfully, for a single physiological factor that might be the underlying cause of all addictions. The prime candidates have been endorphins, morphinelike substances found to occur naturally in the body. Some pharmacologists speculated that people are susceptible to drug addiction if their bodies don't produce a normal level of endorphins. Maybe all addictive involvements elevate your endorphin levels, the theory went.

When it turned out that people could even become addicted to serious jogging, biochemical studies of runners were also done. Sure enough, jogging was found to boost endorphin levels. But endorphins failed to explain the difference between those who stop running when they're injured or it's inconvenient and those who behave like true addicts.

One very lean man, who insisted on running hard every day regardless of inclement weather, family obligations, or his own injuries, explained his addiction to me this way: "I feel great every day I run; but I'm afraid I'll balloon back up to 200 pounds the moment I quit." His desire to run was more than chemical; he saw running as a magical talisman against returning to his former self.

The best explanation of addiction takes both mind and body into account. The effects of a substance can't be isolated from the context of human experience. Thinking of addiction solely as a "disease" or a "chemical dependency" ignores the power of the mind in generating the need for the drug—and in breaking that need.

The cycle of addiction begins as a response to a stressful problem (getting drunk to avoid dealing with a bad job, running to get away from a bad marriage) or as an attempt to produce certain feelings (as Harvard psychologist David McClelland and his coworkers showed, many men feel a sense of power while drunk).

These feelings, in turn, lead into a cycle that makes the addiction harder to escape. For example, a man who abuses his family when he is drunk may feel disgusted with himself when he sobers up—so he gets drunk again to boost his self-esteem. Soon the addictive experience feeds on itself. It becomes central to the person's life, and it becomes a trap.

THE STEPS TO SELF-CURE

How does anyone manage to kick a habit after years of living with it? To find out, San Francisco sociologists Dan Waldorf and Patrick Biernacki interviewed heroin addicts who quit on their own, and sociologist Barry Tuchfield at Texas Christian University talked with some 50 alcoholics who recovered without therapy or AA. And in conducting our own field research with addicts of all types, my associate Archie Brodsky and I have outlined the critical steps in self-cure.

The key word is *self*: taking charge of your own problem. Some psychologists call this self-mastery; others, self-efficacy; others, the belief in free will. It translates into three components necessary for change: an urge to quit, the belief that you *can* quit and the realization that *you* must quit—no one can do it for you. Once you have quit, the rewards of living without the addiction must be great enough to keep you free of it.

The stages of successful self-cure are remarkably similar, regardless of the addiction:

1. *Accumulated unhappiness about the addiction.* Before a change can take place, unhappiness with the addiction has to build to a point where it can't be denied or rationalized away. This phase of the process of self-cure, to use Vaillant's analogy, is like the incubation of a chick. Just because the chick hatches, rather abruptly at that, doesn't mean it happened spontaneously. A lot of changes go on first beneath the outer shell.

   To break an addiction, you must believe the rewards you'll get (from not smoking, from exercising and losing weight, from cutting down on or giving up alcohol or drugs) will surpass what you got from the habit. Heroin addicts who "mature out" typically explain to interviewers that a life of hustling, prison and the underworld was no longer worth it.

2. *A moment of truth.* An alcoholic pregnant woman told Tuchfield: "I was drinking beer one morning and felt the baby quiver. I poured the rest of the beer out and I said, 'God forgive me, I'll never drink another drop.'" Another woman who had quit (and resumed) smoking several times found herself sorting through the butts in an ashtray late one night, desperate for a smoke: "I saw

a snapshot of myself in my mind's eye," she told me, "and I was disgusted." She has not been a smoker for fifteen years now.

Most ex-addicts can pinpoint a moment at which they "hatched" from the addiction and left it behind. It is impossible to distinguish the real moment of truth from the addict's previous vows to quit, except in retrospect. But it is just as foolish to disregard these reports altogether. Because they are part of such a high percentage of successful cures, they seem to have an important meaning to the ex-addict.

Epiphanies that work can be brought on by dramatic, catastrophic events: an alcoholic becomes falling-down-drunk in front of someone he admires, or a cigarette smoker watches a friend die of lung cancer. But most moments of truth seem to be inspired by trivial remarks or chance occurrences. Either way, they work because they crystallize the discrepancy between the addict's self-image and the reality.

3. *Changing patterns.* People successful at self-cure usually make active changes in their environment—they may move away from a drug culture, become more involved in work, make new friends. But some people break a habit without changing their usual patterns. The man whose story began this article—the heavy drinker and smoker—was a musician who continued to spend nearly all his nights in bars. He wrapped himself in a new identity—"I'm a nondrinking, nonsmoking musician"—that protected him from his familiar vices.

4. *Changing the identity of addict.* Once former addicts gain more from their new lives than from the old ways—feeling better, getting along with people better, working better, having more fun—the lure of the addiction pales. One long-time heroin addict quoted in the book *High on Life* quit the drug in his thirties, went to school and got a good job. Later, during a hospital stay, he was given an unlimited prescription for Percodan, a synthetic narcotic. He marveled at how he had no desire to continue the drugs when his pain stopped: "I had a different relationship with people, with work, with the things that had become important to me. I would have had to work at relapsing."

5. *Dealing with relapses.* One of the problems with biological theories of addiction is the image of imminent relapse it creates for the addict—the idea that one slip is a return to permanent addiction. Many of Schachter's ex-smokers admit having a puff at a party. Half of those ex-addicts who had been in Vietnam did try heroin at home, Lee Robins found, but few returned to a full-fledged addiction. The addict who has successfully modified his or her life catches the slip, and controls it.

The steps out of addiction, therefore, are: to find a superior alternative to the habit you want to break; find people who can help you puncture your complacent defenses; change whatever you need to in your life to accommodate your new, healthier habits; celebrate your new, nonaddicted image whenever you can.

The common feature in all these steps is *your* action, *your* beliefs. Self-curers often use many of the same techniques for breaking out of an addiction that formal treatment programs do. But motivated people who have arrived at these techniques on their own are more successful than those in therapy.

Why should this be? One possibility, of course, is that the people who go for professional help are the hard cases—those who have tried to change on their own and found it impossible. People may try to quit smoking a dozen times, or lose and regain a few hundred pounds, before deciding they need help. Therapy often represents only one attempt at cure, whereas people usually come to grips with a problem over a period of years.

But I also think that therapy itself may inadvertently impede cure, by lowering the addict's sense of self-mastery and self-control. In turning to therapy, addicts unwittingly acknowledge that they are powerless to break the addiction. Thus medical supervision of drug withdrawal, for example, can actually inflate the difficulty of doing something that drug addicts accomplish repeatedly on their own.

Therapy can be especially demoralizing when it's based on the notion that addiction stems from an unchangeable biological weakness. Such a philosophy can make quitting even more difficult. Sociologist Charles Winick observed two decades ago that adolescents who failed to mature out of heroin addiction were those who "decide they are 'hooked,' make no effort to abandon addiction and give in to what they regard as inevitable."

We now see why that discovery applies to the general problem of breaking self-destructive habits. Only death and taxes, it now appears, are truly inevitable. Everything else is negotiable—and open for improvement.

References

Abram, H. S. 1965. Adaptation to open heart surgery: A psychiatric study of responses to the threat of death. *American Journal of Psychiatry* 122:659–67.

Ader, R. 1979. Comments at a symposium on "Experimental Ulcer Produced by Behavioral Factors." Los Angeles, Center of Ulcer Research and Education, October.

Ader, R. and L. J. Grota. 1973. Adrenocortical mediation of the effects of early life experiences. *Progress in Brain Research* 39:395–405.

Adler, A. 1930. Individual psychology. In C. Murchison, ed., *Psychologies of 1930*. Worcester, Mass.: Clark University Press.

Alker, H. A. 1967. Cognitive controls and the Haan-Kroeber model of ego functioning. *Journal of Abnormal Psychology* 72:434–40.

Allee, W. C. 1951. *Cooperation Among Animals*. New York: Henry Schuman.

Allport, G. W. 1955. *Becoming: Basic Considerations for A Psychology of Personality*. New Haven: Yale University Press.

Allport, G. W. and P. E. Vernon. 1933. *Studies in Expressive Movement*. New York: Macmillan.

Andrew, J. M. 1970. Recovery from surgery, with and without preparatory instruction, for three coping styles. *Journal of Personality and Social Psychology* 15:223–26.

Andrews, G., C. Tennant, D. M. Hewson, and G. E. Vaillant. 1978. Life event stress, social support, coping style, and risk of psychological impairment. *Journal of Nervous and Mental Disorders* 166:307–16.

Angyal, A. 1941. *Foundations For A Science of Personality*. New York: Commonwealth Fund.

Ansbacher, H. L. and R. R. Ansbacher, eds. 1956. *The Individual Psychology of Alfred Adler*. New York: Basic Books.

Anticaglia, J. R. and A. Cohen. 1974. Extra-auditory effects of noise as a health hazard. In P. M. Insel and R. H. Moos, eds., *Health and the Social Environment*. Toronto: Heath.

Antonovsky, A. 1974. Conceptual and methodological problems in the study of resistance resources and stressful life events. In B. S. Dohrenwend and B. P. Dohrenwend, eds., *Stressful Life Events: Their Nature and Effects*. New York: Wiley.

Asch, S. E. 1952. *Social Psychology*. Englewood Cliffs, N.J.: Prentice-Hall.

Auerbach, S. M. 1973. Trait-state anxiety and adjustment to surgery. *Journal of Consulting and Clinical Psychology* 44:809–18.

Auerbach, S. M., P. C. Kendall, H. F. Cuttler, and N. R. Levitt. 1976. Anxiety, locus of control, type of preparatory information, and adjustment to dental surgery. *Journal of Consulting and Clinical Psychology* 44:809–18.

Averill, J. R. 1968. Grief: Its nature and significance. *Psychological Bulletin* 70:721–28.

—— 1973. Personal control over aversive stimuli and its relationship to stress. *Psychological Bulletin* 80:286–303.

—— 1979. The functions of grief. In C. E. Izard, ed., *Emotions in Personality and Psychopathology.* New York: Plenum.

Averill, J. R. and E. M. Opton, Jr. 1968. Psychophysiological assessment: Rationale and problems. In P. McReynolds, ed., *Advances in Psychological Assessment,* 1:265–88. Palo Alto, Calif.: Science and Behavior Books.

Averill, J. R. and M. Rosenn. 1972. Vigilant and nonvigilant coping strategies and psychophysiological stress reactions during the anticipation of electric shock. *Journal of Personality and Social Psychology* 23:128–41.

Bales, R. F. 1951. *Interaction Process Analysis: A Method for the Study of Small Groups.* Reading, Mass.: Addison-Wesley Press.

—— 1954. In conference. *Harvard Business Review* 32:44–50.

Ball, T. S. and R. E. Vogler. 1971. Uncertain pain and the pain of uncertainty. *Perceptual Motor Skills* 33:1195–1203.

Bandura, A. 1977. Self-efficacy: Toward a unified theory of behavioral change. *Psychological Review* 89:191–215.

Bandura, A. and K. Simon. 1977. The role of proximal intentions in self-regulation of refractory behavior. *Cognitive Therapy and Research* 1:177–93.

Barnett, S. A. 1960. Social behaviour among tame rats and among wild-white hybrids. *Proceedings of the Zoological Society of London* 134:611–21.

—— 1963. *The Rat: A Study in Behaviour.* Chicago: Aldine.

—— 1964. Social stress. In J. D. Carthy and C. L. Duddington, eds., *Viewpoints in Biology,* 3:170–218. London: Butterworths.

Barrow, J. H., Jr. 1955. Social behavior in fresh-water fish and its effect on resistance to trypanosomes. *Proceedings of the National Academy of Science* 41:676–79.

Bartrop, R. W., E. Luckhurst, L. Lazarus, L. G. Kiloh, and R. Penny. 1977. Depressed lymphocyte function after bereavement. *Lancet* 1:834–36.

Basowitz, H., H. Persky, S. J. Korchin, and R. R. Grinker. 1955. *Anxiety and Stress.* New York: McGraw-Hill.

Baum, A., R. J. Gatchel, R. Fleming, and C. R. Lake. 1981. Chronic and acute stress associated with the Three Mile Island accident and decontamination: Preliminary findings of a longitudinal study. Technical report submitted to the U.S. Nuclear Regulatory Commission.

Baum, A. and S. Valins. 1977. *Architecture and Social Behavior: Psychological Studies in Social Density.* Hillsdale, N.J.: Lawrence Erlbaum.

Beck, A. J. 1967. *Depression: Clinical, Experimental, and Theoretical Aspects.* New York: Hoeber.

Becker, E. 1973. *The Denial of Death.* New York: Free Press.

Becker, H. S. 1967. History, culture and subjective experience: An exploration of the social bases of drug-induced experiences. *Journal of Health and Social Behavior* 8:163–76.

Beecher, H. K. 1955. The powerful placebo. *Journal of the American Medical Association* 159:1602–06.

—— 1956. Relationship of significance of wound to pain experienced. *Journal of the American Medical Association* 161:1609–13.

—— 1957. The measurement of pain. *Pharmacology Review* 9:59–209.

Beiser, M., J. Feldman, and C. Engelhoff. 1972. Assets and affects. *Archives of General Psychiatry* 27:545–49.

Bem, D. 1970. *Beliefs, Attitudes and Human Affairs*. Belmont, Calif.: Brooks/Cole.

Benner, P., E. Roskies, and R. S. Lazarus. 1980. Stress and coping under extreme conditions. In J. E. Dimsdale, ed., *Survivors, Victims, and Perpetrators: Essays on the Nazi Holocaust*, pp. 219–58. Washington, D.C.: Hemisphere.

Benoit, J., I. Assenmacher, and E. Brard. 1955. Evolution testiculaire du canard domestique maintenu à l'obscurité totale pendant une longue durée. *Comptes-Rendus Academie des Sciences* 241 (Paris):251–53.

—— 1956. Etude de l'évolution testiculaire du canard domestique soumis très jeune à un éclairement artificiel permanent pendant deux anx. *Comptes-Rendus Academie des Sciences* 242 (Paris):3113–15.

Benson, H. 1975. *The Relaxation Response*. New York: Avon.

Bentley, E., ed. 1952. *Naked Masks: Five Plays by Luigi Pirandello*. New York: Dutton.

Bergmann, T. (in collaboration with A. Freud). 1958. *Children in the Hospital*. New York: International Universities Press.

Berkman, B. 1977. Community mental health services for the elderly. *Community Mental Health Review* 2:1, 3–9.

Berkman, L. F. and S. L. Syme. 1979. Social networks, host resistance, and mortality: A nine-year follow-up study of Alameda County residents. *American Journal of Epidemiology* 109:186–204.

Bernard, C. 1879. *Leçons sur les phénomènes de la vie commune aux animaux et aux végétaux*, vol. 2. Paris: Baillière.

Bernardis, L. and F. Skelton. 1963. Effect of crowding on hypertension and growth in rats bearing regenerating adrenals; *and* Effect of gentling on development of adrenal regeneration hypertension in immature female rats. *Proceedings of the Society for Experimental Biology and Medicine* 113:952–57.

Bierman, H. R. 1956. Parent participation program in pediatric oncology: A preliminary report. *Journal of Chronic Diseases* 3:632–39.

Birnbaum, R. M. 1964. Autonomic reaction to threat and confrontation conditions of psychological stress. Ph.D. dissertation, University of California, Berkeley.

Bishop, L. F., and P. Reichert. 1969. The psychological impact of the coronary care unit. *Psychosomatics* 10:189–92.

Blake, K. 1976. Vitamin C: The case looks stronger, but. . . . *Pastimes* (Air-shuttle edition) (Eastern Airlines) March.

Block, J. 1971. *Lives Through Time*. Berkeley, Calif.: Bancroft Books.

Boklage, M. G. 1970. ICU training program. *Hospitals* 44:78–80.

Borus, J. F. 1973a. Re-entry I. *Archives of General Psychiatry* 28:501–06.

—— 1973b. Re-entry II: "Making it" back in the states. *American Journal of Psychiatry* 130:850–54.

—— 1973c. Re-entry III: Facilitating healthy readjustment in Vietnam veterans. *Psychiatry* 36:428–39.

Bourne, P. G. 1970. *Men, Stress, and Vietnam.* Boston: Little, Brown.

Bourne, P. G., R. M. Rose, and J. W. Mason. 1967. Urinary 17-OHCS levels. *Archives of General Psychiatry* 17:104–10.

Bowers, K. G. 1968. Pain, anxiety, and perceived control. *Journal of Consulting and Clinical Psychology* 32:596–602.

Bowlby, J. 1961. Process of mourning. *International Journal of Psychoanalysis* 42:317–40.

—— 1969. *Attachment and Loss,* vol. 1: *Attachment.* London: Hogarth Press.

—— 1973. *Attachment and Loss,* vol. 2: *Separation: Anxiety and Anger.* London: Hogarth Press.

—— 1980. *Attachment and Loss,* vol. 3: *Loss: Sadness and Depression.* London: Hogarth Press.

Bozeman, M. F., C. E. Orbach, and A. M. Sutherland. 1955. Psychological impact of cancer and its treatment, III. The adaptation of mothers to the threatened loss of their children through leukemia: Part I. *Cancer* 8:1–19.

Bramson, R. M. 1981. *Coping With Difficult People.* New York: Doubleday.

Breen, D. 1975. *The Birth of a First Child: Towards an Understanding of Femininity.* London: Tavistock.

Breger, L. 1967. Functions of dreams. *Journal of Abnormal Psychology Monographs,* 72.

Brehm, S. 1976. *The Application of Social Psychology to Clinical Practice.* New York: Wiley.

Breuer, J. and S. Freud. 1955. *Studies in Hysteria.* Standard Edition, 2. London: Hogarth Press. (Originally published in 1895).

Broadbent, D. E. 1971. *Decision and Stress.* New York: Academic Press.

—— 1978. The current state of noise research: Reply to Poulton. *Psychological Bulletin* 85:1052–67.

Brodsky, C. M. 1977. Long-term work stress in teachers and prison guards. *Journal of Occupational Medicine* 19:133–38.

Bromet, E. 1980. Three Mile Island: Mental health findings. Pittsburgh, Western Psychiatric Institute and Clinic and the University of Pittsburgh.

Bronson, F. H. and B. E. Eleftheriou. 1965a. Adrenal response to fighting in mice: Separation of physical and psychological causes. *Science* 147:627–28.

—— 1965b. Relative effects of fighting on bound and unbound corticosterone in mice. *Proceedings of the Society for Experimental Biology and Medicine* 118:146–49.

Bronzaft, A. L. and D. P. McCarthy. 1975. The effects of elevated train noise on reading ability. *Environment and Behavior* 7:517–27.

Brown, A. H. 1947. Water shortage in the desert. In E. F. Adolph, ed., *Physiology of Man in the Desert,* pp. 136–59. New York: Interscience.

Brown, B. B. 1977. *Stress and the Art of Biofeedback.* New York: Bantam.

Brown, C. C., ed. 1967. *Methods in Psychophysiology.* Baltimore: Williams and Wilkins.

Brown, G. W. 1974. Meaning, measurement, and stress of life events. In B. S. Dohrenwend and B. P. Dohrenwend, eds., *Stressful Life Events: Their Nature and Effects.* New York: Wiley.

Brown, G. W. and T. Harris. 1978. *Social Origins of Depression: A Study of Psychiatric Disorders in Women.* London: Tavistock Publications.

Browne, I. and T. Hackett. Unpublished data.

Buhler, C. 1961. Meaningful living in mature years. In R. W. Kleemeier, ed., *Aging and Leisure*. New York: Oxford.

Byrne, D. 1964. Repression-sensitization as a dimension of personality. In B. A. Maher, ed., *Progress in Experimental Personality Research*. 1:169–220. New York: Academic Press.

Calhoun, J. B. 1949. A method for self-control of population growth among mammals living in the wild. *Science* 109:333–35.

—— 1962. Population density and social pathology. *Scientific American* 206:139–48.

Campbell, D. T. and J. C. Stanley. 1966. *Experimental and Quasi-Experimental Designs for Research*. Chicago: Rand McNally.

Cannon, W. B. 1929, 1953. *Bodily Changes in Pain, Hunger, Fear, and Rage*. Boston: C. T. Branford.

—— 1939, 1963. *The Wisdom of the Body*. New York: Norton.

—— 1942. "Voodoo" death. *American Anthropologist* 44:169–81.

Caplan, G. and M. Killilea, eds. 1976. *Support Systems and Mutual Help*. New York: Grune & Stratton.

Carpenter, C. R. 1958. Territoriality: A review of concepts and problems. In A. Roe and G. G. Simpson, eds., *Behavior and Evolution*, pp. 224–50. New Haven: Yale University Press.

Carter, H. and P. C. Glick. 1976. *Marriage and Divorce: A Social and Economic Study*. Rev. ed. Cambridge: Harvard University Press.

Cassell, J. 1976. The contribution of the social environment to host resistance. *American Journal of Epidemiology* 104:107–23.

Chambers, L. W., W. O. Spitzer, G. B. Hill, and B. E. Helliwell. 1976. Underreporting of cancer in medical surveys: A source of systematic error in cancer research. *American Journal of Epidemiology* 104:141–45.

Chertok, L. 1959. *Psychosomatic Methods in Painless Childbirth*. New York: Pergamon Press.

Chesney, M. A. and R. H. Rosenman. 1980. Strategies for modifying Type A behavior. *Consultant* 20:216–22.

Chitty, D. 1958. Self-regulation of numbers through changes in viability. *Cold Spring Harbor Symposium of Quantitative Biology* 22:277–80.

Chodoff, P. 1959. Adjustment to disability: Some observations on patients with multiple sclerosis. *Journal of Chronic Diseases* 9:653–70.

Christian, J. J. and D. E. Davis. 1956. The relationship between adrenal weight and population status of urban Norway rats. *Journal of Mammalogy* 37:475–86.

Christian, J. J., V. Flyger, and D. E. Davis. 1960. Factors in mass mortality of a herd of Sika deer (*Cervus nippon*). *Chesapeake Science* 1:79–95.

Christian, J. J. and H. O. Williamson. 1958. Effect of crowding on experimental granuloma formation in mice. *Proceedings of the Society for Experimental Biology and Medicine* 99:385–87.

Chu, C. C. 1966. Fear arousal, efficacy, and imminency. *Journal of Personality and Social Psychology* 4:517–24.

Clayton, P. J. 1974. Mortality and morbidity in the first year of widowhood. *Archives of General Psychiatry* 30:747–50.

Cleary, P. J. 1974. Life events and disease: A review of methodology and findings. *Reports from the Laboratory for Clinical Stress Research,* No. 37, Departments of Medicine and Psychiatry, Karolinska Sjukhuset, Stockholm, November.

Cobb, B., R. L. Clark, C. McGuire, and C. D. Howe. 1954. Patient-responsible delay of treatment in cancer. *Cancer* 7:920–26.

Cobb, S. 1976. Social support as a moderator of life stress. *Psychosomatic Medicine* 38:300–14.

Coehlo, G. V., D. A. Hamburg, and J. E. Adams, eds. 1974. *Coping and Adaptation.* New York: Basic Books.

Cofer, C. N. and M. H. Appley. 1964. *Motivation: Theory and Research.* New York: Wiley.

Cohen, A. 1973. Industrial noise and medical, absence, and accident record data on exposed workers. In W. D. Ward, ed., *Proceedings of the International Congress on Noise as a Public Health Problem.* Washington, D.C., GPO.

Cohen, A. K. 1955. *Delinquent Boys.* Glencoe, Ill.: Free Press.

Cohen, F. 1975. Psychological preparation, coping, and recovery from surgery. Ph.D. dissertation, University of California, Berkeley.

—— 1979. Personality, stress, and the development of physical illness. In G. C. Stone, F. Cohen, N. E. Adler, and Associates, *Health Psychology—A Handbook,* pp. 77–111. San Francisco, Jossey-Bass.

—— 1981. Stress and bodily illness. *Psychiatric Clinics of North America* 4:269–86.

Cohen, F., M. J. Horowitz, R. S. Lazarus, R. H. Moos, L. N. Robins, R. M. Rose, and M. Rutter. 1980. *Report of the Panel on Psychosocial Assets and Modifiers of Stress, Committee for Research on Stress in Health and Disease.* Institute of Medicine, National Academy of Sciences, June.

Cohen, F. and R. S. Lazarus. 1973. Active coping processes, coping dispositions, and recovery from surgery. *Psychosomatic Medicine* 35:375–89.

—— 1979. Coping with the stresses of illness. In G. C. Stone, F. Cohen, N. E. Adler, and Associates, *Health Psychology—A Handbook,* pp. 217–54. San Francisco: Jossey-Bass.

Cohen, S. 1978. Environmental load and the allocation of attention. In A. Baum, J. E. Singer, and S. Valins, eds., *Advances in Environmental Psychology.* Hillsdale, N.J.: Erlbaum.

Cohen, S., G. W. Evans, D. S. Krantz, and D. Stokols. 1980. Physiological, motivational, and cognitive effects of aircraft noise on children: Moving from the laboratory to the field. *American Psychologist* 35:231–43.

Cohen, S., D. C. Glass, and S. Phillips. 1979. Environment and health. In H. E. Freeman, S. Levine, and L. G. Reeder, eds., *Handbook of Medical Sociology.* Englewood Cliffs, N.J.: Prentice-Hall.

Cohen, S., D. C. Glass, and J. E. Singer. 1973. Apartment noise, auditory discrimination, and reading ability in children. *Journal of Experimental Social Psychology* 9:407–22.

Cohen, S. and A. Lezak. 1977. Noise and inattentiveness to social cues. *Environment and Behavior* 9:559–72.

Cohen, S. and G. McKay. 1980. Social support, stress and the buffer hypothesis. University of Oregon, manuscript.

Cohen, S. and N. Weinstein. 1981. Nonauditory effects of noise on behavior and health. *Journal of Social Issues* 37:36–70.

Coleman, J. C., J. N. Butcher, and R. C. Carson. 1980. *Abnormal Psychology and Modern Life*. 6th ed. Glenview, Ill.: Scott, Foresman.

Colligan, M. J., M. J. Smith, and J. J. Hurrell. 1977. Occupational incidence rates of mental health disorders. *Journal of Human Stress* 3:34–39.

Collins, D. L., A. Baum, and J. E. Singer. 1983. Coping with chronic stress at Three Mile Island: Psychological and biochemical evidence. *Health Psychology* 2:149–66.

Coover, G. D., L. Goldman, and S. Levine. 1971. Plasma corticosterone increases produced by extinction of operant behavior in rats. *Physiology and Behavior* 6:261–63.

Cormier, W. H. and L. S. Cormier. 1979. *Interviewing Strategies for Helpers: A Guide to Assessment, Treatment and Evaluation*. Monterey, Ca.: Brooks/Cole.

Coser, R. L. 1959. Some social functions of laughter. *Human Relations* 12:171–82.

Cottrell, N. B. and S. W. Epley. 1977. Affiliation, social comparison and socially mediated stress reduction. In J. M. Suls and R. L. Miller, eds., *Social Comparison Processes: Theoretical and Empirical Perspectives*. New York: Wiley, Halstead Press.

Cousins, N. 1976. Anatomy of an illness (As perceived by the patient). *New England Journal of Medicine* 295:1458–63.

—— 1979. *Anatomy of An Illness As Perceived by the Patient: Reflections on Healing and Regeneration*. New York: Norton.

Cox, P. R. and J. R. Ford. 1964. The mortality of widows shortly after widowhood. *Lancet* 1:163–64.

Cox, T. 1978. *Stress*. Baltimore: University Park Press.

Craffey, R. 1960. The cardiac pacemaker. *Massachusetts General Hospital Nursing Alumnae Quarterly* 1:8–11.

Curry-Lindahl, K. 1963. New theory on a fabled exodus. *Natural History* 122:46–53.

D'Amato, M. E. and W. E. Gumenik. 1960. Some effects of immediate versus randomly delayed shock on an instrumental response and cognitive processes. *Journal of Abnormal and Social Psychology* 60:64–67.

Dameshek, W. and F. Gunz. 1958. *Leukemia*. New York: Grune and Stratton.

Davenport-Slack, B. and C. H. Boylan. 1974. Psychological correlates of childbirth pain. *Psychosomatic Medicine* 36:215–23.

Davis, D. E. and C. P. Read. 1958. Effect of behavior on development of resistance in trichinosis. *Proceedings of the Society for Experimental Biology and Medicine* 99:269–72.

Davis, F. 1963. *Passage Through Crisis: Polio Victims and Their Families*. Indianapolis: Bobbs-Merrill.

Davis, M., E. R. Eshelman, and M. McKay. 1982. *The Relaxation and Stress Reduction Workbook*. 2d ed. Oakland, Ca.: New Harbinger.

Davison, G. C. and J. M. Neale. 1982. *Abnormal Psychology: An Experimental Clinical Approach*. 3d ed. New York: Wiley.

Davison, G. C. and S. Valins. 1969. Maintenance of self-attributed and drug-attributed behavior change. *Journal of Personality and Social Psychology* 11:25–33.

Deevey, E. S. 1960. The hare and the haruspex: A cautionary tale. *American Scientist* 48:415–29.

DeLong, D. R. 1970. Individual differences in patterns of anxiety arousal, stress-relevant information and recovery from surgery. Ph.D. dissertation, University of California, Los Angeles.

—— 1971. Individual differences in patterns of anxiety arousal, stress-relevant information, and recovery from surgery. *Dissertation Abstracts International* 32:554.

Dembo, T., G. L. Leviton, and B. A. Wright. 1956. Adjustment to misfortune—A problem of social psychological rehabilitation. *Artificial Limbs* 3:4–62.

DeMeyer, J. 1967. The environment of the intensive care unit. *Nursing Forum* 6:262–72.

Derogatis, L. R., R. S. Lipman, L. Covi, and K. Rickles. 1971. Neurotic symptom dimensions. *Archives of General Psychiatry* 24:454–64.

Derogatis, L., K. Rickles, and A. Rock. 1976. The SCL-90 and the MMPI: A step in the validation of a new self-report scale. *British Journal of Psychiatry* 128:280–89.

Deutsch, C. P. 1964. Auditory discrimination and learning: Social factors. *The Merrill-Palmer Quarterly of Behavior and Development* 10:277–96.

Dick-Read, G. 1959. *Childbirth Without Fear: The Principles and Practices of Natural Childbirth.* 2d ed. New York: Harper and Row.

Dimsdale, J. E., J. Eckenrode, R. J. Haggerty, B. H. Kaplan, F. Cohen, and S. Dornbusch. 1979. The role of social supports in medical care. *Social Psychiatry* 14:175–80.

Dinardo, Q. E. 1971. Psychological adjustment to spinal cord injury. Ph.D. dissertation, University of Houston, Texas.

Doering, S. G. and D. R. Entwhistle. 1975. Preparation during pregnancy and ability to cope with labor and delivery. *American Journal of Orthopsychiatry* 45:825–37.

Dohrenwend, B. S. and B. P. Dohrenwend, eds. 1974. *Stressful Life Events: Their Nature and Effects.* New York: Wiley.

—— 1978. Some issues in research on stressful life events. *Journal of Nervous and Mental Disease* 166:7–15.

Dohrenwend, B. P., B. S. Dohrenwend, S. V. Kasl, and G. J. Warheit. 1979. *Report to the Task Group on Behavioral Effects to the President's Commission on the Accident at Three Mile Island.* Washington, D.C., October.

Donnerstein, E. and D. W. Wilson. 1976. Effects of noise and perceived control on ongoing and subsequent aggressive behavior. *Journal of Personality and Social Psychology* 34:774–81.

Dubos, R. 1965. *Man Adapting.* New Haven: Yale University Press.

Durrett, L. and M. Ziegler. 1980. A sensitive radioenzymatic assay for catechol drugs. *Journal of Neuroscience Research* 5:587–98.

Eastman, M. 1971. *The Enjoyment of Laughter.* Johnson Reprint of 1937 edition.

Egbert, L., G. Battit, C. Welch, and M. Bartlett. 1964. Reduction of post-operative pain by encouragement and instruction. *New England Journal of Medicine* 270:825–27.

Eissler, K. R. 1955. *The Psychiatrist and the Dying Patient.* New York: International Universities Press.

Ekblom, B. 1963. Significance of psychological factors with regard to risk of death among elderly persons. *Acta Psychiatrica Scandinavica* 39:627–33.

Elliot, G. 1972. *The Twentieth Century Book of the Dead.* New York: Ballantine Books.

Elliott, R. 1965. Reaction time and heart rate as functions of magnitude of incentive and probability of success. *Journal of Personality and Social Psychology* 2:604–9.

Ellis, P. E. and J. B. Free. 1964. Social organization of animal communities. *Nature* 201:861–63.

Elton, C. S. 1958. *The Ecology of Invasions by Animals and Plants.* New York: Wiley.

Engel, G. L. 1961. Is grief a disease?: A challenge for medical research. *Psychosomatic Medicine* 23:18–22.

—— 1962. *Psychological Development in Health and Disease.* Philadelphia: W. B. Saunders.

—— 1968. A life setting conducive to illness: The giving up-given up complex. *Bulletin of the Menninger Clinic* 32:355–65.

—— 1973. Sudden and rapid death during psychological stress: Folklore or folk wisdom? *Annals of Internal Medicine* 78:587–93.

Engel, G. L. and A. H. Schmale. 1967. Psychoanalytic theory of somatic disorder. *Journal of the American Psychoanalytic Association* 15:344–63.

Epley, S. W. 1974. Reduction of the behavioral effects of aversive stimulation by the presence of companions. *Psychological Bulletin* 81:271–83.

Epstein, S. 1967. Toward a unified theory of anxiety. In B. A. Maher, ed., *Progress in Experimental Personality Research,* 4:1–89. New York: Academic Press.

Epstein, S. and S. Clark. 1970. Heart rate and skin conductance during experimentally induced anxiety: Effects of anticipated intensity of noxious stimulation and experience. *Journal of Experimental Psychology* 84:105–12.

Erikson, E. H. 1950, 1963. *Childhood and Society.* New York: Norton.

Etkin, W. 1964. *Social Behavior and Organization Among Vertebrates.* Chicago: University of Chicago Press.

Farr, W. 1859. *Influence of Marriage on the Mortality of the French People.* London: Savill and Edwards.

Feifel, H., ed. 1959. *The Meaning of Death.* New York: McGraw-Hill.

—— 1977. Death in contemporary America. In H. Feifel, ed., *New Meanings of Death,* pp. 4–12. New York: McGraw-Hill.

Fenichel, O. 1945. *The Psychoanalytic Theory of Neurosis.* New York: Norton.

Festinger, L. 1954. A theory of social comparison processes. *Human Relations* 7:117–40.

—— 1957. *A Theory of Cognitive Dissonance.* Evanston: Row, Peterson.

Figley, C. R., ed. 1978. *Stress Disorders Among Vietnam Veterans: Theory, Research and Treatment.* New York: Brunner/Mazel.

Fine, B. D., E. D. Joseph, and H. F. Waldhorn, eds. 1969. *The Mechanism of Denial.* Monograph III, Monograph Series of the Kris Study Group of the New York Psychoanalytic Institute. New York: International Universities Press.

Finkle, A. L. and J. R. Poppen. 1948. Clinical effects of noise and mechanical vibrations of a turbo-jet engine on man. *Journal of Applied Physiology* 1:183–204.

Fiske, D. W. and S. R. Maddi, eds. 1961. *Functions of Varied Experience.* Homewood, Ill.: Dorsey Press.

Fleming, R., A. Baum, M. M. Gisriel, and R. J. Gatchel. 1982. Mediating influences of social support on stress at Three Mile Island. *Journal of Human Stress* 8:14–22.

Flickinger, G. and H. Ratcliffe. 1961. The effect of grouping on the adrenals and gonads of chickens. *Proceedings of the Federation of American Societies for Experimental Biology* 20:176.

Flynn, C. and J. Chalmers. 1980. The social and economic effects of the accident at Three Mile Island. Washington, D.C., U.S. Nuclear Regulatory Commission (NUREG/CR-1215).

Folkman, S. and R. S. Lazarus. 1980. An analysis of coping in a middle-aged community sample. *Journal of Health and Social Behavior* 21:219–39.

—— In press. If it changes it must be a process: A study of emotion and coping during three stages of a college examination. *Journal of Personality and Social Psychology.*

Folkman, S., C. Schaefer, and R. S. Lazarus. 1979. Cognitive processes as mediators in stress and coping. In V. Hamilton and D. M. Warburton, eds., *Human Stress and Cognition: An Information-Processing Approach,* pp. 265–98. London: Wiley.

Fox, B. H. 1978. Premorbid psychological factors as related to cancer incidence. *Journal of Behavioral Medicine* 1:45–133.

Fox, R. 1959. *Experiment Perilous.* New York: The Free Press of Glencoe.

Fox, R. P. 1972. Post-combat adaptational problems. *Comprehensive Psychiatry* 13:435–43.

Frankenhaeuser, M. 1973. Experimental approaches to the study of catecholamines and emotions. Reports from the Psychological laboratories, University of Stockholm (392).

—— 1975a. Experimental approaches to the study of catecholamines and emotions. In L. Levi, ed., *Emotions: Their Parameters and Measurement.* New York: Raven Press.

—— 1975b. Sympathetic-adrenomedullary activity, behaviour, and the psychosocial environment. In P. H. Venables and M. J. Christie, eds., *Research in Psychophysiology.* New York: Wiley.

—— 1976. The role of peripheral catecholamines in adaptation to understimulation and overstimulation. In G. Serban, ed., *Psychopathology of Human Adaptation.* New York: Plenum Press.

Frankenhaeuser, M. and B. Gardell. 1976. Underload and overload in working life: Outline of a multidisciplinary approach. *Journal of Human Stress* 2:35–46.

Frankl, V. E. 1955. *The Doctor and the Soul.* New York: Knopf.

Fredericq, L. 1885. Influence du milieu ambiant sur la composition du sang des animaux aquatiques. *Archives de Zoologie Experimental et Génerale* 3:34.

Freedman, J. L. 1975. *Crowding and Behavior.* San Francisco: W. H. Freeman.

Freireich, E. J., E. A. Gehan, D. Sulman, D. R. Boggs, and E. Frei, III. 1961. The effect of chemotherapy on acute leukemia in the human. *Journal of Chronic Diseases* 14:593–608.

Fremouw, W. J. and R. E. Zitter. 1978. A comparison of skills training and cognitive restructuring-relaxation for the treatment of speech anxiety. *Behavior Therapy* 9:248–59.

Freud, A. 1937, 1946. *The Ego and the Mechanisms of Defense.* New York: International Universities Press.

Freud, S. 1917. Mourning and melancholia. In *Collected Papers,* 4:152–70. New York: Basic Books (1959).

—— 1953. *Beyond the Pleasure Principle.* Standard Edition 18. London: Hogarth Press. (Originally published in 1920.)

Friedman, M. and R. H. Rosenman. 1974. *Type A Behavior and Your Heart.* New York: Knopf.

Friedman, S. B., P. Chodoff, J. W. Mason, and D. A. Hamburg. 1963. Behavioral observations on parents anticipating the death of a child. *Pediatrics* 32:610–25.

Friedman, S. B., J. W. Mason, and D. A. Hamburg. 1963. Urinary 17-hydroxycorticosteroid levels in parents of children with neoplastic disease: A study of chronic psychological stress. *Psychosomatic Medicine* 2:364–76.

——— Unpublished data.

Fromm, E. 1947. *Man for Himself.* New York: Holt, Rinehart and Winston.

Fuller, S. S., M. P. Endress, and J. E. Johnson. 1977. Control and coping with an aversive health examination. Paper presented at the annual meeting of the American Psychological Association, San Francisco.

Furst, S., ed. 1967. *Psychic Trauma.* New York: Basic Books.

Gal, R. and R. S. Lazarus. 1975. The role of activity in anticipating and confronting stressful situations. *Journal of Human Stress* 1:4–20.

Gardam, J. F. 1969. Nursing stresses in the intensive care unit. *Journal of the American Medical Association* 208:2337–38 (Letters to the editor).

Garfield, S. R. 1970. The delivery of medical care. *Scientific American* 222:15–23.

Gergen, K. J. and S. J. Morse. 1967. Self-consistency: Measurement and validation. *Proceedings of the 75th Annual Convention of the American Psychological Association* 2:207–8. (Summary)

Gersten, J. C., T. S. Langner, J. G. Eisenberg, and L. Orzeck. 1974. Child behavior and life events: Undesirable change or change per se? In B. S. Dohrenwend and B. P. Dohrenwend, eds., *Stressful Life Events: Their Nature and Effects,* pp. 159–70. New York: Wiley.

Girdano, D. A. and G. S. Everly, Jr. 1979. *Controlling Stress and Tension: A Holistic Approach.* Englewood Cliffs, N.J.: Prentice-Hall.

Girodo, M. 1977. Self-talk: Mechanisms in anxiety and stress management. In C. D. Spielberger and I. G. Sarason, eds., *Stress and Anxiety,* vol. 4. New York: Wiley.

Glass, C., J. Gottman, and S. Shmurack. 1976. Response acquisition and cognitive self-statement modification approaches to dating skill training. *Journal of Counseling Psychology* 23:520–26.

Glass, D. C. 1977. *Behavior Patterns, Stress and Coronary Disease.* Hillsdale, N.J.: Lawrence Erlbaum.

Glass, D. C. and J. E. Singer. 1972. *Urban Stress: Experiments on Noise and Social Stressors.* New York: Academic Press.

Glick, I. O., R. S. Weiss, and C. M. Parkes. 1974. *The First Year of Bereavement.* New York: Wiley Interscience.

Glorig, A. 1971. Non-auditory effects of noise exposure. *Sound and Vibration* 5:28–29.

Goldberger, L. and S. Breznitz, eds. 1982. *Handbook of Stress: Theoretical and Clinical Aspects.* New York: The Free Press.

Goldfried, M. R., E. T. Decenteco, and L. Weinberg. 1974. Systematic rational restructuring as a self-control technique. *Behavior Therapy* 5:247–54.

Goldfried, M. R., M. M. Linehan, and J. L. Smith. 1978. The reduction of test anxiety through rational restructuring. *Journal of Consulting and Clinical Psychology* 46:32–39.

Goldstein, M. J. 1959. The relationship between coping and avoiding behavior and response to fear-arousing propaganda. *Journal of Abnormal and Social Psychology* 58:247–52.

——— 1973. Individual differences in response to stress. *American Journal of Community Psychology* 2:113–37.

Gore, S. 1973. The influence of social support and related variables in ameliorating the consequences of job loss. Ph.D. dissertation, University of Michigan.

Gove, W. R. 1973. Sex, marital status and mortality. *American Journal of Sociology* 79:45–67.

Greenberg, J. S. 1983. *Comprehensive Stress Management*. Dubuque, Iowa: Wm. C. Brown.

Greene, W. A., Jr. 1958. Role of a vicarious object in the adaptation to object loss. I. Use of a vicarious object as a means of adjustment to separation from a significant person. *Psychosomatic Medicine* 20:344–50.

Greene, W. A., Jr. and G. Miller. 1958. Psychological factors and reticuloendothelial disease. IV. Observations on a group of children and adolescents with leukemia: An interpretation of disease development in terms of the mother-child unit. *Psychosomatic Medicine* 20:124–44.

Greenwood, M. 1935. *Epidemics and Crowd-Diseases*. London: Williams and Norgate.

Grinker, R. R. and J. P. Spiegel. 1945. *Men Under Stress*. Philadelphia: Blakiston.

Guillemin, R., T. Vargo, J. Rossier, S. Minick, N. Ling, C. Rivier, W. Vale, and F. Bloom. 1977. B-endorphin and adrenocorticotropin are secreted concomitantly by the pituitary gland. *Science* 197:1367–69.

Gunderson, E., and R. Rahe, eds. 1974. *Life Stress and Illness*. Springfield, Ill.: Charles C. Thomas.

Haan, N. 1963. Proposed model of ego functioning: Coping and defense mechanisms in relationship to I.Q. change. *Psychological Monographs,* vol. 77, no. 571.

—— 1969. A tripartite model of ego functioning: Values and clinical research applications. *Journal of Nervous and Mental Diseases* 148:14–30.

—— 1977. *Coping and Defending*. New York: Academic Press.

—— 1982. The assessment of coping, defense, and stress. In L. Goldberger and S. Breznitz, eds., *Handbook of Stress: Theoretical and Clinical Aspects,* pp. 254–269. New York: Free Press.

Hackett, T. P. and N. H. Cassem. 1974. Development of a quantitative rating scale to assess denial. *Journal of Psychosomatic Research* 18:93–100.

—— 1975. Psychological management of the myocardial infarction patient. *Journal of Human Stress* 1:25–38.

Hackett, T. P., N. H. Cassem, and H. A. Wishnie. 1968. The coronary-care unit: An appraisal of its psychologic hazards. *New England Journal of Medicine* 279:1365–70.

—— 1969. Detection and treatment of anxiety in the coronary care unit. *American Heart Journal* 78:727–30.

Hackett, T. P. and A. D. Weisman. 1962. The treatment of the dying. *Current Psychiatric Therapies* 2:121–26.

—— 1964. Reactions to the imminence of death. In G. H. Grosser, H. Wechsler and M. Greenblatt, eds., *The Threat of Impending Disaster,* pp. 300–11. Cambridge, Mass.: M.I.T. Press.

Haggard, E. A. 1949. Psychological causes and results of stress. In Committee on Undersea Warfare, ed., *Human Factors in Undersea Warfare,* pp. 441–61. Washington, D.C.: National Research Council.

Hahn, M. E. 1966. *California Life Goals Evaluation Schedules*. Palo Alto, Ca.: Western Psychological Services.

Haldane, J. S. 1922. *Respiration*. New Haven: Yale University Press.

Hall, C. S. and G. Lindsey. 1957. *Theories of Personality*. New York: Wiley.

Hall, E. T. 1959. *The Silent Language.* New York: Doubleday.

—— 1964. Silent assumptions in social communication. In D. Rioch and E. A. Weinstein, eds., *Disorders of Communication,* pp. 41–55. Baltimore: Williams and Wilkins.

Hamburg, D. A. and J. E. Adams. 1967. A perspective on coping behavior: Seeking and utilizing information in major transitions. *Archives of General Psychiatry* 17:277–84.

Hamburg, D. A., G. V. Coelho, and J. E. Adams. 1974. Coping and adaptation: Steps toward a synthesis of biological and social perspectives. In G. V. Coelho, D. A. Hamburg, and J. E. Adams, eds., *Coping and Adaptation,* pp. 403–40. New York: Basic Books.

Hamburg, D. A., B. Hamburg, and S. deGoza. 1953. Adaptive problems and mechanisms in severely burned patients. *Psychiatry* 16:1–20.

Hamburger, E. 1962. A two-stage study of plasma ascorbic acid and its relation to wound healing. *Military Medicine* 127:723–25.

Hare, A. P. 1963. *Handbook of Small Group Research.* Glencoe, Ill.: Free Press.

Hartmann, H. 1958. *Ego Psychology and the Problem of Adaptation.* New York: International Universities Press.

Hay, D. and D. Oken. 1972. The psychological stresses of intensive care unit nursing. *Psychosomatic Medicine* 34:109–18.

Haydn, H. 1974. *Words and Faces.* New York: Harcourt, Brace and Jovanovich.

Heard, G. 1963. *Five Ages of Man.* New York: Julian Press.

Hediger, H. 1950. *Wild Animals in Captivity.* London: Butterworths.

Heft, H. 1979. Background and focal environmental conditions of the home and attention in young children. *Journal of Applied Social Psychology* 9:47–49.

Henry, W. E. 1968. Personality change in middle and old age. In E. D. Norbeck, D. Price-Williams, and W. M. McCord, eds., *The Study of Personality: An Interdisciplinary Appraisal.* New York: Holt, Rinehart and Winston.

Herridge, C. F. 1974. Aircraft noise and mental health. *Journal of Psychosomatic Research* 18:239–43.

Hinde, R. A. 1960. An ethological approach. In J. M. Tanner, ed., *Stress and Psychiatric Disorder,* pp. 49–58. Oxford: Blackwell.

Hinkle, L. E., Jr. 1974. The effect of exposure to culture change, social change, and changes in interpersonal relationships on health. In B. S. Dohrenwend and B. P. Dohrenwend, eds., *Stressful Life Events: Their Nature and Effects,* pp. 9–44. New York: Wiley.

Hinkle, L. E., Jr., F. D. Kane, W. N. Christenson, and H. G. Wolff. 1959. Hungarian refugees: Life experiences and features influencing participation in the revolution and subsequent flight. *American Journal of Psychiatry* 116:16–19.

Hinton, J. 1967. *Dying.* Baltimore: Penguin.

Hinton, J. M. 1963. The physical and mental distress of dying. *Quarterly Journal of Medicine* (January), n.s. 32:1–21.

Hiroto, D. S. 1974. Locus of control and learned helplessness. *Journal of Experimental Psychology* 102:187–93.

Hockey, G. R. J. 1970. Effects of loud noise on attentional selectivity. *Quarterly Journal of Experimental Psychology* 22:28–36.

Hocking, B. 1982. An anthropological view of stress diseases. *Community Health Studies* 6:14–18.

Hodges, W. F. and C. D. Spielberger. 1966. The effects of threat of shock on heart rate for subjects who differ in manifest anxiety and fear of shock. *Psychophysiology* 2:287–94.

Hoerr, S. O. 1963. Thoughts on what to tell the patient with cancer. *Cleveland Clinic Quarterly* 30:11–16.

Hofer, M. A., C. T. Wolff, S. B. Friedman, and J. W. Mason. 1972. A psychoendocrine study of bereavement: Parts I and II. *Psychosomatic Medicine* 34:481–504.

Holahan, C. J. 1982. *Environmental Psychology*. New York: Random House.

Holden, C. 1981. Cousins' account of self-cure rapped. *Science* 214:892.

Holmes, T. H. and M. Masuda. 1974. Life change and illness susceptibility. In B. S. Dohrenwend and B. P. Dohrenwend, eds., *Stressful Life Events: Their Nature and Effects*, pp. 45–72. New York: Wiley.

Holmes, T. H. and R. H. Rahe. 1967a. *Schedule of Recent Experiences*. Seattle: School of Medicine, University of Washington.

—— 1967b. The social readjustment rating scale. *Journal of Psychosomatic Research* 11:213–18.

Holroyd, K. A., F. Andrasik, and T. Westbrook. 1977. Cognitive control of tension headache. *Cognitive Therapy and Research* 1:121–34.

Holroyd, K. A. and R. S. Lazarus. 1982. Stress, coping, and somatic adaptation. In L. Goldberger and S. Breznitz, eds., *Handbook of Stress: Theoretical and Clinical Aspects*, pp. 21–35. New York: Free Press.

Homans, G. C. 1950. *The Human Group*. New York: Harcourt, Brace.

Horney, K. 1950. *Neurosis and Human Growth: The Struggle Toward Self-Realization*. New York: Norton.

Horowitz, L. M., H. Sampson, E. Y. Siegelman, A. Wolfson, and J. Weiss. 1975. On the identification of warded-off mental contents: An empirical and methodological contribution. *Journal of Abnormal Psychology* 84:545–58.

Horowitz, M. J. 1969. Psychic trauma: Return of images after a stress film. *Archives of General Psychiatry* 20:552–59.

—— 1970. *Image Formation and Cognition*. New York: Appleton-Century-Crofts.

—— 1973. Phase oriented treatment of stress response syndromes. *American Journal of Psychotherapy* 27:506–15.

—— 1975. Intrusive and repetitive thoughts after experimental stress. *Archives of General Psychiatry* 32:1457–63.

—— 1976. *Stress Response Syndromes*. New York: Aronson.

Horowitz, M. J. and S. S. Becker. 1972. Cognitive response to stress: Experimental studies of a "compulsion to repeat trauma." *Psychoanalysis and Contemporary Science* 1:258–305.

Horowitz, M. J., R. Benfari, S. Hulley, S. Blair, W. Alvarez, N. Borhani, A. M. Reynolds, and N. Simon. 1979. Life events, risk factors, and coronary disease. *Psychosomatics* 20:586–92.

Horowitz, M. J. and G. F. Solomon. 1975. A prediction of delayed stress response syndromes in Vietnam veterans. *Journal of Social Issues* 31:67–80.

Hough, R. L., D. T. Fairbank, and A. M. Garcia. 1976. Problems in the ratio measurement of life stress. *Journal of Health and Social Behavior* 17:70–82.

House, J. S. and J. A. Wells. 1977. Occupational stress, social support and health. Paper presented at a conference on *Reducing Occupational Stress*. White Plains, N.Y., May 10–12.

Houston, B. K. 1972. Control over stress, locus of control, and response to stress. *Journal of Personality and Social Psychology* 21:249–55.

Houts, P. S., R. W. Miller, G. K. Tokuhata, and K. S. Ham. 1980. Health-related behavioral impact of the Three Mile Island nuclear accident. Report submitted to the TMI Advisory Panel on Health Research Studies of the Pennsylvania Department of Health, Hershey, Pa., April.

Huberty, C. J. 1975. Discriminant analysis. *Review of Educational Research* 45:543–98.

Hudgens, R. W. 1974. Personal catastrophe and depression. In B. S. Dohrenwend and B. P. Dohrenwend, eds., *Stressful Life Events: Their Nature and Effects,* pp. 119–34. New York: Wiley.

Huttel, F. A., I. Mitchell, W. M. Fisher, and A. E. Meyer. 1972. A quantitative evaluation of psychoprophylaxis in childbirth. *Journal of Psychosomatic Research* 16:81.

Imboden, J. B., A. Canter, and L. E. Cluff. 1963. Separation experiences and health records in a group of normal adults. *Psychosomatic Medicine* 25:433–40.

Jackson, D. N. 1974. *Personality Research Form Manual.* Goshen, N.Y.: Research Psychologists Press.

Jacobs, J. 1961. *The Death and Life of Great American Cities.* New York: Vintage Books.

Jacobs, S. and A. M. Ostfeld. 1977. An epidemiological review of the mortality of bereavement. *Psychosomatic Medicine* 39:344–57.

Jacobson, E. 1957. Denial and repression. *Journal of the American Psychoanalytic Association* 5:61–92.

Jahoda, M. 1958. *Current Conceptions of Positive Mental Health.* New York: Basic Books.

James, W. 1948. *Psychology.* New York: World.

Janis, I. L. 1949. Problems related to the control of fear in combat. In S. A. Stouffer, ed., *The American Soldier*: vol. 2. *Combat and Its Aftermath.* Princeton, N.J.: Princeton University Press.

—— 1951. *Air War and Emotional Stress.* New York: McGraw-Hill.

—— 1958. *Psychological Stress.* New York: Wiley.

—— 1971. *Stress and Frustration.* New York: Harcourt, Brace, & Jovanovich.

—— 1974. Vigilance and decision-making in personal crises. In G. V. Coelho, D. A. Hamburg, and J. E. Adams, eds., *Coping and Adaptation,* pp. 139–75. New York: Basic Books.

—— ed. 1982. *Counseling on Personal Decisions: Theory and Research on Short-Term Helping Relationships.* New Haven: Yale University Press.

—— 1983. Stress inoculation in health care. In D. Meichenbaum and M. E. Jaremko, eds., *Stress Reduction and Prevention,* pp. 67–99. New York: Plenum Press.

Janis, I. L., A. H. Lumsdaine, and A. I. Gladstone. 1951. Effects of preparatory communications on reactions to a subsequent news event. *Public Opinion Quarterly* 15:488–518.

Janis, I. L. and L. Mann. 1977. *Decision Making: A Psychological Analysis of Conflict, Choice, and Commitment.* New York: Free Press.

Janis, I. L. and J. Rodin. 1979. Attribution, control, and decision-making: Social psychology and health care. In G. C. Stone, F. Cohen, and N. E. Adler and Associates, *Health Psychology—A Handbook*, pp. 487–521. San Francisco: Jossey-Bass.

Jansen, G. 1969. Effects of noise on physiological state. In W. D. Ward and J. E. Fricke, eds., *Noise As A Public Health Problem*. Washington, D.C.: American Speech and Hearing Association.

Javert, C. T. and J. D. Hardy. 1951. Influence of analgesia on pain intensity during labor ("with a note on natural childbirth"). *Anesthesiology* 12:189–215.

Jenkins, C. D. 1976. Recent evidence supporting psychologic and social risk factors for coronary disease. *New England Journal of Medicine* 294:987–94 and 1033–38.

Jenkins, C. D., M. W. Hurst, and R. M. Rose. 1979. Life changes: Do people really remember? *Archives of General Psychiatry* 36:379–84.

Johnson, J. E. 1966. The influence of purposeful nurse-patient interaction on the patients' postoperative course. *American Nurses Association Monograph Series No. 2.: Exploring Medical-Surgical Nursing Practice*. New York: American Nurses' Association.

—— 1977. Information factors in coping with stressful events. Paper presented at the eleventh annual convention of the Association for the Advancement of Behavioral Therapy, Atlanta, December.

Johnson, J. E. and H. Leventhal. 1974. Effects of accurate expectations and behavioral instructions on reactions during a noxious medical examination. *Journal of Personality and Social Psychology* 29:710–18.

Johnson, J. E., J. F. Morrisey, and H. Leventhal. 1973. Psychological preparation for endoscopic examination. *Gastrointestinal Endoscopy* 19:180–82.

Johnson, J. E., V. H. Rice, S. S. Fuller, and P. Endress. 1977. Sensory information, behavioral instruction, and recovery from surgery. Paper presented at the annual meeting of the American Psychological Association, San Francisco.

Jung, C. G. 1933. *Modern Man in Search of a Soul*. W. S. Dell and C. F. Baynes, trans. New York: Harcourt Brace.

Kanfer, F. and M. L. Seiderk. 1973. Self-control: Factors enhancing tolerance of noxious stimulation. *Journal of Personality and Social Psychology* 25:381–89.

Kanner, A. D., J. C. Coyne, C. Schaefer, and R. S. Lazarus. 1981. Comparison of two modes of stress measurements: Daily hassles and uplifts versus major life events. *Journal of Behavioral Medicine* 41:1–39.

Kanungo, R. N. 1970. The concepts of alienation and involvement revisited. *Psychological Bulletin* 86:119–38.

Kaplan, B. H., J. C. Cassel, and S. Gore. 1977. Social support and health. *Medical Care* 15:47–58.

Kaplan, D. M. 1972. On shyness. *International Journal of Psychoanalysis* 53:439–53.

Kaplan, Q. 1964. *The Conduct of Inquiry: Methodology for Behavioural Science*. San Francisco: Chandler.

Kastenbaum, R. and R. Aisenberg. 1972. *The Psychology of Death*. New York: Springer.

Kastenbaum, R. and P. T. Costa. 1977. Psychological perspectives on death. *Annual Review of Psychology* 28:225–49.

Katz, J. L., H. Weiner, T. G. Gallagher, and L. Hellman. 1970. Stress, distress, and ego defenses. *Archives of General Psychiatry* 23:131–42.

Keeley, K. 1962. Prenatal influence on behavior of offspring of crowded mice. *Science* 135:44–45.

Kelley, H. 1967. Attribution theory in social psychology. In D. Levine, ed., *Nebraska Symposium on Motivation*. Lincoln: University of Nebraska Press.

Kendall, P., L. Williams, T. F. Pechacek, L. E. Graham, C. Shisslak, and N. Herzoff. 1977. The Palo Alto medical psychology project: Cognitive-behavioral patient education interventions in catheterization procedures. University of Minnesota, unpublished manuscript.

Kiesler, C. A., ed. 1971. *The Psychology of Commitment*. New York: Academic Press.

Kinderlehrer, J. 1974. Vitamin C: The best thing that ever happened to antibiotics. *Prevention* 26:71–75.

Klausner, S. Z. 1968. *Why Man Takes Chances: Studies in Stress-Seeking*. New York: Anchor Books.

Klenner, F. R. 1971. Observations on the dose and administration of ascorbic acid when employed beyond the range of a vitamin in human pathology. *Journal of Applied Nutrition* 23:61–87.

Knudson, A. G., Jr. and J. M. Natterson. 1960. Participation of parents in the hospital care of fatally ill children. *Pediatrics* 26:482–90.

Kobasa, S. C. 1977. Stress personality and health: A study of an overlooked possibility. Ph.D. dissertation, University of Chicago.

—— 1979. Stressful events, personality, and health: An inquiry into hardiness. *Journal of Personality and Social Psychology* 37:1–11.

Kobasa, S. C. and S. R. Maddi. 1977. Existential personality theory. In R. Corsini, ed., *Current Personality Theories*. Itasca, Ill.: Peacock.

Kobasa, S. C., S. R. Maddi, and S. Kahn. 1982. Hardiness and health: A prospective study. *Journal of Personality and Social Psychology* 42:168–77.

Kobasa, S. C. and M. C. Puccetti. 1983. Personality and social resources in stress resistance. *Journal of Personality and Social Psychology* 45:839–50.

Kobrin, F. E. and G. E. Hendershot. 1977. Do family ties reduce mortality? Evidence from the United States 1966–68. *Journal of Marriage and the Family* 39:737–45.

Koford, C. B. 1963. Rank of mothers and sons in bands of rhesus monkeys. *Science* 141:356–57.

Kornfeld, D. S. 1969a. Psychiatric aspects of patient care in the operating suite and special areas. *Anesthesiology* 31:166–71.

—— 1969b. Psychiatric view of the intensive care unit. *British Medical Journal* 1:108–10.

Krantz, D. S., D. C. Glass, and M. L. Snyder. 1974. Helplessness, stress level, and the coronary prone behavior pattern. *Journal of Experimental Social Psychology* 10:284–300.

Kraus, A. S. and A. M. Lilienfeld. 1959. Some epidemiological aspects of the high mortality rate in the young widowed group. *Journal of Chronic Diseases* 10:207–17.

Kroeber, A. 1948. *Anthropology*. Rev. ed. New York: Harcourt, Brace and World.

Kroeber, T. C. 1963. The coping functions of the ego mechanisms. In R. W. White, ed., *The Study of Lives*, pp. 178–98. New York: Atherton Press.

Krystal, H., ed. 1968. *Massive Psychic Trauma*. New York: International Universities Press.

Kryter, K. D. 1970. *The Effects of Noise on Man*. New York: Academic Press.

Kübler-Ross, E. 1969. *On Death and Dying*. New York: Macmillan.

Kutash, I. L., L. B. Schlesinger, and Associates. 1980. *Handbook on Stress and Anxiety: Contemporary Knowledge, Theory, and Treatment*. San Francisco: Jossey-Bass.

Lacey, J. I. 1959. Psychophysiological approaches to the evaluation of psychotherapeutic process and outcome. In E. A. Rubinstein and M. B. Parloff, eds., *Research in Psychotherapy.* Washington, D.C.: American Psychological Association.

―― 1967. Somatic response patterning and stress: Some revisions of activation theory. In M. H. Appley and R. Trumbull, eds., *Psychological Stress: Issues in Research,* pp. 14–42. New York: Appleton-Century-Crofts.

Lacey, J. I., J. Kagan, B. C. Lacey, and H. A. Moss. 1963. The visceral level: Situational determinants and behavioral correlates of autonomic response patterns. In P. H. Knapp, ed., *Expression of the Emotions in Man,* pp. 161–96. New York: International Universities Press.

Lamm, H. and D. G. Myers. 1978. Group-induced polarization of attitudes and behavior. In L. Berkowitz, ed., *Advances in Experimental Social Psychology,* vol. 11. New York: Academic Press.

Lane, S. R. and W. C. Meecham. 1974. Jet noise at schools near Los Angeles International Airport. *Journal of the Acoustical Society of America* 56:127–31.

Langer, E., I. Janis, and J. Wolfer. 1975. Reduction of psychological stress in surgical patients. *Journal of Experimental Social Psychology* 1:155–66.

Lapidus, L. B. 1969. Cognitive control and reaction to stress: Conditions for mastery in the anticipatory phase. *Proceedings of the 77th Annual Convention of the American Psychological Association* 4.

Lasagna, L. 1962. Some explored and unexplored psychological variables in therapeutics. *Proceedings of the Royal Society of Medicine* (London) 55:773–76.

Lawton, M. P. and L. Nahemow. 1973. Ecology and the aging process. In C. Eisdorfer and P. Lawton, eds., *The Psychology of Adult Development and Aging,* pp. 619–74. Washington, D.C.: American Psychological Association.

Lazarus, R. S. 1966. *Psychological Stress and the Coping Process.* New York: McGraw-Hill.

―― 1974. Psychological stress and coping in adaptation and illness. *International Journal of Psychiatry in Medicine* 5:321–33.

―― 1975. A cognitively oriented psychologist looks at biofeedback. *American Psychologist* 30:553–61.

―― 1976. *Patterns of Adjustment.* New York: McGraw-Hill.

―― 1978. The stress and coping paradigm. Presented at Conference on the Critical Evaluation of Behavioral Paradigms for Psychiatric Science, Gleneden Beach, Oregon, November 3–6.

―― 1979. Positive denial: The case for not facing reality. *Psychology Today* 13:44–60.

―― 1983. The costs and benefits of denial. In S. Breznitz, ed., *The Denial of Stress,* pp. 1–30. New York: International Universities Press.

―― In press. Trivialization of distress. In J. C. Rosen and L. J. Solomon, eds., *Preventing Health Risk Behaviors and Promoting Coping With Illness, Vol. 8: Vermont Conference on the Primary Prevention of Psychopathology.* Hanover, N.H.: University Press of New England.

Lazarus, R. S. and E. Alfert. 1964. The short-circuiting of threat. *Journal of Abnormal and Social Psychology* 69:195–205.

Lazarus, R. S., J. R. Averill, and E. M. Opton, Jr. 1970. Toward a cognitive theory of emotion. In M. Arnold, ed., *Feelings and Emotions,* pp. 207–31. New York: Academic Press.

—— 1974. The psychology of coping: Issues of research and assessment. In G. V. Coelho, D. A. Hamburg, and J. E. Adams, eds., *Coping and Adaptation*, pp. 249–315. New York: Basic Books.

Lazarus, R. S. and J. B. Cohen. 1977. Environmental stress. In L. Altman and J. F. Wohlwill, eds., *Human Behavior and the Environment: Current Theory and Research*, vol. 2. New York: Plenum.

Lazarus, R. S., J. B. Cohen, S. Folkman, A. Kanner, and C. Shaefer. 1980. Psychological stress and adaptation: Some unresolved issues. In H. Selye, ed., *Selye's Guide to Stress Research*, pp. 90–117. New York: Van Nostrand.

Lazarus, R. S., J. Deese, and S. F. Osler. 1952. The effects of psychological stress upon performance. *Psychological Bulletin* 49:293–317.

Lazarus, R. S. and S. Folkman. 1984a. Coping and adaptation. In W. D. Gentry, ed., *The Handbook of Behavioral Medicine*, pp. 282–325. New York: Guilford.

—— 1984b. *Stress, Appraisal, and Coping*. New York: Springer.

Lazarus, R. S. and R. Launier. 1978. Stress-related transactions between person and environment. In L. A. Pervin and M. Lewis, eds., *Perspectives in Interactional Psychology*, pp. 287–327. New York: Plenum.

Lazarus, R. S., E. M. Opton, Jr., M. S. Nomikos, and N. O. Rankin. 1965. The principle of short-circuiting of threat: Further evidence. *Journal of Personality* 33:622–35.

Lefcourt, H. M. 1966. Repression-sensitization: A measure of the evaluation of emotional expression. *Journal of Consulting and Clinical Psychology* 30:444–49.

—— 1973. The function of the illusions of control and freedom. *American Psychologist* 28:417–25.

Lemaze, F. 1958. *Painless Childbirth: Psychoprophylactic Method*. London: Burke.

Leventhal, H. 1963. Patient responses to surgical stress in regular surgery and intensive care units. *Rep. Div. Hosp. Med. Facilities. U.S. Public Health Service*. Mimeo.

—— 1973. Changing attitudes and habits to reduce chronic risk factors. *American Journal of Cardiology* 31:571–80.

Leventhal, H., R. E. Singer, and S. Jones. 1965. Effects of fear and specificity of recommendations. *Journal of Personality and Social Psychology* 2:20–29.

Leventhal, H., J. C. Watts, and F. Pagano. 1967. Effects of fear and instructions on how to cope with danger. *Journal of Personality and Social Psychology* 6:313–21.

Levine, J. and E. Zigler. 1975. Denial and self-image in stroke, lung cancer, and heart disease patients. *Journal of Consulting and Clinical Psychology* 43:751–57.

Levine, S. and G. D. Coover. 1976. Environmental control of suppression of the pituitary-adrenal system. *Psychology and Behavior* 17:35–37.

Levinson, D. J. 1977. The mid-life transition: A period in adult psychological development. *Psychiatry* 40:99–112.

Levy, J. M. and R. K. McGee. 1975. Childbirth as crisis: A test of Janis' theory of communication and stress resolution. *Journal of Personality and Social Psychology* 31:171–79.

Lewin, B. 1950. *The Psychoanalysis of Elation*. New York: Norton.

Lewin, K. 1947. Frontiers in group dynamics: Concept, method and reality in social science; social equilibria and social change. *Human Relations* 1:5–41.

Lewis, N. D. C., and B. Engel, eds. 1954. *Wartime Psychiatry: A Compendium of the International Literature*. New York: Oxford University Press.

Lifton, R. J. 1964. On death and death symbolism: The Hiroshima disaster. *Psychiatry* 27:191–210.

—— 1967. *Death in Life: Survivors of Hiroshima*. New York: Random House.

—— 1970. The scars of Vietnam. *Commonwealth* 91:554–56.

—— 1973. *Home from the War*. New York: Simon and Schuster.

Lindeman, C. A. 1972. Nursing intervention with the presurgical patient: The effectiveness and efficiency of group and individual preoperative teaching. *Nursing Research* 21:196–209.

Lindeman, C. A. and B. Van Aernam. 1971. Nursing intervention with the presurgical patient—The effects of structured and unstructured preoperative teaching. *Nursing Research* 20:319–32.

Lindemann, E. 1944. Symptomatology and management of acute grief. *American Journal of Psychiatry* 101:141–48.

Lipman, R. S., K. Rickles, L. Covi, L. R. Derogatis, and E. H. Uhlenhuth. 1969. Factors of symptom distress. *Archives of General Psychiatry* 21:328–38.

Lipowski, Z. J. 1970. Physical illness, the individual and the coping process. *International Journal of Psychiatry in Medicine* 1:91–102.

Lippett, R., J. Watson, and B. Westley. 1958. *The Dynamics of Planned Change: A Comparative Study of Principles and Techniques*. New York: Harcourt, Brace.

Loeb, M. 1979. Noise and performance: Do we know more? In J. V. Tobias, ed., *The Proceedings of the Third International Congress on Noise as a Public Health Problem*. Washington, D.C.: American Speech and Hearing Association.

Lopata, H. Z. 1973. *Widowhood in an American City*. Morristown, N.J.: General Learning Corporation.

Lucas, R. A. 1969. *Men in Crisis*. New York: Basic Books.

Lynch, J. J. 1977. *The Broken Heart: The Medical Consequences of Loneliness*. New York: Basic Books.

McAlister, A. L., C. Perry, and N. Maccoby. 1979. Adolescent smoking: Onset and prevention. *Pediatrics* 63:650–80.

McDaniel, J. W. and A. W. Sexton. 1970. Psychoendrocrine studies of patients with spinal cord lesion. *Journal of Abnormal Psychology* 76:117–22.

McDonald, D. G., J. Stern, and W. Hahn. 1963. Effects of differential housing and stress on diet selection, water intake, and body weight in the rat. *Journal of Applied Physiology* 18:937–42.

McFall, R. M. and L. Hammen. 1971. Motivation, structure, and self-monitoring: Role of nonspecific factors in smoking reduction. *Journal of Consulting and Clinical Psychology* 37:80–86.

McGrath, J. E. 1970a. Major substantive issues: Time, setting, and the coping process. In J. E. McGrath, ed., *Social and Psychological Factors in Stress*, pp. 22–40. New York: Holt, Rinehart, and Winston.

—— 1970b. Settings, measures, and themes: An integrative review of some research on social-psychological factors in stress. In J. E. McGrath, ed., *Social and Psychological Factors in Stress*, pp. 76–83. New York: Holt, Rinehart, and Winston.

—— 1970c. *Social and Psychological Factors in Stress.* New York: Holt, Rinehart, and Winston.

Mackintosh, J. H. 1962. Effect of strain and group size on the response of mice to "seconal" anaesthesia. *Nature* 194:1304.

McKissick, G. E., G. L. Flickinger, Jr., and H. L. Ratcliffe. 1961. Coronary arteriosclerosis in isolated, paired, and grouped chickens. *Proceedings of the Federation of American Societies for Experimental Biology* 20:91.

MacLean, P. D. 1958. Contrasting functions of limbic and neocortical systems of the brain and their relevance to psychophysiological aspects of medicine. *American Journal of Medicine* 25:611–26.

MacMahon, B. and T. F. Pugh. 1965. Suicide in the widowed. *American Journal of Epidemiology* 81:23–31.

McNeill, D. N. 1973. *Mortality Among the Widowed in Connecticut.* New Haven: Yale University (MPH essay).

Maddi, S. R. 1967. The existential neurosis. *Journal of Abnormal Psychology* 72:311–25.

—— 1975. The strenuousness of the creative life. In I. A. Taylor and J. W. Getzels, eds., *Perspectives in Creativity.* Chicago: Aldine.

—— 1976. *Personality Theories: A Comparative Analysis.* 3d ed. Homewood, Ill.: Dorsey Press.

Maddison, D. C. and A. Viola. 1968. The health of widows in the year following bereavement. *Journal of Psychosomatic Research* 12:297–306.

Maddison, D. C. and W. L. Walker. 1967. Factors affecting the outcome of conjugal bereavement. *British Journal of Psychiatry* 113:1057–67.

Mandler, G. 1975. *Mind and Emotion.* New York: Wiley.

Margolis, G. J. 1967. Postoperative psychosis on the intensive care unit. *Comprehensive Psychiatry* 8:227–32.

Margolis, J. R., W. B. Kannel, M. Feinleib, T. R. Dawber, and P. M. McNamara. 1973. Clinical features of unrecognized myocardial infarction—silent and symptomatic. Eighteen year follow-up: The Framingham study. *American Journal of Cardiology* 32:1–7.

Mariott, H. I. 1950. *Water and Salt Depletion.* Springfield, Ill.: Charles C. Thomas.

Markush, R. E. and R. V. Favero. 1974. Epidemiologic assessment of stressful life events, depressed mood, and psychophysiological symptoms—A preliminary report. In B. S. Dohrenwend and B. P. Dohrenwend, eds., *Stressful Life Events: Their Nature and Effects.* New York: Wiley.

Marlatt, G. A. 1983. The controlled-drinking controversy: A commentary. *American Psychologist* 38:1097–1110.

Marlatt, G. A., B. Demming, and J. B. Reid. 1973. Loss of control drinking in alcoholics: An experimental analogue. *Journal of Abnormal Psychology* 81:223–41.

Marmor, J. 1963. The cancer patient and his family. In H. I. Lief, V. F. Lief, and N. R. Lief, eds., *The Psychological Basis of Medical Practice,* pp. 309–17. New York: Harper and Row.

Maslow, A. H. 1954. *Motivation and Personality.* New York: Harper and Row.

—— 1962. *Toward a Psychology of Being.* New York: Van Nostrand.

Mason, J. W. 1959. Psychological influences on the pituitary-adrenal cortical system. *Recent Progress in Hormone Research* 15:345–89.

——— 1968. Over-all hormonal balance as a key endocrine organization. *Psychosomatic Medicine* 30:791–808.

——— 1971. A re-evaluation of the concept of "non-specificity" in stress theory. *Journal of Psychiatric Research* 8:323–33.

——— 1974. Specificity in the organization of neuroendocrine response profiles. In P. Seeman and G. M. Brown, eds., *Frontiers in Neurology and Neuroscience Research*, pp. 68–80. Toronto: University of Toronto.

——— 1975a. A historical view of the stress field. Part I. *Journal of Human Stress* 1:6–12.

——— 1975b. A historical view of the stress field. Part II. *Journal of Human Stress* 1:22–36.

Mathews, K. E., Jr. and L. K. Canon. 1975. Environmental noise level as a determinant of helping behavior. *Journal of Personality and Social Psychology* 32:571–77.

Matte, I. 1943. Observations of the English in wartime. *Journal of Nervous Mental Diseases* 97:447–63.

Matussek, P. and D. Mantell. 1971. *Die Konzentration-slagerhaft und ihre Folgen.* Berlin: Springer.

Mechanic, D. 1962. The concept of illness behavior. *Journal of Chronic Diseases* 15:189–94.

——— 1976. Stress, illness, and illness behavior. *Journal of Human Stress* 2:2–6.

——— 1978a. *Medical Sociology.* 2d ed. New York: Free Press.

——— 1978b. *Students Under Stress.* Madison: University of Wisconsin Press.

Meichenbaum, D. 1972. Cognitive modification of test anxious college students. *Journal of Consulting and Clinical Psychology* 39:370–80.

——— 1977. *Cognitive-Behavior Modification: An Integrative Approach.* New York: Plenum Press.

Meichenbaum, D. and R. Cameron. 1973. An examination of cognitive and contingency variables in anxiety relief procedures. University of Waterloo: unpublished manuscript.

Meichanbaum, D., B. Gilmore, and A. Fedoravicious. 1971. Group insight vs. group desensitization in treating speech anxiety. *Journal of Consulting and Clinical Psychology* 36:410–21.

Meichenbaum, D. and M. E. Jaremko. 1980. *Stress Prevention and Management: A Cognitive-Behavioral Approach.* New York: Plenum Press.

Meichenbaum, D. and M. E. Jaremko, eds. 1983. *Stress Reduction and Prevention.* New York: Plenum Press.

Meichenbaum, D. and D. C. Turk. 1976. The cognitive-behavioral management of anxiety, anger and pain. In P. O. Davidson, ed., *The Behavioral Management of Anxiety, Depression and Pain.* New York: Brunner/Mazel.

——— 1982a. Stress, coping, and disease: A cognitive-behavioral perspective. In R. Neufeld, ed., *Psychological Stress and Psychopathology.* New York: McGraw-Hill.

——— 1982b. Stress inoculation: A preventative approach. In R. Neufeld, ed., *Psychological Stress and Psychopathology.* New York: McGraw-Hill.

Melville, H. 1850. *Redburn.* New York: Harper and Row.

——— 1851. *Moby Dick.* New York: Harper and Brothers.

——— 1852. *Pierre, or the Ambiguities.* New York: Harper.

Menninger, K. A. 1959. Hope. *American Journal of Psychiatry* 116:481–91.

—— 1963. *The Vital Balance*. New York: Viking Press.

Mikhail, A. 1981. Stress: A psychophysiological conception. *Journal of Human Stress* 7:9–15.

Mills, J. H. 1975. Noise and children: A review of literature. *Journal of the Acoustical Society of America* 58:767–79.

Mischel, W. 1968. *Personality and Assessment*. New York: Wiley.

Mitchell, R. E., R. C. Cronkite, and R. H. Moos. 1983. Stress, coping, and depression among married couples. *Journal of Abnormal Psychology* 92:433–48.

Monat, A. 1976. Temporal uncertainty, anticipation time, and cognitive coping under threat. *Journal of Human Stress* 2:32–43.

Monat, A., J. R. Averill, and R. S. Lazarus. 1972. Anticipatory stress and coping reactions under various conditions of uncertainty. *Journal of Personality and Social Psychology* 24:237–53.

Monat, A. and R. S. Lazarus, eds. 1977. *Stress and Coping: An Anthology*. New York: Columbia University Press.

Moos, R. H., ed. 1976a. *Human Adaptation: Coping with Life Crises*. Lexington, Mass.: D. C. Heath.

—— 1976b. *The Human Context: Environmental Determinants of Behavior*. New York: Wiley Interscience

Morris, L. E. 1970. "Over the hump" in Vietnam: Adjustment patterns in a time-limited stress situation. *Bulletin of the Menninger Clinic* 34:352–63.

Morrow, P. E. 1975. An evaluation of recent NO$_x$ toxiticity data and an attempt to derive an ambient standard for NO$_x$ by established toxicological procedures. *Environmental Research* 10:92–112.

Moss, G. E. 1973. *Illness, Immunity, and Social Interaction*. New York: Wiley

Murphy, L. B. 1962. *The Widening World of Childhood*. New York: Basic Books.

—— 1974. Coping, vulnerability, and resilience in childhood. In G. V. Coelho, D. A. Hamburg, and J. E. Adams, eds., *Coping and Adaptation*, pp. 69–100. New York: Basic Books.

Murray, E. J. 1960. Adjustment to environmental stress in fallout shelters. In G. W. Baker and J. H. Rohrer, eds., *Symposium on Human Problems in the Utilization of Fallout Shelters*, pp. 67–77. Disaster Study No. 12. Washington, D.C.: National Academy of Sciences—National Research Council.

Murray, H. A. 1949. Introduction. Herman Melville's *Pierre, or the Ambiguities*. New York: Henricks House.

Myers, J. E. 1966. *Fundamentals of Experimental Design*. Boston: Allyn and Bacon.

Myers, J. K., J. J. Lindenthal, and M. P. Pepper. 1975. Life events, social integration and psychiatric symptomatology. *Journal of Health and Social Behavior* 16:421–29.

Myers, J. K., J. J. Lindenthal, M. P. Pepper, and D. R. Ostrander. 1972. Life events and mental status: A longitudinal study. *Journal of Health and Social Behavior* 13:398–406.

National Academy of Sciences. 1982. *Research on Stress in Health and Disease*. Washington, D.C.: Institute of Medicine.

National Air Pollution Control Administration, 1970. *Air Quality Criteria for Carbon Monoxide, AP-62*. Washington, D.C.: GPO.

National Center for Health Statistics. 1970. *Mortality from Selected Causes by Marital Status.* Series 20, No. 8. Washington, D.C.: GPO.

Natterson, J. M. and A. G. Knudson. 1960. Observations concerning fear of death in fatally ill children and their mothers. *Psychosomatic Medicine* 22:456–65.

Nefzger, M. D. 1970. Follow-up studies of World War II and Korean War prisoners. 1. Study plan and mortality findings. *American Journal of Epidemiology* 91:123–28.

Neugarten, B. L. 1969. Continuities and discontinuities of psychological issues into adult life. *Human Development* 12:121–30.

—— 1974. The middle years. In S. Arieti, ed., *American Handbook of Psychiatry.* New York: Basic Books.

Neugarten, B. L., J. W. Moore, and J. C. Lowe. 1965. Age norms, age constraints, and adult socialization. *American Journal of Sociology* 70:710–17.

Niederland, W. G. 1968. Clinical observations on the "survivor syndrome." *International Journal of Psychoanalysis* 49:313–15.

Nomikos, M. S., E. M. Opton, Jr., J. R. Averill, and R. S. Lazarus. 1968. Surprise versus suspense in the production of stress reaction. *Journal of Personality and Social Psychology* 8:204–8.

Novaco, R. 1975. *Anger Control: The Development and Evaluation of an Experimental Treatment.* Lexington, Mass.: Heath.

Nuckolls, K. B., J. Cassel, and B. H. Kaplan. 1972. Psychosocial assets, life crisis, and the prognosis of pregnancy. *American Journal of Epidemiology* 95:431–41.

Numerof, R. E. and M. N. Abrams. 1984. Sources of stress among nurses: An empirical investigation. *Journal of Human Stress* 10:88–100.

Offer, D. and D. X. Freedman. 1972. *Modern Psychiatry and Clinical Research: Essays in Honor of Roy R. Grinker, Sr.* New York: Basic Books.

Office of Population Censuses and Surveys. 1977a. Series FM2, No. 1. *Marriage and Divorce Statistics, 1974.* London: HMSO.

—— 1977b. Series DH 1, No. 1. *Mortality Statistics, 1974.* London: HMSO.

Oken, D. 1961. What to tell cancer patients: Study of medical attitudes. *Journal of the American Medical Association* 175:1120–28.

Olin, H. and T. Hackett. Unpublished data.

Olsen, R. L. 1960. The implications of food acceptability for shelter occupancy. In G. W. Baker and J. H. Rohrer, eds., *Symposium on Human Problems in the Utilization of Fallout Shelters,* pp. 167–79. Disaster Study No. 12. Washington, D.C.: National Academy of Sciences—National Research Council.

Orbach, C. E., A. M. Sutherland, and M. F. Bozeman. 1955. Psychological impact of cancer and its treatment, III. The adaptation of mothers to the threatened loss of their children through leukemia, Part 2. *Cancer* 8:20–33.

Oswald, P. and E. Bittner. 1968. Life adjustment after severe persecution. *American Journal of Psychiatry* 124:1393–400.

Parens, H., B. J. McConville, and S. M. Kaplan. 1966. The prediction of frequency of illness from the response to separation. *Psychosomatic Medicine* 28:162–76.

Parkes, C. M. 1972. *Bereavement: Studies of Grief in Adult Life.* London: Tavistock.

—— 1975. Unexpected and untimely bereavement: A statistical study of young Boston widows and widowers. In B. Schoenberg, I. Gerber, A. Wiener, A. H. Kutscher,

D. Peretz, and A. C. Carr, eds., *Bereavement: Its Psychosocial Aspects.* New York: Columbia University Press.

Parkes, C. M., B. Benjamin, and R. G. Fitzgerald. 1969. Broken heart: A statistical study of increased mortality among widowers. *British Medical Journal* 1:740–43.

Parkes, C. M. and R. Brown. 1972. Health after bereavement: A controlled study of young Boston widows and widowers. *Psychosomatic Medicine* 34:449–61.

Parkes, K. R. In press. Locus of control, cognitive appraisal, and coping in stressful episodes. *Journal of Personality and Social Psychology.*

Parsons, T. 1951. *The Social System.* Glencoe, Ill.: Free Press.

Pascal, G. R. 1951. Psychological deficit as a function of stress and constitution. *Journal of Personality* 20:175–87.

Paykel, E. S. 1974. Recent life events and clinical depression. In E. K. Gunderson and R. H. Rahe, eds., *Life Stress and Illness.* Springfield, Ill.: Charles C. Thomas.

Paykel, E. S., B. A. Prusoff, and E. H. Uhlenhuth. 1971. Scaling of life events. *Archives of General Psychiatry* 25:340–47.

Pearlin, L. I. 1959. Social and personal stress and escape television viewing. *Public Opinion Quarterly* 23:255–59.

—— 1975a. Sex roles and depression. In N. Datan and L. Ginsberg, eds., *Life-Span Developmental Psychology Conference: Normative Life Crises,* pp. 191–207. New York: Academic Press.

—— 1975b. Status inequality and stress in marriage. *American Sociological Review* 40:344–57.

—— 1980. Life strains and psychological distress among adults. In N. J. Smelser and E. H. Erikson, eds., *Themes of Work and Love in Adulthood,* pp. 174–92. Cambridge, Mass.: Harvard University Press.

Pearlin, L. I. and M. A. Lieberman. 1979. Social sources of emotional distress. In R. Simmons, ed., *Research in Community and Mental Health.* Greenwich, Conn.: JAI Press.

Pearlin, L. I. and C. Radabaugh. 1976. Economic strains and the coping functions of alcohol. *American Journal of Sociology* 82:652–63.

Pearlin, L. I. and C. Schooler. 1978. The structure of coping. *Journal of Health and Social Behavior* 19:2–21.

Peele, S. 1983. Out of the habit trap. *American Health* (September/October), pp. 42–47.

Pervin, L. A. 1963. The need to predict and control under conditions of threat. *Journal of Personality* 31:570–85.

Peterson, A. P. G. and E. E. Gross, Jr. 1972. *Handbook of Noise Measurement.* Concord, Mass.: General Radio.

Pflüger, E. 1877. Die teleologische Mechanik der Lebendigen. *Natur. Pflügers Archiv für die gesamte Physiologie des Menschen und der Tiere* 15:57.

Pirandello, L. 1939. *Saggi.* Milan, Italy: Mondadori.

Powers, R. W. Jr. and H. A. Alker. 1968. Coping suppression, defensive repression and reports about dirty words. *Cornell Journal of Social Relations* 3:124–28.

Pranulis, M., J. Dabbs, and J. Johnson. 1975. General anesthesia and the patients' attempts at control. *Social Behavior and Personality* 3:49–51.

Rabkin, J. G. and E. L. Struening. 1976. Life events, stress, and illness. *Science* 194:1013–1020.

Rachman, S. J. 1978. *Fear and Courage*. San Francisco: W. H. Freeman.

Rahe, R. H. 1972. Subjects' recent life changes and their near-future illness susceptibility. *Advances in Psychosomatic Medicine* 8:2–19.

—— 1974. The pathway between subjects' recent life changes and their near-future illness reports: Representative results and methodological issues. In B. S. Dohrenwend and B. P. Dohrendwend, eds., *Stressful Life Events: Their Nature and Effects*, pp. 73–86. New York: Wiley.

Rahe, R. H. and R. J. Arthur. 1978. Life change and illness studies. *Journal of Human Stress* 41:3–15.

Rahe, R. H., E. Gunderson, W. M. Pugh, R. T. Rubin and R. J. Arthur. 1972. Illness prediction studies: Use of psychosocial and occupational characteristics as predictors. *Archives of Environmental Health* 25:192–97.

Rahe, R. H., U. Lundberg, T. Theorell, and L. K. Bennett. 1971. The Social Readjustment Rating Scale: A comparative study of Swedes and Americans. *Journal of Psychosomatic Research* 51:241–49.

Rahe, R. H., J. D. McKean, and R. J. Arthur. 1967. A longitudinal study of life-change and illness patterns. *Journal of Psychosomatic Research* 10:355–66.

Rahe, R. H., H. W. Ward, and V. Hayes. 1979. Brief group therapy in myocardial infarction rehabilitation: Three to four-year follow up of a controlled trial. *Psychosomatic Medicine* 41:229–42.

Rank, O. 1936. *Will Therapy and Truth and Reality*. New York: Knopf.

Rees, W. and S. Lutkins. 1967. Mortality of bereavement. *British Medical Journal* 4:13–16.

Reich, W. 1933. *Character Analysis*. New York: Orgone Institute Press (1949).

Richmond, J. B. and H. A. Waisman. 1955. Psychologic aspects of management of children with malignant diseases. *American Journal of Diseases of Children* 89:42–47.

Riskind, J. 1982. The client's sense of personal mastery: Effects of time perspective and self-esteem. In I. L. Janis, ed., *Counseling on Personal Decisions: Theory and Research on Short-term Helping Relationships*. New Haven, Conn.: Yale University Press.

Rodin, J. and E. J. Langer. 1977. Long-term effects of a control-relevant intervention with the institutionalized aged. *Journal of Personality and Social Psychology* 35:897–902.

Rodin, J. R. 1978. Somatopsychics and attribution. *Personality and Social Bulletin* 4:531–40.

Rogers, C. 1959. A theory of therapy, personal and interpersonal relations, as developed in the client-centered framework. In S. Koch, ed., *Psychology: A Study of a Science*. New York: McGraw-Hill.

—— 1968. The significance of the self-regarding attitudes and perceptions. In C. Gordon and K. Gergen, eds., *The Self in Social Interaction*. New York: Wiley.

Rogers, M. P., D. Dubey, and P. Reich. 1979. The influence of the psyche and brain on immunity and disease susceptibility: A critical review. *Psychosomatic Medicine* 41:147–64.

Rogers, R. W. and W. C. Deckner. 1975. Effects of fear appeals and physiological arousal upon emotion, attitudes, and cigarette smoking. *Journal of Personality and Social Psychology* 32:220–30.

Rogers, R. W. and C. R. Mewborn. 1976. Fear appeals and attitude change: Effects of a threat's noxiousness, probability of occurrence, and the efficacy of coping responses. *Journal of Personality and Social Psychology* 34:54–61.

Rogers, R. W. and D. L. Thistlethwaite. 1970. Effects of fear arousal and reassurance upon attitude change. *Journal of Personality and Social Psychology* 15:227–33.

Rokeach, M. 1968. *Beliefs, Attitudes, and Values.* San Francisco: Jossey-Bass.

Rollin, B. 1976. *First You Cry.* New York: New American Library.

Romalis, F. 1942. The impact of the war on family life. Part I: Reactions to change and crisis. *The Family* 22:219–24.

Rome, H. 1969. The irony of the ICU. *Psychiatry Digest* 30:10–14.

Rose, R. M. 1980. Endocrine responses to stressful psychological events. *Psychiatric Clinics of North America* 3:251–76.

Rosen, G. M. 1981. Guidelines for the review of do-it-yourself treatment books. *Contemporary Psychology* 26:189–91.

Rosenberg, M. and L. I. Pearlin. 1978. Social class and self-esteem among children and adults. *American Journal of Sociology* 84:53–77.

Roskies, E. 1980. Considerations in developing a treatment program for the coronary-prone (Type A) behavior pattern. In P. O. Davidson and S. M. Davidson, eds., *Behavioral Medicine: Changing Health Life Styles.* New York: Brunner/Mazel.

—— 1983. Stress management: Averting the evil eye. *Contemporary Psychology* 28:542–44.

Roskies, E., M. Spevack, A. Surkis, C. Cohen, S. Gilman. 1978. Changing the coronary-prone (Type A) behavior pattern in a non-clinical population. *Journal of Behavioral Medicine* 1:201–16.

Rothenberg, A. 1961. Psychological problems in terminal cancer management. *Cancer* 14:1063–73.

Rotter, J. B. 1966. Generalized expectancies for internal versus external control of reinforcement. *Psychological Monographs,* vol. 80, no. 609.

Rotter, J. B., M. Seeman, and S. Liverant. 1962. Internal vs. external locus of control reinforcement: A major variable in behavior theory. In N. F. Washburne, ed., *Decisions, Values, and Groups.* London: Pergamon.

Rowland, K. F. 1977. Environmental events predicting death for the elderly. *Psychological Bulletin* 84:349–72.

Sahud, M. A. and R. J. Cohen. 1971. Effect of aspirin ingestion on ascorbic-acid levels in rheumatoid arthritis. *Lancet* 1:937–38.

Salter, M. 1970. Nursing in an intensive therapy unit. *Nursing Times* 66:486–87.

Sarason, I. G., C. de Monchaux, and T. Hunt. 1975. Methodological issues in the assessment of life stress. In L. Levi, ed., *Emotions: Their Parameters and Measurement,* pp. 499–509. New York: Raven Press.

Schachtel, E. G. 1959. *Metamorphosis.* New York: Basic Books.

Schachter, S. 1959. *The Psychology of Affiliation.* Stanford, Calif.: Stanford University Press.

Schleiffer, S. T., S. E. Keller, F. P. McKegney, and M. Stein. 1980. Bereavement and lymphocyte function. Paper presented at meeting of the American Psychiatric Association, San Francisco, March.

Schmale, A. H., Jr. 1958. Relationship of separation and depression to disease: I. A report on a hospitalized medical population. *.Psychosomatic Medicine* 20:259–77.

—— 1972. Giving up as a final common pathway to changes in health. *Advances in Psychosomatic Medicine* 8:20–40.

Schmidt, R. L. 1966. An exploratory study of nursing and patient readiness for surgery. Master's thesis, Yale University, School of Nursing.

Schmitt, F. E. and P. J. Wooldridge. 1973. Psychological preparation of surgical patients. *Nursing Research* 22:108–16.

Schoenberg, B., I. Gerber, A. Wiener, A. H. Kutscher, D. Peretz, and A. C. Carr, eds. 1975. *Bereavement: Its Psychosocial Aspects.* New York: Columbia University Press.

Schulz, R. and B. M. Hanusa. 1978. Long term effects of control and predictability enhancing interventions: Findings and ethical issues. *Journal of Personality and Social Psychology* 36:1194–1201.

Seligman, M. E. P. 1975. *Helplessness: On Depression, Development, and Death.* San Francisco: Freeman.

Sells, S. B. 1970. On the nature of stress. In J. E. McGrath, ed., *Social and Psychological Factors in Stress,* pp. 134–39. New York: Holt, Rinehart and Winston.

Selye, H. 1936. A syndrome produced by diverse nocuous agents. *Nature* 138:32.

—— 1950. *The Psychology and Pathology of Exposure to Stress.* Montreal: Acta.

—— 1952. *The Story of the Adaptation Syndrome.* Montreal: Acta.

—— 1956, 1976. *The Stress of Life.* New York: McGraw-Hill.

—— 1974. *Stress Without Distress.* Philadelphia: Lippincott.

—— ed. 1980a. *Selye's Guide to Stress Research,* vol. 1. New York: Van Nostrand.

—— 1980b. The stress concept today. In I. L. Kutash and L. B. Schlesinger and Associates, *Handbook on Stress and Anxiety,* pp. 127–43. San Francisco: Jossey-Bass.

—— 1982. History and present status of the stress concept. In L. Goldberger and S. Breznitz, eds., *Handbook of Stress: Theoretical and Clinical Aspects,* pp. 7–17. New York: Free Press.

Shannon, T. X. and G. M. Isbell. 1963. Stress in dental patients: Effect of local anesthetic procedures. Technical Report No. SAM-TDR-63-29. Brooks Air Force Base, Texas: United States Air Force School of Aerospace Medicine.

Shapiro, A. K. 1964. Factors contributing to the placebo effect: Their implications for psychotherapy. *American Journal of Psychotherapy* 18 (Supplement 1):73–88.

Shapiro, D. 1965. *Neurotic Styles.* New York: Basic Books.

Shatan, C. F. 1972. The grief of soldiers. *American Report* 2:1–3.

—— 1974. Through the membrane of reality: Impacted grief and perceptual dissonance in Vietnam combat veterans. *Psychiatric Opinion* 11:6–15.

Shepherd, D. and B. M. Barraclough. 1974. The aftermath of suicide. *British Medical Journal* 2:600–3.

Shils, E. A. and M. Janowitz. 1948. Cohesion and disintegration in the Wehrmacht in World War II. *Public Opinion Quarterly* 2 (Summer).

Shneidman, E. S. 1967. Sleep and self-destruction. In E. S. Shneidman, ed., *Essays in Self-Destruction.* New York: Science House.

—— 1970. The enemy and death questionnaire. *Psychology Today* August:37–41, 62–72.

—— 1971a. Death and you. *Psychology Today* June:43–45, 74–80.

—— 1971b. Perturbation and lethality as precursors of suicide in a gifted group. *Life-Threatening Behavior* 1:23–45.

—— ed. 1972. *Death and the College Student.* New York: Behavioral Publications.

—— 1973. *Deaths of Man.* New York: Penguin.

—— ed. 1976. *Death: Current Perspectives*. Palo Alto, Calif.: Mayfield.

—— 1977. The college student and death. In H. Feifel, ed., *New Meanings of Death*, pp. 67–86. New York: McGraw-Hill.

Siegal, H. S. 1959. The relation between crowding and weight of adrenal glands in chickens. *Ecology* 40:495–98.

Silber, E., D. A. Hamburg, G. V. Coelho, E. B. Murphey, M. Rosenberg, and L. D. Pearlin. 1961. Adaptive behavior in competent adolescents: Coping with the anticipation of college. *Archives of General Psychiatry* 5:354–65.

Sime, A. M. 1976. Relationship of preoperative fear, type of coping, and information received about surgery to recovery from surgery. *Journal of Personality and Social Psychology* 34:716–24.

Singer, J. E., U. Lundberg, and M. Frankenhaeuser. 1978. Stress on the train: A study of urban commuting. In A. Baum, J. E. Singer, and S. Valins, eds., *Advances in Environmental Psychology*, vol. 1. Hillsdale, N.J.: Erlbaum.

Singer, M. T. 1974. Engagement-involvement: A central phenomenon in psychophysiological research. *Psychomatic Medicine* 36:1–17.

Sjoback, H. 1973. *The Psychoanalytic Theory of Defensive Processes*. New York: Wiley.

Sklar, L. S. and H. Anisman. 1979. Stress and coping factors influence tumor growth. *Science* (August 3), 205:513–15.

Smelser, N. J. 1963. *Theory of Collective Behavior*. New York: Free Press of Glencoe.

Smith, A. 1975. *Powers of the Mind*, pp. 11–14. New York: Random House.

Smith, M. B. 1961. "Mental health" reconsidered: A special case of the problem of values in psychology. *American Psychologist* 16:299–306.

Sobell, M. B. and L. C. Sobell. 1976. Second-year treatment outcome of alcoholics treated by individualized behavior therapy: Results. *Behavior Research and Therapy* 14:195–215.

Solnit, A. J. and M. Green. 1959. Psychologic considerations in the management of deaths on pediatric hospital services: I. The doctor and the child's family. *Pediatrics* 24:106–112.

Solomon, G. F. 1969. Discussion. Emotions and immunity. *Annals of the New York Academy of Sciences* 164 (Art. 2):461–62.

Solomon, G. F., V. P. Zarcone, R. Yoerg, N. R. Scott and R. G. Maurer. 1971. Three psychiatric casualties from Vietnam. *Archives of General Psychiatry* 25:522–24.

Spielberger, C. D., R. L. Gorsuch, and R. E. Lushene. 1970. *Manual for the State-Trait Anxiety Inventory*. Palo Alto, Calif.: Consulting Psychologist Press.

Staub, E. and D. Kellett. 1972. Increasing pain tolerance by information about aversive stimuli. *Journal of Personality and Social Psychology* 21:198–203.

Staub, E., B. Tursky, and G. E. Schwartz. 1971. Self-control and predictability: Their effects on reactions to aversive stimulation. *Journal of Personality and Social Psychology* 18:157–62.

Staudenmayer, H., R. A. Kinsman, J. F. Dirks, S. L. Spector, and C. Wangaard. 1979. Medical outcome in asthmatic patients: Effects of airways hyperactivity and symptom-focused anxiety. *Psychosomatic Medicine* 41:109–18.

Steinmetz, J., J. Blankenship, L. Brown, D. Hall, and G. Miller. 1980. *Managing Stress: Before It Manages You*. Palo Alto, Calif.: Bull Publishing.

Stern, M. J., L. Pascale, and J. B. McLoone. 1976. Psychosocial adaptation following an acute myocardial infarction. *Journal of Chronic Diseases* 29:513–26.

Sternbach, R. A. 1966. *Principles of Psychophysiology.* New York: Academic Press.

Stokols, D. 1978. Environmental psychology. *Annual Review of Psychology* 29:253–95.

Stone, A. A. and J. M. Neale. 1984. A new measure of daily coping: Development and preliminary results. *Journal of Personality and Social Psychology* 46:892–906.

Stone, G. C., F. Cohen, N. E. Adler, and Associates. 1979. *Health Psychology—A Handbook.* San Francisco: Jossey-Bass.

Stroebe, M. S., W. Stroebe, K. J. Gergen and M. Gergen. 1981. The broken heart: Reality or myth? *Omega* 12:87–106.

Stroebe, W., M. S. Stroebe, K. J. Gergen and M. Gergen. 1980. Der Kummer Effekt: Psychologische Aspekte der Sterblichkeit von Verwitweten. *Psychologische Beiträge* 22:1–26.

—— 1982. The effects of bereavement on mortality: A social psychological analysis. In J. R. Eiser, ed., *Social Psychology and Behavioral Medicine.* Sussex, England: Wiley.

Suinn, R. M. 1979. Type A behavior pattern. In R. B. Williams and W. D. Gentry, eds., *Behavioral Approaches to Medical Treatment.* Cambridge: Ballinger.

Sullivan, H. S. 1953. *The Interpersonal Theory of Psychiatry.* New York: Norton.

Symington, T., A. R. Currie, R. S. Curran, and J. N. Davidson. 1955. The reaction of the adrenal cortex in conditions of stress. In *Ciba Foundations Colloquial on Endocrinology*, vol. 8. *The Human Adrenal Cortex.* pp. 70–91. Boston: Little, Brown.

Tanzer, D. 1968. Natural childbirth: Pain or peak experience. *Psychology Today* 2:17–21.

Taylor, F. G. and W. L. Marshall. 1977. Experimental analysis of a cognitive-behavioral therapy for depression. *Cognitive Therapy and Research* 1:59–72.

Taylor, S. E. 1983. Adjustment to threatening events: A theory of cognitive adaptation. *American Psychologist* 38:1161–73.

Thiessen, D. D. 1963. Varying sensitivity of C^{57}BL/Crgl mice to grouping. *Science* 141:827–28.

Thomas, C. B. and K. R. Duszynski. 1974. Closeness to parents and the family constellation in a prospective study of five disease states: Suicide, mental illness, malignant tumor, hypertension, and coronary heart disease. *Johns Hopkins Medical Journal* 134:251–70.

Tinbergen, N. 1953. *Social Behaviour in Animals.* London: Methuen.

Toffler, A. 1970. *Future Shock.* New York: Bantam.

Townes, B. D., D. A. Wold, and T. H. Holmes. 1974. Parental adjustment to childhood leukemia. *Journal of Psychosomatic Research* 18:9–14.

Toynbee, A. 1969. *Man's Concern with Death.* New York: McGraw-Hill.

Turk, D. C. 1977. *Cognitive Control of Pain: A Skills-Training Approach.* Master's thesis, University of Waterloo.

—— 1978. Cognitive behavioral techniques in the management of pain. In J. P. Foreyt and D. J. Rathgen, eds., *Cognitive Behavior Therapy: Research and Application.* New York: Plenum Press.

Turk, D. C. and M. Genest. 1979. Regulation of pain: The application of cognitive and behavioral techniques for prevention and remediation. In P. Kendall and S. Hollon, eds., *Cognitive Behavioral Interventions: Theory, Research, and Practices.* New York: Academic Press.

Tversky, A. and D. Kahneman. 1973. Availability: A heuristic for judging frequency and probability. *Cognitive Psychology* 5:207–32.

—— 1974. Judgment under uncertainty: Heuristics and biases. *Science* 185:1124–31.

U.S. Department of Health, Education, and Welfare. 1970. *Facts of Life and Death.* Washington, D.C.: GPO, PHS publication No. 600.

U.S. Environmental Protection Agency. 1974. *Levels Document 550/9-74-004.* Washington, D.C.: GPO.

Vaihinger, H. 1911. *The Philosophy of "As If."* New York: Harcourt.

Vaillant, G. 1977. *Adaptation to Life.* Boston: Little, Brown.

Venables, P. H. and I. Martin, eds. 1967. *A Manual of Psychophysiological Methods.* Amsterdam: North-Holland.

Vernon, D. T. A. and D. A. Bigelow. 1974. The effect of information about a potentially stressful situation on responses to stress impact. *Journal of Personality and Social Psychology* 29:50–59.

Vinokur, A. and M. L. Selzer. 1975. Desirable versus undesirable life events: Their relationship to stress and mental distress. *Journal of Personality and Social Psychology* 32:329–37.

Visotsky, H. M., D. A. Hamburg, M. E. Goss, and B. B. Lebovitz. 1961. Coping behavior under extreme stress: Observations of patients with severe poliomyelitis. *Archives of General Psychiatry* 5:423–48.

Von Kugelgen, E. 1975. Psychological determinants of the delay in decision to seek aid in cases of myocardial infarction. Ph.D. dissertation, University of California, Berkeley.

Voors, A. W., T. A. Foster, R. R. Frerichs, L. S. Weber, and G. S. Berenson. 1976. Studies of blood pressure in children, ages 5–14 years, in a total biracial community. *Circulation* 54:319–27.

Vreeland, R. and G. Ellis. 1969. Stresses on the nurse in an intensive-care unit. *Journal of the American Medical Association* 208:332–34.

Walker, K. N., A. MacBride, and M. L. S. Vachon. 1977. Social support networks and the crisis of bereavement. *Social Science and Medicine* 11:35–41.

Wallston, B., S. Alagna, B. DeVellis, and R. DeVellis. 1981. Social support and health. Bethesda, Md.: Uniformed Services University of the Health Sciences. Manuscript.

Ward, A. W. 1976. Mortality of bereavement. *British Medical Journal* 1:700–2.

Washburn, S. L. and L. Devore. 1961. The social life of baboons. *Scientific American* 204:62–71.

Watzlawick, P. 1976. *How Real is Real?* New York: Random House.

Weiner, H. 1977. *Psychobiology and Human Disease.* New York: American Elsevier.

Weinstein, J., J. R. Averill, E. M. Opton, Jr., and R. S. Lazarus. 1968. Defensive style and discrepancy between self-report and physiological indexes of stress. *Journal of Personality and Social Psychology* 10:406–13.

Weisman, A. D. 1972a. *On Death and Dying.* New York: Behavioral Publications.

—— 1972b. *On Dying and Denying.* New York: Behavioral Publications.

Weisman, A. D. and T. Hackett. 1961. Predilection to death: Death and dying as a psychiatric problem. *Psychosomatic Medicine* 23:232–56.

—— 1962. The dying patient. *Forest Hospital Publication* 1:16–20.

Weiss, J. M. 1970. Somatic effects of predictable and unpredictable shock. *Psychosomatic Medicine* 32:397–409.

Weiss, R. S. 1976. The emotional impact of marital separation. *Journal of Social Issues* 32:135–45.

Welty, C. 1957. The geography of birds. *Scientific American* 197:118–28.

Wershow, H. and G. Reinhart. 1974. Life change and hospitalization—A heretical view. *Journal of Psychosomatic Research* 18:393–401.

Wheelis, A. 1966. *The Illusionless Man: Fantasies and Meditations.* New York: Norton.

White, E. B. and K. S. White. 1962. *A Subtreasury of American Humor.* New York: Capricorn Books.

White, R. W. 1959. Motivation reconsidered: The concept of competence. *Psychological Review* 66:297–333.

—— 1963. Ego and reality in psychoanalytic theory. *Psychological Issues* 3(3), whole no. 11.

—— 1974. *Strategies of adaptation: An attempt at systematic description.* In G. V. Coelho, D. A. Hamburg, and J. E. Adams, eds., *Coping and Adaptation,* pp. 47–68. New York: Basic Books.

White House Conference on Food, Nutrition and Health: Final Report. 1969. Washington, D.C.: GPO.

Wiggins, J. S. 1973. *Personality and Prediction: Principles of Personality Assessment.* Reading, Mass.: Addison-Wesley.

Witkin, H. A., D. R. Goodenough, and D. K. Oltman. 1979. Psychological differentiation: Current status. *Journal of Personality and Social Psychology* 37:1127–45.

Wolf, A. V. 1956. Thirst. *Scientific American* 194:70–76.

Wolfe, S. W. 1972. Avoid sickness—How life changes affect your health. *Family Circle* (May), 30:166–70.

Wolfenstein, N. 1957. *Disaster.* New York: Free Press.

Wolfer, J. A. and M. A. Visintainer. 1975. Pediatric surgical patients' and parents' stress responses and adjustment as a function of psychologic preparation and stress-point nursing care. *Nursing Research* 24:244–55.

Wolff, C. T., S. B. Friedman, M. A. Hofer, and J. W. Mason. 1964. Relationship between psychological defenses and mean urinary 17-hydroxycorticosteroid excretion rates: Parts I and II. *Psychosomatic Medicine* 26:576–609.

Wolff, C. T., J. W. Mason, S. B. Friedman, and M. A. Hofer. 1963. The relationship between ego defenses and the adrenal response to the prolonged threat of loss: A predictive study. Atlantic City, N.J., Presented at the Annual Meeting of the American Psychosomatic Society.

Wolff, W. 1943. *The Expression of Personality: Experimental Depth Psychology.* New York: Harper and Brothers.

Worcester, A. 1940. *The Care of the Aged, the Dying and the Dead.* 2nd ed. Springfield, Ill.: Charles C. Thomas.

Wortman, C. B. and C. Dunkel-Schetter. 1979. The importance of social support: Parallels between victims and the aged. Presented at Workshop on the Elderly of the Future, Committee on Aging, National Research Council, Annapolis, Md., May 3–5.

Wright, B. A. 1960. *Physical Disability: A Psychological Approach.* New York: Harper and Row.

Wyler, A. R., M. Masuda, and T. H. Holmes. 1968. Seriousness of Illness Rating Scale. *Journal of Psychosomatic Research* 11:363–75.

—— 1970. Seriousness of Illness Rating Scale: Reproducibility. *Journal of Psychosomatic Research* 14:59–64.

Young, M., B. Benjamin, and C. Wallis. 1963. Mortality of widowers. *Lancet* 2:454–56.

Zborowski, M. 1969. *People in Pain.* San Francisco: Jossey-Bass.

Zeuner, F. E. 1963. *A History of Domesticated Animals.* London: Hutchinson.

Ziegler, P. 1969. *The Black Death.* Middlesex, England: Penguin.

Zimbardo, P. G. 1970. The human choice. In W. Arnold and D. Levine, eds., *Nebraska Symposiuim on Motivation,* vol. 17. Lincoln: University of Nebraska Press.

Zola, I. K. 1972. Studying the decision to see a doctor: Review, critique, corrective. *Advances in Psychosomatic Medicine* 8:216–36.

Index